D1523113

Battles in the Alps

A History of the Italian Front of the First World War

G. Irving Root

PublishAmerica
Baltimore

First printing

PublishAmerica has allowed this work to remain exactly as the author intended, verbatim, without editorial input.

ISBN: 1-60703-037-3
PUBLISHED BY PUBLISHAMERICA, LLLP
www.publishamerica.com
Baltimore

Printed in the United States of America

Table of Contents

List of Maps

Foreword

In May of 1915 the Kingdom of Italy declared war on the Empire of Austria-Hungary, thus initiating a new battle front in a wider conflict at that time already known as the Great War. Before doing so it repudiated an over thirty year old understanding known as the *Triple Alliance*, in which both nations and the German Empire, had been partners. Austria-Hungary had been at war for ten months, and was fighting on two other fronts at the time of the Italian declaration, but thereafter considered the struggle against Italy as the main one, for the duration of the war. Before it was over 166 combat divisions had made an appearance in this theatre and two and a half million men (and a few women) would become casualties. In addition the modern and powerful navies and air forces of the contestants became involved, widening the scope of the subsequent operations, both geographically and militarily.

For Italy the war zone was known simply as the front; to the Austro-Hungarian command it became the Southwest Front, but for the rest of the interested world it was referred to as the Austro-Italian Front, and since there was not much chance of confusing it with any other, it was often called simply the Italian Front. Because of the topography of the region along the border between the two warring powers, it was sometimes dubbed the Alpine Front. By whatever name it was indicated as, however, it was the setting for a desperate contest between two of the larger countries of Europe, who were home to more than 85 million people.

The Alps, Europe's highest and most rugged mountain system, have long served as a barrier to human passage. As long ago as the Second Punic War a general named Hannibal had led an army across this notorious Range, a remarkable feat of logistical accomplishment that to this day earns him high marks from historians as a leader of great ability. Those who came later included names such as Caesar, Attila and Napoleon, but by and large the mountains by their mere existence have served to quell the aggressive spirits of lesser personalities and have long marked boundaries between racial, linguistic or ethnic groups. The inability of humans to subsistence-farm over much of the area, coupled with the harsh and unforgiving climate of the higher altitudes have kept the Alps an area of relatively low population density, even to this day. In 1915 few roads negotiated the difficult terrain, and even fewer railroads, those lifelines of early 20ᵗʰ Century Armies. Streams in the area, as in all mountainous areas, tended to be icy and fast-flowing; having cut courses into the landscape that were almost always flanked with steep-sided heights over which no vehicle, and few animals, could travel. Rockslides and avalanches are always a problem. And in the Alps, winter is the dominant season, and generally dictates the nature of human activity there.

The enormous difficulty of conducting military operations among high mountain peaks dictated that much of the fighting would take place where the international frontier eased down from the heights to meet the waters of the Gulf of Trieste, at the northern tip of the Adriatic Sea. Here the valley of a relatively small river became the setting for a dozen desperate campaigns with all the resulting death and destruction. Localities such as the small city of Görz, very much in harm's way, were reduced to ruins and took many years to rebuild. Home to perhaps 40 or 45,000 residents in 1915, the place was an empty, blackened ruin by the end of the war, and only regained its pre-war population level more than two decades after the guns had finally fallen silent. In other areas along the border, majestic forests would be leveled, beautiful Alpine villages destroyed, and even mountain peaks would disappear to the devastating forces of modern explosives.

For Americans, far and away the most destructive war in our history was the Civil War, a conflict which claimed roughly 600,000 lives, a figure that surpasses the total losses of all other American wars combined. As the fighting took place on U.S. soil, property loss was catastrophic, as was damage to the economies of the rebellious states. Hardly an American alive during the middle years of the 19ᵗʰ Century was not affected in one way or another by the war; after the event, no one could deny that 1861-1865 had been a defining time in the evolution of the United States. As devastating and as deadly as the Civil War was, however, it was less so than the war on the Italian Front from 1915-1918, yet the latter conflict seems to have gone almost unnoticed in the histories of the 20ᵗʰ Century, indeed, even in the histories of the Great War itself. Most often, this conflict, for those who are even aware of it, is waved off, along with the story of the Eastern, Balkan and Turkish fronts, as a mere 'sideshow' of the First World War, one of the many 'peripheral' campaigns.

Webster's New Collegiate Dictionary defines 'sideshow' as 'an incidental diversion' and 'peripheral' as 'located away from the center or central portion'. Oxford American Dictionary calls a sideshow 'A minor show attached to a principal one; peripheral is 'of minor importance to something'. Indeed. Is it to be believed that the peoples of Italy and Austria-Hungary, who considered the Alpine Front to be the main one, fought so desperately and so long for an incidental diversion? Was Austria-Hungary struggling for its very existence in a minor show attached to a principal one? Did hundreds of thousands of young Italians charge uphill to their deaths over an issue of minor importance? Could 166 divisions have been committed to a battle away from the center of the war?

Enough said. The arrogance of Western opinion that was spawned in 1914 continues to this day; into the 21st Century, confirmed advocates of Western Front strategy are *still* talking and writing about 'sideshows' and 'peripheral' campaigns, but it is high time to do justice to these campaigns by taking a better look at them, and if that is accomplished, perhaps a more complete understanding of the war will be the result.

No one doubts that Germany was the strongest of the powers on its side of the war and that it made its main effort on the Western Front. In opposing her, the United Kingdom, France and later the United States also used the Western Front as the primary one, and these were the nations that financed the war and dictated the peace. Neither Italy nor Austria-Hungary were the strongest powers in their respective coalitions, and as a result neither were able to convince their more powerful partners of the critical importance of the Italian Front. In as much as neither were able to force a decision there as well, at least until the dominos began to fall in the autumn of 1918, the myth of the paramount importance of the Western Theatre was able to be nourished without challenge. Once they had convinced themselves that the only way to kill the beast was with a blow to the head, they were prepared to rule out all other possibilities; it never occurred to them that a blow to the heart, kidneys, knees or groin may have done the job as well, and may have been much easier to deliver.

General histories of the First World War rarely devote much space to the Italian Front, perhaps one chapter, most of which deals with Caporetto, a name they have attached to the Austro-German offensive of October 1917, which lasted well into November. Actually Caporetto is a small Isonzo town at which very little fighting took place. Known as Karfreit before the war, it has been known as Kobarid since 1945, when the local Slovene population was at last allowed to join with Yugoslavia; Italian ownership endured only a quarter-century. Multi-volume histories with much more space do the subject somewhat more justice but rarely enough. For example, one well-known ten volume set devotes only a half-volume to the Italian Front, while providing five and a half for the Western Front. In terms of numbers of men engaged and casualties sustained, the Alpine Theatre was easily the third most important of the war, and thus deserves better recognition. Even so, only a handful of books in English on the subject have ever emerged. It is time to correct this imbalance; the men who labored, suffered from the harsh elements, or bled and suffered great pain for a cause they believed in, deserve to have their story told. Their efforts and their sacrifices must never be forgotten.

The following tale is told in chronological sequence or at least as close to such as was possible for the sake of the narrative. It is a format that I personally prefer to read, especially when dealing with historic events, as I believe a better understanding of the subsequent elapsing of time relative to the actual occurrences is thus gained, and the text becomes more of a story, as opposed to a dry statement of fact. A resultant day-by-day tale is hopefully quite noticeable, and tolerable. Every reader is encouraged to consult vintage maps whenever possible, as all place names are of 1915. In most cases the names have not changed since 1919, but the contested Italian-Slavic frontier is a notable exception. Caporetto has already been mentioned; Görz is another good example. After the war, Austrian Görz became Italian Gorizia, and when the borders moved again in 1945, the city was split between Italy and Yugoslavia. The latter's portion was renamed Nova Gorica; today it is part of independent Slovenia and rivals Gorizia in size. In most cases where there had never been a heavy German presence, names have changed only once; examples include Pola (Austrian/Italian) to Pula (Yugoslav/Croat) and Fiume (Hungarian/Italian) to Rijeka (Yugoslav/Croat).

Another point that begs explanation is my choice of terms when referring to the rival, warring coalitions. Before the war the *Triple Alliance* of the German and Austro-Hungarian Empires and the Kingdom of Italy represented one power bloc, the *Triple Entente* of France, Russia and the United Kingdom another. Throughout the pages below the *Entente* nations and those which fought alongside them (later including Italy and the United States) are called as such. The Austro-German combination, deserted by Italy but later joined by Ottoman Turkey and Bulgaria, is referred to as the *Alliance*. I believe this is more logical than the commonly-used terms Allies and Central Powers. For one thing, the U.S. never considered itself one of the Allies; it became an 'Associated Power', as did some others. For another 'allies' is a term for nations working or fighting together for a common cause and is therefore too generic to be specific. In his memoirs General Ludendorff wrote of 'confederated' powers when denoting his allies in the war, and General Hoffmann wrote of 'Allied' countries or contingents while doing the same. As for 'Central Powers', none of these nations referred to themselves as such until after the war. The well-documented desire of the Germans for a *Mittel Europa* (Central Europe), a large and powerful bloc of countries in east-central Europe, was pretty much frustrated when both Italy and Romania declined to fight for it, and eventually joined the other side. *Entente* leaders began to call their enemies the Central Empires, and at some point in time the designation Central Powers evolved, and found favor, and has been reused until the present day. I hope the reader will agree that my use of terms is less confusing.

While researching this work I made use of sources published from 1916 to the present. Because so few books are devoted exclusively to the subject I found it necessary to piece together the story from whatever tidbits of information were available, yet I must report that for the persistent inquisitor, no such effort can be said to remain incomplete for lack of relevant material, it simply needed to be rounded up and sorted out. It is my sincere hope that the final product represents a worthwhile, medium-length rendition of a story that truly needs to be told more often. The book, like the bibliography that supports it, is not intended to be an exhaustive compilation of data and facts, but a very readable tale of the exploits of two great nations during an extremely traumatic period of European history. I do hope it inspires others, however few, to take a second look at some of the alternative campaigns of the First World War, a conflict that is all too often dismissed as the culmination of a commercial rivalry between Britain and Germany or of a long Franco-German vendetta. Those who served on the Italian Front did not do so to further the interests of the Western Powers (until Western contingents were sent there), but to honor their duties to their country, their communities, and their families. To downplay their efforts and achievements is to abuse their memory, and that of the war itself.

Most sincere thanks go out to all of those persons who assisted directly or indirectly in the creation of this work, over the years of careful preparation. Any errors within are mine alone. Special thanks are due my family, especially my wife Elaine, who spent seemingly endless hours typing and correcting the manuscript. They encouraged me during times of frustration and lack of focus and aided me in a project which by its very nature deprived us of a good deal of quality time together.

Chapter One
Agenda: War

Serious research into the origins of the war fought along the Austrian-Italian frontier during the second decade of the Twentieth Century will necessarily lead the inquisitor back to days deep within the Nineteenth. Ever since modern Europe began to take shape during the Middle Ages, the ground of the Central portion of the continent had always been a patchwork of kingdoms, dukedoms, principalities, Imperial and Free cities, and Church-owned parcels. Such was the frame-work of the Holy Roman Empire, a vast confederation which sprawled over what are the modern states of the Low Countries, Switzerland, Germany, Italy, Czech Republic, Slovenia, Austria, and much of France. For centuries, hundreds of otherwise vulnerable and ridiculously tiny political entities were thus nurtured under the Imperial banner, which, however, did not prevent the almost constant warfare amongst them and other foreign states. Napoleon I finally put an end to the old system; during his interlude the number of governments in mid-continent was reduced significantly, and a relative few were therefore increased substantially in size and strength. Perhaps even more importantly, another force was unleashed during the Napoleonic period: nationalism.

The Congress of Vienna rearranged Europe immediately after the great Frenchman had been finally defeated. The delegates of the Convention, who represented the Great Powers of Europe, there attempted to usher in a new era of stability under the old, that is, pre-revolutionary rules. As might be expected, much of the continent remained restive, especially the still-splintered areas of the bygone Empire. A new wave of revolution shook the old order in 1830, then another even more serious wave in 1848; it is from this latter date that our story really begins.

The ruling Habsburg dynasty of the Austrian Empire had at one time possessed nearly all of the Italian peninsula, including Sicily and Sardinia. Even in the mid-Nineteenth Century it still owned a large portion of the north, and exerted tremendous political influence on the remainder. When as a result of the 1848 disturbances, republics were set up in Venice and in Rome; the Austrian reaction was swift and predictable. Before long, the fledgling republics were forcibly toppled, and the Austrians had gained the enmity not only of those Italians who wished for the end of foreign influence south of the Alps, but also those who preferred constitutional, rather than authoritarian, government. Thereafter, Austria stood for all that was contemptuous to the Latin patriots, an outside force repressive of individual liberties and suppressive of every attempt to obtain self-rule.

Better days were, however, on the horizon. In 1831 a liberal monarch, Charles Albert, had come to the throne of Piedmont, a fairly sizable kingdom which included the western end of the Po valley up to the French and Swiss borders, the Genoa area, and the island of Sardinia. It was the strongest and most progressive of any of the Italian-speaking entities, and enjoyed strong ties to France. As a result of the 1848 revolutionary period, Charles Albert granted a liberal constitution, a time from which his kingdom became the natural leader in the cause of Italian unification and freedom. In 1850 Count Cavour became head of the Piedmontese Cabinet. Cavour was an excellent statesman, shrewd and practical, and well suited for the tasks he would be called upon to perform; he would earn a reputation as 'Italy's Bismarck' for his role in the unification of much of the peninsula.

Cavour realized that Piedmont alone was not nearly strong enough to expel the Austrians from areas they had long since secured, so he began a policy of befriending Prussia, England, and France. When the latter two went to war with Russia a few years later they found an easy ally in Piedmont, troops from which were sent with British and French contingents to the Crimea. By July of 1858, Cavour had coaxed Napoleon III into signing an alliance with him that was directed against Austria. The French Emperor's motives were of course selfish; he believed he could supplant Austrian influence in Italy with that of France, but the Count was wiser. If the Austrians could be defeated, he reasoned, a united Italy would be strong enough to resist French intrigues. At any rate, the allies made war on Austria and won important engagements at Magenta in western Lombardy and Solferino, south of Lake Garda. Apparently aware of the nationalistic enthusiasm that the war had provoked and astute enough to understand that his own designs could not be realized,

Napoleon asked for a peace conference with his opposite number, the young Austrian Emperor, Franz Joseph. The two soon met at the town of Villafranca; southwest of Verona, and concluded peace. Austria was to cede Lombardy to Piedmont; France was to withdraw from the war. Cavour, aghast at this disruption of his plans, resigned in disgust. But others advocated continuing the war, most notably Giuseppe Mazzini, a Genoan with a passion for adventure, and Giuseppe Garibaldi, a soldier of fortune from Nizza. By the addition of Lombardy, Piedmont had increased by half again its size and population, and now referred to itself as the Kingdom of Italy, a magnetic attraction for many Italians who felt the war could still be won. But King Vittorio Emanuel II accepted the Villafranca arrangement; he had already gained a rich province and a new title and had no intentions of restraining the cause of unification.

Events soon moved quickly. By March of 1860, Tuscany, Parma, Modena and Romagna (the northernmost of the Papal States) had shaken off their feeble and unpopular regimes and petitioned to join Italy. Vittorio Emanuel, though pleased, hesitated to annex these considerable lands without the approval of Napoleon. Cavour was recalled for his expertise, and soon a deal was cut by which the new Kingdom was nearly doubled in size; Napoleon's price was the French-speaking province of Savoy and a smaller strip of ground along the seacoast south of the Ligurian Alps and including the city of Nizza, which became French Nice, infuriating its native son Garibaldi. The new boundary between the two realms was fixed at the watershed divide between the Rhone and Po River systems. Garibaldi was almost certainly provoked into action; wisely he directed his energies toward southern Italy and the almost universally despised 'Kingdom of the Two Sicilies'.

Within a month, uprisings in Messina and Palermo had been provoked, and their anticipated suppression was the signal for Garibaldi to strike. He and a relatively small group of followers invaded Sicily and easily overcame its administration, gathering an ever-swelling flood of recruits. By the end of July the entire island was conquered—liberated in the minds of most—and an advance on Naples planned. Once on the mainland, Garibaldi encountered very little resistance owing to the extreme unpopularity of the Neapolitan government. On September 7th, 1860 Naples itself was occupied. Now, somewhat suspicious of Garibaldi and desiring a show of force by regular Italian troops in the south, Cavour recommended an advance from the north. Upon the approach of the Piedmontese, the areas known as the Marches and

Umbria held a plebiscite in October while in the next month it was the turn of Naples/Sicily and in each case the vote was heavily in favor of union with the north. Despite vigorous protests from the Pope, who had lost a good deal of territory to such votes, the union was approved and a united Italy proclaimed on February 18th of 1861. Pope Pius countered by promptly excommunicating the King, Cavour, and everyone else in any way connected with the new Italian government. Undeterred, the Italian patriots wanted to take Latium, the last Papal province, as well as Venetia from Austria. "Free from the Alps to the Adriatic" became the cry, but the King decided to bide his time, despite the early death of Cavour on June 6th, 1861; he well knew that French troops would resist any occupation of Rome, and the Austrian Empire would not surrender Venetia without a definite military defeat.

Garibaldi proved impossible to restrain. The following year he led a military expedition against Rome, but the effort was beaten off and he was wounded. Following the departure of the last of the French troops in December 1866, he would try again, but the second effort also came up short of its purpose. Meanwhile, Austria and Prussia went to war in 1866 and Bismarck had seized the opportunity to conclude an alliance with Italy in order to force Austria to fight on two fronts at once. Nevertheless, it was the Austrians who were victorious at the Battle of Custozza—close by the old battlefield of Solferino—and the naval engagement subsequently known as the Battle of Lissa. Try as they might, Vittorio Emanuel's forces could not find a means to break the powerful Austrian defenses around the so-called Quadrilateral, a position anchored on the four cities of Mantua, Peschiera, Verona, and Legnago. Fortunately for the Italian cause, the Austrians were decisively defeated by the Prussians and forced to yield. Italy demanded the province of Venetia and the southern portion of the Tyrol around the city of Trient, two reasonable stipulations, as both areas were Italian in speech and character. Franz Joseph, however, was not impressed; his forces had beaten off the Italians and since he was not being asked to surrender any ground to the Prussians, who had beaten his army, he naturally felt great reluctance to give in to Vittorio Emanuel. But Bismarck supported his erstwhile allies, and in the end the Austrian had to cede Venetia. He did not yield it directly to the Italians, preferring to save face somewhat by presenting it to Napoleon, who was expected to, and did, give it to Italy. Franz Joseph was able to keep the southern Tyrol.

Austria's Emperor and many of his subjects would eventually more or less forgive the Prussians their moderate victory; they would have a much more difficult time forgiving the Italians their lack of the same. For their part, the latter always felt somewhat shortchanged, as long as Italian-speaking lands were left under Austrian rule. Some of the disappointment was temporarily mitigated four years later when war broke out between France and Prussia, and French troops were finally totally withdrawn from Latium. The Italians quickly moved in to fill the vacuum, despite the most energetic protests from the Pope, and for the first time since the days of the Roman Empire, all of Italy south of the Alps was under a single government, and the entire area was free of foreign soldiers. The capitol was moved from Florence to Rome. Yet another plebiscite of the inhabitants overwhelmingly approved the new arrangements.[1] Soon, new laws were passed guaranteeing the sanctity of the Papacy in the Vatican and Lateran Palaces. The Pope replied by declaring himself a 'prisoner' and threatening with excommunication all those who actively collaborated with the authorities of the government. Also peeved with the French who he considered had left him in the lurch, the Bishop of Rome now took new stock in those remaining heads of state across Europe who could still be considered devoted followers. Among them he recognized the familiar figure of the devoutly Catholic Franz Joseph.

By 1870, then, a newly united Italy had achieved the limits of its European territorial expansion until the outbreak of the Great War. She still looked longingly at the southern Tyrol, and began to notice other, smaller areas of the Austro-Hungarian Empire where Latin-speaking populations resided. Some of her more ardent nationalists even looked to the French-owned island of Corsica (which in itself was larger than the Italian-speaking areas of Austria) as a possible future area of expansion, but interestingly, the government never sanctioned greed for the island, probably because Italy held a substantial French-speaking population adjacent to the common frontier. Any adjustment to the Alpine border would not have been worthwhile for Rome; a line along the watershed crest was far more appealing to hold than the economically backward island in the Mediterranean. At any rate, nearly all desire for further expansion after 1870 was aimed directly at Vienna.

Unfortunately for the expansionists, the Italian government had many very serious internal issues to deal with as priorities for the years following the unification. The system was that of the Piedmonese State, the Constitution of which the King had promised never to rescind. It called for a Parliament consisting of a Senate and a Chamber of Deputies which were supposed to be of equal power. The King appointed the Senators and the Deputies were elected by popular vote, although suffrage was not truly universal at any time before the war. It is pointless for us to study in detail the working system here; suffice it to relate that like all Parliamentary governments it worked slowly and awkwardly, yet somehow worked. Two of the most pressing problems it faced were an intolerably high rate of illiteracy and a wide gap of living standards between the poorer, agrarian south and the more urban, industrializing north. Illiteracy rates may have been as high as 80% in the south in 1870; they were still at 50% by 1914, by which time those in the north stood at around 25%. Poverty was of course common, especially in the rural south, where many forms of agriculture were more difficult, owing to the poorer soils and lesser amounts of rainfall encountered there. Tax bases were often shallow and revenues far short of targets, let alone desires. There was never nearly enough to allot the armed forces, and with such a lengthy, vulnerable coastline to watch, the country was bound to need a powerful navy as well. In one of its first definitive foreign policy decisions, the government determined to never go to war with Britain, possessor of the world's most powerful navy.

On the other hand, the Italians never entirely trusted the French, despite the obvious historical, ethnic, and geographical ties between the two peoples. They reasoned—quite correctly, as things turned out—that France would always tend to play the role of a patronizing older sibling, suspicious and jealous of whatever the younger one might achieve. When the last scramble for overseas colonies took place in the 80's, Italy was among the last to act and accordingly, her share was among the least impressive. When the French leapt the Mediterranean and seized Tunisia, the Italians were bitterly disappointed; as the point on the North African littoral nearest the shores of Sicily they felt Tunisia was rightfully theirs. Moreover, it had been the heart of the Carthaginian realm, bought and paid for with Roman blood. Determined to protect themselves from further French encroachments, they sought out Bismarck, who arranged for Italy to join the three-year-old Dual Alliance with Austria-Hungary, converting it into a Triple Alliance. Now they needed not fear France; Bismarck had kept that nation diplomatically isolated in Europe. Although the Triplice served the three signatory nations very well, and attracted the Romanians and even the Serbians for awhile, it did have one negative effect on Austria-Hungary. Once the Italians had become the *bona fide* allies of Austria, the spirit of irredentism[2] grew markedly. Apparently the expansionists believed that a friendly Austria would be easier to reduce than would a hostile one. Whatever the case, Franz Joseph never had the slightest intention of surrendering any more land; he still resented the loss of Venetia if not Lombardy as well.

During the long period of Italian unification, which roughly coincided with that of the German, the Austrian Empire stood as an anomaly in an age of nationalism. Originally a widely scattered collection of Habsburg family lands across west-central Europe, the Empire had steadily lost detached lands in the west while gaining contiguous ground in the east. By 1848 it still held sizeable areas in Italy, but nearly lost its very cohesion to revolutionary movements, the most difficult of which to contain was the Hungarian bid for independence, a serious enterprise which took a year to defeat and only then with the help of Russian troops. A decade later the unsuccessful war with France and Piedmont shook the Habsburg State yet again. A third round of troubles came with the defeat of 1866 and more territorial loss to Italy. Certainly, history teaches that the surest way to topple regimes is to inflict serious military defeats upon them. Bismarck was well aware of Austria's vulnerability after the 1866 campaign, and purposely tried to mitigate his former enemy's difficulties in defeat. Franz Joseph hardly had time to mourn the loss of Venetia; his multi-ethnic state seemed likely to crumble into linguistic fragments. He clearly saw the need to placate the various nationalities, especially the stronger, more self-conscious ones. A first move involved the Hungarians. As a result of the so-called *Ausgleich* of 1867, the Empire was split into two roughly equal halves; the Magyars would enjoy full autonomy, and the Emperor would add King of Hungary to his long list of titles. A year later the Magyars arranged somewhat of an *Ausgleich* of their own when they allowed self-rule to the troublesome southwestern ten percent or so of their half, an area known as Croatia and Slavonia. Such moves could only provoke demands for concessions from other ethnic groups, but Franz Joseph had not intended to placate only the Hungarians. In 1870 the Austrian government revoked the 1855 Concordat with the Vatican, a stroke intended to please his numerous Protestant, Orthodox, and Islamic subjects. The following year the Czechs of Bohemia and Moravia were approached with an offer of autonomy in exchange for the Emperor to be crowned 'King of Bohemia' in Prague. This was probably a wise move, but it was bitterly opposed by the Austrian Germans—especially those who lived in Bohemia/Moravia—and the Slovenes, who desired equal treatment, as well as the Hungarians, and the project was abandoned. Austria-Hungary would plod along, with Hungary home to five major ethnic groups (one dominant, another autonomous) and Austria home to six (one dominant). Of these six the Italians were by far the smallest, and represented less than three percent of Austria's population, and only one and one-half percent of the total Imperial population. They did, however, represent one linguistic group too many, as we shall see.

Following the signing of the treaty creating the *Triple Alliance* on May 22nd, 1882, Franz Joseph took care never to go to Rome, in order to avoid any awkward developments which might arise from the friction between the Italian government and the Vatican. It was never intended to be a slight to either and apparently both understood his position. But if the Emperor was devoted to his Church, he never trusted his southern neighbors, and continued to lament the loss of his onetime Italian possessions. The government in Rome did nothing to help him save face or reduce his anxieties, and worse, it did nothing to stifle the noisy irredentists. Even so, the *Triple Alliance* was renewed in 1887. All seemed well within the framework of Europe. Then in 1890 came Bismarck's dismissal; suddenly the man who had played the leading role in the unification of Germany and a peripheral role in that of Italy, the architect of the *Triple Alliance* and guardian of the peace of Europe for twenty years, was gone. It would probably be an exaggeration to suggest that the fall of the old German Chancellor caused the economic depression of the early 1890's, but the act was most definitely a contributing factor in the subsequent slump. Italy, still very weak economically, was hard hit.

The early Nineties were characterized by economic difficulties around the world, but of the two nations of our focus, Italy was the worse off. Hard times led to civil unrest and disorders across the land. By 1894 steps had been taken to suppress the Socialists and other more extreme groups. The able Francesco Crispi was Premier by then; a proponent of the Triplice, he used his Austro-German connection to pursue colonial endeavors which might divert national attention from the daunting domestic issues. This tactic worked well until an Italian expedition into Ethiopia was resoundingly defeated at Adowa in 1896, a disaster that led to Crispi's downfall. A successor government tried to conciliate the extremists without result, leading to a virtual insurrection in the city of Milan on May 6, 1898 where hundreds of citizens were killed or injured. Within two years, fanatics had assassinated the King (Humbert 1878-1900) in the same location. He was succeeded by his son, Vittorio Emanuel III, an amiable, liberal-minded man who was determined to avoid trouble, especially at home. The new monarch entrusted the liberals with power, ushering in the era remembered as the 'Giolittian period' for the dominant personality of that time, Giovanni Giolitti. Although Giolitti's premiership was broken several times from 1901 until 1914, those who filled the intervals were more or less of the same mind. Those years were characterized by a free press, enlargement of the voting enfranchisement, and economic and political stability. Italy's desire to be included within the ranks of Europe's Great Powers seemed a goal which might well be attainable.

Unapparent at the time was the Giolittian foreign policy. As early as 1894, the *Triple Alliance* faced a possible hostile coalition in the form of the Dual Alliance of France and Russia. Uncomfortable with Italy's role in league with two Empires opposing the more liberal-minded French, the Giolittians decided to approach the latter, and the result was a secret treaty signed in 1902 in which the Italians pledged not to take part on Germany's side in any new Franco-German conflict, even if the circumstances leading to it were similar to those of 1870, when the French had been the first to declare war. This was a clear violation on Italy's part of the terms of the Triplice, hence the secrecy. Rome also promised to support France's claim to Morocco, in exchange for French support of Italian desires for Tripoli and Cyrenaica, the last remaining remnants of the Ottoman Empire on the North African littoral. The French assured their new friends that they were free to move against the two provinces whenever they desired. It was not until the results of the Moroccan Crisis of 1911 that French were finally confirmed as possessors of Morocco; through no coincidence did the Italians decide to strike against the Turks that year. The resulting war is beyond our interests here, except in the way it upset the stability of the *Triple Alliance*.

Germany had long been looking towards the Balkans and Turkey as the logical direction in which her influence might be spread. The Kaiser in particular had taken great pains to befriend Constantinople and to try to divert Russian ambitions away from the region and out into central and eastern Asia. These plans had been largely successful; German officers had long been drilling Ottoman troops, the controversial Berlin to Bagdad Railway was well under construction, and the Russians had come into conflict with Japan—a British ally—and been obliged to wage unsuccessful war. The eastern Mediterranean seemed ripe for domination by the *Alliance* if not for the British in Egypt. But by declaring war on a potential ally, the Italians had upset the applecart. The French and Russians might well be pleased, but the British, who now had a new neighbor on the Egyptian/Libyan border, were not so sure, and the Austro-Germans were more than disappointed. Italian duplicity had long been suspected, and now it seemed confirmed.

Luckily for the Austro-Germans, Italian ineptitude came to the rescue. Unable to secure the provinces from the fanatical resistance of the inhabitants, Rome asked for diplomatic support. The French could do little without revealing the substance of the secret treaty and the British were unwilling to risk offending the Turks. Italy had little choice but to turn to her official allies who then promised their support for a price. If Italy would return to the fold of the *Alliance*, she could have full diplomatic support and could even annex some of the islands of the Aegean. Rome agreed, Constantinople was bought off with promises of other territories for the future, and the crisis passed. The *Triple Alliance* continued, incidentally, to be renewed every five years; its final renewal was signed in 1912. Thus was maintained the façade of unity of the *Alliance* until the outbreak of the Great War in 1914. Germany and Austria-Hungary felt they still had Italy as an ally, though they certainly did not trust her. France and Russia were equally unsure of Britain, but as long as Grey was British Foreign Minister they need not have worried. The Italians, for their part, kept a foot in each camp, and were determined to support whichever party they felt would best protect their interests. Premier Salandra referred to the policy as one of *sacro egoismo* (sacred egoism) once war had broken out, but before Italy had joined in. The Austrians in particular would have agreed with the egoistic part; they would not have concurred regarding the 'sacred' description. For all the belligerents, a question which most seriously concerned them now was: What will Italy do?

For decades, historians have wrestled with the circumstances surrounding the outbreak of the Great War, searching and straining for some explanation of how such a calamitous event could have so disrupted such an apparently prosperous and progressive society as Western Civilization. From another perspective, it is difficult to imagine how it could have *not* occurred. The case of the Austro-Italian conflict is, however, unique. France doomed herself and Germany to war by her refusal to forgive the latter its victory in 1871. Bismarck had shielded his Empire for twenty years by keeping the French diplomatically isolated, but once his steadying influence was gone, it was inevitable that Paris would combine with St. Petersburg; the latter being on an equally dangerous collision course with Germany's only firm ally Austria. As long as the odds were two-on-two there was no real danger; a Triplice Italy and an aloof Britain would see to that. It was when the two odd men out began to make unprecedented foreign policy moves that conflict became possible, even likely.

Britain settled her long standing differences with France with the famous *Entente* of 1904, but there is some evidence that the two were beginning a fundamental understanding as early as 1897. Then came the *Entente* with Russia; France's ally, in 1907; up to and even after the outbreak of war, British leaders were always scrupulously consistent in insisting that Britain had no formal commitments to anyone, that her hands were free. And technically, all this was true; realistically it was anything but. Only a few men knew the truth and they were not talking—ever. The point is that the Germans could be forgiven for not understanding the actual British position; if they had, they almost certainly would never have gone to war against such odds. But there was more, much more. We know that the Italians had vowed to never go to war with Britain and they had allowed the French to leak this information to London. With it in hand the British had no qualms about concluding an agreement with France wherein the French navy was to guard the Mediterranean, while the British opposed the main enemy (German) fleet. But this arrangement only makes sense if Italy is assumed to *not* be an enemy, the *Alliance* notwithstanding; the combined Austrian and Italian fleets would have matched up rather well against the French. And Britain was not about to allow an important lifeline such as the Mediterranean to be thus imperiled.

Very few people in or out of government—any government—had any idea of what was really going on behind the scenes. Less than two years after the *Triple Entente* had been worked out, the Italians and the Russians came into understanding in the Racconigi Agreement of 1909. It provided for the two nations to cooperate in opposing Austro-Hungarian designs in the Balkans. Italy agreed to support the Russian claim to the Straits (Turkish territory) in return for Russian support for its schemes involving Tripoli and Cyrenaica. For the first time, all four future major *Entente* partners were linked. The Austro-Germans always suspected Italian shenanigans, but considering their actions when the crisis came in 1914, it is hard to believe that they knew for sure that the odds would be four to two. But both Berlin and Vienna/Budapest had seriously underestimated just how much resentment had been fermented in Rome and St. Petersburg with the Austro-Hungarian annexation of Bosnia and Herzegovina in 1908. Both of the latter were furious and vowed to never again allow any Habsburg aggrandizement unless they too were equally compensated. For old Franz Joseph, the annexation of the two primitive, former Turkish provinces—which were not incorporated into either Austria or Hungary, but formed in themselves a third parcel of the Empire—was poor compensation for the loss of Lombardy and Venetia earlier in his reign. It surely never occurred to him, who only wanted to keep his inheritance more or less equally spacious, that he had provoked two resentful neighbors. When Austria-Hungary moved against Serbia in July 1914, even though virtually all impartial observers agreed she had every right to do so, the Russians and Italians were not willing to allow her freedom of action. Russia backed Serbia, and firmly so. The Italian reaction was much less straightforward.

As we have seen, Giolitti was more or less master of Italian politics from the turn of the century. In March of 1914 he withdrew and began to travel in earnest; his successor as Premier was Antonio Salandra, a man of similar, but not identical leanings. When the crisis of July arrived, the Salandra government determined to press the issue of compensation by Austria to Italy, should the former take any advantage of Serbia or in the Balkans in general. As early as the 27th, that is, before Vienna had declared war on Belgrade, Rome had made its position clear, at least if Salandra is to be believed, and on this point there was no reason for him to be untruthful. One would assume then that the Austrians expected to 'compensate' Italy from the first. But there is another, strong possibility: Vienna was counting on Rome's support in the war, and was well prepared to agree to approve a worthwhile share of the spoils for Italy. If this was the case, they were by no means alone, for on the 31st the Italian Commander in Chief of the Army, General Luigi Cadorna, dispatched his battle plans to the King for approval. These plans called for deployment along the Franco-Italian frontier in the Alps and for one army (two Corps) to be sent to the upper Rhine, from where it would assist the Germans against the French.

In fact, the government was deeply divided amongst those who favored fighting with the allies of the *Alliance*, those who wanted the nation to stay neutral for the time being, and those who preferred immediately throwing off the mask and declaring for the *Entente*. But by August 1st when it was felt some sort of stance needed to be taken, the British position was still not clear, so Salandra and his group opted for the middle road—neutrality—and this was subsequently announced on August 2nd. That same day the King approved Cadorna's plans, which for the moment, and in the end forever, would remain only plans.

The announcement stunned the Austro-Germans, and not a few Italians as well. Baron Sidney Sonnino, a prominent figure who had twice held the Premiership briefly, was angered and declared that the move had 'dishonored' the government. The two *Alliance* Emperors could not believe their fellow monarch Vittorio Emanuel would casually abandon them in their hour of danger. Although neither was particularly well informed of the events that rapidly unfolded in the final rush to war, each clung to the belief that antique codes of honor still superseded any inclinations of self-interest. Genuinely hurt, they grumbled and sputtered, vowing never to again have any dealings with the Italian King. The men of their administrations were not nearly as surprised, grounded as they were by heavier doses of reality. Nevertheless, news of Italy's neutrality was received across Central Europe to a good deal of disappointment and disgust. Too late did the Austro-Germans realize that they should never have trusted their erstwhile allies. When Britain entered the war on August 4th, the shock was complete.

Austria-Hungary's reaction was relatively speedy. By the 13th, a veteran General (Rohr) had been given command of the border districts and ordered to begin preparing all necessary defenses. Next day Baron Karl von Macchio was shuttled to Rome with an urgent diplomatic mission: Remind the Italians that even if they refused to support their *Alliance* partners, they were still bound by one of the Treaty's clauses which called for at least 'benevolent neutrality' in cases of non-belligerency. Von Macchio was shown another clause of the text which called for the signatories to maintain the status quo in the Balkans and 'reciprocal compensation' if any of the three obtained any special advantages there. The Baron's argument that Austria had not at that time achieved any advantages anywhere fell on deaf ears. By simply declaring war on Serbia, the Italians maintained, Vienna had upset the status quo and therefore owed Rome. It did not take much insight to determine which way the winds of politics were blowing. By mid-September, Austria had scraped up a force of 300,000 troops with which to guard the southern border. On the 19th, they were sent, and Rohr finally had something to work with.

Summer gave way to autumn. Gradually, those who in Italy had favored the *Alliance* cause gave way to increasing numbers of neutralists and those who leaned toward the *Entente*. A grandson of the famous Garibaldi of the days of unification persuaded 4,000 men to enlist with him into the French Foreign Legion; this force ended up on the Western Front aside the French before winter. When the Ottoman Empire joined the *Alliance* in October, additional sympathies for the *Entente* were generated. The tribesmen of the recently Turkish provinces of Tripoli and Cyrenaica had never been subdued, and with Turkish participation in the war they began an insurgency with renewed vigor. All through the autumn and winter fighting raged in the deserts of North Africa. One native group in particular—known as the Senussi—was rather successful in resisting the Italians, practically expelling them from all areas distant from the seacoast. These humiliating defeats only hardened Italian feeling against the Turks, and indirectly against their allies.

On October 16th the long-time Italian Foreign Minister San Giuliano died. He was replaced by Baron Sonnino, who apparently had gotten over the dishonor he had felt when the country had not gone to war with her allies against the *Entente*. Sonnino was not a typical Italian. His mother had been English and he was a Protestant in a nation almost entirely Catholic, and he had no patience for the expressive emotionalism of his countrymen. Nicknamed 'The Taciturn' by his colleagues, he had little to say unless he felt it important. When confronted with opinions contrary to his own, his tactics were to avoid argument and remain silent. Proper to the core, he was all for maintaining agreements to the letter. Having failed to convince his people to fight, he now could be counted on to adhere to the principle of benevolent neutrality; he could also be counted on to insist on compensation from Austria.

As time passed and neither of the warring camps were able to secure the quick victory they so sincerely expected, many Italians began to debate the benefits of continued neutrality versus those of participation in the war. Participation now meant joining the *Entente*. The first issue of a newspaper dated November 15th, 1914 strongly advocated war. Its editor was a man named Benito Mussolini, a right-wing nationalist who believed that Italy would miss a golden opportunity to strengthen itself and claim her just spoils if she failed to involve herself. Mussolini found an increasing number of Italians to agree with him. As the debate raged across the country, Premier Salandra decided to reveal part of his hand, and on December 5th informed the Chamber of Deputies of an incident he claimed occurred in August of 1913. As the story went, Austria had asked for Italy's assent for an attack on Serbia, a nation recently enlarged by annexations following the Balkan Wars, and increasingly hostile to Austria. Italy had refused, he said, and made it perfectly clear that she would countenance no Austrian actions in the Balkans. He now used the incident to point out that Austria must have known well that her recent war on Serbia was bound to provoke Italy. He did not mention that a decision had already been taken to begin negotiations with Vienna for the purpose of settling the compensation issue. An appeal from the Pope (Benedict XV had succeeded Pius X who had died on August 20th) to broker some sort of Christmas truce for all the nations at war, came on the 6th, but received scant support.

Secret negotiations between Rome and Vienna began on December 12th; Sonnino was involved and informed his ambassador in Austria, the Duke of Avarna, to contact his opposite number, Count Berchtold. Soon after Berchtold knew, so did the Germans, who quickly recruited a suitable candidate to travel to Rome and influence events. The man for the job was former Chancellor von Bülow, a well-mannered and charming personality who was married to a Sicilian lady, often spent the winter months in the Mediterranean, and spoke the language fluently. Bülow would be well-received they reasoned, and in fact he was. By the time Bülow reached his destination on the 20th, the talks were barely off the ground, the main Italian points thus far had been a consistent demand for compensation, and a warning issued on the 14th that they would not tolerate an Austro-Hungarian absorption of Serbia. On the very day of the German's arrival, tempers cooled noticeably, and Berchtold agreed to continue the talks on the basis of allowing for compensation to Italy. Few persons in Italy felt any antipathy toward Germany; indeed, many respected well her martial reputation, powerful navy, and rapidly growing economy and were aware of the extent of German financial interests south of the Alps. But Bülow's task would not be easy. The Italian demands were steep. First, they proposed to annex about 40% of the Tyrol, an area they referred to as the Trentino. They foresaw a new boundary as leaving the old at Mt. Cevedale and running east by northeast to the town of Klausen; from there south, then due east to meet the old line just northeast of Cortina on the Ampezzo River. Secondly, they wanted an area north of the Gulf of Trieste, including the City of Görz, the towns of Cormons, Monfalcone, and Gradisca, and above all, the seaport of Trieste. Thirdly, certain small islands in the Adriatic were asked for. In return, they promised to continue their 'benevolent neutrality' throughout the war. They then proposed a recess for the Holidays while the Austrians thought about the proposals.

The Austrians were not amused. They accepted the recess and agreed to begin face-to-face talks in Rome on January 7th, but were not inclined to consider any of the Italian proposals, which were deemed to be excessive. Little did they realize that while they were left to consider giving away territory, Rome was considering entering the war. Austria-Hungary's poor military showing in the first five months of war had weakened her bargaining position. On January 6th, 1915, the Italian leaders authorized the call-up of 300,000 troops. The screws around Austria were beginning to tighten.

When talks resumed in Rome on the 7th, Bülow, Macchio, and Sonnino began a three way give and take. Bülow asked if Italy would be satisfied with the Trentino alone. Sonnino indicated that any offer should include at least Trieste. Within a week the men of the *Alliance* had forwarded an official proposal; as it did not include Trieste, it was rejected. Sonnino was informed that as Trieste was Austria's only seaport it could not be surrendered; the Empire would prefer war. Then at the Austrian Foreign Ministry, Berchtold was replaced by Baron Burian, a stubborn, tough negotiator, and the talks bogged down while Burian initially voiced some unworkable proposals. Sonnino began to feel frustration, and wondered whether Vienna was serious about diplomacy. Typically, he began to speak less and trust more sparingly. Sonnino's subsequent behavior would make a lasting impression on Bülow, who later said that despite the Italians' reputation for bubbly speech, "it was my misfortune to strike the one Italian who did not talk".[3] The Duke of Avarna was given the unenviable task of explaining, painstakingly, the Italian position to Burian, whose next tactic was to attempt to deflect his neighbor's interests to the Balkans, where he claimed, Austria was prepared to offer a good deal. Hopefully, for the sake of his memory, he was only attempting to stall, although it is hard to understand why at that time he would want to. Already on January 28th serious riots erupted in Bosnia over the issue of conscription. In the end it was decided to send these Slavic troops to the Italian border where there was yet no war, rather than risk sending them against the Russians, let alone the Serbs.

Soon Sonnino had been stalled long enough. On the 12th of February he addressed a warning to the Austro-Hungarian government in which his government's position regarding the future of the Balkans was made crystal-clear. Expecting to be contacted, he was not, and repeated the warning in different words five days later. Meanwhile on the 16th, the first contact with the British was made for the purpose of discussing possible Italian participation in the war on the side of the *Entente*. Finally on the 27th, Burian made some futile proposals and a few more were forthcoming on March 3rd, prompting Avarna to conclude that further negotiation with the Austrian was hopeless. But just then Burian's position began to weaken when he realized that the Winter offensives on the Eastern Front had irretrievably broken down and the fortress of Przemsyl was doomed. On March 9th, he announced he had accepted the principle that compensation to Italy must be made from Austrian territory. Sonnino demanded that serious talks be resumed at once, and without German (i.e. Bülow's) interference. This final round began on the 15th over Bülow's protestations, however, five days later he notified Sonnino that Germany would underwrite any deal cut between Italy and Austria. At last Sonnino could speak again.

A week later, on March 27th, the German Chancellor announced that Austria had a fresh offer to make. It included: All territory of Italian speech in the Trentino and at the head of the Gulf, Trieste to become a free city within the Empire and enjoy an administration of Italian character and have an Italian university. Albania was to come into the Italian sphere of interest. All Italian nationals from the annexed territories were to be repatriated. Eagerly the Austro-Germans awaited Sonnino's response. It was not what they wanted to hear; 'too vague' commented the Italian. By April 2nd, the proposal had been resubmitted with specific boundaries mentioned. Six days later Vienna had received a new response, in the form of an ultimatum listing all of Italy's minimum demands. They were: The Trentino, with a northern boundary identical with that of the Napoleonic Kingdom of Italy of 1811, Gradisca, Görz, and Trieste and their environs. The Carzolari Islands in the Adriatic. Italian hegemony in Albania. The territory in question was to be transferred immediately. Italy pledged neutrality throughout the war and offered 200 million lire for loss of government property. On the 16th came Burian's reply. It was generally negative, except for the Albanian stipulation and an unspecific offer of slightly more ground in the Trentino. It could barely be considered a counter-offer and predictably, it was rejected on the 21st as insufficient. Two days later Cadorna ordered the mobilization of eight Army Corps, and all eyes focused on the *Entente*. Burian continued to parley with the Italian ambassador for a few more days, but negotiations had run their course. Simply put, Austria was unwilling to meet Italy's minimum demands; from another perspective Austria had refused to be blackmailed by the Italians.

One is left to wonder why the two sides could not come together over the momentous issue of war, especially inasmuch as they were never all that far apart. Only one mountain ridge separated the final Austrian offer from the Italian demands in the Trentino. Albania was never much of an issue, nor were the Islands. That left only the territory at the head of the Gulf, and it was here that lay the real issue. This region is where Latin speech gives way to Slavic, and the Slavs were absolutely adamant that they not be handed over to Italy; such a development would certainly have provoked a revolt of the Slovenes and Croats within Austro-Hungarian territory. While Rome was not demanding any Slavic lands *per se*, it did insist on several cities and towns, where Latin was the speech of the majority, but to have annexed them was to annex a sizeable Slovene minority in the necessary contiguous surrounding territory as well as in the population centers. And Trieste was Austria's only seaport worth mention; Fiume belonged to Hungary. Trieste and vicinity then, was the real issue, and one for which both parties were willing to fight.

The fight could now not be long delayed. On April 26th, Italy and the *Entente* nations signed the Treaty of London, despite some grumbling by the Russians as to whether all the Italian demands were worth meeting in order to 'admit' her into the conflict. They did have a point. Rome's price was high: The Trentino, including all property south of the line of the Adriatic watershed (which included a quarter-million Germans), the entire Istrian Peninsula (inhabited by Slovenes and Croats) which of course included Trieste, etc., Northern Dalmatia (Croats) and numerous islands off the coast of the same, a sphere of influence in Turkey, an expansion of her North African possessions, and Valona and Sasemo Island in Albania.[4] But for the *Entente*, giving away enemy territory was no problem; it was in fact good insurance to have another greedy power on its side. And if it were to lose, the promises would be worthless anyway.

By the end of April Giolitti had been informed that the nation intended to enter the war, and he immediately burst into action, trying desperately to save the peace. He had hesitated for too long in believing that a deal with the Austrians would be worked out. On May 3rd Sonnino contacted Vienna to formally repudiate the *Triple Alliance*. Rabble-rousers in several major cities—Mussolini and the poet D'Annunzio among them—organized mobs of unemployed and extremist citizens in mass demonstrations for war, giving birth to the myth that the government had been forced into war to avoid revolution. In reality the average Italian, at least the average literate one who may have had some opinion on international politics, had no reason to clamber for war, and had he been honestly informed of the circumstances of Italy's entry into it, he almost certainly would have favored a peaceful settlement. But in Italy as in all the nations that went so willingly to war from 1914 to 1918, the populace was simply swept up by events, and carried with the tides of war hysteria.

There was no stopping the avalanche into war. On May 5th the Italian General Staff were told of the London Treaty. On the same day a massive demonstration organized by Gabriele D'Annunzio near Genoa was cancelled by the authorities for reasons the poet/playwright correctly assumed meant war. Then on the 7th, Giolitti announced that he had worked out a deal with Bülow practically guaranteeing all of Italy's desires. The war was unnecessary after all, he pleaded, to no avail; he could not have known his efforts came far too late. Two days later he was still begging the King and Salandra to change their minds, without result. His next strategy was to rally his still considerable support in the government to protest the war and to bring down Salandra.

This he proceeded to do, and had no real difficulty in gathering the necessary majority, proof positive that the warmongers were still a clear minority. Meanwhile, Austrian and German citizens in Italy at that time were advised by their respective consulates to leave the country without delay. On the Eastern Front, *Alliance* forces broke the line between the Carpathian Mountains and the Vistula River and advanced rapidly, turning the Russian retreat into nearly a chaotic rout. Salandra's position was undermined to the extent that he offered his resignation on May 13th. Parliament was scheduled to meet on the 20th. With a week in which to work his magic, Giolitti believed for a moment that he had succeeded. Then the King, the only person who could have derailed the peace train, intervened. He refused to accept Salandra's resignation, and he ordered the denunciation of the *Triple Alliance* to be made public. From that moment, everyone knew what was coming. Even so, the King did not allow the terms of the Treaty of London to be made public; he knew that many Italians would not have been willing to fight for such extravagant terms. And one of the stipulations for Italy was that she declare war within one month of its signing.

By the next day, May 16th, no one in or out of government retained any doubts as to Italy's new position *vis a vis* the war. Giolitti left Rome, still in disbelief that so many of his old associates such as Salandra and Sonnino could have allowed their attitudes to have been so drastically altered. Everyone held their breath until the 20th, and the meeting of the Parliament. In the event, Salandra got his vote of confidence and a measure was passed whereby full authority to wage war was conferred upon the standing Ministry. Full military mobilization was ordered on the 22nd. Already on the 10th of the month a naval agreement had been signed in Paris which specified the respective roles of British, French, and Italian sea power in the Mediterranean.[5] The ground forces enjoyed a similar head start, but the government wanted to give its soldiers every last minute necessary to be ready for the break. Finally, at 4:00 p.m. on May 23rd, 1915, the Kingdom of Italy declared that it was in a state of war with the Empire of Austria-Hungary. It did not immediately declare hostilities against the other *Alliance* powers.

At last the deed had been done. For many Italians the conflict was seen as a final chapter of the *Risorgimento*, that national movement which had led to unification. Everywhere there were demonstrations of patriotism and the enthusiastic crowds as experienced by the original warring nations in August of 1914. Had they only known the truth…

Across the frontier, the feeling of most Austrians was that they had been jumped from behind by a former ally while fighting for their lives against two other opponents. Many citizens who had previously been lukewarm at best for the war—much of its large Slavic population—now felt a new patriotism and a new determination to help the Empire defend itself. The elderly Emperor Franz Joseph considered the declaration a personal affront from Vittorio Emanuel against him, and called the act "Perfidy whose like history does not know."[6]

For the Germans the primary emotion was disappointment. No one since the days of the formation of the *Triple Alliance* in 1882 had ever believed Italy would be of much great help against France; Bismarck himself had once written that the best that could be expected of Italy was that she might send buglers and drummers to the crest of the Alps to make some noise which might worry the French and possibly divert *some* strength away from Germany. Now, even this modest hope was gone and another nation added to the ranks of her enemies. Chancellor Bethmann-Holweg gave a speech in which he admitted he was angry, and accused the Italians of treachery and of suppressing the majority of Deputies who stood against the war. Bülow, who had at the eleventh hour offered virtually everything the Italians were asking for, spoke of the bad faith of the latter and the intrigues of the *Entente*.

Salandra publically answered these invectives with a lengthy address in which he carefully outlined and justified Italy's position, and in flowery language basically admitted that Italy did not trust its former allies and to have kept to the *Triple Alliance* was to have accepted a position of submission to Germany. He did not, of course, mention the Treaty of London. The war of words was over. The war of bullets had already begun.

Chapter Two
War Zones and War Machines

The uplands of northern Italy have reportedly long been home to the sounds of cannon fire. That is, the natives have long reported what they say sounds like cannon fire, although like many such locations around the world no cannons have ever been discovered, and it is plain to all but the most superstitious that the noises are of natural origin. These reports long predate the modern era and probably predate the gunpowder era, but for most who have experienced them, there is more or less general agreement that the phenomena do indeed sound like distant cannon discharging, usually heard on clear, calm days. Interestingly, such sounds have come to be associated with guns in several global locations, including Lake Seneca in western New York State and near the town of Barisol in the present nation of Bangladesh. When pursued, the booming sounds always seem to be somewhere else, not unlike the end of a rainbow. None of the absurd explanations advanced by the inevitable skeptics has ever satisfied the locals, however, who certainly know the difference between the sound of a thunderstorm or an avalanche and that of a cannon. In Italy the phenomena are known as *brontidi* and at one time were the subject of an intense study by serious scholars, who when they had been informed by mountain residents that often the sounds seemed to emanate from the very mountains themselves, advanced some very earthy explanations.

But for forty-two months, from late May of 1915 until early November of 1918, no new reports of *brontidi* would be forthcoming. For during that interval there would indeed be many cannon in the Alps and they would, unfortunately, fire millions of rounds which were a good deal more destructive than any natural forces of human memory. The Great War had come to Italy, and before it was over, the landscape would be altered considerably. In many cases, the way of life would as well.

An examination of the ground over which two of Europe's great nations were about to do battle makes for a fascinating study. The Austro-Italian frontier of 1915 ran almost exclusively over the tops of mountain peaks and along mountain ridges. Of course, it necessarily cut across numerous rivers and streams and thus traversed many valleys, but the tradition was that great heights separated the two realms. If one could have hiked the jagged, curving line from the Swiss border to the Adriatic Sea, he or she would have completed a journey of about 765 kilometers (475 miles) over some of the most rugged, and some of the most beautiful, landscapes of the continent. The route would have appeared on a map as distinctly resembling a letter 'S' lying on its left side, and over 90% of its course would have required an individual of the utmost experience and stamina, used to prolonged exertion in the thin air of high altitudes. Of all the European international frontiers of the time, perhaps only the one separating Norway and Sweden could be considered as less appropriate for a battle line between two powerful military establishments. Yet once war had been declared, this is exactly what the frontier had become. It then only remained to be seen which of the hostile camps had a plan and the means to commence operations somewhere within this Alpine panorama. Let us briefly examine the geography of this region, that we might better understand the nature of the campaigning which was about to commence.

Europe's Alps Mountains are without question the most notorious range in the world. Though not nearly as high as Asia's Himalayas, nor nearly as long a chain as South America's Andes, nor nearly possessed of such a huge area of expanse as North America's Rockies, they nevertheless have long enjoyed the distinction of consideration as among the foremost of the earth's natural features. This is certainly due in part to the fact that recorded history in the area of the range predates that in most other areas of the surface of the planet. By the time of the Roman Empire the entire area was within the boundaries of its civilizing influence, and the mountains have affected the flow of events ever since. Some of the most colorful Western literature, folklore, and tradition originates in or concerns these rugged uplands. Their magnificence, splendor, and serenity have inspired wonder, admiration, and industry throughout the ages, and even in the Twenty-First Century their magnetic attraction continues to draw vacationers and tourists as well as every sort of outdoor person, from the climber or biker to the canoeist or camper. Probably no other European topographic feature is as well known, unless it is the Rhine River which, of course, rises in the Alps.

According to the *Britannica World Atlas* (William Benton, 1968) which features an excellent fold-out map of the region, the Alps Mountain System consists of at least twenty-five major ranges, and at least as many more lesser ones, with innumerable sub-groups and clusters. From the Mediterranean Sea at the Franco-Italian border, the range sprawls to the north, then to the east, encompassing a wide swath of ground before yielding to less formidable foothills which themselves seem to flatten out before the Central European or Hungarian Plain is reached. It is debatable whether the Dinaric Group which extends down into the Balkans and the Apennine Ridge which runs the length of the Italian Peninsula should be considered sub-ranges of the Alps, but even without them the core area represents the single most imposing feature on a topographic map of the continent west of the Caucasus. The entire Italian Peninsula including the Po Valley is effectively set apart from the land beyond the mountains and Italy is practically isolated from all its neighbors by the presence of the lofty peaks. As the ancient Romans expanded their power and influence, the region was slowly assimilated into their control, but was not entirely conquered until about the time of the founding of the Empire. The Imperial Roman regime was, incidentally, the only government to ever possess the entire area of the Alps. Since its fall, the mountains have always been a frontier area dividing various nationalities, language groups, and cultures. But the Romans preferred to anchor the borders of their Empire on large rivers, notably the Rhine and Danube, both of which draw a considerable percentage of their waters from Alpine sources. These two cover the north slope of the range, flowing in opposite directions, to the North and Black Seas, respectively. The western slopes are drained by France's Rhone, while the southern side feeds its runoff into the Adriatic, and it is around this latter watershed that our story will unfold. Far and away the largest stream to empty into the Adriatic is the Po, the valley of which accounts for much of the land of northern Italy. Moving from this river to the northeast along the seacoast to its northern extremity at the Gulf of Trieste, one encounters many other lesser rivers, the largest of which are the Adige, the Brenta, the Piave, the Tagliamento, and the Isonzo. Beyond the Gulf, the running waters do not originate from the Alps. Also beyond the Gulf, ground relevant to our story becomes hard to find, and as we shall see, this is no coincidence.

The Adriatic Sea watershed then, is our principal concern. If we begin at the extreme western end of the Austro-Italian border where it meets the Swiss frontier, we are among some of the highest peaks of the eastern Alps. From Bormio Italy, which is in the valley of the Adda River (a Po tributary), a carriage road was constructed which led into Austrian territory and the Etsch River valley. The Etsch is a major north-to-south running stream which drained half of the Austrian Tyrol and the valley of which was the setting for all the major towns south of the Brenner Pass and a railroad connecting them. This road was the only link between the two river systems for many miles and was only painstakingly constructed through a gap in the high ridge subsequently known as the Stelvio (or Stilfser) Pass. This so-called pass is over 2,750 meter (9,000 foot) high and required countless hairpin turns on both sides for the road to traverse it. The Swiss border is only a kilometer or so distant, and at this point where the three nations met was found the Dreisprachenspitze, a mountain which supposedly divided lands in which three languages—Italian, German and Romansch—were spoken, the Romansch being the vernacular of the Swiss in that area. From the Pass the border ran along the spine of the Ortler Group, a snow capped, glacier ridden ridge featuring peaks such as Cristallo (3,900m, 12,800 ft) and Cevedale (3,765m, 12,300 ft) in a generally southeasterly, then southerly, direction. As far as Cevedale the international frontier was also the linguistic frontier, but as the line cut due south it ran into land of purely Italian speech. South of the Ortlers, the elevation diminished somewhat, the glaciers disappeared, and the terrain became somewhat less formidable at the Tonale Pass an 1,885m (6,180 ft) road bearing-gap which also connected the Po and Adige[7] watersheds, though its path is far less difficult. But south of the Tonale, the border once again climbed uphill to cross the imposing Adamello Group, another glacial wilderness attaining heights of 3,660m (12,000 ft). Only riding trails crossed this area, to be used sparingly in the best of weather. As the line continued south, however, it slipped away from the main ridge and followed a lesser one, passing east of the peaks of Cornone and entering a vale from which it emerged to just touch the northern shore of the alpine Lake Idro, a clear body of water at 365m (1,200 ft) which formed the southern terminus of a pristine valley known as Val Guidicaria. Then the line rose again to the tops of the nearby mountains, several of which topped at 1,980m (6,500 ft) or so. Here it halted its southerly course and turned to the east sloping down to cross Lake Garda, a large, warmer body of freshwater at only 47m (154 ft) elevation.

Garda is a gorgeous lake, rimmed by mountains along its more northerly shores, but jutting into the Plans of Lombardy at its southern end. Over 90% of the water was on the Italian side of the line, but Austrians held the northern tip as well as the largest town on the shoreline. Both peoples used the idyllic setting for vacationing, and even today so many German speakers visit the lake for recreation that the locals still facetiously refer to it as 'Garda See'. It is within, but on the very edge of, the Po watershed; its outlet the Mincio River has been the scene of much strife between Italian and Austrian.

As it left the waters of the lake, the borderline climbed high onto the Baldo *Massif*, a voluminous mountain ridge separating the Mincio and Adige watersheds. Often referred to simply as Mount Baldo, this feature actually displayed several distinct peaks, including the 2,075m (6,800 ft) Mt. Altissimo and the 2,200m (7,200 ft) Mt. Maggiore. Then it dipped down to cross the Adige at its extreme southernmost point, and promptly rose onto the heights of Mt. Corno and the ridge to the east, the southerly slopes of which fell gently to the plain. Here was the setting for the medieval 13 Communities, an area in which large numbers of Germans had settled as they established a trail of commercial ventures from southern Germany, over the Brenner Pass and down the Etsch valley and on to the sea. By the beginning of the Twentieth Century, however, nearly all traces of German speech in the 13 Communities had vanished as the inhabitants either emigrated or were assimilated by the Italian culture which surrounded them. Had the '13' been sited a few kilometers to the north, on the Austrian side of the border, it may have retained its German character for a longer time period, but as we have seen, the Corno ridge was as far south as the Austrian Tyrol extended.

From this point to follow the border to the east is to follow a winding, twisting line for over 200 kilometers in a generally northeast direction. Near Valarsa it was cut by the Frugazze Pass, a relatively low (1,160m, 3,800 ft) trail just south of the majestic Mt. Pasubio, a 2,230m (7,300 ft) obstruction beyond which lay the Barcole Pass, connecting Val Terragnolo on the Austrian side with the Posina River valley on the Italian side. The Posina is a tributary of the Astico which in its northern reaches formed part of the frontier in the area of the Folgaria and Lavaronne Plateaus. This area is a very convenient short-cut for travelers or traders coming down the Etsch valley but wanting to end up in Venice. To follow the Etsch to the sea was to travel too far south. But to leave the Etsch just south of Trient by way of the Val Terragnolo or by way of the Plateaus to the Astico was to reduce the journey's distance considerably. For this reason, another German settlement, this one known as the Seven Communities (*Setti Communi*)[8], grew up on what became known as the Asiago Plateau. This island of German speech had not nearly disappeared, as had the 13 Communities, by 1915, and as we shall see would play a major role in determining Austrian strategy. It is worth noting that although the Asiago Plateau was fairly easily connected to the Tyrol by routes to the west and northwest, to its immediate north were the nearly impassible ridges formed by Spitz Tonezza (1,433m, 4,700 ft), Mt. Mandriola (2,050m, 6,700 ft), Mt. Kempel, Mt. Ortigara (2,100m, 6,900 ft) and others. But there is no incentive for the traveler to attempt such an undertaking, since a few kilometers to the east flows the Brenta River, which rises well to the north and empties into the sea near Venice. The Brenta valley represents the best route to the island city for a trader from the north, and the gap which it has eroded into the mountains, which is known as the Val Sugana, extends north by northwest nearly all the way to Trient. It is small wonder then that the Seven Communities flourished in an area located halfway between the Astico route and the Brenta route.

North of the Brenta, the line resumed its irregular course over the crests of mountains, passing over Agaro (2,065m, 6,775 ft), Pavione (2,835m, 9,300 ft) and others before briefly forming the watershed line between the Piave and Etsch drainage systems. These mountains are known as the Dolomites and offer as breathtaking scenery as any in the world. Before the Great War, however, very few roads crisscrossed this relatively remote area. Rolle Pass (1,970m, 6,460 ft) lay easily on the Austrian side, but the strategically important Valles (2,030m, 6,670 ft) and San Pelegrino (1,920m, 6,300 ft) Passes straddled the frontier, as did the dominating 3,500m (11,500 ft) Mt. Marmolada, a snow-capped peak of enormous mass. To control Marmolada was to control the Fedaja (2,030m, 6,660 ft) and Sella (2,245m, 7,365 ft) Passes beyond, and possibly the nearby border town of Caprile and the pass of the same name. But now we have reached an area which no longer represented a homeland of Italian speech. From just south and west of Marmolada northeast to Lake Landro and including most of the upper Ampezzo River valley resided a people who used Ladin as a vernacular. Ladin, as its name implies, is a Latin language more closely related to Romansch than Italian. It is also related to Friulian, although the latter used a higher proportion of Italian words. Only in these remote, rugged locations could such pockets of ancient languages have survived into the Twentieth Century, and probably because they still existed outside of the Italian State, incorporation into which would no doubt doom them within a few generations. However, the Italian government badly wanted to annex the Ladins as it had annexed most of the homeland of the Friulians, the latter without incident. Today, one can only wonder what the feelings of the small Ladin community might have been a century ago, as they contemplated a forcible annexation to Italy.

But to return to our frontier journey, we have now reached the area east of Cortina around Mts. Cristallo (3,220m, 10,560 ft) and Piano (2,300m, 7,525 ft). As we approach Mt. Croce and the pass beyond of that name, we leave behind that portion of the Tyrol, to the west that is drained by the watershed of the Adriatic; from now on, as the border continues on eastward, Austrian territory is now strictly to the north, and it is drained by the Danube River. For a ways, along the spine of what are known as the Carnic Alps, the line follows exactly the crest of the mountains, that is, all the drainage on the Italian side flows to the Adriatic, and all the same on the Austrian side swells the Black Sea. Remarkably, the linguistic divide also conforms here, making for an international border which would be hard to challenge. In fact, this is the only section of border where the Italians made no further claims, and it has survived until the present day. The Romans named these mountains for a 4th Century B.C. tribe who had descended from them to occupy the coastal plain below. In time, these *Carni* were driven off or assimilated by the Romans, who would designate the mountain range as the provincial boundary between Venetia and Noricum. Ever since, the Carnic Alps have served as the border between the Germanic north and the Latin south. Although not a terribly high range—most of the high peaks top out at between 2,500 and 2,750 meters (8 and 9 thousand feet)—the chain is continuous and traversed by few roads and even fewer railroads. Val di Inferno Pass crossed the divide at mid-range, but the lack of a major population center on either side dictated that the road was not the best. Somewhat farther east was Plöcken Pass, at 1,357m (4,450 ft) a much lower and less winding route. Then the border left the crest of the range near the Rosskofel (2,235m, 7,330 ft) and jutted to the southeast, along a minor tributary of the Fella River, then crossed the main stream and the railroad which paralleled it, near the Italian town of Pontebba. The railroad was only the third so far to have crossed the border; the other two followed the Adige and Brenta Rivers far to the west.

From the Mittagskofel just east of Pontebba, the line turned sharply to begin its final, southerly course to the sea. Here it came very close to the only geographic point in Europe where sub-groups of the three great language divisions of the continent concurred; the Germanic, Latin (or Romance), and Slavic branches of the Indo-European Family met just within Austrian territory. To the north lived the German speaking residents of Austria's province of Carinthia. To the west were the Latin speaking Friulians of Italy's Venetia. And to the east the ground was home to the Slavic Slovenes of Austrian Carniola. From this point south, the German element disappeared and the latter two groups vied for predominance. The frontier attained the mountain ridge which divides the Fella, or more properly, the Taglimento system from that of the Isonzo, but did so a few kilometers west of the important Predil (Predeal) Pass through which the only road across the heights ran. Austria, therefore, controlled the Pass, the northern key to the Isonzo valley; throughout its course the river ran exclusively in Austrian territory. Even the name of this unimpressive stream was far from universal. To the Friulians it had since at least Medieval times been called the Lisonzo. As the similar Italian tongue gradually supplanted the Friulian, it was more often referred to as Isonzo. To the Slovenes, whose language could be heard along much of its course, it was the Soca.

But the frontier line was never nearer the river than the nearest high ridge above its western bank. From the lofty and glacial peaks of Rombon (2,210m, 7,250 ft) and Canin (2,585m, 8,480 ft) it traversed Mt. Maggiore, the easy Starasella Pass, and Mts. Matajur and Cucco before dropping from the heights to the headwaters of the Judrio River. This relatively small stream had been fixed as the frontier nearly 400 years before (1521) with little to recommend it except that it pretty much was a fair division of the ethnic groups. The Judrio itself also flows into the Isonzo, but before it did, the border line jumped it and cut across the coastal plain to the Ausa River and along the latter to the Adriatic Sea at its very most northerly point.

Such, then, was the Austro-Italian border in 1915, a twisting, curving, irregular path across glaciers, lakes, snow-capped or barren-topped mountains and wooded back country, except for a 35km (22 mi) stretch where it met the sea. Besides the three railroads mentioned above, two more crossed the line on the level ground near the sea, but five railways for a 765km (475 mi) front is hardly ideal; moreover as a general statement it could be said that the entire line was protected by formidable natural barriers to great depths. It was also a very traditional border in the sense of time, for whatever that was worth (The Austrians certainly felt it was worth something). We have considered the antiquity of the Carnic frontier. But other sections of the line, while not ancient, were certainly quite old; with so much as cursory glances through historical atlases, one can recognize the distinctive shape of the pre-war borders from as early as the Thirteenth Century, and the linguistic divide from at least the Tenth. One might also notice that the long-standing Venetian Republic, the possessions of which the Italians had long argued formed the basis of their claims to the eastern littoral of the Adriatic, did at no time hold some of the lands—including Trieste and Fiume—which they purported to so passionately desire. Indeed, in the words of one writer, Trieste had "given itself over to Austria from 1382"[9] in order to protect its commerce from a strong Venetian rivalry. It was probably useless for the Austrians to advance such arguments, of course; the Italians could always go back further in time and point out the fact that the Julian Alps (within Austrian territory) had been named for Caesar, and that in his day the provincial boundary for the Trieste area had been far to the east in Istria, along the river Arsa (they still would have come up short regarding Fiume). At any rate, once war had been declared the onus was on the Italians to somehow advance over the common frontier and physically seize the areas they desired. Now it was up to the soldiers.

Although the land frontier between the two nations ended at the coast of the northern tip of the Adriatic Sea, that very body of water also serves as a dividing line, extending far to the south, all the way in fact to the heel of the Italian Peninsula. Here, the sea narrowed to the Straits of Otranto. Austrian territory stopped short of the Straits by 160km (100 mi) or so; before 1912 the Balkan side was owned by Turkey, but after the Balkan Wars it was ground of the new state of Albania, designs upon which were coveted by Austria, Serbia, and in particular Italy. Control of the straits would ensure control of the entire Sea, the same by either of the former would allow them free passage of the Straits. For Austria the issue was critical, as the Adriatic was her only outlet to the Mediterranean and the oceans beyond. Italy's intense interest could be traced to the 1866 war, when she had suffered a terrible naval defeat near the island of Lissa. Determined to never again be outdone at sea by Vienna, Rome could be counted on to wrest every advantage possible in the area. Geography certainly seemed to favor the Austrians; the eastern shore of the Adriatic is dotted with inlets and bays, often overlooked by mountains which allowed no coastal plain, and much of the shoreline is obscured by irregular groups of islands surrounded by deep water. It represented an ideal land-and-seascape to harbor a fine navy. On the Italian side, the coast was relatively smooth and without any of the other advantages. Moreover, it was, unlike Dalmatia, heavily populated and thus exposed to attack.

Upon the outbreak of war both sides were pretty much aware of the content of the forces against them. The respective Chiefs of the naval staffs had recently met in person to discuss cooperation against the *Entente* in case of war. They now needed a new strategy, and Austrian Admiral Anton Haus could be counted on to adopt a cautious one designed to preserve his inferior fleet for the purpose of defending the home waters. Counting units still under construction, he disposed of three modern battleships and three more semi-dreadnoughts, six older battleships, seven cruisers of various types, eighteen destroyers, at least forty torpedo boats (some sources claim as many as 85), and at least a half-dozen submarines. This powerful force of nearly 350,000 tons was backed by almost 20,000 naval personnel. And the number of submarines available would soon increase, as the Germans began to rail components to the main Austrian naval base at Pola, on the Istrian peninsula south of Trieste, and others arrived from out of the Mediterranean. Already on May 13th Captain Hersing had reached the base at Cattaro after an eighteen day voyage from Germany in *U-21*, an Austrian destroyer steaming out to hail him.[10]

Haus's opposite number was Vice Admiral Paolo Thaon di Revel, commanding a comfortable, though not crushing, superiority over his enemy. Italy then possessed three Dreadnoughts, eight older battleships, twenty-one cruisers of all types, roughly thirty-five destroyers, at least twenty submarines, about seventy-five torpedo boats, and ten or so minesweepers. Total tonnage reached a half-million, with 40,000 trained personnel. Revel's main difficulty was devising a plan whereby he could lure the Austrians away from their protective coastline and out into the open sea where they could be destroyed. Any dispersion of his fleet might well cancel his advantage. But once the war was on, he had to allocate at least some strength to watch Italy's long west coast and large island shorelines, and he needed to establish a blockade of the Straits of Otranto, as well as cooperate with his allies. For both sides, the task at hand would certainly not be easy to accomplish.

Italy in 1915 was a nation of about 35 million inhabitants, 15% or so of whom lived in cities of 100,000 or more. Her railroad mileage per one million citizens was 500 km (310 mi); pig iron production had reached 350,000 (metric) tons per year, and important steel working firms such as Terni and Ansaldo were booming, as were other modern industries across the northern half of the country. The south was still mainly agricultural and poor, despite a system of elementary education established in 1877, and we have seen how bad the problem of illiteracy was. In 1908 a severe earthquake had ravaged Sicily, killing 150,000 people and destroying the fragile economy, which had yet to recover by the war's outbreak. It was from these southerly regions, riddled by unemployment and infected with organized crime that the bulk of the Italian army was recruited; physically fit, undereducated peasants used to privation and hardships, made good soldiers. Conscription had been established back in the 1870's, but during the years of peace the supply of manpower far exceeded the demand for it, and as late as 1911 fewer than one-quarter of those eligible for training were actually called to service.[11] And this was in a period of considerable emigration; at least 350,000 Italians left their homeland in the year 1900 and the number had escalated to over 530,000 in 1911. By then the grand total since 1890 was well over 5.5 million. Even so, the country did as much as it could afford to do; it was a time of rising debt to mostly foreign lenders, particularly the British and Germans, the latter claiming investments to the equivalent of 600 million dollars before the war.

Manpower, then, was never a problem for Rome, especially considering the fact that its new enemy had already been fighting on two other fronts since the previous August. Cadorna soon had twelve Army Corps at his disposal— nearly 900,000 troops—to face a foe who had already suffered something like 2 ¼ million casualties versus other opponents. Before a shot was fired, he already outnumbered the enemy by three to one. A force of 39 infantry and cavalry divisions were available for deployment in May, 1915. The news was not all good however; the Italian Army lacked cohesiveness. It was still a curious collection of soldiers from geographic areas with unique traditions, most of who resented what they believed was favoritism shown to Piedmontese contingents, in particular their officers. There rarely was much pride in service such as enjoyed by the Germans, to the contrary, the army was considered an instrument of political repression (it had often been used to quell domestic unrest), and a dead-end vocation suitable only for the unemployed.

Moreover, discipline was harsh, the officers were all too often aloof, and pleasant diversions were rare. Small wonder then that in the last year of peace (1914), at least one in ten of those called for service simply failed to appear.

As was the case in most other establishments of the time, Italy's military gradually evolved towards smaller units to operate as self-contained forces in the field. By 1915 divisions were replacing Corps[12] as the smallest such units, and the war would accelerate the trend. A typical Italian Infantry Division consisted of two brigades of three regiments of three 1,000-man battalions, an artillery regiment of two groups of two or three six-gun batteries, plus engineers, communications sections, medical personnel, and supply trains for each brigade. As experience dictated, machine-gun companies were formed at brigade level, but by the war's end, these were being assigned to regiments and even battalions. Other evolving units included mortar sections for each battalion, and by 1917, platoons or companies of *Arditi* were being attached to every regiment. *Arditi* (intrepid ones) were hand-picked from groups of volunteers for their physique, enthusiasm, and skills in close combat. They were very heavily armed with the finest weapons. By 1918 Infantry battalions had been reduced from four companies to three. All told, an average Infantry Division in 1915 fielded over 14,000 men, 1,400 horses, thirty guns of 75mm and eight machine guns. These numbers had been reduced considerably by the last year of the war, except for machine-guns, which had increased exponentially to 144. Also on the plus side by 1918 were several batteries of heavy mortars and three batteries of heavy, 149 mm artillery pieces for the Field Artillery Regiment of each Division.

Other elite infantry included the *Bersaglieri*, distinguished by their wide-brimmed hats to which poultry tail feathers were attached. They were light, highly mobile troops often issued bicycles, whose regiments were widely distributed among infantry divisions; only one entirely *Bersaglieri* division existed throughout the war. *Alpini*, as their name suggests, were recruited from mountainous areas of Italy and specially trained as units capable of negotiating the roughest of terrain. Their acclimation with the thin air of high elevations ensured a stamina for such tasks which was completely lacking in soldiers native to lowlands. *Alpini* also wore distinctive headgear, adorned with eagle feathers. As with the *Bersaglieri*, the use of these feathers was discontinued in September of 1915[13] when the war was only four months old. *Granatieri di Sardegna* (Sardinian Grenadiers) units were perhaps the most prestigious of all Italian Army formations. Their standards were so high that only two regiments were raised.

In 1908/1909, infantrymen of the Royal Italian Army were issued a new uniform in a new color. Thus began the tradition of the *grigio-verde* (gray green) which would serve the nation for several generations. It was similar to the German gray-green only perhaps slightly lighter. The color so impressed one observer that he wrote he would have failed to see groups of soldiers resting along the roads had they not been pointed out to him, on several different occasions. The enemy, he claimed, would fail to see Italian troops "in broad daylight at fifty yards."[14] As in all armies of the day, a soft cap was initially worn; it featured a leather visor and chin strap and displayed a regimental number above the forehead. In the spring of 1916 the decision to adopt the French 'Adrian' steel helmet was taken, and by August most of the army had been outfitted. Later that year Italian industry had begun to produce a domestic version of the Adrian which was easier and faster to manufacture, and soon thereafter *grigio verde* helmet covers had appeared. One firm—Elmo Farina of Milan—made a distinctively Italian headpiece of thick armor designed to protect the forehead and sides of the face. It also produced body armor for the shoulders and chest, as well as portable shields. Wearers of these Farina products more closely resembled medieval, than modern, troops. Leather ankle boots were the norm, with puttees, although *Alpini* were often issued spiked boots with long woolen socks. Calf-length lace-up boots were also not uncommon. For winter, many soldiers enjoyed all-white (including hats but not boots) uniforms, and of course, heavy protective greatcoats. Before they had learned to become inconspicuous, many officers still wore blue capes and carried swords.

Personal equipment was similar to that of other armies of the day. A belt which suspended ammunition pouches and a sheathed bayonet was worn, and a heavy backpack containing all items necessary for a camp-like life in the field, and a knapsack to which a water bottle was attached was slung around the neck. Once the static nature of the campaign had been established, the backpack was usually unnecessary, and the entrenching spade was moved from it to the belt, under the bayonet. As time elapsed, a gas mask was carried in a metal case slung around the neck, and the knapsack was more and more likely to be filled with hand grenades. The canteen was flattened and aluminum replaced wood as material for its design. It is said that *Arditi* often filled it with brandy.[15]

Most Italian infantry carried a 6.5 mm Mannlicher-Carcano six-shot bolt-action rifle of 1891 design. It was slung over the shoulder when carried on the march. A reliable weapon, it was nonetheless somewhat less powerful than other standard infantry weapons of the war, yet weighed 3.8 kg (8 lb., 6 oz.) and was a lengthy 1290 mm (51 in.). Initially, secondary weapons were almost unheard of in the Italian Army, but the nature of the fighting ensured that grenades, knives, and trench clubs of all kinds quickly became popular among the rank-and-file. As early as 1915, the world's first submachine-gun was available to the troops, but typically, their leaders failed to appreciate the potential of the new weapon, and it only came into use very gradually, and then in the role as a true machine-gun, complete with bipod. This early design—known as the Villar Perosa—was superseded in 1918 by a more traditional-looking Beretta which was capable of fully automatic fire.

Heavy machine-guns were few in 1915, a mere 750 or so for the entire Army. The standard design was an M95 6.5mm Revelli, manufactured by Fiat of Turin. It closely resembled most other water-cooled weapons of the day, but it was less powerful and somewhat unreliable, and weighed 17kg (37 lbs., 8 oz.) without its tripod. The Italians quickly turned to their allies to help make up the deficiency, and soon all sorts of rapid-fire weapons were on the front lines. By the war's end, Rome could boast of possessing 17 times as many machine-guns as it did at its outbreak. Other weapons which had proliferated during the conflict included flame throwers and trench mortars; the former were based on a French design, the latter a mixture of French, British and homemade types of various calibers.

Italian cavalry were organized into divisions of two brigades of two 800-man regiments. Each regiment contained a machine-gun section. An artillery group of two four-gun (75mm) batteries and a *Bersaglieri* bicycle battalion rounded out the combatants. Engineer, Medical, and supply troops were also included, making for a total of about 4,200 men with 4,200 horses, eight machine guns and eight 75 mm artillery pieces.[16] Cavalry uniforms were similar to those of infantry except for the use of leather gaiters instead of puttees, and the headgear, which initially was either a fur/felt hat or a combed helmet not unlike those worn by French dragoons. By mid 1916, the old headgear had all been replaced by either the steel helmet or an infantry-type cap. Firearms were a shorter, or carbine, version of the infantry rifle, but with a fixed, hinge-out bayonet; these supplemented traditional weapons, either sabers or lances. It was not long before the sabers and lances were discarded.

The standard Italian field piece was the 75mm M1911 gun. A smaller 65mm weapon had been developed for use in mountain warfare; it was easily dismantled in order to be packed, in pieces, by mules. The components of each gun could be carried by six animals. There were never enough of these guns, but the most serious shortage lay in the heavier varieties, and it is reported that the nation went to war with only 112[17] heavy guns, mostly 149mm with a few 210mm howitzers included. The Ansaldo-Schneider '149' was fairly well liked by the troops, and its production was vastly expanded throughout the war, as was that of the 100mm field howitzer. Eventually a collection of 120mm, 149mm, 152mm, 155mm and 380mm guns were available, as well as 152mm and 305mm howitzers, the latter so huge as to have inspired a railway mounting to have been created for it. Indeed, for the Italians, moving artillery in the rugged terrain of the north would prove a task every bit as difficult as manufacturing it.

What Italy could manufacture apparently as well as anyone else in the world, was motor vehicles. As early as 1911, Isotta-Graschini had developed an armored fighting vehicle featuring a rotating turret equipped with a machine gun. A good design capable of achieving 60kph (37 mph), some of them saw service in Libya in 1912. Not to be outdone, Fiat soon had a similar design available, but the Ansaldo firm created the most widely used type in the war; dubbed the Lancia IZ it was spacious enough to accommodate three machine guns and a crew of six. Bianchi of Milan represented yet another manufacturer of the new contraptions, however, for all of these companies the chief contribution to the war effort regarding motor vehicles was in regard to the large number of trucks they created. Trucks were used as troop transports, for pulling wheeled artillery, as ambulances, as communications aids, as mobile kitchens, for self-propelling large guns, and a whole host of other duties. But far and away the most important function served by the trucks was that of supply, a means to move the enormous quantities of material with which it is necessary to supply an army. In general, Italy was very well served by her automobile industry.

Once other *Entente* nations began using tanks, the Italian Command became somewhat interested in the concept, and requested an example of the French Schneider for trials and study. Fiat was given a contract to reproduce a domestic version, but nothing came of the project except a desire by the firm to create its own design. By the late summer of 1918, several Renault FT's had been acquired, and Fiat was again contracted to begin production of a 1,400 unit lot to be completed by the following May. When the war ended, the order was cancelled, roughly 100 having been built. Meanwhile two examples of the Italian design—called Carro Armato Fiat Tipo 2000—were ready. This massive vehicle weighed 40 tons and needed a crew of ten to function properly, with a 65mm gun in the turret and seven machine-guns protruding from the four sides of the hull. It was seriously underpowered and could attain only 7.2kph (4.5 mph).[18] It is perhaps needless to relate that tanks did not play a worthwhile role on the Italian Front in the First World War.

Italian engineers certainly did play a worthwhile role; their work can still be observed a century later, in the form of the countless roads constructed on mountainsides along what was the front line of the fighting. Some of these roads traverse slopes so steep that it is truly amazing to imagine how they were built under hostile fire, even sporadic hostile fire or the occasional air raid. Winding, twisting trails aside sheer precipices and into solid rock in often extreme weather conditions are difficult enough to travel in semi-primitive vehicles; add high winds or ice into the formula and it is nearly inconceivable that they were carved into places where not so much as a goat-trail had preceded them. Another remarkable feat performed by the engineers was suspending steel cables between peaks or across precipitous gorges and ravines. These cables enabled cable-cars to be used to transport all sorts of material, human and otherwise, across topographic features which could have been all but nonnegotiable without them. The Italians called these cableways *Teleferica*; to the Austrians they were *Seilbahnen*, but however referred to they definitely saved enormous exertions.

Sources differ as to how many aircraft Italy entered the war in possession of; what is certain was that she had been the first nation to use airplanes for military reconnaissance and from which to drop bombs on an enemy. This occurred during the recent war in Libya in 1911. Three years later two military flying schools had been established and fourteen airfields were in use. By May of 1915, fifteen air squadrons were operational, which suggests something in the order of 90 planes were available, plus three airships. The navy disposed of another thirty or so units, half of which were seaplanes, and two airships. As in all the major powers, aircraft production intensified as the war dragged on, and the design and construction of bombers received increasing attention.

In 1915, fewer than 400 airplanes were produced in the country, but by 1918 the number approached 6,500.[19] Some of the latter were the best that technology could deliver at the time, including the massive Caproni three-engine tri-plane bomber. Excellent home-grown fighters such as the Ansaldo A-1 and Pomilio PE ensured that Italy's dependence on allied aircraft would wane as time passed, although plenty of British and French types were always in evidence. By the end of the war, 75 *Entente* air squadrons had been formed and were in service on the Italian Front.

In summation, the Kingdom of Italy put forth a first-class effort in service of the *Entente* cause. It raised a total of 72 Infantry divisions, of which 70 saw deployment on the main front. Eight spent at least some time on other Fronts; one in Macedonia, two in France, and five in Albania. Of these, only one division served its entire tenure in Albania, and one other division was disbanded before it participated in any action. In addition, Italy's four Cavalry Divisions—which had been raised in pre-war days—also outlasted the three-and-a-half years of conflict, although three of the four were eventually dismounted. These ground forces were supplemented by a naval force which was somewhat more powerful than that of the main opponent, and which was critical to maintaining *Entente* control of the Mediterranean Sea, which in itself was crucial in order to validate the usefulness of the Suez Canal and to create war zones in the Aegean and Adriatic Seas. It is difficult to understand how all this could have been accomplished had Italy stayed within the *Alliance*; it would have been difficult enough had she remained neutral.

Another important and often overlooked Italian asset was her merchant marine, a fleet seventh largest in the world. In 1914 it consisted of over 1,050 ships of over 100 tons each, and many smaller ones, making for a total tonnage of about 1.7 million. Here was another tool available for use by the *Entente*. Taken together with her manpower, sea power, air power, and industrial capability, Italian commercial strength could now be committed to seek a decision in war. Few at the time, and even fewer ever since, at least outside of Italy, ever appreciated the extent of the national strength which had been thrown onto the scales of war, which were as a result irretrievably tipped to upset the old balance.

The Empire of Austria-Hungary was the largest state entirely within Europe. It sprawled over 676,250 sq. km (261,100 sq. mi) and was home to roughly 51 million people, the third most populous on the continent. As we have seen it was composed of two fairly equal halves each of which enjoyed its own parliamentary and administrative apparatus but both recognizing the Habsburg Emperor Franz Joseph. Hungary was possessed of more traditional boundaries and was framed by mountains and rivers. It included just two provinces, Hungary proper and Croatia-Slavonia, which had its own Diet and governor. The latter was at least mostly Croatian in character, but the former was home to large numbers of Germans, Slovaks, Serbs, Ruthenes, and especially Romanians, and none of these minorities felt adequately represented in Budapest. Bosnia/Herzegovina was a third piece of the Empire independent of both main halves; it was peopled by Serbs and Croats and technically enjoyed a limited self-government, though the governor was a choice of the Emperor. Austria was a geographic nightmare, consisting of fifteen provinces as scattered as Bukovina beyond the Carpathians, Voralberg on the Swiss frontier, and Dalmatia, the Adriatic littoral extending as far south as Montenegro. Only five provinces were almost exclusively peopled by Germans. The Czechs, who represented about 23% of the total, predominated in three, the Poles and Ruthenes in two, and the Slovenes and Croats in one apiece. Vienna had an opportunity to rid itself of most of its Croats when the latter asked to be given Dalmatia in 1905, but the request was refused. It was the Latins then, who were the only groups who were not a majority in any Imperial province; Romanians in Bukovina were too few to over-shadow the Ruthenes, Italians were a minority to Germans in Tyrol and were one of three groups (with Slovenes and Croats) in Küstenland. But both of the Latin groups lived in areas adjacent to independent nations of their linguistic brethren, whereas of the Slavs, only the Serbs/Croats did. The three south Slavic populations did, however, have one overriding concern in common: none wanted to see 'their' lands along the Adriatic littoral annexed by Italy. With few exceptions, most Austro-Hungarian citizens were content to live within the Empire, and most of those who were discontented wanted only to change the existing system, not destroy it.

Army service was based on universal conscription like most European nations of the day. Those exempt included teachers, priests, and men with dependant families. The latter were considered part of the *Ersatz* Reserve, for which they trained but were not placed on active duty. Army service plus active reserve service (*Landwehr*) lasted from the age of 18 to the age of 33, where after came the inactive reserve (*Landsturm*) until age 55. Infantry served two years active and ten in reserve, while cavalry served three active, seven reserve. Any fit man not called up was considered *Landsturm* between the ages of 19 and 37; the unfit paid a tax in lieu of service. Men with acceptable levels of education could volunteer and thus serve only one year before becoming reservists; many of these became officers of the reserve. Since most men preferred to serve the minimum two years active required, officer and non-commissioned officer training schools had to be set up to ensure a constant supply of leadership. In general, the Emperor's officers were well-trained, patriotic, and devoted to their *Kaiser*.

Austro-Hungarian infantry went to war wearing a bluish appearing uniform. It was officially called *hecht-grau* (pike grey). Boots, belts, straps and cap visors were a natural brown leather. Troops from Bosnia/Herzegovina often wore a fez. Attached to the belt were four ammunition pouches, a haversack, a bayonet and an entrenching tool, while slung over the shoulders hung a knapsack, greatcoat, tent section, and eating utensils. Later, a gas mask was usually carried, and grenades as well. Counting the rifle, the total load for each man was about 28 kilos (62 lbs.).

In 1914 some soldiers still carried the older M88/90 or M90 rifle, but these had pretty much been superseded by the Mannlicher M1895 model, an 8mm five-shot weapon using a steel core bullet with a lubricated steel jacket. Cavalry used the shorter carbine version. They compared quite favorably with most contemporary arms. A large number of Mausers, produced under license for export and other types were in use as well.[20]

Officers were often armed with handguns, one of a wide variety of available types ranging from small caliber automatics to large bore revolvers. In the early days of the war, many still carried swords, a practice soon discontinued, like so many others. Another old tradition which was killed after two months of war was the art of the drummer. These youths were obliged to trade their drums for rifles.[21]

Soon, the old uniform was also discarded in favor of a 'field green' replacement, similar in color to the Germans' and Italians'. In late 1916 the new Emperor Karl insisted yet another color be adopted; his choice was khaki. It is believed that Karl was motivated by a desire for his troops, who were increasingly being mixed with German units and placed under German command, to at least have a distinctive appearance. His initiative was quietly ignored except with regards to the color of the new steel helmets arriving at the front. Even then, Karl was ultimately disappointed; the original, distinctively Austrian-style helmet was soon succeeded by a German-looking one, except that the brown was retained. Officially, this was done to speed and ease production, but unofficially, German pressure was suspected.

A typical Austro-Hungarian infantry division counted roughly 15,000 men and 44 artillery pieces. As in other armies, the tendency as time passed was to add more specialized troops in order that the division be self-contained if it needed to be transferred from one front or sector to another. For this reason the number of engineer, telegraph, railway, air service, and automobile troops increased considerably during the war. One source lists a division of 1918 as consisting of 21,765 men, 7,281 horses, 112 machine guns, 68 mortars, 46 guns, 34 howitzers and 20 heavy guns/howitzers.[22]

A 1914 cavalry division fielded about 7,000 men and an equal number of horses., Every tenth or eleventh animal drew a vehicle. It also carried a few machine-guns and pulled a dozen or so light artillery pieces. Initially the men still carried the lances or swords typical of their formations, whether heavy or light horsemen, or scouts and reconnaissance troops. They also went to war in colorful uniforms and various types of headgear. Later only firearms were retained as weapons and several divisions were dismounted, and they began to appear more and more like infantry.

All the combatants soon realized the importance that artillery would represent in the war, and the Austrians were no different. Industrial output was increased as quickly as possible, boosting the inventory from perhaps 2,600 pieces in 1914 to 4,000 within two years. Numbers continued to rise until mid 1918 when serious economic pressures and wartime shortages took their toll. Firms such as Steyr in upper Austria put out high quality products, as good as anything the *Entente* could counter with. Skoda of Pilsen in Bohemia was another outfit whose weapons earned the respect of friend and foe alike, but it is hardly surprising if, as one historian wrote, "Bertha (Krupp, German armaments maker) and the Schneiders (French armaments maker) owned as much of Austria-Hungary's Skoda Werke as any Austrian."[23]

Unique amongst the belligerents, the Empire's artillery included a very high percentage of mountain guns. These shorter, lighter weapons were often assigned to the cavalry. One excellent 75mm model weighed only 620 kilos (1,365 lbs.), but could fire a 6.3 kilo shell seven kilometers (4.3mi). A 104mm model shot a 15.5 kilo (34.2 lb) round eight kilometers (4.9mi). Regular field guns included 80 and 104mm examples, and 100 and 150mm howitzers. Then there were the heavies. Skoda made a 305mm siege weapon which had to be dismantled after use and hauled in three pieces by trucks. A battery of these monsters consisted of only two units, but required 20 trucks to lug all the necessary equipment, supplies, and ammunition. When in service, the 25.5 metric ton (28 ton) giant could hurl a 384 kilo (846 lb) shell 12 kilometers (7.5mi)! This '305' was one of the more infamous big guns of the time, but the Austrians enjoyed other, similar types. They were also well supplied with mortars. Small, reasonably portable 12cm trench models were manufactured, as well as large wheeled ones of 22.5 and 24cm. All in all, the artillery, like the rest of the nation's equipment, was of good quality.

Austria's choice of a machine-gun became the model 07/12 Schwarzlose, an 8mm belt fed, water cooled device on a tripod mount. A protective shield was provided, but not always used, mainly because of the extra weight it represented. A reliable gun, the Schwarzlose was lighter than either the German or Italian choices, but was less powerful than the former, if slightly more potent than the latter.

In the domain of armored warfare the Empire contributed the least of any Great Power. The unsuitability of the terrain in the Balkans and on the Italian Front was doubtless a factor in the lack of such initiative, but considering the extent of armored car deployment on the Eastern Front by the Russians, one might expect that a similar effort from Vienna/Budapest would have been forthcoming. In fact, the Habsburg military had experimented with the idea of armored fighting vehicles during the pre-war years, but without any resultant production. Apparently a few types were built from 1915 on, in very small numbers. Neither was any tank production ever seriously contemplated, another indication of the largely defensive role the High Command expected its army to play. Austria did endeavor to make good use of armored trains, however, and a number of these were armed with powerful naval ordnance. Most of these would be used in the East.

Naval forces in the Dual Monarchy in 1914 amounted to six battleships, two armored cruisers, five light cruisers, eighteen destroyers, about sixty torpedo boats and a half-dozen submarines, for a total tonnage of around 350,000. We have seen how this force was inferior to that of Italy, and its commanders had no intention of exposing it unnecessarily to danger. A role of coastal defense was planned, with the occasional quick, offensive jab at specific targets.

Unlike Italy, Austria-Hungary had never used aircraft in combat situations before 1914. It did not even possess an air force until the results of a 1912 study recommended that the need was real and urgent. At the outbreak of war the Empire was still trying to attain an air arm comparable to that of other Powers; nine companies had been created, but no more than 40 airplanes and one dirigible were available, plus a few observation balloons. Even after Italy's entry into the war, the primary task of aircraft was reconnaissance or spotting for the artillery. The desire to avenge Italian disloyalty prompted more and more emphasis on bombing runs, with production following accordingly. Fortunately for the Austrians, a wealthy industrialist from Trieste had recently purchased a German aircraft manufacturer[24], an act which gave the Empire an industrial base from which to develop and expand, so that technical parity with enemy was able to be maintained. Numerical parity, however, was another matter; in this regard the Italians always held the advantage. For one thing, Austria-Hungary was already fighting on two other fronts when Italy intervened. Even more importantly, the Empire managed to produce only one-fourth as many airplanes as did Italy alone. Despite the fact that at least 75 flight companies had been raised by 1918, the Habsburg air force was almost invariably outnumbered over the Italian Front. A naval air force also existed and at one time was built up to about 200 machines, but like the fleet it served, it was hampered by its inability to fight an offensive war.

Before the war was over, Austro-Hungarian forces of at least divisional size had been employed on all five major European fronts. Some idea of the relative importance Vienna attached to the Italian Front may be gleaned from how it deployed its troops. Of a total of 12 Cavalry Divisions and 79 Infantry Divisions raised by the Empire, 72—8 Cavalry and 64 Infantry—saw action on the south side of the Alps, a commitment of 79% of the entire lot. Of these, eleven spent their entire tenure between May 1915 and November 1918 facing the Italians. There can be no question as to the importance of this theater in the minds of the Austro-Hungarian (and Italian) leaders. By contrast their allies were unimpressed; Germany sent a total of eight divisions but for a very limited time period. For the *Entente*, Britain would send five, France five, the Czechs would supply two and the United States would make a showing with one regiment. Overall then, 87 *Entente* divisions would eventually oppose 80 *Alliance* divisions, making the Italian Front the third most important battle zone of the war; once Russia had collapsed, it became second most critical. Without question, this was a struggle which neither side could afford to neglect.

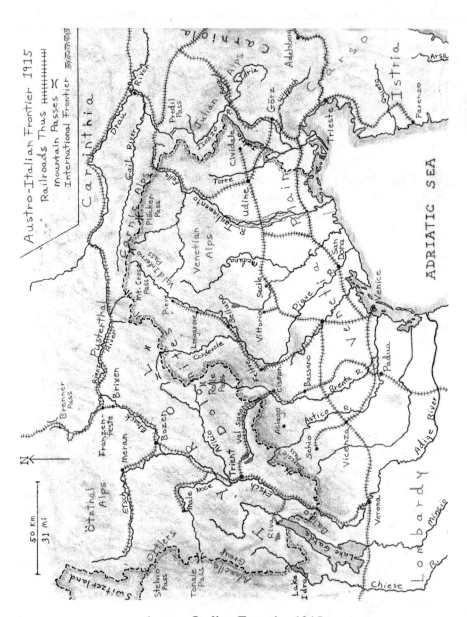

Austro-Italian Frontier 1915

Chapter Three
For Want of a Strategy

When war came to the Austro-Italian frontier in May 1915, no one in either country was less surprised than the Chief of the General Staff of the *Kaiserlich-und-Königliche Armee* (Imperial and Royal, i.e. Austro-Hungarian Army), General Franz Conrad von Hötzendorf. He was an old soldier by that time, having been born in 1852 and enrolled in a Cadet-school before his eleventh birthday, and having been commissioned Lieutenant before his nineteenth. During his long career he had been stationed all over the Empire, including at Innsbruck deep in the Alps, and at Trieste, where he learned a little about the Irredentist movement. Open-minded, intelligent, and utterly devoted to his Habsburg masters, Franz Conrad proved an able officer with a strong work ethic and an acute understanding of the political and military problems facing the Dual Monarchy. Fluent in several of the languages spoken within the country, including Italian, he had long since concluded that Italy would never fight alongside Austria, and called her adherence to the *Triple Alliance* a 'farce'. Having attained the premier position in the Army in 1906, he was not inclined to be a mere figurehead and was soon calling for preventative wars against two neighbors—Serbia and Italy—he was just sure Austria would have to fight sooner or later. The Chief believed sooner was preferable to later, as the political situation deteriorated, but was rebuked by the Emperor when he pushed hard for war against Serbia during the Bosnian annexation crisis. Two years later he was strongly advocating war against Italy when the latter declared on Turkey; again he was chastised, Franz Joseph insisting that he was a man of peace. Refusing to be silenced, he was dismissed, and then recalled eight months later.

For New Year's 1914, the Chief had prepared a written analysis of the military situation. It was almost certainly meant to be seen by the Emperor; its conclusions were pessimistic, to the effect that a war waged within the near

future could not be successful. When war did come that summer, two of the
six available armies were sent to oppose the Serbs and the other four were
railed to face the Russians, in each case a force inadequate to secure a quick
decision. There was little left with which to man an Italian Front. By the time
of Italy's entry, the pre-war Austrian army had been almost completely wiped
out, the Empire had already mobilized over two and one-quarter million men
who were desperately needed to replace the enormous losses on the two
original fronts, and the level of training of new recruits was already beginning
to slip. Nevertheless, a force of eleven divisions had been scraped together to
oppose the 39 initially at the disposal of the new enemy. They worked
frantically to construct defensive positions over terrain which was usually not
suitable for digging trenches. Most often, gun pits and troop shelters had to be
blasted into the solid rock, or stone and timber walls set up across stretches of
literally solid ground. Trees had to be felled to create fields of fire. Barbed wire
and defensive materials and weapons of all kinds had to be hauled to the crests
of mountain ridges. And of course roads for supply had to be etched into the
often sparsely-populated frontier areas. Later, when army commands had
been set up, mechanical drilling and boring equipment became available. It was
a godsend to the engineers attempting to hollow out bunkers, dig tunnels, and
secure gun battery emplacements. Pneumatic drills driven by gasoline engines
were the norm, but the heavier, faster drills and the tunnel-boring machines
were sometimes fully gear-driven and were usually self-propelled; one model
ran on a narrow-gauge railway. Visiting the front in August 1916, Lord
Northcliffe observed a rock drill which was "unusually light and strong",
displaying a "new type of Mercedes engine".[25]

Railroads were another major problem, as these were of utmost importance
if the troops were to be adequately supplied. But railroads cannot negotiate
steep grades, and the presence of the main Alpine Range between Austrian
industrial and agricultural centers and the northern Italian plains allowed for
few routes to the south. Only one line crossed the mountains from the north,
by way of the Brenner Pass into the Etsch/Adige valley. Another had been
engineered from the northeast, the Vienna area, to Villach on the Drau; it
crossed the gap between the Carnic and Karawanken chains and entered the
coastal plain via the Tagliamento valley. An east-west track connecting these
two lines ran rather close to the border; if the enemy crossed the Carnic Range
it could be easily cut, leaving half of the frontier area without lateral

communications. South of the mountains toward the seacoast the situation was even worse, since the railroad to the ports and naval base at Pola ran close to the enemy border. There were other lines from the east, but these followed roundabout courses for trains with north-south destinations. When General Rohr demanded more manpower to construct a new railway in a less exposed location, he was sent several thousand Russian prisoners of war who were promptly put to work on it, while his own men consumed huge quantities of explosives trying to carve a defendable front line out of the inhospitable countryside.

Fortunately for the *Alliance* cause, Hötzendorf made a wise choice when he appointed a commander for the new Fifth Army forming on the eastern end of the Front, a veteran of the Eastern Front who had been replaced after complaining too much about unrealistic orders to attack in the Carpathian Mountains in the dead of winter. His name was General Svetozar Boroevic Edler von Bojna, and he was from a family of military men who had served the Habsburgs for centuries. As his name suggests, he was a south Slav (Croat), whose presence could only tend to galvanize the spirit of the south Slavic troops of the Empire to defend the border areas against the despised Italians. Like his Chief, he had entered cadet-school at age ten, and had risen in the ranks due to his competence and intelligence. Slight of build, he nevertheless earned a reputation for possessing an iron will and a gritty toughness. His insistence on proper appearance and behavior had already before the war gained him a sober nickname (The Straightrazor) and an ungrudging admiration from his men.[26] Even before Boroevic had had a chance to survey his new command— he only arrived in the Carniolan provincial capitol of Laibach on May 27th— he issued orders that the troops of Fifth Army should bolster their positions to the best of their ability and prepare to remain in them for the foreseeable future.[27]

Hötzendorf had correctly assessed that his enemies would concentrate on the eastern end of the line. Farther west, Rohr retained command of a weak 'Carnic Force' to watch the mountain barrier, and in the south Tyrol a very lengthy section of line was entrusted to the so-called 'Tyrolese Force' under General Dankl, barely two divisions strong centered about the city of Trient. But the Chief knew his enemy well; Trieste, he reasoned, would be the focus of the Italian Army.

He was right. We have seen how Trieste was the real reason for the war, the one area regarding which neither side was willing to yield. But what made Trieste so special, such a focus of both camps, so worth fighting for? It was not a terribly impressive prize, for it had long been overshadowed by Venice, that island-city across the water, and had only become a modern port city in the Eighteenth Century. By the beginning of the Nineteenth Century, it and Muggia, another port a few kilometers to the south, were abandoning their traditional Friulian speech in favor of Italian. Within a few decades the economy was booming with trading and shipbuilding activities, and in 1850 the city was granted a Constitution which guaranteed self-government. A pivotal event occurred in 1907, when the Cosulich shipyard was opened in nearby Monfalcone, the population of which expanded from 4,000 to 12,000 in a short time. Boomtowns of course attract those seeking employment, and Trieste, Monfalcone, Gradisca and Görz were all towns where Italian speakers constituted a majority which could easily be diluted by the large influx of Slovenes, whose lands they lay so very close to. As the Slovene numbers increased, the Italian speakers feared their culture would be overwhelmed just as that of many of the old Venetian towns on the eastern shores of the Adriatic had been. Their feeling—as well as that of those in Rome—was that unless they were annexed by Italy, their culture would be replaced by another. They pointed to the near-by town of Aquileia, a once thriving provincial capitol in Roman times, which had lost its preeminence following its destruction by barbarians, to towns further inland. In 1914, some 800,000 Italian, Friulian, and Ladin speakers resided in Austria-Hungary. Perhaps 375,000 lived in the Trentino and 120,000 in Trieste. Most of the remainder lived in a rough triangle from Aquileia to Görz (called Gorizia by the Italians) to Muggia. The remainder were scattered along the Adriatic's eastern littoral. Many Italians agreed these people needed to be 'liberated'. Apparently not all those earmarked for liberation agreed; in Tyrol alone, some 3,500 Latin-speakers joined home-defense organizations to fight against the invaders.[28]

While the Austro-Hungarians braced for the blows they knew were about to be delivered, the Italian Commander-in-Chief of the Army, General Count Luigi Cadorna was suffering no difficulty in having to completely alter his battle plans at the eleventh hour. Technically he was subordinate to the King, but Vittorio Emanuele was not a man to interfere with the wishes of his highest-ranking soldier, and when Italy opted for neutrality the previous August,

Cadorna seems not to have been too bothered, and simply began planning a campaign directed against Austria. But it was in his nature to be imperturbable, and having been born in 1850, he was getting somewhat advanced in years to waste much energy on unnecessary emotion. Like his enemy counterparts, he had come from a family with a history of military service, in his case in the service of Piedmont. He was well-trained and dedicated to his vocation. A strict disciplinarian, he tolerated no unwelcome suggestions and no insubordination. Those who knew him rarely loved him, often feared him, but invariably respected him. And for Cadorna, only one strategy made sense: Hold the line from the Swiss frontier to the Julian Alps with light forces, advancing whenever possible towards the vital rail centers. South of the Julians, smash forward and capture Gorizia and Trieste, then push on to Laibach and ultimately to Vienna. The fact that no one in this war had, after the initial onrushes, been able to advance much at all, seems not to have influenced him. Accordingly, he sent his weak First Army under General Brusatti to the west of Lake Garda and a comparable group known as Fourth Army (General Nava) to cover the line from the Lake to where the Dolomites give way to the Carnic Alps. The latter range was watched by a collection of units under General Lequio appropriately named 'Carnic Corps'. And facing the Isonzo River on the northeastern frontier he reserved for his best armies, the Second, bossed by General Pietro Frugoni, and the Third, under Emanuele Filiberto di Savoia (the Duke of Aosta). Cadorna established his headquarters at Udine, the largest city of the border area of Friuli, and a point close behind both of the main armies. Udine then boasted a population of about 50,000 and lay just 19 km (11.8 mi) from the international frontier at the Judrio. The time had arrived at last to march into *Italia Irredenta*.

The Treaty of London, signed by the Italians on April 26th, had committed the country to war within one month. By the end of the third week of May the deadline was fast approaching, and having been informed by Cadorna that the army was in position to initiate hostilities, the Salandra government decided to take the plunge. Late on the afternoon of Sunday, May 23rd, the deed was done; for the troops on both sides of the border, it had been simply a matter of waiting for the word that it was official. Just as soon as the signal had been given, units of various sizes began limited movements designed to secure advantage at points deemed of significant military importance. Rohr's men in the Carnic Alps jockeyed for position, but the first engagement of the war was said to have occurred at Forcellini di Montozzo, a remote outpost on a peak commanding the north side of the Tonale Pass on the far western frontier. Apparently, elements of the Italian First Army scaled the difficult heights, drove away the Austrian defenders, and began a maneuver for full possession of the Pass. The following day, capture of both the Tonale and Stelvio Passes was reported, and Italian newspapers could print tales of the war's first 'successes'. The reality was that these two gaps in the mountains, which lay on each end of the imposing Ortler Range, led to practically nowhere. The Austrian commanders in the area were content to surrender the high summits of roadways, provided the roads could be blocked at lower elevations on their side of the ridge. In both cases, the many hairpin turns on the approaches were easier to defend than the actual pass; let the enemy deal with the problems of supply and shelter on the arctic-like mountaintops, while they dug in on less challenging obstacles at lower, wooded elevations.

One Austrian commander who was frantic to strike a quick but powerful first blow was Admiral Haus. As soon as he received the news of the anticipated state of war, he ordered his fleet to prepare to sail, and gave the actual command at 8:00pm, as darkness was falling. Within hours, the fleet was off numerous targets on the Italian east coast, and it opened fire before daylight on the 24th. The torpedo boat base at Porto Corsini, just north of Ravenna was heavily shelled as was the city of Ancona, the cathedral of which was damaged. Other locations hit were Rimini, Senigallia, Porto Recanati, Civitanova, and Venice, where the arsenal and oil tanks were bombed. A few of the lighter, faster Austrian vessels even reached the far south, attacking Vieste, Manfredonia, Barletta, and Bari. Three of these ships, led by the cruiser *Helgoland*, encountered the Italian destroyer *Turbine* near Pelagosa Island on the return trip, and sank it. The dirigible base at Chiaravalle was also the object of an air raid.[29] Haus's lightning strike, which was over within two hours, had caught the Italians more or less flat-footed; their only naval success of the day being a destroyer raid on the minor town of Porto Buso lying on an offshore island at the border between the warring countries. Within hours, the unharmed Austrian fleet was back upon its bases, the most important of which was Pola, near the tip of the Istrian Peninsula.

In other action of May 24th, Fourth Army began its advance into the Trentino by way of the Brenta River valley and that of its tributary, the Cismone. The former led through the Val Sugana, a deep gorge which extended perilously close to Trient, the latter led only to difficult mountain ridges. Along the Carnic Range, Lequio's men pushed hard to secure the two best passes, the Plöcken, where they were repulsed, and the Val d Inferno, which they claimed to capture. Here was one stretch of front where the Austrians enjoyed a distinct advantage; behind the spine of the mountains flowed the Gail River, running west to east, the valley of which allowed for excellent lateral movement and communications. Nothing comparable existed on the Italian side. To the south, Second and Third armies also began to move, both crossing the border on the first full day of war. Second Army advanced over the low Starasella Pass and into the Isonzo valley without serious opposition. Before the day was done it had taken the towns of Kreda and Karfreit.[30] The Isonzo had been reached within 24 hours. Third Army crossed the Judrio and took Cormons on the railroad between Udine and Görz. No determined enemy resistance had yet been encountered.

On the morning of the 25th, Vittorio Emanuele left his capitol to join his soldiers. The move was largely symbolic, but it made for good press. As the day passed reports from all along the line were coming in magnifying minor Italian advances. In the west, troops crossed the low Guidicari Pass and marched into the valley of the same name north of Lake Idro, trying to force the back door to Trient. At the front door, the Baldo *Massif* was alive with *grigioverde* as they pushed their opponents off a border peak known as Altissimo. Far below, in the valley along the Adige, others skirmished with Austrian rearguards, who sniped from every advantageous topographic feature. And farther east, Fourth Army units scrambled up the rugged country of the upper Astico River, which formed the border for several kilometers, in an attempt to assault the town of Lavaronne, itself only one ridge distant from either the Adige or the upper reaches of Val Sugana. If all went well it seemed that Trient would soon be Italian.

Still smarting from the unexpected Austrian naval raids of the 24th, Admiral Revel attempted to mitigate the embarrassment somewhat on the 26th, by announcing that henceforth a tight naval blockade of the entire enemy coastline was to be enforced and the Otranto Straits closed. The *Alliance* was to be deprived of its last doorway to the open sea. No doubt, the British and French would have done so anyway, had the Italians not. Elsewhere that day Fourth Army reported the capture of the 2238m (7,342 ft) high Giau Pass, between Caprile and Cortina in the northern Dolomites.

May 27th brought the first reports which much pleased Cadorna. Both Second and Third Armies had taken bridgeheads over the Isonzo and the delta area was being overrun. A battle for Grado, a small but strategically located fishing village across the Gulf from Trieste had begun; it would fall the next day and become an excellent base for small naval craft. In Carnia the Plöcken Pass was declared secure, and Fourth Army had advanced to within 8 km (5 mi) of Borgo in Val Sugana. First Army took Condino in Val Guidicaria, and was approaching a position from which to outflank Riva and the northern tip of Lake Garda. Lastly, Italian troops had fought their way into Ala, the first sizeable town on the trek north up the Adige. Ala would, however, require two more days to completely conquer; the whole affair at Ala illustrates a certain lack of urgency in the minds of the attackers during these early advances. Following the three-day delay, the Austrians left behind only 60 casualties to be dealt with by the 'victors'.[31]

Anxious to disable the railroad connecting Monfalcone and Trieste as his troops approached the former, Cardorna ordered an air raid to strike it at its most vulnerable point, where it hugged the coast in the Nabresina area. This act brought retaliation in the form of a second raid on Venice, so a naval force was quickly summoned to begin softening up the enemy fleet base at Pola, which was duly attacked on May 30th/31st by air elements of the navy, and by at least one dirigible. During the same time period the Carnics were alive with activity. Rohr, having received some reinforcement, counterattacked his tormentors at the Monte Croce Pass, beginning an extended round of fighting with *Alpini*. The reason for the considerable Austrian concern for this area was that it represented the closest point on the border to the lateral railway in the Pusterthal which connected all of Carinthia and points east, to the Tyrol line through the Brenner Pass at Franzenfeste. To see the Pusterthal line cut was an unacceptable scenario if the war against Italy was to be waged with any hope of success. Should the enemy be allowed to breach the Pass in any strength, he would surely attempt to at least bring the railroad under artillery fire. Consequently, all available help was sent to Rohr, who was able to stabilize the front after some hard fighting. Somewhat to the southwest, other Italian units pushed up the Ampezzo River trough and captured Cortina, long renowned for the magnificent scenery of the surrounds, on May 30th, and a day later were claiming to have 'liberated' 40 small towns in the immediate vicinity.

The month ended with one final piece of politicking. Apparently General Brusati of First Army had been critical of Nava's failure to concentrate Fourth Army's resources for a coordinated drive on Trient; he was rewarded by being given about half of Fourth Army's section of front. The idea was that one commander alone should focus on Trient, which was threatened on three sides by a hostile advance.

June began with a good deal of Italian aggressiveness at sea; the middle and southern portions of the Dalmatian coast were bombarded by the fleet, but this act only provoked a retaliatory bombing of Bari and Brindisi during the next night. Italy also lost the submarine *Medusa*, sunk by a German sub that day. The German vessel was among several which would eventually join the Austrian fleet; some sailed in from the open Mediterranean despite the blockade, while others were railed in pieces to Pola, there to be assembled for use. On the 5th Revel's ships struck again, bombarding lighthouses, ports and stations along the coast and among the Dalmatian Islands. Monfalcone was also shelled from the water, then again on the 7th, as the army closed in on the city. A third round of bombardments occurred on the 9th, mostly in Dalmatia. During this time period the only Austrian counter was another air raid against Venice on the 8th, but Haus was careful not to expose his big ships to risks, as he expected something much more serious from the enemy before long.

Cadorna's gaze was fixed on his two main armies which, finally up to full strength as mobilization was completed, began earnest movement against the foe. Second Army broke free of its bridgehead over the Isonzo at Karfreit and began to scale the sheer, barren heights of the Julian Alps beyond. The capture of the main ridge was the objective, and at first little opposition was encountered and the more westerly peaks were taken on June 1st. When *Alpini* and *Bersaglieri* units tackled the highest peak of the chain—the 2245m (7,365ft) Mt. Nero (or Mt. Krn)—the next day, however, they ran into a withering hail of small-arms fire and were stopped. Despite several more assaults over the next few days in which the Italians suffered a total of over 2,000 casualties, Mt. Krn remained in Austrian hands. Frustrated, invaders rounded up the Slovene residents of several nearby villages and deported them to Italy. In one town, the male population was decimated for alleged guerilla activity.[32]

Farther south Frugoni's men captured another bridgehead at Plava, a town about which the Isonzo takes a sharp loop to the west. By June 4th, engineers had constructed a pontoon bridge with which to press a further attack. Another group reached the river opposite Tolmein, but met heavy enemy fire from the far side and was unable to cross. On the extreme right, all attempts to seize the high ground on the west bank near Görz were similarly frustrated.

Third Army was able to cross the Isonzo at all points along its very narrow front. Monfalcone, with its important shipbuilding facilities and on the railroad to Trieste, fell to the Italians on June 9th; there were no natural obstacles from which a heavily outnumbered force could defend it. Gradisca was taken on the same day. These were the last relatively easy captures, as now the army had reached the western bluff of an upland known as the Carso Plateau, and Boroevic, having abandoned the lowlands, was not about to yield an inch of the heights without a bitter struggle.

Cadorna was still receiving encouraging reports from his rear. News of a financial summit at Nice on the 4th seemed to ensure that Italy would receive the necessary capital from her *Entente* allies for a prolonged effort, if one was needed. In the Cortina area, Mt. Piano was listed as captured on the 7th, and the Falzarego Pass leading to points west on the 9th. First Army claimed to have gained ground in a battle upon the glaciers south of Tonale Pass. And in the Carnics, fighting around Freikofel peak led to the capture of two more secondary passes on the 8th, although the Austrians had counterattacked and reached Mt. Paralba on Italian soil within a week. As if to offset this, the Carnic Corps had gained ground east of Pontebba, on the railroad to Villach, and brought the town of Malborghetto under shellfire on the 12th. Also, a probe towards the Predil Pass at the northern tip of the Isonzo watershed was undertaken. In the Adige Valley Mori had been reached on the 12th as well. Clearly, the pressure was being applied, all along the front line.

The Italian Chief also wanted support on his seaward flank, and continued to press the navy for it, but Revel's resources were being stretched to the limit. Effective Senussi activity in Libya needed to be countered, *Entente* schemes in the Mediterranean needed to be supported and of course the submarine threat dealt with. An Austrian sub torpedoed a British cruiser on June 9th, and surface ships were still raiding the Adriatic coast as late as the 18th. Before the month was out, three German-made U boats would be ready for action, having been assembled at Pola. For the moment, the best the navy could do was support the airship raids on the enemy fleet base, which were carried out on June 12th to 14th.

Second Army, farther from the coast, began a new series of assaults from the Plava bridgehead on the 10th. For three days desperate fighting occurred on the heights above the river's east bank, but in the end, after seven separate attempts, Frugoni's men were beaten off with heavy loss. On the 16th a fresh division was committed to the attack which once again swept up the blasted, corpse-covered slopes and in a struggle of sheer attrition reached the Austrian positions which were taken in bloody, hand-to-hand combat. Twenty-four hours later the depleted but determined defenders returned and re-took that which they had lost, again in close-quarter fighting. After a week of struggle for the Plava heights, 10,000 men were casualties, three-quarters of them Italian. The landscape had been altered to create a scene of utter devastation. Frugoni's only real success came on the 16th when, helped by a thick fog which reduced visibility to nil, *Alpini* once again fell on the defenders of Krn, and overwhelmed them in yet more hand fighting.

Aosta's Third Army fared no better. It began attacking the Podgora position as early as the 15th, without result. Reports that Mebrosina had been 'reached' or that the railroad terminus at Divaccia had been 'destroyed' could mean anything and were not likely to placate Cadorna, yet the Chief seems not to have been much disturbed by his armies' bloody repulses, despite the fact that he had lost perhaps 20,000 men in less than a month. Typically, he gave the order for a major attack designed to take Görz, considered a preliminary necessity to the advance on Trieste. Both Second and Third Armies would take part in the drive, which was to come between Tolmein and the Gulf of Trieste. Frugoni was to seize the bridgehead opposite Tolmein, then the town itself, plus make his main effort at Görz. Aosta was given the task of capturing the Doberdo Plateau, which is the westernmost extension of the Carso, from which he could outflank both Görz and the well-defended coast road to Trieste.

On the other side of the line, Boroevic's men worked frantically to improve their defenses, in particular to construct shelters in which to hide during the inevitable bombardment. Although he had sustained at least 5,000 casualties by now, and was outnumbered in infantry three-to-one, 'The Straightrazor' had no intention of retreating. To the contrary, his strategy was to hold his ground, period. He knew that his army was a hodge-podge of nationalities from all over the Austro-Hungarian Empire, but to a man they were determined to deny the Italians any victory, unless it was to come over their dead bodies.

On June 23, 1915 the Isonzo Valley trembled under the explosions of thousands of artillery shells, a deadly rain that continued for seven days. It seemed to cause an atmospheric disturbance, as a period of fog and rain began only a day or two after its commencement. Amidst the awful din, Italian troops attacked the Plava heights at least ten times between the 24th and 26th and were neatly mown down by machine guns as they struggled up the tortured slopes.

In an effort to dilute the blow against Boroevic which was easily anticipated, Hötzendorf implored Rohr and Dankl to launch diversionary attacks however limited in nature. Rohr responded by hurling some recently acquired battalions against Freikofel, a good observation point he disliked sharing with the enemy. The affair led to several days of engagements without producing the desired result. Meanwhile Lequio hit back somewhat to the west, and claimed the capture of the peak of Cresta Verde on the 24th. Another mountain known as Zellenkofel was reportedly taken ten days later by only 29 *Alpini* who attained the summit by using ropes to scale the sheer precipices by aid of moonlight.[33] For the moment Dankl was unable to respond, or perhaps unwilling, if he realized that any effort he might waste strength on could not possibly alter the battle on the Isonzo.

The big push began on the morning of June 30th. Second Army smashed vainly into the Austrian defenses on the Podgora bluff and on Mt. Sabotino, a height just to the north but also on the west side of the river. Apparently the defenders had dug themselves deep enough into the rock to have survived the week-long barrage, even if their positions were rather shattered. Upstream, attacks on Tolmein and the rail junction town St. Lucia were also beaten off, as was another effort to advance in the Julian peaks. Within a few days, the Italians had been stopped in their tracks. Third Army fared no better. Repeated assaults on the Doberdo Plateau gained little for terrible losses, and an attack up the 275m (900ft) high Mt. San Michele on the northern fringe was likewise defeated. A further effort on July 4th brought the attackers to the western edge of the Plateau, where they clung to the flats by the barest of margins, with the steep bluffs at their rear, up which any supplies had to be lugged. About all Cadorna had to show for his effort thus far was a slight gain of ground east of Sagrado up to Castelnuovo. The latter town was, incidentally, the birthplace of an Austrian airman named Gottfried von Banfield, who on June 27th, recorded his first of many air victories when he shot down an Italian observation balloon near the mouth of the Isonzo.[34] Other Austrian planes bombed Cormons on July 2nd, attempting to disrupt enemy communications.

But Cadorna was not yet satisfied, and demanded another push on the 5th. It became the defining event of the entire operation. Frugoni threw everything he could scrape up into the fray, against the Podgora-Oslavia-Sabotino line before Görz. Following another short, sharp barrage the *grigioverde* rushed the Austrian defenders, who slaughtered them by the thousands. The attacked staggered, then halted, without a meter of gain to show for the landscape of corpses. Aosta's men tried hard to expand their toehold on the Doberdo, but it was an exercise in futility. On the 6th the madness was suspended and thus ended the battle history remembers as 'The First Battle of the Isonzo'. Both sides were utterly exhausted, especially the defenders, who were receiving no replacements and could not be re-supplied during the fighting. Boroevic had won round one, but unless he could be reinforced, it would be a pyrrhic victory. Casualties are usually listed as approximately 15,000 for the Italians and 10,000 for the Austrians, but at least one source suggests that they were probably twice as high.[35] Whatever the case, the losses could fairly easily be made good by Italy, but only with great difficulty by Austria.

On the same day that Cadorna reluctantly called off First Isonzo, the government at Rome declared the entire Adriatic to be a war zone. The Austrians certainly needed no convincing. A day later one of the recently-assembled German subs from Pola torpedoed the Italian cruiser *Amalfi* not far from port. Although the sub flew the Austrian flag and carried an Austrian designation (*U 26*), its crew were Germans, a fact known by few at the time. On the 11th, Venice was bombed for the fourth time. All the while Revel was distracted by an operation one of his subordinates had come up with, a landing on the tiny island of Pelagosa mid-way between the two coasts and off to the south. The place was occupied without a fight on July 11th; two days later an Austrian airplane reported the landing, and Haus knew something was in the wind. His suspicions were confirmed several days later when another plane reported the departure of an Italian cruiser force from Brindisi. By the time the vessels had crossed the Sea, Austrian U-boats were in place to greet them. One of these, the *U4*, was able to sink the cruiser *Garibaldi* on the 18th. Haus then sent a fleet of his own to raid the middle portion of the enemy coastline, the Tremiti Islands, and Pelagosa. The attacks were delivered on the 23rd and again in different localities five days later. Pelagosa resisted reoccupation successfully, but the defense of it cost the submarine *Nereide*, sunk by the *U5*,[36] on August 5th. About the only success for Rome at sea during this period was the destruction of a sub-station on Lagosta Island on July 26th. This act was, however, accomplished by a French vessel.

When news of Cadorna's rebuff on the Isonzo reached the eyes and ears of his subordinates who commanded forces to the north and west, they knew instantly that the Chief was bound to be furious. And when Cadorna was angry, officers were often degraded, demoted, or dismissed, and enlisted men punished or even shot. They reacted by immediately ordering their troops into action, even for no apparently good reason. Soon the 'good news' began to reach the Chief: Italian *Alpini* were 'advancing' in Carnia. On July 9th came a report of the capture of Malga Sarta and Costa Bella, obscure topographic features of dubious military value in the shadow of Mt. Pasubio. A note from the 12th claimed Italian cavalry had raided to within 5 km (3 mi) of Trieste. The most interesting story, however, and one that turned out to be completely factual, came out of the Dolomites. A grandson of the *Risorgimento*-famous Guiseppe Garibaldi, who had survived the near destruction of the *Legion Italienne* in France the prior winter, was back in the country and of course up at the front. Colonel Peppino Garibaldi was given command of a battalion which had marched over the Austrian border in the Caprile area and advanced up the Cordevole Valley just east of the mammoth Mt. Marmolada. Then it was halted at the base of a "white triangle of towering mountain. A true granite Alp among the splintered Dolomites".37 This peak was the Col di Lana, and Garibaldi was ordered to secure it at all costs; the subsequent valiant efforts of the *Alpini* and their heroic commander were well covered by the Italian press and became a much-needed source of inspiration on both the home and battle fronts. For the time being, Col di Lana was successfully defended, but Garibaldi vowed to capture it, and few in Italy doubted that he would do so.

Cadorna, meanwhile, had replenished and resupplied his armies on the Isonzo and was already planning another big push. Within ten days of the end of the First Battle, he was ready for a second. Certain that all that was needed for success was more men, more ammunition, and above all more determination, he ordered Third Army to seize Mt. San Michele and the Doberdo Plateau; Second Army was to gain Mt. Sabotino, the Plava heights, Tolmein, and mountains to the north. If he struck quickly enough, he reasoned, Boroevic would not have had time to re-fortify his positions. In the event, this reasoning would prove to be correct.

Boroevic and Fifth Army were granted just a week and a half to repair the damage caused by a week of shelling and two weeks of fighting. Trenches had become featureless depressions, their wooden or sandbagged reinforcement blasted to smithereens. Dugouts and underground bunkers had often caved in, or partially so, and barbed wire barriers had been cut, crushed or blown up. Vast quantities of food, water, medical supplies and ammunition needed to be brought up and stored securely, as none could reach the front lines while an attack was in progress. And where the Italians had gained a few meters or yards, entirely new positions had to be built. Even so, the men of Fifth Army were as determined as their commander to defend every stone and tree. They were for the most part devoted to their Emperor and cause, and were ready to die rather than retreat.

On the eve of the Second Battle of the Isonzo, Austro-Hungarian strength in Italy had reached 16 divisions in all, nine of which were stationed along the river. Italy retained the 39 with which she had begun the war, and had kept them up to strength, but the odds had been shaved from three-to-one to about 2.5-to-one, both overall and in the east.

Hoping to distract enemy attention or disrupt some of his communications, Italian aircraft bombed the coast road between Monfalcone and Trieste on July 16th and 17th. In the wee hours of the following day, every artillery piece Cadorna could muster opened fire on the front, especially the Doberdo Plateau and Mt. San Michele. Within hours, tens of thousands of shells had exploded among the defenders; Mt. San Michele alone had been pounded by 2,500 of them.[38] Thick clouds of smoke and dust were raised, blinding and choking those who were fortunate enough to survive the dense hail of flying steel and rock splinters. Many men were deafened by the awful roar, blinded with foreign matter to the eyes, or buried by shifting earth and stone. The barrage was far less lengthy, but far more accurate than that of the First Battle. Clearly the Italian artillerymen were improving their skills. By midday it had ceased, and thousands of infantry began to advance.

Only a precious few minutes were available to the defenders between the lifting of the cannonade and the inevitable approach of the foot soldiers. Only a few minutes to shake off the trauma of bombardment, clear the eyes, nose, and ears, rush out of the dugouts with weapons and ammunition, take up position, and begin firing. Despite all the handicaps, particularly their depleted numbers, the Austrians were able to meet heavy attacks on the Doberdo, Mt.

San Michele, and Mt. Sei Busi with accurate rifle and machine gun fire. As successive attacks were beaten back, Italian artillery opened fire again, forcing the Austrians to seek shelter. Aosta continued to throw fresh units into new assaults, until the defenders were too exhausted to energetically resist, and in this manner the advance crept ahead slowly. By the 20th, Mt. San Michele had been taken in close fighting and 500 defenders had been made captives.

To the north, Second Army was also suffering from heavy casualties. Attacks on Podgora and Mt. Sabotino were shot up and dispersed. These would continue with the same results for several days. Nor could Frugoni advance from Plava; his forces there gained barely a few meters. High in the Julian Alps, other units tried again to take the entire main ridge. This time they won one nameless peak, but failed to break the enemy's main line. Losses, as usual, were heavy.

When on July 21st an Austrian counterattack regained Mt. San Michele, Cadorna decided to commit his reserves in that area and ordered Aosta to renew the offensive. Reluctantly, the Duke complied; he had already sustained frightful losses in the area. It was forthcoming on the 25th against the weary, depleted men who had been in action for a week, and the renewed assault was simply too much for them to withstand. On that day both Mt. Sei Busi on the southern end, and Mt. San Michele on the northern end of the Plateau were taken by the Italians in savage hand-to-hand combat. Boroevic was furious and ordered counterattacks, but his army was too weak to provide for them, and only the San Michele effort was successful, on the 26th. Mt. Sei Busi could not be retaken, and these attacks cost Fifth Army another 3,000 casualties, men it could not afford to lose. Over the next several days, the Italians slowly brought up artillery to the newly-won areas while the Austrians re-grouped. Soon the battle had degenerated into an artillery duel, not as exhaustive, but every bit as nerve-wracking, for the men of both sides. One day—August 2nd—500 Austrians were killed by shrapnel, but clearly the offensive was winding down, to the great relief of everyone but Cadorna, who seems to have adopted a Haig-like belief that just 'one more push' would be enough to destroy the enemy.

Aerial bombing was becoming increasingly popular with both commands. Nabresina, on the coast road to Trieste, and the railroad center of San Polaj were both hit by Italian airplanes during the height of the Second Battle, on July 22nd. A much more daring long-range raid was carried out against Innsbruck, capitol of Tyrol, the following day. The Austrians countered with raids on Verona on the 25th and 27th. Italian seaplanes, which had been brought to Lake Garda, attacked the lakeside town of Riva, within Austrian territory. All these air actions were relatively minor, but both sides were gaining valuable experience for the future.

Senussi actions were another distraction for Rome during July; an engagement on the 5th was unfavorable, and on the 23rd, several garrisons of occupation in Libyan towns were fallen upon and massacred by the rebels.

Elsewhere about the battle line the news was a mixture of good and unfavorable. Austrian attempts to recapture Pelagosa on the 28th/29th ended in failure, as did an Austrian diversionary attack in the Carnic Alps on the 28th. Farther west, Fourth Army advanced slightly at the San Pelegrino Pass separating the Piave and Adige watersheds near Paneveggio. This movement supported efforts to the southwest as Italian troops neared the crest of the main Dolomite Range well inside enemy territory, where they met determined resistance from the heights of Cima d'Asta, (2,844m, 9325ft) and Mts. Cauviol and its twin peak, Cardinal (2,491m, 8170ft). Supporting efforts were also made in the Cordevole Valley near Col di Lana, on the 28th, and in the Cadore, on the 29th, where the heaviest guns the Italians could deploy lobbed shells towards the town of Sexton. Subsequently, hard rains put a damper on these actions, and by August 1st, all was quiet along the Italian Front.

A combination of the poor weather and his own shortage of artillery shells finally induced Cadorna to call off the slaughter on the Plateau on August 7th. Despite the disappointing results along the Isonzo nothing had occurred which in any way moved him to reconsider his battering-ram strategy. To the contrary, he was still convinced that his enemy was about to collapse; accordingly, he ordered Second Army to renew its attacks in the upper valley. He gave it less than a week to prepare. Second Isonzo had 'officially' cost him 42,000 casualties against 45,000 Austrian, but the Italian figure is highly suspect, and may very well have been half again as much. But the Chief was willing to pay any price to achieve his objectives; Boroevic was equaling willing to pay any price to stop him, but the Austrian was literally running out of soldiers.

On August 3rd, the government at Rome sent an unfriendly note to Constantinople, and at last it seemed as though Italy might declare war on another of the *Alliance* powers. Tensions mounted until the 20th, when war was declared. The act had no immediate effect on the war as a whole, but

Italy's *Entente* allies were encouraged. Now they hoped for a similar declaration from Rome against Germany, but for the moment it was not forthcoming.

First Army began a limited attack towards Trient on the 4th of the month by attacking Folgaria from the rugged country of the upper Astico. Other units claimed to have hauled heavy guns high above the Tonale Pass. Just what they hoped to accomplish with such lofty ordnance might have been a reasonable question. In Val Sugana attackers secured Mt. Cima Cista on the 28th, an act that threatened the town of Strigno. Two days later, elements of the Folgaria force reported that they had driven the enemy off Mt. Maronia.[39] Fourth Army, not to be outdone, announced that it had gained ground in the Sexten area north of Mt. Croce Pass as well as in the Rienz Valley, north of the Misurina Pass. Both the latter advances brought Italian troops perilously close to the Pustertal railroad in the Toblach area.

At sea it was the Austrians who took the initiative during August. Haus sent a fleet to recapture Pelagosa; it heavily bombarded the island on the 17th and the Italians withdrew their rather small garrison the following day. He did, however, lose two submarines during the month, one to a mine near Venice, the other to an enemy destroyer, far to the south.[40] *Status quo anti bellum* seemed to have been achieved after three months of war in the Adriatic.

In the air, activity continued to increase. On August 5th, Austrian naval personnel forced an enemy airship to land near Pola, and captured it. Two days later, however, Pola was raided nine times for the loss of only two Italian airplanes. Trieste was also hit on the 7th, receiving 200 kilos of bombs, a fair amount for those early days of tactical bombing. Austrian aviators hit back the next day, when they attacked Monfalcone. Seaplanes bombed Venice again on the 15th, and Brescia, a supply center, on the 25th of the month.

During all of August 12th and 13th the constant thundering of artillery heralded Cadorna's newest scheme on the Isonzo. This time the region selected for attack was the northern portion of the valley, between Tolmein and the town of Flitsch, in the shadow of Mt. Rombon. For 48 hours the guns belched their destructiveness amidst the beautiful scenery of the Julian Alps. One major objective was the Austrian foothold on the west bank of the river at Tolmein; this was to be overrun, the stream crossed, and the rail junction of St. Lucia on the east bank captured. The assault began on the morning of the 14th and continued, scarcely unabated, until the 21st. Although the Italian Corps attacking the Tolmein area consisted of about 50% elite *Alpini* and *Bersaglieri* troops, the multi-lingual Austro-Hungarian defenders could not be routed. Almost in desperation did the Italian Commander, General Nicolis di Robilant order another barrage and attack on the 22nd. It, too, failed.

North of the bridgehead other *grigioverde* were sent to attack the unconquered peaks of the Julians. It was a hopeless task. One participant wrote that his *Bersaglieri* unit began to refer to Mt. Nero as Monte Rosso "because so much blood has been spilled here." He described one assault up a steep slope and into barbed wire while under accurate artillery and small arms fire. In horror, he witnessed dozens of his comrades cut down until the dead were piling up. When they decided to retreat, many more were killed or wounded. "What a massacre!" he wrote, "So many young lives wasted."[41] The man was able to survive by hiding in a ravine, where he spent the night exposed to a soaking rain. The next day he realized the extent of the carnage and related that his battalion had been reduced to about 50 survivors. And the fate of this particular unit was by no means unique. Di Robilant gained no ground in the Julian Alps, and the last of the futile efforts came on the 29th.

Near Flitsch the Isonzo cuts through a deep gorge eroded over the eons between the peaks of the western Julian Range. Overlooking this channel on the west bank are the twin spires of Mt. Kanin (2,585m, 8,480ft) and Mt. Rombon (2,210m, 7,250ft), a towering massif which is often snow covered near the summit, even in summertime. Beyond this barrier lay the Predil Pass, straddling the ridge separating the Isonzo watershed from that of the Danube, a prize clearly worth fighting for. Early in the war, Italian troops had occupied Flitsch without a fight, but they were under constant fire from Rombon. For Cadorna, the capture of Mt. Rombon would lead to the capture of the Predil, which in turn would put his army on the road to Vienna, or at least Villach. Naturally, he ordered the deed to be done.

The action kicked off on August 24th when Di Robilant tried to advance up the valley towards the Pass and outflank Rombon; the effort was stopped. Then came the advance up the mountain on the 27th. At first it seemed to be successful, but as the attackers neared the summit, Slovene troops rose up from their positions and caught the Italians without cover on the treeless, wind-swept mountaintop, and shot them down in droves. The brave and resourceful *Alpini* tried again on the 29th, but to no avail. Rombon would remain Austrian, guarded by Slavs. Still, Cadorna was unwilling to admit defeat. His response to lack of success was simply to increase expenditure. Like any modern-day bureaucrat, his favorite word for dealing with a problem was 'more', in his case more men, more guns, more ammunition, and more fighting spirit. It never would have occurred to him that perhaps the manner in which he used his resources was flawed, that his strategy was unsound. No, he would reinforce his armies to the point from which he could not fail. All that was needed, he believed, was to continue the battering and pounding.

Boroevic in his own way was just as obstinate, but with far better reason. Not everyone in the Hapsburg command structure agreed with his stubborn resolve to hold every meter of ground; some were not afraid to say so. In Boroevic's defense, however, it might be said that his options were extremely limited. Trieste was fewer than 30 kilometers from the front, and if it fell to the enemy, Pola, Fiume, and the entire Austrian naval presence would be in extreme danger. If the enemy could push on to Villach or Laibach, communications to the seacoast would be similarly threatened. In Boroevic's mind the enemy had to be engaged somewhere, and that somewhere might as well be as far forward as possible.

At the beginning of the month of September, the French informed Cadorna that their own Chief of Staff General Joffre was coming to confer with him. The Italian was not excited; he had little to say regarding the *Entente* cause, and was not particularly interested in anything outside of his own command. Probably in order to have an operation underway, a fact which might preclude him from wasting too much unwanted time with Joffre, he decided to renew the offensive which had so recently stalled. Accordingly, the Tolmein bridgehead was once more assaulted on September 4th and 5th. Once the initial charged had failed, a more powerful effort was made on the 9th; before it was over the elite mountain troops of both sides had clashed in furious hand-to-hand fighting. The defense prevailed. Two days later Italian artillery pounded the unbeaten defenders for another 24 hours, and on the 12th, the infantry attacks commenced again for another long day. When the dust and smoke finally dissipated and the red-hot barrels of Schwarzlose machine guns were allowed to cool, the only Italians on the battlefield were corpses. Meanwhile Joffre had made his visit on the 6th, the essence of which was to ask Cadorna for a supporting offensive on the Italian Front to coordinate with an upcoming French attack later that month. Cadorna politely refused, citing logistical difficulties; he should have refused citing the futility of it.

Once it became clear that Tolmein would not be captured, Italian attention shifted back to the Julians, where minor actions had been flaring since the 4th. A new drive to secure Mt. Lipnick began on the 13th, supported by heavy artillery, a rarity in Italian hands up until then. The big guns blasted big gouges out of the rock, but these sometimes caused slides which only hampered the attackers; the defenders caught on and began to roll stones and debris down the slopes. When enemy units approached too closely, they often mixed in hand grenades. By September 20th, the battle was over.

Otherwise, September was relatively uneventful along the front, only minor engagements took place in the Trentino, and mostly early in the month. On the 7th an aviator whose name would soon be on the lips of thousands of Italians experienced his first air combat. The engagement was a disappointment for him when his machine gun jammed and, remarkably, a similar episode on the 13th prevented him from success a second time within a week. His name was Francesco Baracca, and he would go on to become a Major, and Italy's leading air ace. For the moment, Baracca could only complain about his weapons, but he was gaining valuable flying experience.

Neither side was very active in the Adriatic during September. German U-boats did manage to sink eight small vessels during this period but no advantage worth mention resulted. On the 27th, however, the Italian navy was shaken when one of its battleships—the *Benedetto Brin*—suddenly exploded and sank while at harbor at Brindisi. Once submarine action had been discounted, sabotage was suspected, but Rome preferred to remain silent on the matter, probably to avoid embarrassment. The disaster may well have been the result of a freak accident. Whatever the case, the loss of the battleship came at a time when Italian naval strategy was being hotly debated, and it only contributed to the confused atmosphere. Two weeks later on October 11th, Revel resigned in favor of a local command. A new policy needed to be implemented soon; in October, enemy submarines sank 18 *Entente* ships in the Mediterranean.[42]

Pressure on Cadorna to launch another all-out offensive began to build in early October, when the *Alliance* powers, reinforced by Bulgaria's entry into the war, attacked Serbia. The Chief was easily warmed to the idea, as he knew the Austrians would have sent whatever units were available to the Balkans. In addition, he was anxious to drive in Boroevic's front before the onset of winter. Once again, Second and Third Armies were bolstered with every man, gun, and provision that could be scraped up. All the while, his other armies were pleading for enhancement; they believed, with some good reason, that they were capable of achieving a limited success in the mountains. For example, First Army continued to crawl forward in the Trentino towards the immediate objective of Roverto, the capture of which would have upset badly the defense of Trient. A village here, a town there, continued to fall; Pregasina near Lake Garda was reported captured on the 15th. But Cadorna was not interested, and allowed only the barest amount of resources to be directed to the theater to his rear. He saw nothing of essence to be gained there. Predictably, he ordered a third major offensive on the Isonzo and augmented his two armies there with virtually everything available. The first two weeks of October were spent on resupply as hundreds of Fiat trucks and thousands of horse-drawn wagons creaked and groaned under the strain of hauling hundreds of thousands of tons of war material over the dusty roads and up to the front. Autumn rains transformed the dust into mud, and in the higher elevations snow and ice began to fall.

Much of the same transpired on the other side of the front, except that the front line more often ran over higher ground, necessitating a liberal use of pack animals or carts with less heavy loads in order to be able to negotiate the steep slopes. An absence of good roads hampered Boroevic's men, but he kept his engineers busy constructing mostly shelters blasted into solid rock, that his troops might survive the terrible effects of enemy artillery. On the eve of battle, Austria had increased her strength on the Italian Front to 20 divisions; no more could be expected while the Serbian Campaign was underway. Approximately two-thirds of this strength lay with Fifth Army. By contrast, the Italians had not yet increased the number of divisions committed to the front, but they had for the most part kept them up to strength. Italy's advantage had shrunk from 3.5 to one in May to about two to one in October.

By mid-month Cadorna had amassed an impressive collection of artillery, and for the first time in the war, about one-fourth of it was heavy, he having begged, borrowed, or stolen it from anyplace it was available. These weapons began their work on October 18th, at midday. The entire front from the seacoast to beyond Tolmein began to tremble under the most extensive barrage this theater had yet suffered. Reports that the roar could be heard as far away as Venice and Pola may well have been correct. Its effect on the poor Austrian infantry at the front can only be imagined; thousands were killed, crippled, deafened, or blinded and of course even those who were unscathed were unable to sleep or even communicate properly. For three days the hell continued without an energetic response from the Austrians, who were unable to see in the thick smoke and dust. Italian aircraft added to the confusion, bombing and strafing targets beyond the wall of shells, especially enemy airfields. On the 19th, under intense *Entente* pressure, Italy declared war on Bulgaria. Now the nation was officially at war with three of the four *Alliance* countries; only Germany had escaped her wrath thus far.

When the shelling finally ceased on the 21st, Italian infantry leapt out of their positions and advanced on a zone of tortured earth, reasonably certain that no living thing had survived to oppose them. They were wrong. Although Boroevic had lost the equivalent of perhaps an entire infantry division to the carnage, his veterans had not lost their will to defend and everywhere met the attacks with thick and sustained small-arms fire. Tolmein and the Plava heights were successfully defended again, as was Mt. San Michele and the Doberdo Plateau. Austrian troops took more than 600 prisoners on the first day of the offensive, the Third Battle of the Isonzo. Undeterred, Cadorna ordered another bombardment and attack on the 22nd at Mt. San Michele. It too was stopped, as was an effort along the coast road. A third barrage and attack was sanctioned for the 23rd. It was also eventually beaten off, but only after an exhausting day-long struggle often at close quarters. The tired defenders, their ranks depleted, were clearly weakening. When still another heavy artillery preparation and attack were forthcoming on the 24th, it seemed the defense would at last break; somehow it did not, despite hours of severe combat with knives, trench clubs, and grenades. One more determined attack would almost surely have captured the mountain, but it was not immediately to be, giving the Hungarian defenders a critically needed breathing spell.

Turning his attention to Second Army, Cadorna demanded a renewed effort in the north and a knockout blow from the center. The northern effort at Plava and Tolmein, delivered between the 24th and 27th ended as all earlier such drives had ended, in a deadly hail of Austrian defensive fire. In the center, the main Italian push crashed into the familiar defenses at Podgora, Oslavia, and Mt. Sabotino. Beginning on the 24th Italian heavy guns had softened up Sabotino. Wave after wave of attackers advanced on the 25th, and for two days beyond. The question became who would run out of what first; the Italians out of men or the Austrians out of ammunition. Then on October 28th a further assault on Sabotino was undertaken using *the* elite unit of the nations' military, a brigade of Sardinian Grenadiers. Struggling up the inclines littered with the remains of splintered trees, fragmented rock which had slid down from above, and the bodies of those who had gone before them, the Grenadiers met their fate, felled by 8 mm projectiles and grenade and stone fragments. Podgora and Oslavia also remained unconquered. Another drive on Podgora the following day was shattered by Austrian artillery fire.

October 25th was also host to another massive attack on Mt. San Michele, following a barrage of several hours duration. Partially successful against the weakened defense, it was renewed the next day and very nearly carried the hilltop. Exhaustion of both sides ended the battle, but only for a few days. By the 1st of November the Italians surged forward again for two days, and again they could not dislodge the Hungarian defenders. Morale in both armies was beginning to sag, and the fighting more or less just withered away. During the same time period, Podgora, Oslavia, and Sabotino were threatened once more; these attempts were also less energetic than those of a week earlier and by the 3rd, they were spent. The last action of the campaign took place on the 4th near Plava, where a new round of assaults had begun October 31st. At first, Second Army units gained ground south of the town, but they were soon thrown back, the tide turned by a single fresh battalion of Viennese whose commander would win the Knights Cross of the Order of Maria Theresia, Austria-Hungary's most prestigious decoration.[43] In the end, the front line remained where it had been for months.

Once again, Boroevic's Fifth Army had survived the best punch the Italians could throw at it. The cost had been extremely high, however, at over 40,000 casualties, and Boroevic feared for the future. He knew his opponent well by now and expected yet another offensive at any time. Hötzendorf was even more nervous; Austria could not trade Italy man for man or gun for gun, not even at a two-for-one ratio. If the enemy continued his war of attrition, Austria-Hungary must surely be overwhelmed. Even so, neither man considered any other course but fighting on, to the bitter end if necessary. And both would have loved to have been able to concentrate all of the nation's strength on the Italian Front.

For Luigi Cadorna, the task before him was equally clear. He would continue to butt heads into the proverbial brick wall until the wall crumbled. Carefully concealing his enormous losses from the King, the government, and especially the press, he continued to insist that more was better. He would gladly have sacrificed his entire army had it meant achieving his objective.

To this day no one can say how many Italian casualties were suffered during the Third Isonzo campaign, but estimates as high as 80,000 or even more are not unreasonable, considering his enemy's losses which were generally half or less, as extensive. Even considering 75,000 as a bare minimum, the tragedy of it all is that all this suffering produced no gain of ground save a few shell-pocked meters here or there, and not one militarily important height or position of any sort. But Cadorna, like Haig on the Western Front, was just certain that his strategy was working, that he was wearing down an opponent who was always near exhaustion and collapse. There was of course a point to this type of reasoning, at least from a mathematical standpoint, but it took absolutely no account of the needs of the soldiers, who were after all, human beings with hopes, dreams, and desires of their own. So far they had done his bidding and had paid a high price in blood for their devotion. How long could they be expected to maintain their morale if they were to be herded like sheep into the slaughterhouse? Had he provided substantial off-duty activities and entertainments for them, they might have been expected to accept their duties, however reluctantly. But he did not. In fact Cadorna rarely ever visited the front; he considered time thus spent as wasted and distracting, an unpleasant chore, or worse. Even the King had put himself in harm's way more frequently than had the Chief. As soon as the Third Battle had savaged his armies to impotence, the Chief began planning a fourth.

Chapter Four
For Want of a Reason

Once the Third Battle of the Isonzo had faded away in early November, many commanders on both sides of the front lines expected that active military operations would be suspended for the winter. It was a reasonable enough assumption; traditionally armies did not fight, because they could not fight, in bitterly cold weather. But everything about this war seemed to break with tradition. Already on both the Eastern and Western Fronts the struggle had continued unabated throughout the first winter of war, due in large part to the static nature of the fighting, which enabled soldiers to dig themselves into the ground where they could at least survive the elements of inclement weather. We have seen how the situation in the high mountains was somewhat different, yet it was similar enough to allow for a year-round bivouac even in the extreme atmospheric peculiarities of the Alps. In all but the highest elevations, the numerous forests provided timber for shelters and fuel for thousands of fires so essential for survival. Snow could always be melted for drinking water in locations high above the closest stream. Provided the necessary clothing was available, the soldiers could, and did, pass the season without much change in their routine. This is not to suggest that there were no problems. Snow and ice seemed to be falling constantly, making the easiest inclines difficult to negotiate; steep grades could cause men and animals as well as vehicles, to slide to injury, death, or destruction. In the course of the war hundreds of men and horses broke legs or worse, by falling. Many, of course, fell long distances to their deaths, often never to be seen again. Snow slides and avalanches were always a problem, and could sweep away entire units or bury entire positions. Both sides soon learned how to inflict such a calamity upon the enemy. Often, artillery would be fired at points above a known enemy stronghold in order to cause snow and ice or just general debris to fall upon them. Sniping and sharpshooting became popular at targets well outlined against a snowy landscape. As time went on, more and more white clothing was used, but it was most effective during stormy or foggy days. Wounds sustained at low temperatures can lead to all sorts of problems not common in summertime, and usually meant death or disability for those injured along the remote frontier ridges. In addition, weapons and ammunition would often not function properly in the cold. Artillery pieces sometimes had to be warmed prior to firing, lest the crew risk an explosion of the barrel. Frequent high winds exacerbated most other difficulties and could reduce visibility to only a few meters. Prolonged darkness contributed to the incidence of accidents and generally compounded all other problems.

There was little activity in the way of offense, from the Stelvio to the Predil. One story that did come out of the Dolomites in November involved Colonel Garibaldi and the Col di Lana. Apparently the Colonel had received substantial reinforcement in late October, and began an advance, once again, on the mountain. By about the 6th, he claimed to have taken three sides of the peak, but not the summit, which he described as presenting "a sheer wall of rock, more than 200 meters high."[44] Nevertheless, the Italians were able to wipe out an enemy machine gun section at the top of the cliff with artillery fire, after which *Alpini* troops scaled the height and captured the summit and 130 prisoners who had emerged from their shelters too late. Soon an Austrian counterattack regained a portion of the summit, which Garibaldi described as being "bisected by a ten-meter-high ridge."[45] That little ridge became the new front line for the time being, from November 8th. The only other action of any consequence occurred south of Trient, where slow but steady First Army pressure led to the evacuation of the civilian populations of Mori and Roverto by Dankl's men. Mori was practically on the front line by now and Roverto had become the southern terminus of Austria's sole Trentino railroad, and was always bristling with military activity. It is likely that Dankl was motivated by the fear of the presence of spies in this Latin-speaking region at least as much as he was driven out of concern for the well-being of the civilians of these towns. At any rate, many of the residents had long since fled before the official exodus was undergone on the 23rd.

Cooler weather did not end air activity by either side. Bombing was becoming more and more of a normal routine, less of a novelty. Verona, south of the 'Thirteen Communities', was hit on the 14th, Brescia was targeted again, by two Austrian planes, on the 15th. Two days later three locations were bombed; Grado, Verona, and Vicenza all sustained very minor damage. On the 19th, it was the turn of Udine, site of Cadorna's headquarters. These raids were pretty much acts of frustration, carried out as some sort of offensive action by people who were constantly on the defensive, and often (Fourth Isonzo was then underway) under heavy attack. Francesco Baracca, the Italian flyer whose equipment had twice failed him in September, was once again to be similarly disappointed on November 19th, when an intended victim was able to escape. Baracca had yet to shoot down an enemy machine, but before the year was over, his numerous reports detailing the limitations of his aging aircraft had won for him a more modern airplane to fly. He was pleased with the new weapon.[46]

If it seemed that Austrian aggression in the air during the waning days of 1915 was being unanswered by the Italians, the same could certainly be said for *Alliance* aggression at sea. As we have seen, German submarines had been causing havoc in the Mediterranean throughout the year, and flew the Austrian flag whenever a desired target was Italian. Another such incident sank the liner *Ancona*. This action caused quite an international stir, as the passengers were multinational; about 20 American lives, for example, were lost. Other subs brought money and provisions to the Libyan shores, to be used by the Senussi who had become a serious nuisance to the Rome government. One account relates the passage of two camels from the tribesmen via submarine to the naval base at Pola![47] Aside from transporting such gifts to the *Kaiser*, the subs performed militarily useful tasks; steamers and patrol boats along the coasts were regularly sunk, and of course *Entente* shipping in the Mediterranean seriously disrupted. In November, at least 44 ships, and in December 17 ships, were sent to the bottom of the sea by submarines, and at least one other by a mine laid by a sub.[48] Since Italy had entered the war nearly 100 *Entente* ships had been lost in this theatre, over half of them British. The crushing naval superiority that Italy was supposed to have brought to her warring partners had certainly not made itself evident thus far. On December 3rd, an agreement was signed in Paris which allocated different sections of the Mediterranean to British, French, or Italian responsibility. The latter were limited to patrolling their own coasts and those of Libya, but no one could doubt that Rome's main seaward interests lay in the Adriatic. And on the Adriatic coast the city of Ancona, which had already been pounded from the air and sea in this war, was bombed again on December 10th by seaplanes. The raiders escaped unscathed.

Although Rome's resolve in the air or at sea might be questioned in late 1915, the same could not be said of the ground campaign. For it was during this time period that Cadorna set his armies in motion for the Fourth Battle of the Isonzo. Launched just one week after the end of the Third Battle, it represented a continuation of the prior struggle, with hardly a pause in the bleeding. Even the attackers had not sufficient time to regroup, resupply, or integrate replacements, though they were infinitely better off than the defenders, who barely had a chance to remove the dead, evacuate the wounded, lug fresh quantities of ammunition forward, and try to get some rest and a decent meal. There was simply no time to rebuild shattered trenches and strong points, let alone construct new ones. Even more serious was an outbreak of cholera, said to have been brought to the area by Austrian troops sent in from the Eastern Front. It ravaged men on both sides of the line for weeks, particularly in November; typhus, trench foot, and digestive infections also took their toll. An Italian soldier named Benito Mussolini was one victim of the germs, which nearly killed him, an act that the enemy had thus far been unable to accomplish. There was of course the weather to deal with as well. Dust of summer had given way to the sticky mud of late autumn, and the rains were cold and unwelcome. And into this setting of exhausted, sick and miserable human beings, Cadorna would initiate a new attack. Gone were the days of patriotic enthusiasm, but the average Italian would still obey his orders; he knew he had no other choice but a firing squad. On the Austrian side, a stoic determination to resist the invaders still lingered in most minds, but the persistence of the far more numerous foe was beginning to raise serious doubts as to the certainty of victory.

By late 1915 Italy's war effort was beginning to gain momentum. Industries were beginning to turn out more and more equipment and supplies, in amounts quite adequate to replace combat losses and still outfit new formations. The army training camps were releasing the first echelons of the nation's vast manpower reserves, enough men to maintain all of Cadorna's divisions, in spite of the already staggering losses; even a large reserve was being created for the Chief to draw upon in the frequent moments of need. It was precisely this availability of resources which enabled him to initiate the Fourth Battle so soon after the end of the Third. Just as quickly as unit rosters had been filled he struck again, confident that the enemy lines could be broken before Boroevic could reinforce them. The reasoning was not entirely illogical; it was based, however, on the optimistic belief that the Austrians were close to collapse.

The tenth of November was host to the commencement of the new offensive, which began as usual with a fierce artillery barrage. Between Plava and Mt. San Michele the air filled with shell splinters and shrapnel, fragments of rock and stones, and bits and pieces of debris of all sorts. Following four hours of pounding and churning, the Italian infantry attacked. At Plava, a day and a half of carnage was punctuated by the breakdown of the attacks under accurate Austrian artillery fire. In the center Mt. Sabotino was successfully defended again by Polish and Ukrainian troops, though not without difficulty. The heaviest fighting took place on a direct route to Görz, at the Podgora height and at the village of Oslavia, which was obliterated by the shelling. Without adequate time to prepare proper defenses, the Austrians resorted to all sorts of measures to hold their high ground; at Podgora they rolled barrels of kerosene or other flammable liquids down the slopes and ignited the contents with artillery fire or by throwing grenades along behind the containers.[49] Soon, the fighting had become so close that it was decided with bayonets, knives, and clubs. Slight Italian gains were nullified by prompt Austrian counterattacks, so after four days of vicious combat, the front lines remained unchanged.

The only location at which the attackers gained anything worth mention was Mt. San Michele, where repeated assaults slowly overwhelmed the defenders. Even so the frightful losses were hardly worth the limited gains, and in the end the highest part of the mountain remained to the Austrians. By November 16th, a relative quiet settled over the Isonzo. But Cadorna, as mentioned above, was a man out of the same mold as Douglas Haig; any slight gain was seen as a major victory, any advance however inconsequential, was proof of imminent defeat of his foe. Accordingly, the offensive was ordered renewed on the 17th, to begin the next day. The primary objective was the city of Görz.

Görz had long been the object of Italian desires. Behind Trieste and Trient, it was the third largest city in *Italia Irredenta*; at only 14.5km (9 mi) from the old border it was easily the closest. Lying on high ground on the east side of the Isonzo, its center was just 1.5km from the river and only a few kilometers west of the Latin/Slavic linguistic divide. Of a prewar population of at least 40,000, perhaps 70% of the inhabitants spoke Italian as their native tongue, while the remainder were divided between Slovene and German speakers. Up until November, the city had been spared deliberate Italian bombardment—the latter would have preferred to have captured it intact—but subsequently it came under intense artillery fire and was the target of bombing attacks beginning on the 18th. The remaining civilians who had decided for whatever reason not to evacuate the city were forced to hide underground to escape the awful shelling. Within a few hours half of the city's 2,500 buildings had been rendered uninhabitable and hundreds of people killed or injured. When the dust cleared, only 3,000 of the original population remained, and many of these represented the infrastructure, the offices of which had "retired into cellars". "The Police Headquarters had been reduced to a space two yards square."[50]

Next day, the 19th, the rain of steel was redirected to the front lines beyond the Isonzo. Austrian artillery tried to answer whenever the crews themselves were not immediately threatened by the barrage, and the air force delivered bombs to Venice's seaward defenses on Alberoni Island, but Cadorna would not be distracted. He waved his divisions forward again on the 20th, against the Podgora-Sabotino positions, where they were again bloodied by Austria's Slavic defenders. Mt. San Michele also received several waves of assaults, all of which were beaten off by the Hungarian troops dug in on the heights. Everywhere, the lines were held, but at a terrible cost to the Fifth Army as well. Boroevic simply had no fresh troops with which to relieve his weary men. Cadorna's battering-ram tactics were slowly beginning to prevail, or so it seemed.

But the question had become one of which implement would break up first, the battering-ram or the wall it was striking. Italian morale was beginning to crack under the strain of so many futile attacks, producing so many casualties for so little gain. One regiment apparently mutinied at this time; a few deaths by firing-squad were performed in order to convince it to return to its duties.[51] Once again, Cadorna was incapable, or unwilling, to read the handwriting on the wall. A few more blows, he reasoned, and the enemy would be finished.

This final effort to reach the ruins of Görz before the snows fell commenced on November 25th with artillery fire falling on Austrian positions from Tolmein to the Doberdo Plateau. Second Army smashed at Tolmein and and Plava again, only to sacrifice more thousands of its soldiers uselessly. Even heavier attacks broke upon the Podgora-Sabotino lines, where every unit Cadorna could call upon was committed in a desperate attempt to overrun the weary defenders. Italian gains were measured in meters, for very heavy casualties, yet the onrushes continued until even the attackers could find no replacement units with which to continue. Consequently, the battle wound down as successive attacks grew weaker. In early December, Frugoni was allowed to disengage. Overall gains had been minimal, losses incredibly high.

At the southern end of the front, Third Army fared no better. All of the shelling, both past and present, had cleared Mt. San Michele of most of its trees, which lay shattered on its slopes, their jagged, broken remnants everywhere amongst the corpses and the pock-marked acres. Austrian visibility was thus enhanced when the latest attacks were delivered; spotters called in friendly artillery fire to help stop the assaults. Machine guns, rifles, mortars and grenades did the rest. Very little ground changed hands. For several days, the Duke of Aosta's army persisted, and heavy fighting developed around the village of San Martino, on the southwest flank of San Michele. No breakthrough could be attained, even after two more weeks of shelling and attacking on and around the mountain; sheer exhaustion dictated an end to the Fourth Battle on December 14th. Winter had arrived, and even Cadorna realized that further offensive action was at least temporarily impossible. Reluctantly, he refrained from ordering any further attacks for the calendar year, and the war lapsed into a static phase where the only actions consisted of sniping, occasional sporadic shelling, and a few infrequent probes and trench raids. Elsewhere along the front, the only action of much consequence took place in the Ledro Valley, northwest of Lake Garda, where elements of First Army tightened their hold on the town of Bezzecca from the time of its capture in November until the last forward movement was achieved about December 10th. That same day, Austrian seaplanes bombed the port city of Ancona again. By mid-month both antagonists had suspended strategic operations.

Fourth Isonzo exacted a terrible toll from both the Italian and Austro-Hungarian armies. Cadorna, as usual, was careful to conceal his losses from everyone, and it was only much later that the official figure of 49,000 killed, wounded, or missing was established, and this number probably represents only half the actual toll, which is now believed to be somewhere near 90,000. Ninety thousand men sacrificed for advances which could nowhere be measured in more than meters. Neither Görz nor Trieste had been secured for the loss of almost the equivalent of an entire army. And for the first time in the war, Italian soldiers had surrendered in large numbers; roughly one casualty in ten had been a captive of the enemy. Worse still, morale was at an all-time low.

For the Austrians the battle had been a very costly defensive victory. Boroevic admitted a loss of 25,000 troops, but again the real figure was much higher, at least 35,000 and probably 45,000, or about half that of the attackers. Those men now lost to the defense could have staffed three to four divisions. Still, Fifth Army had prevented the enemy from achieving any strategic advantage, and Boroevic saw no need for a change of tactics on his part; he had after all held his ground in the face of a significant numerical superiority and had inflicted greater punishment upon his enemy than he himself had suffered. Provided he continued to receive adequate manpower and munitions, he felt his forces could hold out indefinitely.

Far behind the front lines in the mountains, many Italian civilians had begun to wonder by the autumn of 1915 why *Italia Irredenta* remained unredeemed. Most people had assumed that the war would simply be a march into, and seizure of, the lands the nation desired to own. The enemy was tied down against the Russians on one front and the Serbs and Montenegrins on another, and was not expected to be able to sustain a third battle line against Italy. When hundreds of thousands of families were informed of a dear soldier's death, disfigurement, or unaccounted-for absence, a good deal of concern began to build among the populace. When by late autumn Monfalcone was still the best prize the army could boast of having captured, many began to wonder if all was not well within the nation's military. Discontentment began to foment, and it spilled over into the ranks of the soldiers, however slowly. By November, it was clear to many members of the government that something needed to be done to reinforce the nation's resolve. A first step came on December 1st, when Sonnino of the Foreign Office gave a speech to the Chamber of Deputies in which he revealed for the first time publically, the existence of the Pact of London. Most of the details of the Pact were not mentioned; his purpose was to hammer home the article which bound all the signatories not to seek or sign a separate peace with the *Alliance* Powers. Sonnino was making it perfectly clear that Italy was not at liberty to consider peace with the Austrians alone. Indeed, Italy was fully committed to the war, come what may. The message was not lost on the Deputies, but not universally appreciated by the general population.

The Italians were of course not alone in their frustrations. Every nation that had gone to war since July of 1914 had expected easy, early victories, and everyone had been just as disappointed. All had long since been claiming that they were fighting a purely defensive struggle; no one but the enemy was an aggressor. The hypocrisy of it all came to a head in December at Chantilly, France, where the *Entente* nation's representatives were called for a strategic conference on how to achieve victory. Cadorna sent his Chief of Staff General Porro to sit for Italy; the conference began on the 6th. Porro had no difficulty in getting into line with his British, French, and Russian colleagues who all agreed that the best way to defeat the enemy coalition was to launch simultaneous offensives on all three main fronts so as to prevent the *Alliance* from switching its reserves from one theatre to another when necessity called. By coordinating their attacks, they reasoned, they could all break through the enemy lines and drive on to victory. The fact that the only times thus far that anyone had broken the front had been as a result of an *enemy* offensive seems to have eluded them all. As soon as good weather arrived in the spring, they agreed, the attacks would begin. Cadorna was not displeased with Porro's subsequent report. He was planning to attack as soon as the weather permitted anyway, and if the others wanted to do so as well, so much the better.

In fairness to the Italian government, it should be noted that it did make some effort to try and rein in the unimaginative Cadorna. Prime Minister Salandra himself proposed that future strategy be arrived at by a committee composed of both military men and civilians (politicians), an unconcealed attempt to establish some limits to Cadorna's dictatorial powers. It failed because the Chief was legally subordinate only to the King, who would not sanction the move. The nation's war effort remained solely in the hands of one man.

Saturday January 1st, 1916 dawned cold and grey over much of the Italian Front. There was little or no fighting, as soldiers turned their energies to improving their living quarters or simply to staying warm. Italy had been at war for 222 days, yet was apparently not much closer to achieving her objectives of the campaign, though lack of results had not been due to lack of resolve. The nation had in fact geared up for all-out war without much of a hitch. As early as May 19th, all railroads had been placed under military control; on July 7th the same applied to all factories which produced war material. The first national loan was issued on June 28th, a second followed in the autumn, and by February 6th, 1916 a third raised indebtedness to five trillion lire. Before the war, Italy had imported more than three-fourths of the food she consumed, and despite determined efforts to increase domestic production from 1915, nutrition quickly became a national concern as prices soared. When a speedy victory at the front proved elusive, the government began to take more extreme measures to prop up the economy. Although neither Rome nor Berlin had yet declared a state of war, something like three billion dollars worth of German investments in Italy were frozen, and later seized. Soon, on leap year day 1916, a very provocative action was taken when Rome confiscated 36 German merchant ships which had been interned in Italian ports since the country's entry into hostilities. They represented more than 175,000 tons of shipping, and they were soon back at sea, flying flags of various *Entente* nations with the reasoning being that the newly acquired ships offset somewhat the heavy losses the *Entente* had suffered at the hands of *Alliance* sea action, up to that point. Still, Germany refrained from declaring war on Italy.

On the other side of the front, Austria-Hungary had now been at war for seventeen months, or more than twice as long as Italy. Accordingly, she was nearer exhaustion. Although before the war the Empire had been more or less self-sufficient in the matter of foodstuffs, serious manpower shortages had hurt the agricultural industries badly, and early losses of prime farmland made the problem that much worse. As early as May 19th, 1915, before Italy had even declared war, Vienna experienced its first 'meatless day', a day during which the public was asked to consume no meats, and none were offered for sale. A month later it was Hungary's turn when on June 24th the price of foods shot up drastically. Domestic unrest began to brew. To make matters worse, an outbreak of cholera in Galicia soon spread, with returning wounded troops, to several Austro-Hungarian cities. Spring and autumn 1915 were times of particularly virulent epidemics. All the while the economy was severely strained; by mid-July Austria had made a second war loan in an effort to raise another 625 million dollars (equivalent). Later that month the Imperial government took steps to regulate the economy and confiscated the 1915 vegetable crop. The beginnings of rationing had arrived.

Militarily, at least, the news was not all bad. A massive *Alliance* drive on the Eastern Front had evicted the Russians from most of Galicia and shoved them deep within their own territory, inflicting nearly two million casualties and capturing vast stores of equipment, munitions, and provisions in the process. Subsequent Russian counterattacks had all been easily defeated. Following Bulgaria's entry into the conflict, a well coordinated German-Austrian-Bulgarian offensive had broken the Serbian Front and overrun all of Serbia and

Montenegro, carrying the *Alliance* armies into Albania and to the Greek frontier. In less than a season, Austria had been able to reduce her warfronts from three to two with one—Russia—apparently stable for at least awhile. And farther to the southeast, the Gallipoli Front, which the *Entente* had chosen to create a year before, was also eliminated when the British and French decided to evacuate it. The hard-pressed Turks continued to fight on three other fronts, but three was better than four. For the *Entente* the only face-saving move during this time period was a violation of Greek neutrality, when the port of Salonika was occupied, in an effort to forestall an enemy occupation of all of the Balkans.

The new year began, then, with the people of the *Alliance* nations able to take heart that despite the heavy odds arrayed against them, they appeared to be holding their own, or better. The Western and Italian Fronts were stalemated, but elsewhere the news was good. It seemed that they might be able to knock out their enemies one by one. For Franz Conrad von Hötzendorf, the time seemed ripe for an opportunity he had long dreamed of: an offensive against Italy. He wanted to take forces from the defunct Serbian Front and the quiet Russian Front, and reinforced with Germans from the same locations, launch a strategic offensive from out of the south Tyrol to the Adriatic Sea near the mouth of the Adige. All of Cadorna's Second, Third, Fourth and Carnic Armies would be cut off and destroyed, and the war won against the despised Italians. Then Germany and Austria-Hungary could concentrate all of their forces against Russia and perhaps secure a separate peace in the East. Ultimate victory might still be attainable, he believed, but if so Italy had to be knocked out of the war. Historians of the war usually dismiss Hötzendorf's plan as over-ambitious, unattainable, foolhardy, or worse. It was none of the above. In fact it represented one of the few strategically intelligent plans of the war, and had it been implemented the way he envisioned it, it would almost certainly have succeeded, as subsequent events were to prove. But it never had a chance. Falkenhayn, Germany's Chief of the General Staff at that time, was committed to the Western Front, like so many unimaginative commanders of his day. He was planning a major offensive against Verdun, for which he wanted every available German soldier. Nothing was to be spared for Italy; besides Germany and Italy were still not officially at war. It was a great excuse, but a terrible omission. Franz Conrad would have no more than his own forces with which to attack to the south. The Austrian was bitterly disappointed, but he began to plan the attack anyway. If the Empire was to be defeated, at least let the Italians suffer its best effort. Slowly, throughout the winter and spring, the number of divisions facing Italy was increased. Four arrived during February. Four more appeared in March, though one was sent away that month. Still, by April 1st, 27 divisions were on the line in the Alps.

General Cadorna was also increasing the numbers available to him, but not because he had anything resembling a new plan, he simply took whatever the war effort could provide for him. As of April 1st he disposed of 43 divisions, all pretty much at full strength. At this time, the odds in favor of Italy had slipped to 1.6 to one, or less than half as favorable as when war broke out. Just how the Chief expected to win his objectives with a comparatively ever-decreasing force when he had failed to do so under far more favorable circumstances, was a question he preferred not to confront. He needed no strategic planning, he knew what he wanted to do, and he cared little about his allies or other war fronts; he cared even less about whatever price his nation would be required to pay, that his bidding might be done. When in January Austrian press releases suggested a million Italian casualties thus far in the war, Cadorna made little effort to reassure his people, even those in the government, that the numbers had been exaggerated, if indeed they had. Instead he clung to his policy of silence regarding losses. By the end of the month he had thrown a sop to the press with an 'official' statement claiming 30,000 enemy prisoners to date, five artillery pieces and 65 machine guns captured, plus large quantities of munitions and war material of all sorts. It was hardly a reassuring counter to an enemy claim of a million casualties inflicted, but the Chief was never much interested in the thoughts of others, especially civilians.

All was not exactly quiet at the front, even in the dead of winter. Once he had been allowed a short breathing spell, Boroevic decided that he wanted to recover even the minimal gains the enemy had made in November and December, so he sanctioned local attacks which commenced on January 14th. The ruins of the village of Oslavia were assaulted several times over the next ten days until a more determined attempt won the old position on the 24th. Both armies suffered in this battle in fog and mist; the Italians much more so, and they had lost a position which had cost them dearly to take in the first place. Boroevic could hail a minor triumph.

In other minor actions of the winter, Austrian ski troops surprised and routed an *Alpini* battalion high on Mt. Canin on February 12th, then had to endure a week of counterattacks, supported by persistent artillery fire, before the Italians gave up and conceded the snowy, freezing heights to them. At the Col di Lana, Garibaldi's men, suffering from exposure and anxious to do something to improve their lot, began a tunneling project on January 15th, designed to advance upon the enemy in a subterranean manner, unexposed to the elements. They were aided by a number of men with considerable mining experience, some of whom had labored in operations as far distant as the United States and Canada. Soon the Austrians realized what they were up to and began to shell the location, prompting the *Alpini* to use all their skills to haul up mountain guns of their own, one of which was able to silence a particularly dangerous enemy weapon, before it too was disabled. Despite occasional heavy Austrian shelling, Garibaldi's men pressed on with the drilling throughout the winter. To the west, First Army units advanced under fog cover and fought their way into the towns of Romchi and Roncegno in Val Sugana. Other ground was gained in the vicinity of Mt. Collo on the northern rim of the valley. They were closing in on Trient from the east and Dankl was beginning to grow concerned for the safety of the city, but Hötzendorf was saving all of his strength for his strategic offensive, and declined to reinforce his scanty forces in the Trentino. Meanwhile, unchallenged Italian aircraft bombed Austrian supply and communications centers. Breguzzo, in the valley of the stream which runs into Lake Garda, was bombed on January 13th, and two days later six other locales were similarly hit. General Brusati felt that with modest reinforcement, he could fall upon Trient from three sides and capture the place. But Cadorna would have none of it; his eyes continued to focus on the Isonzo.

Bombing attacks were not confined to the Trentino; the Adriatic winter is not too severe for such operations. Austrian planes again raided naval installations at Rimini on January 12th and on February 14th. Another group of aircraft bombed the north coast on February 12th, and two days later extensive runs were made in the Milan area where not only the city itself was targeted, but also the nearby towns of Monza, Treviglio, and Bergamo. Rome decided to retaliate for these rather un-military hits, and sent a force of Caproni bombers to bombard Laibach four days later. Normally, attacks such as these caused very few casualties and did little damage of value to the war efforts of either side, but they could cause temporary panic amongst the inhabitants of the target areas, and did contribute to the growing cynicism towards the war in the minds of many.

On the 21ˢᵗ of February 1916, Falkenhayn initiated his Western Front offensive against the fortified French town of Verdun, thus beginning a three-season-long battle of attrition. It was the most serious German attack in the West since August 1914, and it was designed to cripple the French army for good. The blow caught the *Entente* nations somewhat off guard and spoiled their own offensive hopes for months to come. Paris cried out to all of its allies, and invoking the Chantilly agreements of two months earlier, demanded they take the offensive immediately, in order to ease the enemy pressure on Verdun. Soon, the British, Russians and Italians had all responded positively, though they all insisted that they were unable to take immediate action. As far as Cadorna was concerned, he was only too happy to resume his Isonzo madness; he had already begun to plan a Fifth Battle, and the inconvenience of having to advance his timetable by two or three weeks was not too troubling. Hötzendorf was already sending additional forces to south Tyrol when Boroevic began to warn of another impending attack. Austrian troops of Fifth Army knew well by now the telltale signs of another Cadorna adventure, and they began to send ominous reports up the chain of command in the early days of March. Within a week the first probes were conducted, as the Italians sought out weak spots in the defense. On March 8ᵗʰ, a small diversionary attack took place between the Tofana Peaks north of Cortina. Artillery fire shook Austrian positions in the Carnic Alps and in the Fella valley near Malborghetto.

Both Second and Third Army's artillery opened fire on March 11ᵗʰ; about 1,300 guns in all.[52] All throughout that day and the next, they pounded enemy fortifications along the Isonzo while the weather worsened. At first, deep snow in the mountains accumulated while ice and sleet pelted the lower elevations. By the time the infantry assaults began on the 14ᵗʰ, a warm front had shrouded the entire area of the lower river in thick fog and the upper basin in a grey-looking mist. Neither attacker nor defender could see the other until they were only meters apart; when the Austrians heard the enemy approaching they often opened fired into the gloom at the sounds. At San Martino, Mt. San Michele, Podgora, Tolmein, and in the Julians the story was the same: determined resistance and no gains. After a week of staggering around in the awful weather, Cadorna's men were pulled back. Still spoiling for a fight, Boroevic ordered counterattacks behind other clouds of a man-made sort, and his guns began dropping gas shells on the Italians.[53] Three more days of fighting—March 19th to 21st—on the Doberdo Plateau yielded little, as did two counters at Tolmein on the 22nd and 26th. Some ground was gained however in the Podgora area, and a number of captives taken. A last-ditch Italian drive in the Julian Alps was easily defeated at about the same time; as if to punish the Fifth Army, Second Army guns pounded Görz on the 22nd. Three days later it was Third Army's turn to lash back with concentrated fire on the Doberdo and Mt. San Michele, where sporadic fighting was still in progress. Minor attacks by both sides tired the troops of both contestants, then on the 28th, Aosta launched a fresh offensive where so many before it had failed, against what he hoped was an exhausted defense. It gained a few meters of blood-drenched soil east of the village of Selz, then was stopped. By the 30th of March, the Fifth Battle of the Isonzo was over. Both sides had made the slightest of gains for the loss of two to three thousand men.

The Fifth Battle was conspicuous by both its relative brevity and its relatively low cost. Cadorna had not insisted, as he had in the earlier battles, upon endlessly repetitious attacks on inflexible defenses, nor had he pumped his numerous reserves into the fray. If his behavior was untypical, it was certainly not because he had learned not to waste his men on hopeless attacks, or that he had learned to call off a doomed attack when the defense showed no signs of cracking. Not at all. He allowed the Fifth Battle to come to a mercifully quick end simply because his heart had never been in it to begin with; the French, more than he, had dictated its timing. Once the Chief felt that he had honored his obligations to his allies, he was happy to let the whole affair be forgotten. It was of no interest to him that the battle had not in any manner aided the French, whom he was not inclined to trust at any rate. Even the Russian response to Verdun, which was carried out at the same time as Fifth Isonzo, was a far more determined effort, although it was shattered in the mud and snow near Lake Narotch. And the Russian army was much more limited in its means at the time than were the forces of Italy. Unfortunately for the twelve or fifteen hundred Europeans who lost their lives as a result of the Fifth Battle, and the three times as many more who were badly injured, the offensive is rarely ever mentioned in general histories of the Great War, and usually earns only the briefest of descriptions even in the multi-volume accounts. At least Boroevic's men were proud of their achievement; Cadorna's would never have been allowed to be.

As was usually the case when the Italians applied pressure on the Isonzo, Austrian troops in other areas along the line made local attacks to try to distract the enemy command. One of these was delivered on March 23rd in the Terragnolo Valley. It broke against the First Army defenses at Moriviccio and all fighting ended two days later. More successful was a limited move in the snows east of Plöcken Pass in Carnia, where white-clad Austrian ski and snowshoe troops broke through the thin line in the mountains in an effort to outflank the roadway, on the 25th. *Alpini* counterattacked, aided by artillery fire, but were unable to regain their original lines. An Austrian press release of the 27th claimed 500 Italian dead littered the snowfields. Boroevic's airmen also began to step up their activity. Encouraged by Hötzendorf, who wanted somehow to disrupt enemy communications to the Isonzo, an air campaign was initiated in late March. Its first objectives were railroad bridges and junctions in Venezia; the first sizeable attacks came on the 26th and 27th, but were costly to the Austrians in terms of aircraft lost. As the Italians had recently bombed Trieste again (March 15th), another big raid on Ancona was planned as retaliation, but in the event, the raiders were met with a dozen or more enemy fighters and the formation was scattered, on April 4th.

Despite the strict censorship policy of Cadorna, or perhaps because of it, a growing number of people in and out of government were beginning to suspect that all was not well with Italy's war effort. On March 3rd the Chamber of Deputies had met to discuss the possibilities of the presence of a German campaign of intrigue in the country; scapegoats needed to be found. A month later it was announced that General Morone had been appointed Minister of War. If the move was intended to rattle Cadorna, it failed, as did all attempts to limit the dictatorial powers of the Chief. Meanwhile, Britain's King George had requested an audience with Italy's powerful military leader, and Cadorna found the time to be opportune to be received by the Monarch. His Majesty urged greater inter-*Entente* cooperation, and spoke of a new conference of multi-national heads of government scheduled to meet in Paris a few days later. Premier Salandra and Foreign Secretary Sonnino attended for Italy, but the whole affair, like the problems faced by the French and British, was of no particular interest to the Italian Army boss. For the moment, he was planning no new Isonzo offensive.

Cadorna's short term strategy was to poke and jab for awhile instead of another all-out attack. Perhaps he noticed that enemy units were being withdrawn from the Isonzo and were appearing in the Trient area. If so, he may have guessed what Hötzendorf was up to, but curiously, he sent only marginal reinforcement to the west; not even his strategic reserve was moved. Had he known that a new enemy Army Group was being put together far to his rear, he could not have failed to respond more decisively. Habsburg Archduke Eugen was given the Army Group command; its forces consisted of Dankl's command, now raised to Army strength and called the Eleventh, and Third Army from the now-defunct Serbian Front, commanded by General Kovess, another veteran of the Eastern and Balkan Fronts. By mid April, these units had been assembled. Dankl's men faced south from the east shore of Lake Garda to the Folgaria Plateau, while Kovess was to drive southeast into the Seven Communities and into the Val Sugana. Then suddenly the weather turned sour before the attack was launched, forcing a postponement.

No one in the Italian command structure was behaving as though they were about to be attacked. Görz was heavily shelled again on April 6th, and Italian Second Army probed in the Julian Alps on the 9th. Artillery duels raged up and down the Isonzo for much of the month. Third Army probed at San Martino, Selz, and of course at Mt. San Michele, which was now generally referred to by the Italians as 'Mt. San Morde'. For the rest of April, fighting continued on the Doberdo Plateau and in the Selz and San Martino areas, especially between the 22nd and 24th. It was during these relatively minor attacks and counters that two future flying aces scored their first confirmed victories. First, Francesco Baracca shot up an Austrian two-seater and forced it to land on his side of the line, on April 7th. Baracca even landed near his victims and waited with them for Italian ground troops to arrive and take them prisoner.[54] Three weeks later, it was the turn of Viennese Benno Fiala, who machine-gunned an Italian two-seater out of the skies over San Daniele.[55] On this occasion, Fiala was the observer/gunner of the plane; it was Austro-Hungarian policy to credit both personnel of a two-man aircraft with a kill.

The story was much the same on sectors distant from the Isonzo. A determined attack in the foul weather by Austrian Alpine troops on April 7th forced the Italians to abandon the Rauchkofel, a Carnic peak on the Austrian side of the frontier. Farther to the west, and high on the Col di Lana, Peppino Garibaldi's men had finally finished their months-long project of tunneling deep into the mountain summit, half of which was still in the hands of the enemy. Once they had completed their digging, the last several dozen meters were packed with explosives and the charge was sealed with tons of stone to contain it. During the night of April 17th-18th the 'mine' was exploded; the force of the blast obliterated the Austrian half of the summit, somewhat like the eruption of a volcano would accomplish. "A crater 150 feet in diameter and sixty feet deep"[56] was created and was immediately stormed by Garibaldi's men, who subsequently held their ground in the face of several Austrian counterattacks over the next several days. About 200 soldiers had been killed outright by the gigantic explosion, and more than 150 dazed survivors were made prisoner. After nine months of persistence, Colonel Garibaldi had finally taken Col di Lana.

Another interesting story of the same period came out of the mountains far to the west, just south of the Tonale Pass. Here, on the towering heights of the Adamello *Massif,* an American observer recorded an account of a journey up to the front, which became a combination of exhausting hikes and dizzying rides on several *teleferica* before he reached even the base camp, itself a former Alpine Club encampment at 2,517m (8,260 ft). From there he trudged through heavy snow, ever higher, until he glimpsed an emplacement between two peaks into which the Italians had somehow managed to mount a 149mm gun; he referred to it as "the highest piece of artillery in the world".[57] Eventually his party reached the glaciers of the *Massif* at Lobbia Bassa, where he heard accounts of recent fighting in which such topographic features as the lonely Brizio Pass and Mts. Lares, Fargorida, and Fumo were taken with almost superhuman efforts in the most challenging atmospheric conditions. All of the action had taken place in the second week of April, and came to a climax on about the 11th. Later he climbed another "three thousand feet of almost sheer snow-covered rock"[58] to Lobbia Alta, a vantage point from which he watched the extremely elevated Italian artillery lob shells down the east face of the *Massif* into the Val Genova. The difficulties of transporting ammunition for these guns, as well as all the essentials to sustain the lives of their crews in this glacial landscape were phenomenal. By April 17th the *Alpini* had taken and secured Mt. Val di Fumo Pass at 3,400m (11,160 ft); this 'pass' was basically only a gap through the heights on a hiking trail, but the Italian press sensationalized stories of this nature.

Not all the fighting occurred in such remote areas. There were healthy exchanges of artillery fire on April 10th to the 13th in Val Sugana, where First Army units continued to crawl forward, apparently unaware of the concentration of Archduke Eugen's armies. And northwest of Lake Garda, other units of Brusati's force advanced in the Concei Valley at Lake Ledro and assaulted Mts. Pari Cimadore and Sperone, two spires of less than 2,000m (6,500 ft) and no longer completely snow-capped. Sperone in particular became the setting of a savage contest, where the combat was hand-to-hand before it tapered off after several days, on the 16th. Even so, slight advances in the Concei coupled with other slight advances in the Adamello Group meant that Austrian defenses in the Guidicaria Valley in between, were being squeezed, and the Italians initiated some late-month action in the area, hoping to encourage the defenders to withdraw. But the latter were sent just enough reinforcement to enable them to hold, and by the end of April the Trentino was reasonably calm again.

As April gave way to May 1916, larger operations on the Italian Front relaxed in favor of the usual sniping, skirmishing and occasional shelling. The only action of note took place on May 10th, when Second Army brass, still angry over the loss of ground during the previous winter around Mt. Rombon, sent several battalions up the slopes of Mt. Canin in a surprise attack. The summit was recovered. At sea, the anti-submarine nets at the Otranto Straits recorded their one and only confirmed success of the war when the Austrian *U6* was trapped on May 13th.[59] In the skies over the front, pilot Baracca was frustrated when a victory he reported to have scored on the 2nd was not confirmed. The next day the Italian airship *M4* flew to Laibach for an overnight bombing run but was shot down by gunner Benno Fiala, flying with Captain Adolf Heyrowski. Having been set afire, the dirigible crashed to the ground east of Görz near Merna, killing its six crewmen. It was Fiala's second 'kill', and Heyrowski's third.[60]

If the front lines were relatively calm, the nerves of many of the senior commanders were not. Hötzendorf was pacing forth and about, impatient to launch his *Südtyroloffensive*, the weather notwithstanding. He well knew that in a prolonged delay, he would almost certainly lose his element of surprise; if the enemy correctly assessed his intentions, he would surely withdraw from the Isonzo and Carnic areas and block the intended passage to the sea, spoiling completely the strategic plan. For years, the Austrian leader had wanted to attack Italy, and now it seemed that the opportunity might be lost, for want of good weather. Boroevic too was anxious; he had been obliged to surrender several divisions for Hötzendorf's scheme, and he was worried that Cadorna would attack him again soon. His concerns were not without foundation. Everyday came new reports of increased Italian strength within Second and Third Armies. If the trend were allowed to continue, he could not guarantee a successful defense. But the General who was without a doubt the most frantic during those early days of May was Roberto Brusati of the Italian First Army. For months, Brusati had been pleading with Cadorna to reinforce First Army, he had been sent a battalion here, a few companies there, not enough of course, to achieve his primary objective, the city of Trient. An early capture of the place would have eliminated the very type of danger that the Austrian command was now planning, since the next nearest rail center capable of serving as a terminus for an entire army was Bozen, far to the north, too far in fact, to be much of a threat to the north Italian plains. Even without proper strengthening, First Army had slowly closed in on three sides around Trient, and Brusati believed that two or three divisions might have made all the difference. Lately, however, he had been forced to cry for help for another reason: daily he was receiving alarming reports regarding an enemy buildup around Trient. Even Cadorna, who disliked hearing unpleasant news, was sufficiently moved by Brusati's incessant incantations to inconvenience himself to the point of taking the journey to First Army headquarters to settle the matter. It was well known that the Chief was quite unreceptive to suggestions which seemed to conflict with his own beliefs, and was thoroughly bored with listening to alternative points of view. Not surprisingly, Cadorna dismissed Brusati on the spot, citing non-compliance with his instructions for standard defensive postures. General Pecori-Giraldi succeeded to army command. The date was May 8th, and the weather was improving rapidly. Cadorna returned to Udine and hoped that he would not be troubled further by noisy subordinates or by *Entente* entreaties for support. He was anxious to plan a new attack on the Isonzo, a new offensive which would surely break the Austrian defense once and for all.

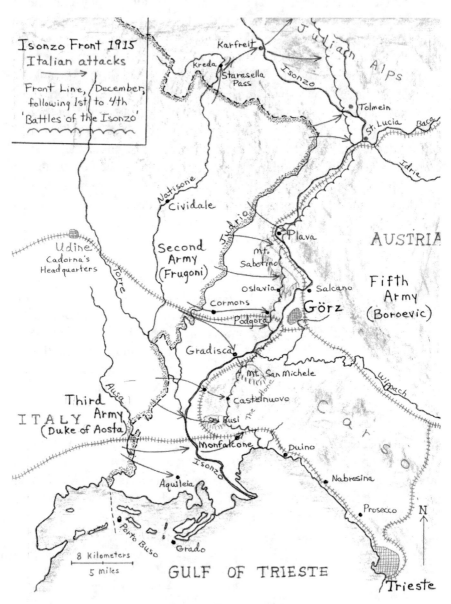

Isonzo Front 1915

Chapter Five
For Want of a Means

For even the least talented of strategists who have ever glanced at a map of the Italian Front from the years 1915 to 1917, a glaring weakness in the shape of the line cannot fail to gain attention. Ever since 1866, the boundary between Italy and Austria-Hungary had formed two adjoining salients which jutted to a position from which each was exposed on three sides by foreign soil. When the two nations went to war, then, each possessed a province that could theoretically be easily overrun by an enemy who attacked the vulnerable province with converging attacks, or who simply advanced from his most forward territorial extension to cut off the opposite salient at its base. For this reason, it would seem illogical for either side to place its main military forces deep into an advanced location from which they might be subjected to isolation by an enemy move to their rear. The entire concept is strategy 101, but as was so often the case in this war, all logic seems to have been abandoned early on and never recovered. Not only did Italy's Supreme Commander commit his main forces to the extreme end of the salient—in Italy's case represented by the province of Venetia—he did so in an area of coastal plain, with his right flank on the sea itself and his left among mountains which were by no means secure from enemy troops. When reports of an enemy concentration far to his rear reached him, he felt the unwelcome information scarcely worth a backward glance; his business was to the east, and nothing was going to distract him. Of course, had he gathered his own considerable superiority to converge on three sides of the enemy buildup, he could have both destroyed half of his opponent's strength and conquered much of an entire province (Tyrol) in one powerful, well-coordinated blow. There is no evidence that any such thoughts ever occurred to him. To the contrary, he continued to send four-fifths of all new strength to his armies on the Isonzo. Besides Second and Third Armies, the Fourth and the 'Carnic Group' were also dangerously positioned;

only First Army fronted most of the three sides of the Tyrol salient.

All of the above was certainly not lost on Cadorna's opposite number, Franz Conrad von Hötzendorf, who had been wanting to attack Italy for a decade. He had considered every aspect of such a war and he knew just what he wanted to do, but he had always lacked the means with which to accomplish his goals. Now, however, with the Eastern Front still quiet and nothing much doing in the Balkans, Hötzendorf could not resist the temptation to strike at Italy. Despite his extreme disappointment in being unable to obtain the seven or eight German divisions he had requested from Falkenhayn, he had decided to go it alone. By May of 1916 he could account for 27 divisions on the Italian Front; of these only six were left to Boroevic for the time being, four more constituted the newly-designated Tenth Army under Rohr, and the others were packed into the south Tyrol. Fourteen of these would be available for the *Südtyroloffensive.* They were augmented with all the independent heavy artillery batteries the high command could scrape up, including about twenty of the very effective 305mm Skoda batteries, and some super-heavy weapons mounted on railcars. In all, some 300,000 men backed by 1500 guns, a third of them heavy, were ready for action. Although the Italians had increased their front line strength by now to 46 divisions, First Army, which would absorb the coming punch, disposed of only five when the snows melted, and Cadorna had even sent one of these to Macedonia in April.[61] By so doing, he had placed his entire command in grave danger.

Hötzendorf's strategic plan called for a breakthrough on the relatively weak enemy lines south and east of Trient and a push to the Venetian Plains. Eleventh Army was to advance south along the Adige and through the Valarsa, take Verona, then pivot to the east cutting railroads and other communications facilities as it went. Third Army was to smash past defenses in the Astico and Brenta River valleys and continue on to Bassano and Vicenza. It was further hoped that the two groups could link up and drive to the sea somewhere in the Venice area, but even an advance short of the Adriatic was considered adequate, provided the supply routes to Cadorna's armies on the Isonzo could be captured, or at least brought under long-range artillery fire. Either way, the Italians would have to withdraw from Boroevic's front and the latter could then apply pressure from the east. The plan's main weaknesses were a lack of reserves for the forces with which initial attacks had to be made, and perhaps most of all, the relatively wide zone of assault chosen. The fifteen hundred guns were simply inadequate to prepare the nearly sixty kilometers (37 mi) of front selected for destruction. Even so, the Austrian generalissimo was reasonably confident of success. At worst, he felt, the offensive would upset the enemy timetable and force him to disperse his reserves. It might delay another Italian attack on the Isonzo for months to come.

Like nearly all big attacks of the Great War, Austria's *Südtyroloffensive* was betrayed by a few of the soldiers who were supposed to have taken part in it. The malady was common to all armies of the warring powers; troops who believed that they would soon be killed once they left the comparative security of their own trenches often crossed no-mans-land between the lines and surrendered to the enemy, hoping that their reports of worthwhile information would ensure decent treatment by their captors. Such intelligence was generally only marginally useful, since it often came too late to be of much value, but it could still be somewhat worthwhile. Out of the darkness of the early morning hours of Sunday, May 14th came a handful of such men, frightened Austrian conscripts who warned of the impending firestorm. Their tales came far too late to help General Pecori-Giraldi, who had been First Army commander for less than a week. At any rate, by the time Giraldi could digest the report, Archduke Eugen's powerful barrage had begun.

Boroevic and Rohr were ordered to carry out a new round of 'diversionary' attacks also on the 14th, those useless, manpower-wasting exercises of which the Austrian command was so fond. Accordingly, Fifth Army units struck on the Doberdo Plateau, surprising dismounted Italian cavalrymen and capturing nearly 200, before they were driven off. Rohr responded with two weak attacks, one in the Julian Alps and one in an upper valley of a Tagliamento River tributary in Carnia, where Tenth Army held a small area on the Italian side of the border. Additionally, Austrian aircraft roamed the skies over Venetia, bombing railroad junctions and stations. One group of these raiders was intercepted by Francesco Baracca and his squadron as it approached Udine on the 16th. Three Austrian vehicles were shot down, including one by Baracca, his third air victory.

All along the front line between Lake Garda and the Val Sugana, the Austrian barrage tore away at First Army from dawn on the 14th. Smaller caliber guns shelled trenches and barricades at lower elevations, while the heavy pieces pounded away at the mountaintops. So furious was the drum-roll of explosions that many of the simple *grigioverde* believed that they had incurred the wrath of the Almighty; no enemy could be capable of such fury. Soon, many Italian troops were sarcastically referring to the enemy offensive as the *Strafexpedition* (punitive expedition); other soldiers, including the Austrians, picked up on the wordplay and inferred that the Italians were being punished for deserting the *Alliance*, and the name came into widespread use.

Once the cannonade had ceased, Eleventh Army units brushed aside the weak, battered defenses on the Adige and attempted to drive to the south, but were soon halted by a withering fire from the heights of Zugna ridge, especially Zugna Torta. A push up the Valarsa was similarly delayed. At Val Terragnolo, the bombardment had practically obliterated the defenses and progress was better. Third Army was generally more successful, and shoved the defenders away from Mt. Collo on the first day. Other gains were made on the more forgiving landscape around Folgaria and Lavaronne. The front had begun to crack.

Zugna Torta would hold out for two more days. Several Austrian attacks up the mountain were shot up, then the heights were bombarded again by heavy guns on the 17th. Next day the defenders withdrew to the south, when Austrian Alpine troops captured a ridge on the Baldo *Massif*, in support of other units which advanced about seven kilometers along the east shore of Lake Garda and into Italian territory. Across the Valarsa, the 2,110m (6,920 ft) Col Santo fell on the 19th, and the aggressors moved on to Mt. Maggio. Another 'diversionary' action took place at the same time northeast of Tonale Pass in the extreme upper Noce valley, where Austrian units reclaimed some ground that they had lost earlier in the war. By the time the sun set on May 19th, Vienna was claiming to have taken 13,000 prisoners and more than 100 guns in five full days of battle. Rome did not dispute the figures.

Chief Cadorna had been taken by surprise, although he never would have admitted as much; Brusati, now disgraced, had been right all along. On May 20th, the Supreme Commander authorized an orderly withdrawal by First Army, and began to strip the over strengthened Second and Third Armies of division after division, which he sent to the Bassano-Vicenza region in order to create a new army with which to stop the Austrian offensive. He also sent an immediate appeal to his *Entente* allies, that they might in the spirit of Chantilly apply pressure to his enemies in other theatres. How soon had he forgotten how half-hearted was his own response to *their* appeals. The new army being created was called the Fifth, and its command was given to the idle

Brusati, for lack of a more immediately available candidate. Six days into the *Südtyroloffensive*, Hötzendorf had already succeeded in one of his secondary purposes, that of drawing major strength away from Boroevic.

Barcole Pass, straddling the watershed between the Terragnolo valley and that of the Posina, was captured by the Austrians on the 20th. Armentara Ridge overlooking the Val Sugana was also overrun, as was more of the plateau around Lavaronne. Aircraft bombed Vicenza. Morale among the First Army defenders was breaking, and ever-increasing numbers of prisoners were being taken . Even the nearly impregnable mountain ridge between the Astico and Brenta Rivers was starting to look un-defendable, given the circumstances. On its western edge, Mts. Mandriola, Campamalon, and Spitz Tonezza were all lost to the defense by the 22nd. A quick evacuation of much of the Val Sugana was now imperative; Roncegno was given up on the 22nd and Borgo two days later. Mt. Salubrio and Strigno would soon follow, once the attackers had gained the commanding heights on the south side of the valley. By May 23rd, when the town of Campolono, with its important metal working industries had fallen, 24,400 Italian prisoners had been taken, along with 251 artillery pieces and 101 machine guns.[62]

For Italy the news was bad, but not entirely so. After the initial onrushes in the Val Lagarina and Valarsa, Eleventh Army units had run into a dogged defense. Despite several more days of hammering at it, they had been unable to prevail against the hail of fire which descended from the Baldo *Massif* and Zugna Coni. A new desperate effort of assault was launched on May 24th. It was designed to outflank Zugna Coni from the south by way of the Buole Pass which commanded the height between the two valleys, and which would have turned the Italian defense of Chiese, the most southerly town worth mention in the Valarsa. Despite a devastating preparatory barrage and a gallant performance by the attackers, the movement was checked. Chiese was captured from the north the following day, but as all the heights remained to the defense, no large-scale advance through the valleys by Eleventh Army was possible. But Hötzendorf was not too worried by the failure of the right wing; the left was in motion, and he therefore removed an entire Corps from the Eleventh and augmented Third Army with it. Dankl's command would advance no more, having gained a few kilometers of ground, most of which had been Austrian soil before the war.

Third Army continued to move forward. Following the capture of Cima Cista and Strigno on the 25th, the Austrian left was in a position to outflank enemy positions in the upper Maso and Cismone watersheds if it so chose, but Kovess would not be distracted from the drive to the southeast. Even so, the Italians evacuated their troops from the Maso to a point about even with Mt. Cauviol. They determined to defend their hard-won ground east of Mt. Cardinal. To the south, once the rugged fastness of the area around Mt. Kempel and Mts. Corno di Campo Verdi and Corno Di Campo Bianca had changed hands (24th-26th) there was no stopping an invasion of the *Setti Communi*.

As mentioned in an earlier chapter, the Seven Communities was an area on the Italian side of the frontier which had been settled by German-speaking wayfarers who occupied the trade routes between points north, and the Adriatic Sea at the important commercial center of Venice. It was an island of German speech amid a Latin sea. A few isolated towns on the Austrian side, such as Pergine and Fersina in the western Val Sugana, and Casotto on the upper Astico were the last remnants of German language in the Italian Trentino, but here on the Italian side of the frontier, remained seven towns on the plateau above the escarpment which fell off to the plains below. Six of the seven lay on a fairly straight line running west to east: Rotzo, Roana, Asiago, Gallio, Foza and Enego. The seventh, San Giacomo, sat below the edge of the escarpment.[63] Clearly, if the Austrians could occupy the Seven, they could practically achieve their purpose for the offensive. The more Hötzendorf and his lieutenants looked at the area, the better they liked what they saw. Three roads ran from the Trentino into the Seven Communities, and a fourth, via the Val Sugana, carried a railway as well. The Austrian commanders were certain that the presence of German speech in several localities on the plateau would facilitate the advance of their troops. In addition, it was believed that the locals would not be unhappy to welcome invaders whose vernacular was the same as their own.

Whatever the residents of the so-called Asiago Plateau may have thought about the return of Habsburg administration, no one was asking them for an opinion. As early as May 25th, the town of Bettale in the upper Posina valley, which was one of the gateways to both the plateau or the plain, was captured. Now the enormous and lofty peak of Pasubio, on the old frontier, would be subjected to attacks from three sides. Small Austrian units attacked the mountain; the real prizes were now farther to the east. On the 27th, Third Army soldiers were pouring down the Val d Assa, past the confluence of the Galmarara and the main stream, and onto Mt. Moschicce, which overlooked the principle plateau town of Asiago. Asiero, at the junction of the Posina and Astico Rivers also fell on that day. Kovess's men were now only 19 kilometers (12 mi) by road from the small city of Schio, at the edge of the Venetian plains.

Hötzendorf continued to hope for the best, but he knew his offensive would soon run out of steam, its momentum slowed by heavy casualties, supply difficulties in the rugged terrain, and general fatigue. Once the Italian defenders of Mt. Civaron had been overcome (May 26th), he urged Kovess to forget any further movement down the Val Sugana and concentrate on the Seven Communities, as the quickest route to the plain. Eleventh Army had obviously stalled, especially by the 30th, when a last day of attempts to take the Buole Pass ended in frustration, the attackers unequal to the task of dislodging the intrepid soldiers of the Italian 37th Infantry Division. But the center was still advancing, and all available reinforcement was directed there. When Mts. Sebio and Moschicce were declared secured on the 28th, it seemed as though one final push might just sweep across the plateau and down onto the plains.

Such reasoning was not entirely illogical, however, Cadorna's new Fifth Army was beginning to make its presence felt. Hundreds of Italian-made trucks were hurrying division after division from the Isonzo to the assembly areas in the very path of the Austrians. They would ensure that even if Kovess did reach the lowlands, he would never be able to drive on to the sea. However, the final days of May still belonged to the Austrians. Gallio was entered on the 30th, and Mt. Pria Fora stormed. The latter was the final height before the escarpment. Asiago, now seriously outflanked, was evacuated by the evening of the same day, and Third army troops cautiously entered it the next day. There were no German-speakers to be found for them to converse with; the place resembled a ghost town. May ended with four of the Seven Communities in Austrian hands, and Hötzendorf could be proud of the latest reports he received, which insisted that since the beginning of his pet offensive, 30,000 enemy troops and 300 artillery pieces had been captured.

Action at sea during late May was very limited. One Austrian steamer was sunk by an Italian torpedo boat at Trieste on the 28th. As if to balance the score, six Austrian warships attacked the line of vessels holding anti-submarine nets at the Strait of Otranto, and sank one, on the 31st.[64] Italian 'naval superiority' continued to appear fictitious.

June opened with the Italians holding on to a line of low mountains on the southern edge of the Asiago Plateau. Mts. Pau, Cengio and Ciove were all successfully defended, with the help of fresh troops, who were now beginning to be committed in large numbers. Ciove was attacked incessantly for three days; the Austrian assailants were able to advance to a point from which they could see Schio, in the valley beyond. It was a location which for them represented victory, but they would never reach the town. Late on the 4th, the attacks were called off, and Mt. Ciove remained to the defense. Several more days of indecisive fighting in and above the Astico Valley gained nothing for Third Army, and with each passing hour the numerical strength of the Italians increased.

Kovess did everything in his power to overcome what was now one final group of heights north of the escarpment. Enemy camps and road junctions were bombed, as well as the cities of Vicenza and Verona, on June 2nd. Three days later more bombs fell on railway facilities at Ala, and at Verona and Vicenza again. In the middle of the plateau, renewed attacks south of Asiago gained some ground, including the town of Cesuna, on the 3rd, a day another 5,600 prisoners in all were reported as captured, by the Austrian press. Victory seemed so close; the plains were just beyond the next hills. Not surprisingly, the Austrian commanders were loath to quit with apparent success so tantalizingly close. Hötzendorf himself was frantic; his grand plan would be defeated for want of a few more divisions with which to exploit the breakthrough.

On the Italian side, Cadorna had regained his composure by early June, when it became clear that the enemy attacks were losing momentum. On the 3rd he issued an order which was more of a press statement—calling for an end to retreat and an energetic defense of national soil. Coming three weeks as it did after the start of the enemy drive, its timing suggested a political rather than a military motive. The Chief was well aware that heads were bound to roll in the wake of the setback; the enemy had conquered as much territory in three weeks as Italy had captured from him in a year. Before any scapegoats could be found in the army, Italy must retake the offensive. Accordingly the new Fifth Army was positioned between Thiene and Bassano where the danger was most acute. It was ready for action by June 7th, and Cadorna immediately waved it forward. There was not a moment to lose. Already on June 4th, the Russians had finally begun their first large scale offensive since the first French

112

appeals for help had come in late February. Now it could serve as a dual-purpose response to both French and Italian needs. The massive blow came on a sprawling section of line between the Pripet Marshes and the river Dniester, and immediately scored a significant breakthrough, taking tens of thousands of prisoners. So desperate was Austria's need to plug the hole in the Eastern Front, that Hötzendorf reluctantly ordered Kovess to transfer two divisions from his command on the 8th.[65] Cadorna ordered heavy attacks of his own for the 9th. Meanwhile, the Italian government was in turmoil. The Chamber of Deputies had convened on the 2nd, and following several days of furious debates, the existing leadership lost a vote of confidence taken on the 10th. Two days later Premier Salandra, who had done so much to bring the nation into the war on the side of the *Entente*, resigned. He was replaced by the less controversial Paolo Boselli. A man named Vittorio Orlando became Interior Minister. Curiously, Sidney Sonnino retained his post as Foreign Minister. No one challenged Chief Cadorna or his methods or 'strategy'.

The outcome of the *Südtyroloffensive* was by now a foregone conclusion. Despite a series of determined assaults on Mt. Lemerle to the southeast of Asiago, from the 9th to the 13th, the entire height was never taken, an outcome that nullified the meager gains. Other, similar contests raged at Mts. del Busiballo (southwest of Cesuna), Ciove, and Brazome (south of Arsiero), with similar results. All along the line, Italian counterattacks were strengthening, and some were beginning to regain lost ground. Far to the east, Boroevic did his best to assist the beleaguered Third Army by launching a surprise attack on the Doberdo Plateau, directed towards Mt. Sei Busi. Although it came behind a short but intense bombardment, it gained only 500 prisoners and little ground. Italian counterattacks prolonged the battle from the 14th until the 17th of June. Bombing planes brought moderate destruction to the cities of Venice, Vicenza, Thiere, and Mestre on the 11th; other squadrons attacked Grado on the 12th. But no amount of distraction could now influence the battle on the Asiago Plateau, where additional units were withdrawn for the Eastern Front also on the 12th. The strategic initiative had again passed to Italy, and Cadorna.

General Pecori-Giraldi would have preferred to see Fifth Army used for a drive up the Val Sugana to the rear of the enemy force on the plateau, a move which would have forced the Austrians to retreat to the west, over difficult border ridges, and where First Army divisions might take them in flank. Cadorna, of course, would have none of such imaginative thinking, and in the event, only a few *Alpini* battalions were assigned to the area. Even so, these made decent progress on the weak Austrian left, advancing north of the Val Frenzela and back onto Mt. Magari from June 16th-18th. First Army counters began at the same time; a modest gain in the Arsa Valley reclaimed Chiese, and a push on the Posina River east of Mt. Pasubio resulted in more favorable positions being attained. In the skies overhead, dozens of Italian airplanes swarmed over the hapless Austrian ground troops, bombing the numerous bridges of the few good mountain roads and strafing the endless, narrow columns of soldiers as they tried to retreat towards Trient. One of these aircraft was shot down near Mt. Cimone by an as yet obscure Hungarian pilot named Josef Kiss on June 20th. Three others fell at the hands of Ernst Strohschneider that month. For the former, it was his first of many air victories; for the latter, only two of the three could be confirmed, but he too was just getting started.

Now that the Italian command knew of Austrian troop transfers out of the Tyrol, another effort was made to cut the Pustertal railroad near Toblach, the location nearest Italian lines. Accordingly, Fourth Army carried out a series of attacks in the valleys north of Cortina, hoping to cross the watershed between them and the railway. Heavy artillery blasted away at the rails from vantage points high above the Rienz River, which flows due north to Toblach. Poor weather hampered the campaign a day or two after it had begun, on June 19th, before any worthwhile results had been achieved. Finally on the 25th, the long-awaited main attack of Fifth Army was delivered on the plateau. Asiago was retaken within 24 hours, as was Cesuna. Austrian troops were also driven away from Mts. Lemerle, Cengio and Cimone, and Arsiero was recaptured by the morning of the 27th. Later that day Posina changed hands, while Pedescala, 5km (3 mi) north of Arsiero on the Astico, was entered by cavalrymen on the 28th. Desperate to stem the enemy counter advance before it had regained all of the ground so recently won, the Austrian command resorted to the first use of chemical agents in the area, calling for a cloud of hydro-cyanide gas on the evening of June 28th. The barrage caught the Italians napping, and inflicted 6,000 casualties before the wind shifted unfavorably for the artillerymen.[66] Over the next several days the defense hardened in the frontier areas north and west of the Asiago Plateau, but on the flanks, the Italians continued to slowly move forward, securing all of Mt. Civaron in the Sugana Valley by the 29th, and driving to Zugna Torta again, in the Valarsa. Out of the early morning gloom of the 29th, an Italian battalion approached enemy lines at a small industrial facility in the Arsa valley, while a few of its officers barked commands in flawless German. They were able to penetrate the local Austrian command bunker but one man quickly sounded a general alarm before he was bayoneted through the throat for his trouble. His actions led, however, to the Italian troops being overpowered and taken prisoner before they could perform an identical maneuver versus the defenders.[67] On the final day of the month only minor combats were fought, mostly among the boulders and crags high above the Astico and Assa rivers of the western plateau.

Events at sea continued to unfold unfavorably for the *Entente*. On June 23rd, an Austrian submarine (U-15) torpedoed and sank an Italian cruiser and a French destroyer at the Otranto Strait. These sinkings contributed to the awesome total of 100 ships that *Alliance* U-boats had sunk in the Mediterranean area since the month of April.[68] Altogether, nearly 200,000 tons of *Entente* shipping was lost in this period. It was beginning to seem as though submarines, not surface ships, would decide the war on the waves. And above the waters of the Gulf of Trieste, Austrian naval air ace Gottfried von Banfield scored victories on June 23rd and June 24th, when he forced down enemy flying boats in a Lohner machine. A later version of the Lohner would become Banfield's favorite airplane to fly. It was produced locally, at the naval arsenal at Pola.[69]

North of the Gulf, Boroevic was preparing to deliver another diversionary attack on the Doberdo Plateau, similar to the one of June 14th. This time he decided to also use poison gas, but the prevailing winds were unfavorable, so the venture was postponed until atmospheric conditions allowed it. Finally, on the 29th the blow was struck, supported by 6,000 cylinders of phosgene.[70] Hungarian infantry protected by gas masks broke through the lines of the enemy, who possessed no such defense against the asphyxiating chemicals. A modest advance on the slopes of Mt. San Michele was the result of the one-day battle, along with nearly 7,000 Italian casualties, whose bodies littered the broken woods of the surrounds. Boroevic had won another temporary, tactical victory.

Hötzendorf was not cheering. It was galling enough that his Italian enterprise had failed, but now he had a full-blown crisis on the Eastern Front to deal with, which meant that all available Austro-Hungarian resources needed to be diverted to that theatre, and that no new buildup against Italy was possible. A great strategic opportunity to use the advantageous geography of the *Welschtyrol*[71] had been lost. Moreover, unaffordable numbers of casualties had been sustained. Most sources list Austrian losses during the Tyrol offensive of May/June at 81,000 and those of Italy at 147,000, with the total lost to capture 26,000 and 56,000 respectively. These figures may of themselves be too low, however, and at any rate do not include other sectors of the front other than the Tyrol/Trentino. Actual total casualties for May and June were certainly 90-100,00 for Austria-Hungary and at least 160,000 for the Kingdom of Italy. Since each side had played the roles of both attacker and defender, the imbalance still easily favored the Empire, but at a price it could no longer afford to pay. By July 1st 1916, Hötzendorf could count only 22 divisions on his southern front, while his enemy had raised his commitment to 47.

While the Austrian Chief of Staff tried to stem the Russian tide in the east, the Italian Chief was growing impatient to attack again on the Isonzo. He was tired of looking over his shoulder towards the Trentino, and anxious to order the return of the many divisions he had so recently and so reluctantly been obliged to send there. By the first of July at least half of the ground lost in May and June had been recovered, and it was obvious that no great force was any longer needed to protect his rear. On June 24th thousands of British and French guns had begun a massive bombardment on the Western Front; everyone realized that they heralded another major campaign. With three big operations—Verdun, the Russian offensive, and now the Somme attack—underway, Cadorna knew the *Alliance* would have absolutely nothing to spare for his front, and he was eager to take full advantage of the situation. Although he allowed the First Army to continue to attack in the west, he began to dismantle the Fifth Army which had so recently been created, and return most of its best units to the Second and Third Armies. Italy's excellent fleet of trucks were serving her very well for the transfer of troops and were much faster than the railroads; during the exodus to the west, entire divisions were reportedly moved within a single day by using 360 trucks per brigade.[72] Italian press reports claimed that between May 17th and June 22nd, 540,000 men, 70,000 horses and mules, and 900 artillery pieces had been transported by truck or rail, to the west.[73] Now the process was reversed. Fifth Army was downgraded to a 'Command', and placed under General Ettole Mambretti; Brusati found himself out of a job for the second time in two months. It was all politics, of course, and the 'Mambretti Command' continued to field more strength than any other of Cadorna's armies for most of the summer. Even so, before the month was over twelve divisions and a host of independent units had been sent to the Isonzo.

While Cadorna rebuilt his Army Group on the eastern frontier, fighting raged elsewhere along the front. Italy's Carnic Force engaged elements of Rohr's Tenth Army in the Seebachtal, north of Mt. Rombon, and in the valley of the Fella near Malborghetto on July 1st, then sporadically throughout the month, especially on the 19th. The forts around the latter location had long been the object of frequent artillery fire, and the trend continued. In the northern Dolomites, Fourth Army began a campaign to clear all of the upper Ampezzo Valley of enemy troops. It began on the 8th, with ground gained among the Tofana Peaks and a couple of hundred prisoners taken. Three days later an incident reminiscent of the Col di Lana explosion occurred when a tremendous blast removed the summit of Col di Bois peak, along with more hundreds of Austrian defenders, and attacking infantry pushed the front back to the mouth of the Travenanzes stream, while all counterattacks were frustrated. Fighting in the area, which boasts some of the most beautiful scenery in all Europe, went on for another two weeks, for only minor additional Italian gains, while bombardments splintered the handsome forests. The side door to the Pustertal remained barred.

Somewhat to the southwest, combat raged from Mt. Marmolada to Mt. Cardinal, as other Italian formations tried to cross the watershed into the valley of the Avisto, a tributary which joins the Etsch just north of Trient. Mt. Cavallazza was heavily shelled for three hours on the morning of the 21st[74], while *Alpini* troops scaled the heights leading to Rolle Pass and the neighboring Mt. Colbricon (2,650m, 8,700ft). A day of bitter fighting in the thin mountain air won the Pass, the mountains, and 500 or so prisoners for the Italians. A day later Mt. Stradone was also taken; nothing could now prevent an advance into Val Travignolo. Without proper reinforcement in this remote, mostly roadless wilderness, the Austrians could do little to hinder the enemy drive on Paneveggio, the obvious target. Nevertheless, a day of delaying actions was fought out on the 30th, before the town was abandoned. Italian troops marched in on the 31st.

Back on First Army's front, Austrian withdrawals and Italian advances in the wake of the recent offensive, were continuing. Every day brought news of a fresh recapture, as First Army units attempted to hop from height to height.

Mt. Maggio was declared as secure on the 1st, Mt. Calgari on the 3rd, and Mt. Seluggio on the 4th. A general advance between the Adige and the Brenta was the idea; the results were less impressive. There was heavy fighting in the Posina and Astico valleys, as well as on the north edge of the plateau. The obscure Agnella Pass was reached on the 8th, and the entire perimeter of Mt. Corno was secured about the 10th, this action completely outflanking the defenders of Mt. Pasubio. Barcole Pass and Pasubio then became the object of the next round of battle, until violent thunderstorms on the 14th and 15th halted the bloodletting. In the Astico valley, Vanzi was captured on the 15th, but in several more days of misery amongst the boulders and jagged ledges of the upper river, Italian advances were stopped. On July 24th, Cadorna ordered all counterattacks in the Trentino area to cease. He wanted more artillery pieces for his upcoming Isonzo attack, and demanded their transfer. Pecori-Giraldi dared not disobey, but he did stall for three days before loading his precious guns on rail cars on the 27th. First Army's days of offense were over, at least for the calendar year.

Apparent Italian success on land, however, did not tell the whole story of the course of the war. At sea, *Alliance* pin-pricks continued to harass Rome's navy. On July 9th the Austrian cruiser *Novara* attacked the submarine blockade at the Otranto Strait and sank two of the ships involved in it.[75] A day later, the submarine *U-17* destroyed the Italian destroyer *Impetuoso* in the south Adriatic.[76] In addition, Austrian naval aircraft bombed Padua on the 14th, and struck Bari and Otranto on the 27th. One of the most remarkable submarine runs of the war began on the 26th, when a German commander in *U-35* left his Adriatic base for a cruise which lasted until August 20th. During that time this one resourceful crew accounted for 54 vessels of various types, totaling an amazing 90,150 tons[77] of *Entente* shipping. All the while, craft like this continued to maintain contact with the distant Senussi, who in turn forced the Italian government to at least maintain some military forces in Libya. Then on August 2nd, the worst naval disaster to that moment in the war befell Italy, when the modern battleship *Leonardo Da Vinci* exploded, caught fire, capsized and sank in Taranto harbor. Enemy sabotage was suspected, but not proven; at any rate it was a terrible blow to Italy's navy. Rome's sole response throughout the entire time period of these setbacks was a moderately strong bombing raid on Fiume, Hungary's only seaport, on August 1st. It could in no way compensate for the continuing carnage in the Mediterranean, where another Italian steamer, the *Letimbro*, was sent to the bottom on the 4th. Before the summer was over, another two dozen of the nation's ships would be lost, mostly to submarines. Taken together, they represented another 35,000 tons of production which was thus denied to the *Entente.*

At *Commando Supremo*, General Cadorna was not concerned with naval matters, be they pleasant or unpleasant. He was proud to have presided over the effort which had stopped Hötzendorf's *Strafexpedition*, and was happy to receive all the acclaim forthcoming from the grateful nation. He, along with most other *Entente* leaders, and even many *Alliance* leaders as well, had considered the enemy plan to have been foolhardy, and executed with inadequate forces in the wrong location at the wrong time. After the fact, he could point to the Austrian rebuff, the Russian Southwest Front offensive, or the Somme attack to prove his point. The real war, he insisted, was being fought on the eastern frontier, and now that all the fuss in the mountains had died down, Italy could get on with the business of winning it. If he ever considered just how close he had come to a catastrophic strategic defeat at the hands of a badly outnumbered and outgunned foe, his subsequent actions certainly did not betray it. For want of a half-dozen or so additional divisions the Austrian strategy had been frustrated, and the Italian nation given new resolve to prosecute a war that for the first time in a year, seemed absolutely winnable. Had Cadorna moved more quickly to exploit the temporary enemy paralysis, he would almost certainly have broken through Boroevic's weakened lines and driven beyond. Moving quickly, however, was not characteristically Cadorna, and long before he struck his next blow, the enemy had noticed the Italian buildup.

Even so, the superiority of Cadorna's armies was impressive. On August 1st 1916, Boroevic could count only seven divisions on the line, plus two independent brigades and one division in reserve. Against this force, Second Army fielded five divisions and Third Army disposed of sixteen more in place or arriving. And Cadorna could also call on the five divisions of the Reserve of the Supreme Command, and of course the many others still lingering to the west in the 'Mambretti Command'.[78] In terms of artillery the disparity was even worse, fewer than 600 guns versus more than 1,800. The latter would be further supplemented by another 150 or so pieces demanded by the Chief from the western forces during July. To make matters worse for the Austrians, Fifth

Army had not been adequately resupplied since Fifth Isonzo, as all men and materials had been diverted to the south Tyrol. As if a three-to-one superiority were not enough, Cadorna could of course concentrate on any narrow sector or sectors of front for an attack, while Boroevic was obliged to defend every meter from the high Julian Alps to the head of the Gulf.

Chief Cadorna was pleased with his new mission on the Isonzo. Too much time had passed, in his opinion, since the last drive here, and he was ready to get going again. Besides his crushing superiority in manpower and war material and munitions of all kinds, he also may have enjoyed, for the first time, an edge in morale as well. The under strength, under supplied Austrians were somewhat demoralized by the failure of the western offensive, but mostly by the fact that they had had to surrender so much strength to it, units that had not returned. They correctly feared that in the event, most would never return. The Italians were lifted by a genuine spirit of national rejuvenation and a determination to aid the war effort in any way possible. Training camps were turning out steady numbers of soldiers, and factories were producing record numbers of small arms, trucks, and guns. For the first time in the war, Italy's army even looked like that of a modern-day Great Power when increasing numbers of troops were being issued hand grenades, gas masks, and steel helmets, the latter patterned after the French 'Adrian'.

With the advent of August, all was ready. Cadorna's plan was straightforward, seize Görz (Gorizia to the Italians, Gorica to the Slovenes) and push on up the valley of the Wippach (Vipacco Vipava) River, an east-bank tributary of the Isonzo, splitting the Austrian defense in two. Once in the upper reaches of the valley, the attackers could approach Trieste from its rear; the door to Laibach would also be wide open.

On the morning of August 4th the first attack was made, behind the inevitable artillery barrage. It was delivered on the south slope of the Doberdo Plateau, at the long-contested ground around Selz. All day the battle raged; Third Army gains were limited to a few meters and about 150 prisoners. It was only a feint, designed to draw the meager Austrian reserves to the area. The main punch began with a pulverizing artillery preparation begun at 5:00pm on the 5th, directed at the entire line between Mts. Sabotino and San Michele. In the small hours of the night it subsided somewhat, only to be renewed with maximum intensity just after first light of day on the 6th. For another six hours in some sectors, eight in others, the guns spat their lethal high-explosive projectiles at known defensive positions, where trenches were filled in by collapsing walls and other debris, sandbagged and wooden reinforcement to strong points was shredded and dispersed, and even the blockades to entrances of dugouts carved in solid rock were blown in. Stone and metal splinters large and small flew everywhere through the air. When the deafening pounding and churning was finally over, thousands of Italian infantry surged forward screaming "Viva Italia".

Mt. Sabotino was the object of the first assault, in mid-afternoon. Despite suffering heavy losses at the hands of the surviving Croat defenders, the summit was won and cleared that afternoon with 1,200 prisoners, most of whom were too dazed by the bombardment to offer prolonged resistance. The few survivors of the mountaintop battle retreated down the east slope and formed a perimeter at the west end of the still intact railroad bridge at Salcano. Farther south, the blood-drenched soil around the Podgora height was hit by successive waves of *grigioverde* which were shot down in droves before they could ascend the hills. This time, unlike prior attempts, there seemed to be no end to the persistent attacks, each of which reduced slightly the number of defenders. One Austrian account of the battle, written shortly thereafter, was denounced as fraudulent when it described ten-to-one odds at Podgora, furiously charged by desperate men who knew that they would be killed by their own machine guns if they turned and retreated in the face of an immoveable Austrian defense.[79] Today, it is known that the estimate of odds was either accurate or even understated, and that Cadorna was not above using such tactics to ensure attainment of his goals; he had after all reintroduced the ancient practice of decimation as a means to punish units he felt had underachieved. At any rate the Podgora position was about to be overwhelmed when its flanks were both turned, forcing the few remaining Croat defenders to evacuate it under cover of the darkness of the night.

Two hours after the big push on Görz began, Third Army's center burst forth from the trenches in the shadow of Mt. San Michele and advanced up the tortured slopes. The battered, confused, choking Hungarian units in the path of the massive attack were overpowered, following a two-hour melee amidst the shell-holes and broken debris on the infamous low mountain. Before the sun set on August 6th, the high ground on both the north and south flanks of Görz was in Italian hands.

Boroevic reacted to the bad news in a typical manner, by ordering counterattacks to retake all the lost positions. But reserves were too few to plug the gaping holes in the old front, and what resulted was no concentrated effort, only a series of widely dispersed battalion-sized counters that were all easily thrown back by the Italians. The brave men who participated in this round of counterattacks were mostly lost, and their sacrifice only worsened the situation for the Austrians. Nevertheless, small groups of fanatical defenders managed to delay the enemy closing up to the river for another whole day. The question now became one of bridges over the Isonzo. Could they be destroyed before they could be captured?

Besides the railroad bridge at Salcano, three kilometers north of Görz, there were two others connecting Podgora with the city. One, an old roadway structure, featured seven stone arches crossing the stream, the other was a modern six-span steel railroad work, about one-half kilometer downstream. Under the embankment leading to the west end of the steel bridge, a stone lined tunnel had been constructed, in which 600 Austrians had sought shelter, hoping to emerge at the appropriate moment to take advancing enemy troops in their rear.[80] The plan was foiled, however, and the tunnel became a trap, forcing the surrender of the 600 under threats of being burnt out. Without a moment to spare, the structure at Salcano was the first to be destroyed, well before dawn on August 8th. Two spans of the second railroad bridge were blown down next, followed at 5:30am by the second span, from the east side, of the stone bridge. Unfortunately for the Austrians, destroying the road-crossings did not mean stopping the enemy at the water's edge. August is the driest time of year at Görz, and Italian troops were able to simply wade the river at certain locations. By noon on the 8th, thousands of Aosta's soldiers had done just that, anxious to march on into the outskirts of the city, which lay immediately ahead.

The struggle for the west bank of the Isonzo had cost Fifth army close to 10,000 men lost as prisoners alone, as well as perhaps 20 guns and 100 machine guns now in the hands of the enemy. There was no point in further sacrifice; Görz was as good as lost. Accordingly, the city was ordered evacuated, an undertaking which went surprisingly smoothly. One account claimed "only six guns, on fixed emplacements, had to be destroyed and left behind".[81] All throughout the afternoon of the 8th, the exodus continued. Army command also threw every airplane at its disposal into the skies overhead, hoping desperately to retard the enemy offensive, on August 1st, and again on August 6th. On the latter date, naval ace von Banfield was credited with shooting down an Italian bomber, and on the 15th he accounted for a flying boat. Captain Heyrowski became an ace during the Sixth Battle. He had scored three kills by the 10th, but had himself been shot down twice, all of the combat in the Doberdo/San Michele sector. Like Banfield, he brought down another enemy on the 15th.[82] Other pilots flew bombing runs, at targets near and far. Venice was raided once more on the 12th, and again on the 19th of the month.

As Boroevic withdrew his mangled units to a partially completed second defensive line a few kilometers to the east, advanced battalions of the Duke of Aosta's army cautiously entered Görz on the morning of the 9th. Engineers set to work feverishly to span the river with pontoon bridges, so that vehicles and supplies could be brought across. They encountered no Austrians that day, and very few residents of the 'City of Violets' remained to welcome the Italians to 'Gorizia'. It was a day later that the place was finally declared secure, and entered by the Duke riding a horse at the head of his army into a round of celebrations and festivities.[83] The whole scene must have appeared somewhat bizarre, with an Italian mayor being named amid the ruins of the once-lovely city, which was still very much within range of even light Austrian artillery. But for the moment Fifth Army personnel were too busy preparing the second line to worry much about harassing the enemy; once they were ready, there was time for such actions later.

Second Army finally joined the battle on the 9th, behind a half-day of intense shelling at the Plava bridgehead. Despite the long drum-roll of powerful explosions, the infantry attacks that followed were no more successful than any that had come before them had been. So heavy was the slaughter on the heights that all assaults were abandoned on the same day they began. General Settimo Piacentini, the recently appointed boss of the Second, was beginning to understand what his predecessor had experienced. After the fall of Gorizia, Piacentini was given command of the left Corps of Third Army (which had previously been under Second Army until the Fifth Battle) and ordered to capture the mountain ridge to the northeast of the city, including Mts. St. Katerina, San Gabriele, and San Daniele. All of these features were within the Austrian second line.

The center of Third Army were the only Italian troops still moving forward on the 10th. The village of Rubbini near the mouth of the Wippach was taken that day, as was San Martino and what was left of the Doberdo Plateau. Then they ran into a deep, sharp ravine known as the Vallone, a natural gouge in the Plateau which carried a stream running north to south, towards the Gulf. The Vallone separated the Doberdo from the main portion of the plateau to the east, where it was known as the Karst (Carso). It was a difficult enough natural feature to cross under the best of circumstances; with a determined enemy defending its far bluff, it was well-nigh impossible. To try to go around the north edge of the ravine was the best bet, but here a high hill known as Nad Logem blocked the way. Soon, bitter fighting raged around the hill and at the edge of the ravine. To the lasting credit of the Italian infantry and the furious bombardment which both lowered the hill and rounded off the sharp bluffs of the Vallone, both features were captured in two days of intense, merciless combat (August 11th-12th). Thereafter, Aosta's men were stopped before the towns of Lokvica and Opacchiasella and another line of nameless hills by a well-placed multi-ethnic defense, and their own sheer exhaustion. Over 1500 Austro-Hungarian prisoners had been captured.

Cadorna was anxious for both armies to continue moving forward, and effect a breakthrough. Austrian shellfire originating from the second line was now raining down on Italian pontoon bridges over the Isonzo, severely hampering the efforts to repair the older steel and stone structures. One eyewitness described the results of the shelling, how it caused many casualties and was intense enough for the shrapnel to "churn the water into foam".[84] Second Army obliged by attacking northeast of Gorizia on the 12th, but gained little ground. Third Army spent most of the 13th rounding up dazed and wounded Austrian prisoners; about 800 were eventually counted. Cadorna impatiently ordered a fresh round of assaults to begin on the 14th. Fortunately for Boroevic, a division from the Tyrol had arrived for reinforcement, and two more from the Russian Front were detraining to the rear. Morale among the Austrians improved noticeably. Despite a long and heavy barrage preceding the attack, Mt. St. Katerina was easily defended, as were the Plava heights again on that bloody Monday. On the western end of the Carso, Aosta's men hurled themselves at Lokvica and Opacchiasella. These attacks were supported by a number of armored cars, the first time such machines had been used in any quantity on the Italian Front. Through no fault of the vehicles, the effort was defeated. Furious, the Chief insisted the armies begin a new drive; Italian commanders could only shake their heads and obey.

August 16th began with more bombardments of Mt. St. Katerina and the western Carso plateau. This time Boroevic's artillerymen were ready for a barrage of their own, having been reinforced, re-munitioned, and having gotten the range. When the enemy troops rushed forward out of the smoke and dust, they were caught by the deadly effects of exploding shrapnel shells as well as hundreds of thousands of rounds of small-arms fire. The carnage was mercifully stopped by darkness of the evening. It was the last action of the Sixth Battle of the Isonzo. Boroevic had prevented—thanks to his last-minute reinforcement—an enemy breakthrough once more.

It has long been contended that by attacking in May in the Tyrol, Hötzendorf allowed the capture of Görz, that he had forfeited the City of Violets for a folly in the mountains. This reasoning is hard to justify. Actually the Austrian Chief of Staff would have been better off to remove Fifth Army entirely and place it with the strike force in the west, if such reinforcement might have ensured success for the strategic plan. He could have allowed Cadorna to take Görz, Trieste, Laibach or anywhere else *if* Archduke Eugen's army group could break through to the sea and cut off Cadorna far to his rear. From what we know today it is not unreasonable to suggest that another half-dozen divisions might well have been enough to achieve Hötzendorf's strategic objective. Of course, the Italians would almost certainly have noticed the absence of the greater part of Fifth Army, and even Cadorna may have adopted a policy of reserved caution, and no one can say what might have happened. But at bottom, to consider Hötzendorf's strategy as unsound is unfair; if anyone's strategy was basically flawed, it was surely Cadorna's, a plan that was costing the nation hundreds of thousands of casualties without a worthwhile return. It is true that after the capture of Gorizia, the *Entente* press hailed the deed as a great triumph, elevated Cadorna to the status of a great conqueror, and proclaimed the door to victory had been opened. Beneath all the hype, though, was the fact that in fifteen months of war, the Italian Front had produced no other 'victories' worth mention. In the west, Italy's prosecution of the war had been considered as lacking vigor and resolve. Now, an advance of a few kilometers and the seizure of one war-torn, empty small city could be raised to the headlines along with all the other strategic triumphs the *Entente* was currently enjoying (1916 had produced only a pyrrhic victory in the east by that time). Sixth Isonzo officially cost Italy 51,000 casualties and Austria-Hungary 37,500, but the actual totals may very well have been double that for Cadorna and 50,000 or so for Boroevic.[85] It is perhaps needless to relate that Cadorna was certain that what was needed next was another offensive, and then as soon as possible.

One last consequence of the capture of Gorizia and the resulting boost in Italian morale came on August 28th, when the emboldened government at Rome finally took the plunge and declared war on Germany. This formality surprised no one, but it did render Vienna somewhat of a favor by removing one excuse Berlin could point to when asked by its ally for help against *Welschland*.

Throughout August most sectors of the line were fairly quiet while the Sixth Battle raged. There was some action in the Tofana Peaks especially on the 7th, when *Alpini* troops registered some minor gains. Additional encounters were fought on the 22nd and 24th. Lord Northcliffe visited this part of the front at that time, and reported that all of the fighting was invariably at night, due to the danger of exposure to snipers in daylight.[86] He also wrote that the Italians claimed to have captured 500 towns and villages on Austrian soil up to that time. The Tyrol, where so much campaigning had so recently been undertaken, was disturbed only by the occasional artillery fire and bombing that typified an inactive sector. One Italian Caproni bomber never returned to its airfield on the 25th; it became the 2nd 'kill' of Josef Kiss near Pergine in the Val Sugana.[87] At about the same time, a future Italian ace named Fulco Ruffo shot down his first enemy airplane, an Austrian reconnaissance machine buzzing the hills opposite the Tolmein bridgehead. Ruffo was flying in a group of three aircraft that day (August 23rd); each of the three pilots would eventually rank among the top eight Italian aces of the war.[88]

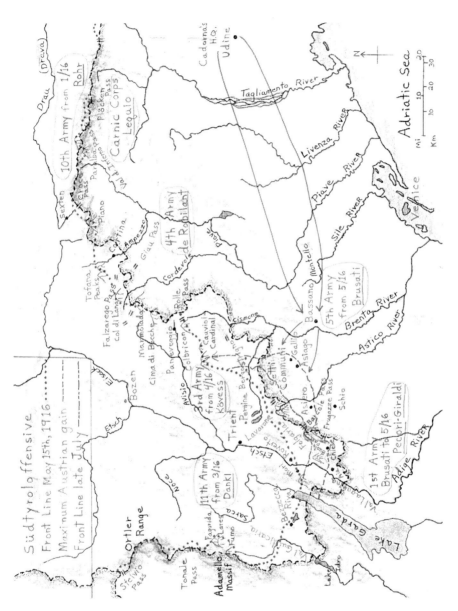

Südtyroloffensive

Chapter Six
...Seven, Eight, Nine...and Beyond

Although no one could have noticed it at the time, a turning point in the fortunes of the Great War was certainly reached during the waning days of August, 1916. During a three-day period at that moment in time, the occurrence of several events would forever alter the course of the fighting. First, on August 27th, Romania emerged from two years of neutrality and declared war on Austria-Hungary at the very moment that those in Bucharest felt that the overstrained Habsburg Empire was at its most vulnerable. Russia's Southwest Front Offensive was nearly three months old, the war was over two years old, and the Imperial Army had suffered appalling losses and was expected to break with one more fresh, new force of 23 divisions thrown against it. That the reasoning was flawed, that the timing was tardy, and that the idea in a war of all the world's Great Powers, that the efforts of one small, backward nation could make much difference when committed to one side or the other was ridiculous, seems not to have occurred to anyone in *Entente* circles. The Romanians were basically just playing follow-the-leader, but at a time of maximum convenience to themselves. They were a nation which had only comparatively recently been made independent, and were anxious to show their preference for Western Civilization, insisting that they represented descendants from Roman colonists of the Second Century. Pointing to their Latin-based language, they were quick to correct anyone referring to them as Rumanians; they wanted very much to be known as Romanians. Since independence had been achieved from the hated Turks, they had pretty much tried to emulate Italy and the Italians, who were at any rate the closest Latin nation to them geographically and with whom they shared (or so they believed) much in common. When Italy joined the *Triple Alliance* in 1881, it was only one year later that Romania also associated herself with that group; when Italy refused to adhere to it in 1914, so too did Romania. Both nations claimed territory within Austria-Hungary, the inhabitants of which they were confident were desirous of being joined to their own. But when Italy had declared war in May, 1915, the Russians were in retreat in the east, and the moment for Romania to follow suit was inopportune. Now their time had finally come, and Bucharest immediately undertook an invasion of the Hungarian province of Transylvania, an act which stretched Austrian resources to the absolute limit.

On the very same day in Berlin, *Kaiser* Wilhelm II announced that he had ordered submarine attacks on non-military ships to cease. Fearful of neutral opinion, especially that of the United States, the Emperor felt he was obliged to override the decisions of his own naval experts; Germany could afford no new enemies. It may have been a fatal decision. There can, of course, be no such thing as true 'neutrality' in war; by trading with the *Entente* nations and not with those of the *Alliance*, the U.S.A. and other nations were clearly showing their preference for one side over the other. And war material was certainly reaching the *Entente* on non-military shipping, as the famous example of the *Lusitania* would eventually prove. As we have seen, the submarine campaign in the Mediterranean alone was causing the *Entente* serious headaches by mid-1916, its crushing naval superiority notwithstanding. Had Wilhelm and his advisors held even a little better understanding of U.S. politics, they would have realized that under no circumstances could the American government have declared war during an election year.

The next day, August 28th, Germany declared war on Romania, in support of her ally. The Rome government, buoyed by the news of Romanian participation and encouraged by the 'victories' in the Tyrol and at Gorizia, declared war on Germany. What had been real enough for a year, was now official.

Two days after reigning in his U-boat fleet, the German *Kaiser* also made a basic change at the head of his army. On the 29th, General Falkenhayn was relieved of his position as Chief of the General Staff. He was replaced by the most popular man in the country, Field Marshal Paul von Hindenburg, a hero of the Eastern Front. Hindenburg and his number-two man General Erich Ludendorff (who would be the actual new boss and who created the rank of First Quartermaster General for his new position), had long been at odds with Falkenhayn over the strategic direction of Germany's war effort; now they were granted the opportunity to see if they could do better. The former Chief was given command of an army in Transylvania, the new battleground with

Romania, and for a while it seemed that the new duo would pursue the eastern strategy they had long advocated. One thing was certain: with Ludendorff at the helm, *Alliance* strategic planning was bound to embark upon a new course. Within a few days, Ludendorff was able to convince all of Germany's allies to recognize *Kaiser* Wilhelm as supreme commander of all *Alliance* military forces. What that meant, naturally, was that he, Ludendorff, was in reality now supreme *Alliance* commander.

If none of the above made any immediate difference to the war on the Italian Front, it was at least a precursor of things to come. In the early days of September, the fighting went on as before. The skies over Val Dogna, south of Pontebba, were the setting for the attainment of a fourth victory for Raul Stojsarljevic, when he shot down an Italian two-seat airplane on the 1st.[89] Italy's Carnic Force tested the defense beyond the Plöcken Pass on the 2nd, to no avail. Other soldiers of Rome pushed ahead in the Cismone Valley, hoping to retake the ground they had willingly surrendered in May, when fear of flank attack had caused the withdrawal. Nearly all of the watershed was occupied by the 5th; then heavy fighting developed among the high peaks of the divide with the Etsch drainage system. Austrian counterattacks at Mt. Civaron were held, but all attempts to seize Mt. Cauviol came up short, in the face of accurate defensive artillery fire. The 2,350m (7,720ft) Mt. Cardinal, which the Italians had never entirely quit, was recaptured in its entirety by September 15th. Soon, heavy snows would put an end to all movement at these great heights. Other Austrian probes were met at Mt. Corno on the 7th and in the Travenanzes Valley on the 8th. Fourth Army responded to the latter action with an attack of its own which yielded minor gains of ground on the 12th and 13th. Some measure of redemption for the loss by demolition of the two mountaintops in the Dolomites was gained by the Austrians on a peak which jutted up from the Pasubio-Santo ridge. In the early morning hours of the 23rd, a mine was detonated, which blasted off the outcropping, causing 500 Italian casualties, and burying adjacent emplacements. Two could play that game.

All of these minor actions were of little interest to General Cadorna, who was, as usual, mainly concerned with his latest offensive on the Isonzo. He ordered virtually all of Italy's artillery to open fire on September 10th, from as far west as Lake Garda, all along the front to the sea. If the move was supposed to confuse the enemy as to where he would launch his main attack, it was not likely to work; Boroevic had come to know his opponent very well. But this newest offensive would in fact be different from the first six in one regard. The Chief had come to believe that the key to his success was to pound enemy positions into oblivion before unleashing his infantry, a tactic that had seemed to work outside of Gorizia. He apparently preferred to forget that it had not worked against the enemy second line a few days later. Irregardless, a genuine attempt was made to coordinate artillery barrages and bombing by aircraft, for the first time. And for this next, Seventh Battle, the stretch of frontline to be assaulted was narrowed considerably. This time, only the ground from the Wippach to the sea would be attacked. Now that Gorizia had been taken, all that remained was to smash through to Trieste. Third Army would do the bulk of the fighting, while Second Army applied just enough pressure farther north to keep any enemy reserves from being diverted to the south.

The first assaults came as early as the 11th, against the heights at San Grado, just east of Gorizia. Five days of close combat followed during which some 1,800 exhausted Austrian defenders were captured, along with many hundreds of meters of trenches they had defended. Two dozen Caproni bombers struck one of Boroevic's airfields, at Parenzo, on the 13th, while simultaneous raids hit naval installations and dockyards at Trieste and Muggia. Italian torpedo boats and other light naval craft also attacked the coast in support of the air forces. These raids were ineffective; one bomber was lost and several of the boats were struck by defensive fire. Air ace von Banfield also claimed to have destroyed a Nieuport fighter on that day, but it was one of several of his victories which would forever remain unconfirmed.[90] Another raid on Trieste on the 14th was little more than a local nuisance. By contrast, an Austrian air attack on Venice on the 13th caused some panic and destroyed several buildings.[91] At sea the *Entente* was worsted again on September 15th, when Austrian aircraft sank the French submarine *Fourcault* about 15 kilometers off the Dalmatian coast.

Aosta's Third Army artillery spoke again at 6:00am on the morning of the 14th, delivering a fierce bombardment for eight hours, from the northern edge of the Carso Plateau to the coast road. Thereafter, waves of Italian infantry advanced on objectives identical to those sought in the late stages of the Sixth Battle. In 24 hours of savage, often hand-to-hand combat, Nad Logem hill was finally overrun, as was another height overlooking the coast road. Beyond this, the attackers could not gain, as Austrian small arms and artillery fire mowed down line after line of *grigioverde*-clad soldiers sent like lambs to slaughter.

Further battles on the 16th failed to break the defense; one source describes the day's action as "the most intense [of] the Seventh Battle".[92] No advance worth mention was achieved. The following day Third Army tried once more, following more big-gun preparation, but the attacks foundered, then subsided. Neither Cadorna nor Aosta was pleased, but they allowed the offensive to fade away into what amounted to no more than energetic skirmishing for the next few days.

Piacentini's Second Army began its attacks two days behind those of the Third, on September 16th. It made two efforts, one of which assailed the lines at Mt. St. Katerina, to no avail. The other struck Mt. Rombon in the Julians, from Italian positions on neighboring Mt. Kanin. As had happened before, the scrambling soldiers were easy targets for the Slavic defenders on the bare-topped mountain and were killed by the hundreds. Overhead, Francesco Baracca and two other pilots watched the futile attack until they spotted an enemy Lohner approaching. The three all contributed to its destruction. Another attack on Rombon occurred on the 18th, and was similarly stopped. Italy also lost yet another Caproni bomber on the 17th of the month, at the hands of the Hungarian flyer Josef Kiss.

Thus ended the Seventh Battle of the Isonzo, on about the 20th of September, although some sources list the 26th as the official end of the action. Either way, the heaviest of the fighting was over by the 18th, after only five days of inexcusable carnage, which deprived the Austrian Fifth Army of another 15,000 or so men, killed, wounded or captured. Cadorna carefully concealed the extent of his own losses; much later he would admit to 17,500, a figure ridiculously low, and probably less than half of the real total. For a maximum gain of about a kilometer in one section, perhaps a half-kilometer in two others, Italy had sacrificed probably 30 to 40,000 soldiers. Cadorna's estimation of the battle was that another was needed, as soon as possible, before the approaching winter deprived him of suitable weather. All of his *Entente* allies were still heavily engaged on other fronts, and his enemies were handcuffed by the draining commitments against the Russians and Romanians. Italy needed to give battle at this opportune time, so as to keep up the appearance of solidarity with her partners.

General Boroevic had not much worried about an enemy breakthrough during the Seventh Battle, but once it was over, he became quite concerned for his Army's ongoing powers of resistance. Having lost the equivalent of an entire division as a result of the September fighting, he was now granted another, to arrive in October, but replacements for his depleted units were simply not arriving quickly enough to maintain Fifth Army's strength. Other material losses, particularly artillery pieces, were also being suffered somewhat faster than they could be replaced. And every time Austro-Hungarian troops were forced to give ground, the overtaxed engineers were called upon to hurriedly construct new positions, and the work had exhausted them and the foot-soldiers alike. What Boroevic desperately needed more than anything else was time, time to regroup, resupply, rebuild and above all, rest. What his intelligence reports indicated during the last week of September, was that the enemy was not going to allow him any.

Austro-Hungarian Troops, Photographed in the Autumn of 1915

One problem faced by attacker and defender alike was that now that the fighting had moved east of the Vallone, the front lines ran across the top of the plateau which lay between the Wippach valley to the north and the narrow strip of level seacoast to the south. They therefore spanned the western edge of the region known as the Karst (Carso, Kras), which extended off to the southeast towards Fiume. Astride the Austrian provinces of Küstenland and Krain (Coastalland and Carniola), the topography of this area is unique. As the name implies, it is a region dominated by the presence of limestone, a solid yet porous rock. On the surface, the plateau features no ponds or lakes, which cannot be contained upon it, and few streams, which tend to run underground. Without topsoil on the stony, barren surface, few plants and almost no trees could survive to soften the appearance of this harsh, wind-swept upland. Over the eons, as rainwater collected in certain depressions and eventually sank into the limestone, chemical action produced a pock-marked surface of crevasses and depressions which retained runoff for hours and even days, after a storm. Many of the indentations were funnel-shaped, some not, but collectively they were known as *dolinas* to the natives, and welcomed as a natural source of cover from biting winter winds or scorching summer heat.

This uninviting landscape was both an advantage and a handicap for the Italians and Austrians alike, as they struggled for control of it. At least the *dolinas* offered some natural protection for Fifth Army troops, who used them for mortar emplacements and machine-gun nests on ground totally unsuitable for digging trenches. A lack of timber precluded the use of wood to reinforce parapets and entrances to shelters blasted into the rock, so sandbags or bags filled with stones were piled up; often steel shields were concreted onto the surface as frontal protection. Even stonewalls were built using the plentiful, scattered material lying on the ground. For the Italians, the plateau was a formidable topographic feature to have to assault, but it did give them one advantage, by its very nature. Superiority in artillery here could be devastating. As high explosive shells with contact fuses hit the soft rock, they tend to penetrate slightly, in the milliseconds before detonation, causing an explosion which shattered the surface of the limestone, much as a hammer striking sandstone tends to shatter the substance into hundreds of free-flying fragments. And because explosions on hard surfaces dissipate horizontally, as opposed to those in soft ground which expand more vertically, the result is thousands of rock and shell fragments propelled parallel with the surface of the ground. This produces an effect which is deadly to any humans in the immediate vicinity, unless they are very well protected. Magnified by tens of thousands of times representing the shells of a barrage, the scene can scarcely be imagined. By the autumn of 1916, every Austrian soldier on the plateau knew he was much more likely to be killed by enemy artillery than by enemy bullets.

Head wounds comprised a large percentage of all injuries suffered during the Great War. Consequently, most armies discarded traditional headgear for steel battle helmets during the conflict, and we have seen how, beginning with Sixth Isonzo, the Italians had followed the French lead. Envious Austro-Hungarian troops soon began to demand similar protection; the battle helmet was specifically designed to protect the head from flying debris resulting from explosions, whatever their source. Germany's helmet covered a greater portion of the head and was superior ballistically to the other main types of the day, and eventually several Austrian firms were licensed to produce it. By the time of the Eighth Battle of the Isonzo, it had begun to appear at the front in small, but increasing numbers. Unlike the grey-green of the German model, Austria's, and later Hungary's, versions were issued in light brown, a most effective color for trench warfare. Italian helmets, like their French predecessors, were painted horizon blue.

Long before Boroevic's men could begin to complete their work on the new defensive positions, Italian artillery opened fire once again, thus forcing all such efforts to come to an end. The pounding began on September 30th and would last for ten long, painful days in varying degrees of intensity. While the earth trembled under the rumble of hundreds of guns and thousands of explosions, Fifth Army troops pressed all available protection to their eyes and ears, hoping to prevent blindness and deafness. They could do no more. In support of Cadorna's Army Group, Italian armies to the west launched attacks of their own, attempting with limited resources to attain certain goals of local importance, and to prevent the transfer of enemy troops to Boroevic. Fourth Army units north of the Tofana Peaks determined to conquer all of the upper Ampezzo basin once and for all, pushing ahead in the Travenanzes Valley on the 1st of October. Other battalions reported the capture of the 2,650m (8,700ft) Colbricon on the 2nd, and gains of ground in the parallel San Pelegrino and Travignolo Valleys on the 4th and 5th. Cold, gloomy weather ended these minor actions very soon after they had begun. Carnic Force also reported forward movement at this time and claimed to have captured an "unnamed peak of more than 8,000 feet, between Monte Cogliano and Pizzocallima".[93] First Army did its part as well, attacking west of Barcole Pass, around the long-contested slopes of Mt. Pasubio and Mt. Cosmagnon. Beginning on the 11th, these battles raged off and on in bad weather until the 20th, when ice and snow put an end to the see-saw nature of the fighting. Both sides claimed success; in truth, nothing resembling success was possible for either in winter conditions at extreme elevations. Whether this or that mountain belonged to this or that army could hardly affect the issue, especially at that time of year, when all movement had itself become more than difficult and extremely hazardous.

On October 9th, the last day of Cadorna's barrage, the artillery fire on the Carso Plateau had reached its most intense, a roll as of a hundred drums. As if the smoke and dust were not enough to inhibit visibility, a thick fog descended on the plateau that night, completely concealing the Italian infantry advances of the next morning from what was left of the troops in their path. The advanced degree of devastation caused by the 10-day bombardment inhibited the attackers more than did the dazed, shell-shocked defenders, who were soon overrun, all along the line. Once Boroevic realized the extent of the disaster, he quickly released all of his modest reserves, who bravely counterattacked in battles lasting all day of the 11th. Caught in the open, treacherous ground of the Carso, the Italian infantry were stopped, then pushed back in some sectors. North of the Wippach, fighting raged around the river Vertoiba, a small tributary stream running north to south, parallel with the front line. Its waters ran red on those awful days, until the breakthrough had been contained, on the 12th. The Italians managed to hold on to some of their gains here, including the village of Sober. On the plateau, Nova Villa was also held, Lokvica was not. Aosta's Third Army attacked again on the 12th, but the handful of defenders were just numerous enough to frustrate the new drive. October 13th hosted no major assaults by either side, only the skirmishing and jockeying for position typical of post-battle activity.

For Boroevic and Fifth Army, Eighth Isonzo was an ominous sign of things to come. They had just barely managed to prevent an enemy strategic breakthrough and certain defeat, perhaps an annihilation. Rome claimed 8,000 prisoners for what was basically a three-day offensive, some indication of how destructive the preparatory barrage had been; for the first time more Austrian casualties had been caused by shelling than by fighting. Few sources offer casualty figures for the Eighth Battle, one however, suggests over 30,000 for Austria and twice as many for Italy.[94] Cadorna continued to conceal his losses and the official Austrian figure was a suspiciously round 20,000. At any rate, Boroevic could not afford to pay the price, coming as it did so soon after the previous battle. It seemed that Cadorna's battering-ram tactics, however primitive, were about to prevail. Fifth Army simply could not withstand another blow of this magnitude, unless it could be strongly reinforced right away, or unless the enemy could be stalled indefinitely. On the 16th, Boroevic appealed to Hötzendorf, pointing out the seriousness of the situation, and predicting that the enemy might strike again within a week, as he had done the last time. Hötzendorf would have liked to have thrown all his strength at Italy, but his hands were tied in the east, where the Romanian Campaign was fast approaching a climax. By robbing Peter to pay Paul, the high command allotted one more division for Boroevic for November, so that a total of twenty-five for the entire Italian Front was maintained. By contrast, Cadorna was able to count a Front total of 49 in the same month. And most of Cadorna's were nearer full strength, and were better supplied. But neither their morale nor the weather was very good by late October, and few believed in the prospects for an imminent victory over their opponents. Many Italian soldiers were exhausted by the constant fighting and all of the physical activity connected with military operations. Most were cold and wet and many were ill. Cadorna realized that he probably had only one last chance to break Boroevic's line before the winter put an end to all hope of major offensive action. Predictably, he gave the order for a Ninth Battle to begin within ten days of the end of the Eighth.

While the Italians struggled to bring forward the thousands of tons of munitions and supplies necessary to sustain another big attack, the multi-lingual Austrian Fifth Army attempted to prepare for yet a further battle of attrition. Its ranks were so depleted by now that it too suffered a crisis of morale. Cold autumn rains inhibited work on defensive positions; even without the weather, time was too short for these to be properly constructed. Ammunition was in short supply as well, and replacements were too few to fill unit roles. Food was also getting scarcer, and medical supplies were barely adequate. Sickness and disease were beginning to infect the ranks whose resistance was weakened by exhaustion, exposure, and a poor diet. Still, most Austro-Hungarian troops were determined to stop the enemy or die trying to do so. Few were surprised when on October 25th, after two days of delay caused by poor atmospheric conditions, Cadorna's artillery opened fire again, pounding the line between Mt. Santo and the sea.

If most Austrian ground troops needed to huddle in dugouts and bunkers to escape certain death from the shelling, men of the air service were under no such restrictions. Many of these took to the skies when hostile guns began to sound, hoping to discover enemy battery locations, so as to inform friendly guns for an effective counter-battery fire, or simply to try to locate and attack enemy troop concentrations or supply depots. Two of these machines were piloted by Lieutenant Ernst Strohschneider and Lieutenant Franz Gräser. The former was already an ace and the latter would eventually become one. On that day, October 25th, the two men jointly destroyed an Italian seaplane near Grado, although since Gräser did not claim his first victory until February 1917, he must have deferred to Strohschneider. At any rate, the two men would fly together many more times, much to the detriment of the Italians. In mid-November, the duo accounted for another 'kill', which was recorded as Strohschneider's tenth.[95]

Low clouds and heavy rains plagued the attackers for several days, and interrupted the artillery barrage on several occasions. Even so, Cadorna would not be denied, and whenever conditions permitted it, the shelling was resumed. On the 30th, as the weather cleared it intensified, and continued at a furious pace throughout the following day and well into November 1st. The Carso Plateau was particularly hard hit, by much of Third Army's ordnance, and all semblance of an Austrian defense line was virtually obliterated. And for the first time in the war, the Italians made widespread use of gas shells. By the late morning of the 1st the guns fell silent, and tens of thousands of *grigioverde* rose from their trenches and advanced on the blasted remains of the enemy defensive line. East of Gorizia, Second Army's only contribution to the offensive faltered almost immediately; the long bombardment had been least effective in that area, and the Austrian lines held. On the left flank of Third Army the small Vertoiba River became the scene of heavy fighting once more, as assaulting infantry waded the stream in several places and engaged the defenders dug in on the east bank in close-quarter combat. Following several counterattacks, the front line remained much the same within a couple of days.

Far and away, the heaviest fighting occurred on the Carso, where the initial advance overran a few dazed and shocked defenders half-buried by the barrage. For once, the advances could be measured in hundreds of meters, and in a few locations over one kilometer of ground was gained. By immediately committing all of his scanty reserves, Boroevic hoped to restore the situation in a series of counterattacks, delivered on the night of November 1st-2nd. These obtained only mixed results, however, and the Austrians were too few to hold the shell-tortured, corpse-strewn landscape that had only recently comprised the main line of resistance. Accordingly, a retreat to the second line was reluctantly authorized, once fresh Italian attacks began at midday on the 2nd, and there was no prospect of holding the old line. Bitter rearguard and holding actions raged on for another twenty-four hours, before the bulk of Fifth Army's remaining forces could establish themselves in this rearward position, the center of which covered the town of Kostanjevica. By retiring to this line, Boroevic knew he was surrendering many localities which had long anchored his army, such as Mt. Volkovnjak, Mt. Pecinka, Faiti Hrib (a high hill) and Lokvica, but he had no choice. Giving up this otherwise-useless ground meant survival for his command and a chance to stop the enemy on the new line. Even then, considering the ragged state of his forces, a solid, unbending defense seemed questionable. If the enemy broke through, there was no longer any force capable of preventing the loss of Trieste. Already on the 2nd, as if to signal the imminence of such an occurrence, Austria's main naval base at Pola had been raided by a disturbingly large number of Italian aircraft.

Cadorna's next push came on the morning of November 3rd, following the customary artillery preparation. Had he realized just how close to decisive victory he had come on that day, he almost certainly would have pressed home his attack, using any and all available reserves, munitions, aircraft and whatever else he could hurl at the enemy. In the event, the assaults of the 3rd seemed to lack the necessary vigor to achieve the desired results. The fact that the weather was poor and the troops uncomfortable and tired no doubt played a part, but such nuisances had never bothered the Chief before; perhaps he too had lost faith in victory that autumn. All the attacks of the 3rd were eventually beaten off. One final effort on the following day was similarly defeated, by accurate Austrian artillery fire,[96] which prevented the waves of Italian infantry from closing with the weary defenders. After only four days of combat, the Ninth Battle of the Isonzo was stalled, and called off by the army commanders, who were not overruled by Cadorna. Skirmishing continued for another ten days or so, further bleeding both sides of men and material. On one day—

November 14th—trench-raiding Austrians claimed to have inflicted over 1,000 casualties on Second Army troops on Mt. San Marco.

This, the latest 'Battle of the Isonzo' (which had come to be very much a misnomer by autumn 1916) like all of its predecessors, was a very costly affair. Boroevic admitted the loss of 28,000 men, but this figure is almost certainly too low, as nearly 10,000 were taken prisoner by the Italians. Cadorna later claimed to have lost about 29,000, a total unrealistically deflated, probably to justify his 'strategy' of attrition by showing that the enemy was suffering as much as Italy was. As we have seen, however, Cadorna's methods usually produced two to three times as many casualties as the defenders sustained, and a more accurate number would probably reach at least 60,000, and quite possibly far more. In December, the Chief announced that his forces had taken a total of 42,000 prisoners and 60 guns on the Isonzo during the Seventh, Eighth, and Ninth Battles. For once, he did not immediately plan a further offensive, and preferred to remain passive for the winter while he again built up his strength.

Once again, Boroevic had escaped breakthrough and probable annihilation by the slimmest of margins. His army had survived, but only barely. Having yielded a maximum of three kilometers (2 mi) on the Carso, he had halted yet another major enemy offensive and saved Trieste for his country. The advent of winter meant that his positions were probably safe for the next several months. This was the good news. The bad news was that having sustained another 30,000 casualties—two entire divisions—he simply did not possess enough strength to stop another determined enemy drive. The icy winds of winter might protect his men for awhile, but when spring arrived, unless help were forthcoming, his command would become extremely vulnerable to attack. His nation was still heavily engaged against the Russians and Romanians, and had troops of occupation in the Balkans and on the line in Macedonia. He must have often asked himself how long his superiors could expect him to hold out. He must have also known that more and more military strategy was being dictated from Berlin, and the Germans were known to not be too concerned with matters on the Italian Front. It cannot have been a happy time for Svetozar Boroevic.

It was not in fact a happy time for those in leadership roles within the Austro-Hungarian Empire. On October 21st the Austrian Prime Minister Count Karl Stürgkh was dining when he was assassinated by a certain

Friedrich Adler, who was son of Viktor Adler, leader of the progressive Social Democratic Party. Stürgkh was an ultra-conservative whose deference and respect for Franz Joseph had earned him the sincere admiration of the Emperor. The old monarch, who had lost so many persons who were close to him to the hands of murderers, was clearly moved by the loss of yet another of his friends. Exactly one month to the day later, he too would be dead, but not as the result of a crime. His age had caught up with him. Born August 18, 1830, he was then in his eighty-seventh year. He had come to the throne during the tumultuous year 1848, while his nation was fighting with Italians, and during his reign he had been dragged into three additional wars with the same people, and now died in the midst of the third one. Perhaps more than any other monarch of the time excepting England's Queen Victoria, his life and reign had come to symbolize an era, especially for the people of his own country. In an age of rising tides of nationalism and socialism, Franz Joseph represented the traditions and values of a bygone time, and did so with absolute dignity and purpose of character. He had always been a peace loving man, only forced into war by the actions of others who would have injured that which he stood for. Earlier in his tenure he had lost the provinces of Lombardy and Venetia; later he felt he had atoned for these losses by acquiring Bosnia and Herzegovina. It was very important to him to try to keep his inheritance intact before he should pass it along. Keeping the faith was also extremely important to him, and it is not an exaggeration to suggest that the long close Habsburg family ties to the Vatican represented the real reason the Catholic Church maintained a distinctly pro *Alliance* attitude throughout the war. And of the four *Alliance* powers, only Austria was populated by a Roman Catholic majority.

For Austro-Hungarian military men and government officials alike, the passing of a man who had ruled for sixty-eight years was a severe psychological blow; most of these people had sworn an oath of allegiance to him and many could not imagine a Dual Monarchy without him as its monarch. Although he was never a decisive, energetic and beloved leader along the lines of a Frederick the Great or a Napoleon, Franz Joseph, to the average Austrian or Hungarian stood for moderation, temperance, and sanity, all of the attributes necessary for a ruler to see his land through difficult times such as were then being experienced. A breakup of the Empire while the old king was alive was for most people—in and out of its borders—unimaginable. Following his death, all the various nationalities of both halves of the realm began to pursue rather more parochial interests. In the Twenty-First Century we often hear that 'anyone can be replaced', but a century ago such was not the case. On November 21st 1916, an era truly came to a close.

The new Emperor was the twenty-nine year old Archduke Karl, one of the most improbable heirs to a throne in all human history. In order for him to succeed Franz Joseph three other men needed to die before the old gentleman: Rudolf, the Emperor's son, who supposedly committed suicide in 1889, Archduke Franz Ferdinand, the man assassinated at Sarajevo in June 1914 by Serbian terrorists, and Karl's own father, who would also be spared advancement into old age. Karl was not possessed of a strong will or personality and was pretty much under the influence of his wife Zita, a princess of Bourbon-Parma, his mother and his mother-in-law. Certainly no military man, Karl despised the war and disliked the overbearing influence of the Germans in his realm. He also disliked the long-time Chief of the General Staff, Conrad von Hötzendorf. Fearing an immediate backlash, Karl for the time being made no major changes in governmental or military personnel, but he could ride his great-uncle's coattails for only just so long. Everyone from Hötzendorf on down believed that sweeping policy changes were now altogether probable, if not absolutely inevitable.

While the Imperial government reshuffled its cards, the war, of course, went on, albeit at an abbreviated pace. The remainder of November was relatively quiet at the front, aside from the constant sniping by day and the occasional trench raids by night. Artillery exchanges were typical and ongoing, and though these rarely did any significant damage to the enemy, artillerymen were happy to fire their weapons which produced warm spent shell casings which could be hugged and fondled for comfort. Air activity also continued unabated. On November 25th, Francesco Baracca became a bona fide ace when he shot down an enemy Albatross two-seater which was bombing Tolmezzo, behind the line in the Carnic Alps. It was Baracca's fifth confirmed victory.[97] On December 2nd a squadron of Italian bombers attacked the railroad towns of Dornberg and Tabor in the upper Wippach Valley, hoping to disrupt communications behind the Austrian line. A day later another group delivered "a ton and a half"[98] of explosives to railway stations inland from Trieste, which was also targeted at its seaplane facilities. One of the Capronis was shot down by Gottfried von Banfield, in cooperation with Godwin Brumowski. The kill was von Banfield's 8th (confirmed), Brumowski's fourth.

Another raid on Trieste came on the 6th, but was ineffective. The Austrians countered with bombing runs on Monfalcone and Adria on the 4th, and on Aquileia on the 6th.

Off the coast, the fortunes of war continued to favor the *Alliance*. On December 11th, the Italian battleship *Regina Margherita* was steaming off the port of Valona, Albania at the Otranto Straits when it collided with a mine. The resulting explosion tore open the armored hull, causing the powerful ship to list and eventually sink. Without having fired a shot, the Austro-Hungarian navy had gained an important advantage; it had not yet lost a comparable vessel. Later that month six Austrian destroyers attacked the anti-submarine blockade line at the Straits, prompting the convergence of six French destroyers, five Italian destroyers, and a British light cruiser against them. Despite the heavy odds opposing them, the Austria ships all managed to make good their escape, while three of the *Entente* units became involved in collisions with one another.[99] Other than by the ramming, neither side suffered much damage.

Five days after the embarrassing maneuvers in the Straits, a German submarine, *UB 47*, torpedoed and sank the French battleship *Gaulois* out in the Mediterranean. It was December the 27th. Thus ended a year of outstanding success for *Alliance* submarines cruising the Middle Sea. Since July, over 250 ships, representing over 660,000 tons had been destroyed.[100] About half of these had been lost in the autumn alone. The situation had become so serious that the British admiralty began, as of December 11th, to divert much of the Mediterranean ship traffic to the long, slow route around the continent of Africa. Meanwhile, for the entire year 1916, The Austro-Germans lost only two submarines in that theatre, neither of which were confirmed to have been destroyed by enemy actions.[101]

Winter 1916/1917 was particularly harsh on the European continent. For those who experienced it, the weather was the harshest in living memory. All of the battlefronts suffered lower than average temperatures, deeper than average snowfalls, and bitter, biting winds. In the higher elevations, blizzards raged throughout the season, while in lower-lying areas fierce gales pelted the earth with ice and sleet. Of all the war zones, the Italian Front was the most elevated and was therefore the most severely affected by the elements. Even the generally-milder climate of the Adriatic became far more inhospitable and stormy. Both armies reacted to the inclement weather in much the same way; staying warm, avoiding frostbite, and guarding against avalanches became priorities which even the military bosses could not ignore. For the first time, the elements and not the enemy became the principal opponent. Offensive operations, even passive ones such as probing, were curtailed drastically. When temperatures reached new lows, artillery action was suspended for fear that the metal of the breaches, brittle with cold, might shatter if stressed by firing. More complicated mechanical devices such as machine guns and automobile engines often froze or would not function properly. Grenades became unreliable. Tinned food became difficult to consume, and of course water rations tended to freeze solid. Bathing and cleaning became virtually impossible. And wounds and injuries in arctic conditions could lead to all sorts of complications, especially for those posted to heights which had become practically inaccessible. It is little wonder then that during the winter months, especially December and January which were particularly severe, little ground fighting took place along the Austro-Italian border.

Other aspects of the colder weather were somewhat more appealing. For one thing, the awful stench produced by thousands of unburied, decaying corpses in no-mans-land and in inaccessible terrain or that which could not be excavated was muted once the tissue froze. Frozen bodies also meant less horrifying filth thrown into the air when the artillery did fire, and less of the germ-laden fluids which often accompanied it. Snow tended to cover most of the disgusting sights of the battlefield, and it could be melted for relatively clean drinking water. Some of the communicable diseases that thrived during the warmer months were more easily controlled. The need to bathe was felt less frequently. But for the average soldier, the greatest advantage to the winter season lay in the absence of major offensive operations by either side. For the moment, his chances of survival were far better.

The year 1916 had been a horribly costly one for all of the belligerents. On the Western Front, the Verdun and Somme campaigns had dominated strategy for the British, French and Germans alike, yet had produced no breakthrough or strategic victory for anyone. In the east, Russia's Southwest Front offensive had lasted all summer, bleeding the Austro-Hungarian and Russian Armies half to death, and spurring the entry of Romania into the war. Italy had precipitated five major attacks on the Isonzo and Austria had responded with one of her own in the Trentino. Turkey had held her own against the British in Mesopotamia and Sinai and against the Russians in Armenia. Bulgaria was holding off the *Entente* forces based on Salonika. The naval blockade was beginning to strangle the *Alliance* nations, but the latter were sinking alarming numbers of ships, laden with all sorts of supplies. It seemed that after two and one-quarter years of war, no one had gained a decisive advantage; no one could say which side would win.

Once it had become quite clear that they would not achieve victory within the year, the *Entente* leaders called for a new round of conferences designed to coordinate policy and strategy towards the enemy. A second Chantilly Conference was called, to be attended by the military chiefs, and an 'Inter-Allied' Conference was promoted for the political heads of government. Both groups met simultaneously on November 15th and 16th. General Porro once again represented Italy for the absent Cadorna at Chantilly, where the results of the talks bore an amazing similarity to those of the previous year. But the Germans had upset all the prior planning when they launched their Verdun operation in late February, and this time it was resolved to "undertake joint offensives from the first fortnight of February 1917".[102] Unfortunately for the interests of the *Entente* this resolution was watered down by references to "climatic conditions" and other "circumstances" which could easily enable any of the contracting parties to wiggle out of it. And While the generals discussed formulating a cooperation that they never intended to practice, the politicians at the Inter-Allied Conference were agreeing that they, and not the military, should control the direction of the war. Italy had sent Minister of the Treasury Carcano, Minister of State Tittoni, and her French ambassador, Marquis Salvago Raggi; all of these men would have known that Cadorna was a virtual military dictator in their country, at least as long as he enjoyed the King's support, but none alluded to this fact. At any rate, the politicians decided that the best way to win the war was to knock the weakest of the enemy powers—Turkey and Bulgaria—out of the equation first, an act that would thoroughly demoralize Vienna and Berlin, and lead to an early peace. Tittoni even went so far as to suggest that the "Italian Government [had always considered] that the Balkan theatre was that in which the war would reach its decision".[103] It was exactly what Briand of France and Lloyd George of Britain wanted to hear, and Tittoni probably knew so. He also knew that as long as the Haigs, Joffres and Cadornas of the *Entente* held the real power to make war, the strategy never had any chance of being adopted. Both conferences broke up with the usual handshakes and niceties; both had been a complete waste of time. If anything at all had been accomplished, it was that the Italians had managed to convince their allies of the need to subsidize the Italian war effort. They called for a further conference at Rome for January.

While the *Entente* leaders were preaching that which they never intended to practice, the *Alliance* scored another military success in Romania. By year's end Bucharest's entry into the war had backfired upon itself, and the city along with two-thirds of the entire country, was occupied. The army had been badly mauled and had lost nearly all of its heavy equipment. The rich croplands, woodlands, and oil fields of Wallachia were now at the disposal of the *Alliance*, all four powers of which had cooperated in the autumn campaign. Another small nation, like Belgium, Serbia and Montenegro before it, had been all but vanquished, and its capitol occupied. With the Italian Front still holding, and both Eastern and Western Fronts deep within enemy territory, it seemed as though the *Alliance* was winning the war. Reacting to the new set of circumstances, each side chose an entirely different approach.

For the *Alliance* nations, late 1916 seemed like an appropriate time to offer a negotiated peace, for they could bargain from a position of relative strength from the recent successes. As early as September German Chancellor Bethmann-Hollweg was considering how best to offer mediation through a neutral country, preferably the United States. Within a month the Austrian Premier Baron Burian was suggesting a direct offer to the enemy coalition. *Kaiser* Wilhelm was next to jump on the peace bandwagon, apparently he too entertained serious doubts about a final German victory. All that was needed now was a favorable opportunity to present the proposal, and that came with the fall of Bucharest on December 6th. Six days later Bethmann-Hollweg was addressing a special session of the German Parliament (*Reichstag*). His speech was a formal proposal of peace which he contended had been communicated to the enemy powers through several neutrals, including Spain, Switzerland, the United States, and the Vatican. Although the remainder of the address was moderate and conciliatory in nature, it was soon being severely criticized from all quarters. One American account of the speech sarcastically referred to it as a "specious display of magnanimity",[104] and it was among the milder of responses. Most *Entente* reaction was derisive, and it was promptly denounced as vague and insincere by each of the *Entente* governments. For

Italy, Baron Sonnino affixed his signature to the formal reply of the *Entente,* which was delivered to the United States ambassador in Paris on December 30th. In Austria, the man who had succeeded the murdered Stürgkh, only weeks earlier, suddenly resigned on the day after the speech in Berlin. He was von Koerber, and his removal probably had much to do with the fact that the new Emperor was determined to rid himself of all those who he believed to be obstacles to peace.

Entente reaction to the events of late 1916 showed just how far removed from reality many leaders of the anti-German coalition had allowed themselves to drift. In Russia, the Duma unanimously rejected the peace proposals. France's Poincaré unconditionally denounced them. Britain's new Prime Minister Lloyd George declared that his nation, with its new cabinet, was not interested in making peace, but in making war. The U. S. President Wilson was the only leader to seize upon the opportunity to advance a reasonable agenda, when he sent notes to all of the warring powers asking them to state conditions upon which they might be willing to negotiate, and their war aims. Official replies to Wilson were polite, but uncompromising. Behind the scenes, the military men still ruled, and the war would go on.

The Italian Front had in fact found a new proponent in the person of Lloyd George. It was he who insisted upon another Inter-Allied Conference while attending the Anglo-French sessions of December 26th, and it was he who arranged that the latest discussions be held in Rome on January 5th, 6th, and 7th of 1917. The British leader was tired of the massive battles of attrition on the Western Front, which cost so many lives, and was convinced that by attacking there, the British and French were simply hammering away at the enemy at his strongest point. He was sure there was a better way to wage the war, and the more he looked at the fronts in Italy and the Balkans, the more he liked what he saw as greater possibilities there. Accordingly, he argued incessantly for an increased *Entente* commitment in Italy and at Salonika. He found few supporters. His French and British colleagues could not redirect their gaze away from France, and most surprisingly, the Italians were indifferent. Although Sonnino eventually allowed that he felt it 'possible' that the enemy might make a major effort in Italy, Cadorna was unimpressed. Sensing that the Italian Chief would be reluctant to be upstaged on his own soil, Lloyd George then offered 250-300 pieces of heavy artillery, of which the Italians were known to be short, if Cadorna would launch his own offensive in the late winter or early spring. Cadorna, however, would not be cornered, and voiced concerns that he might be obliged to return the weapons before he was done with them, and that at any rate the guns could not be sent to the front without discovery by the enemy (as if that were reason enough for not employing them). Ultimately, the Prime Minister's Italian scheme was rejected by simply being ignored by politicians and generals alike. Another conference was called for, however, this time for Petrograd in Russia in February. Within two weeks of its adjournment, the Russian Revolution erased any possible effect upon the war it may have had.

January at the front may have been cold, snowy, and relatively quiet, but men continued to die. On the 1st, Austrian artillery loosed a short but very heavy bombardment on the ruined city of Gorizia for no apparent reason, other than to wish the Italian occupiers a Happy New Year. The same day brought Francesco Baracca his sixth victory, when he shot down an Albatross near Kostanjevica on the Carso. Some kilometers to the south, Baracca's friend Fulco Ruffo also destroyed an enemy airplane over Duino, on the coast.[105] A day later it was the turn of the Austrian, Godwin Brumowski, who became an ace with his fifth kill near Lake Doberdo.[106] Poor weather kept most airplanes grounded for much of the month. The 11th, however, was clear and both sides made bombing runs; the Austrians attacked the training camps at Aquileia, and the Italians targeted the airfield at Prosecco and the seaplane hangers at Trieste. One Austrian seaplane fell to anti-aircraft fire.[107] A few days later, flying in cold windy conditions, two opposing aces had a chance encounter near Gradisca. Baracca and Gottfried von Banfield exchanged some machine gun fire before the weather caused both to break off the inconclusive combat; Banfield always claimed he had clearly seen Baracca's insignia.

Both sides continued to probe the other's lines whenever they felt it appropriate. January 4th was witness to Austrian movements on the Baldo *Massif* and on the hills east of Plava. On the Carso Plateau, Italians advanced slightly on the 4th, a gain nullified two weeks later by a counter on the 18th. Four days later the Austrians struck again and secured a slight gain of their own near Kostanjevica, precipitating a round of skirmishing which continued until the 30th of the month.

Ten days after the delegates to the Rome Conference departed for their respective nations, Luigi Cadorna forwarded a formal request to the western powers for troop and weapons support for Italy's armed forces, specifically, for use on the Italian Front. This was indeed the same man who had expressed no interest in similar offers made to him, in person, by *Entente* leaders in Rome. The reasons for this sudden about-face are to this day still unclear, although it seems likely that someone had certainly involved the King in some way. Vittorio Emanuele was, after all, one of the few persons alive whom Cadorna dared not dismiss out of hand and who could be expected to secure the ears of the Chief. Sonnino may well have been involved; it was he who had negotiated the Treaty of London. Or the whole affair may have been just a great exercise in drama, to spare Cadorna the onus of appearing to be uncooperative with the other *Entente* allies, while he believed all along that the military leaders of those very allies would never agree to a diversion of strength away from the Western Front. At any rate, nothing came of the request, much to the dismay of Lloyd George, who only recently had referred to Cadorna's apparent lack of interest in British offers of aid as "disgusting". Still, there is some evidence which suggests that even Cadorna may have been beginning to lose faith that his unimaginative strategy was winning the war, that perhaps the war could not be won in that manner. It is possible that, having considered the matter somewhat, he changed his mind about accepting French and British aid. No doubt his reasons were selfish if this is true, but something or someone seems to have influenced him during the Conferences of November to January. One thing is for sure; for the moment he was planning no new Isonzo offensives irregardless of the Chantilly agreement. For the time being, he was content to build up his armies and play a waiting game. Political events of the next few months seemed to justify his doing just that.

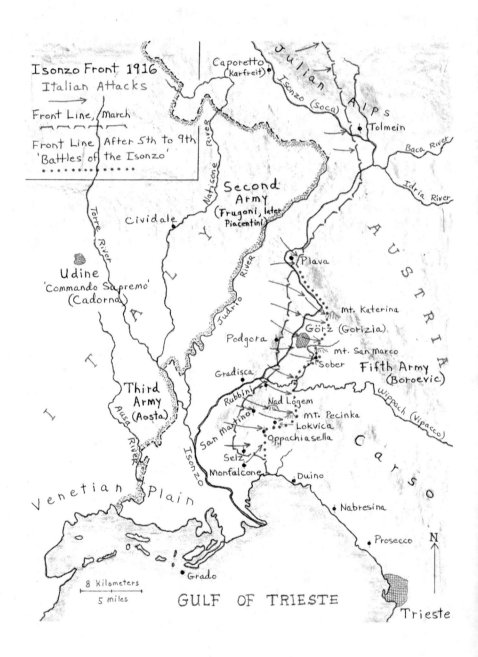

Isonzo Front 1916

Chapter Seven
Peace Efforts, War Efforts

The winter of 1916/17 was certainly one of the most pivotal seasons of the Great War. In the United States, the re-election of President Woodrow Wilson meant that America, her leader's hands now untied by political concerns, was now likely to intervene. Wilson, who had been campaigned on a slogan reminding Americans that 'he keeps us out of war', was now seeking to neutralize the submarine campaign by threats of participation in the war on the side of the *Entente*. Desperate to cripple British control of the seas, the German leaders decided in midwinter to resume the practice of unrestricted submarine warfare, despite the risks. No sooner had they done so, than did Wilson recall his ambassador in Berlin, and diplomatic relations between the United States and Germany were severed. Now, at the slightest pretext, it seemed likely that Washington would declare war. In Britain, the Asquith government fell in December, and a new cabinet was formed with David Lloyd George as Prime Minister, a man whose views on the war sharply contrasted with those of the nation's principal military leaders. Direction of the war effort in France was also in transition; the unorthodox Robert Nivelle was entrusted with the supreme command of the army. And in Russia, weakened by the need to come to the aid of the hapless Romanians, a stricken economy and a listless military establishment ensured that enthusiasm for the war had considerably eroded. The rising tide of Revolution would sweep away the Monarchy before the snows melted, and Russian participation in the wider conflict began to wane. By early 1917, the winds of change were clearly blowing. For those who cared to notice, a new era was unmistakably on the horizon.

Things were much the same south of the Alps, where many Italians were beginning to entertain second thoughts about the nation's participation in the war. After a million casualties, Italy had conquered neither the Trentino nor Trieste, neither the Adriatic Islands nor the Dalmatian coast. The war at sea had gone unfavorably. No end to the slaughter was in sight. Even Cadorna, as we have seen, was having his doubts, and was at last obliged to realize that the staying power of the country, and the army in particular, was not unlimited. Privately, the King expressed doubts about the wisdom of having joined the *Entente*, and initiated a secret campaign for advice on how to best sound out the Austrians with proposals for peace. Careful to avoid all those who he felt were in any way inclined to support further fighting, Vittorio Emanuele proceeded slowly and carefully to create a small but influential circle of men about him who could be trusted to keep the peace efforts in the strictest confidence.

No doubt the King was somewhat influenced in the timing of his initiatives by the death of old Franz Joseph, a man so rigidly bound by codes of honor that he would never have consented to do business with a man who he always felt had betrayed him when Italy had declared war in May of 1915. The new Emperor, however, was a man of a different sort, young, inexperienced in matters of state, ignorant of military concerns, and possessed of a wavering, indecisive personality. Basically a decent man, Karl from the moment of his coronation was desirous of peace. Heavily influenced by his wife and mother-in-law and thus by people with a French-Italian connection who despised the Germans, he was bound to be subjected to a good deal of *Entente*-friendly conversation. But Karl was no fool; he knew an *Entente* victory necessarily meant an Austro-Hungarian defeat and he did feel honor-bound to his allies. He and his wife wanted to keep their thrones and be able to pass the scepter to their son. The best way to ensure this, they were convinced, was to somehow extricate their country from the war. No sooner had the new Emperor succeeded his predecessor, than he was motivated to address his subjects, assuring them that he would do everything in his power to secure an honorable peace. Within two weeks of this declaration he allowed his mother-in-law to contact one of her sons (Empress Zita's brother), Prince Sixte of Bourbon. The Bourbons had been the ruling family of France until the Revolution of 1789 had toppled them. They had been restored briefly by the conquerors of Napoleon, only to be overthrown again in favor of Republican government. Out of power by 1914 for many decades, they nevertheless still held claims to the throne of France and still retained many supporters. Thus always suspicious of this family, successive French administrations had endeavored to keep them at arm's length, or further, from administrative matters. Most of the Bourbons, even those of Zita's family who were native to the Italian Duchy of Parma, still considered themselves Frenchmen, and when the Great War broke out, Sixte volunteered for service in the French army. The offer was declined. He then applied to King Albert of Belgium to whom he was distantly related, and was able to find service in the Belgian army. At the time he was contacted by his mother, he was serving as an officer of artillery. Over the course of the next few weeks, arrangements were made for the two to meet in Switzerland.

Kaiser Karl did not limit his efforts to his brother-in-law. Lloyd George in his memoirs tells of a story about Austro-Hungarian efforts to initiate peace feelers through the neutral Scandinavian governments. An Austrian diplomat in Copenhagen apparently spoke with the King of Norway about the matter, and the British government felt the whole story was interesting enough to send an official of its own, to investigate. The Englishman traveled to the Norwegian, Swedish, and Danish capitols, and supposedly "had several meetings with the alleged agents of Austria",[108] none of which led to any serious negotiations. A good deal of time was wasted before the British official finally met with the Norwegian King on March 6th and learned that Austria was indeed interested in talking peace, but still, nothing came of the opportunity. The Prime Minister is unclear as to why these possibilities were not pursued, but only states that by then, all efforts had shifted to the Sixte connection.

On January 29th, Prince Sixte and his mother the Duchess of Parma, came face to face in neutral Switzerland. The woman informed her son of the Emperor's earnest desire for peace, and handed him a letter signed by the Royal couple. Sixte promised to deliver the note to the proper French authority and to return in two weeks. This he did, and was back on the neutral ground on February 13th, facing a courier of Karl's who carried an offer, complete with terms. When Sixte read the document, he realized immediately that the terms would not have satisfied either Germany or Italy, and he insisted that if a secret agreement were to be made, he would need the credentials of high-ranking Austrian government officials with which to present it to the French. Within a week, the courier was back with two more documents, one signed by Karl himself and one signed by Count Czernin.

Czernin was one of the new faces in Vienna. On December 14th, Karl had made sweeping changes in the old clique, replacing Prime Minister Ernst von Körber with the less willful Count Clam-Martinitz, and Foreign Minister Baron

Burian with Count Ottokar Czernin. The latter was of Czech nationality, that group often considered the most disaffected of all of the Empire's multiple peoples. He had been the best of friends with the murdered Archduke Franz Ferdinand, who was well known to harbor desires to convert the Dual Monarchy into a Triple Monarchy in which the third piece would be composed of the nation's numerous Slavic peoples. Karl had high hopes for Czernin, believing that if anyone represented his vision of the future Monarchy, it was the Foreign Minister. As things turned out, however, it was Czernin's note that received a most unfavorable response in Paris. Neither Karl's nor Czernin's offers extended any concessions at all to the Italians.

President Poincaré of France read the correspondence on March 5th, and consulted with Foreign Minister Briand. A counter-offer was prepared, and returned with Sixte, who this time was accompanied by his younger brother Xavier. The two men traveled all the way to Vienna this time, for a personal interview with Karl, reaching their destination on March 24th. Three brothers-in-law held a lengthy discussion at the Habsburg Luxemburg residence, where the Emperor prepared yet another note very friendly to French interests. Curiously, the French had also neglected to mention Italy, and of course Karl did not do so, since most Austrians were eager for peace with France and Britain with whom they had no direct quarrel, but would never have agreed to any concessions to the hated Italians, who were considered the main enemy of the war. Just how either party expected to make peace *without* Italian participation is a question which neither, apparently, cared to consider at the time.

On the final day of March, Sixte and Xavier were back in the French capitol, meeting with the President and Minister Ribot (who had recently replaced Briand). This time, the French decided that the British should be informed of the Sixte connection and consulted on further possible action. Ribot did not meet with Lloyd George until April 11th, and it was at this meeting that the initiative was probably killed, for the Englishman insisted that the Italians be informed and consulted as well. When Sixte heard of this development on the following day, he knew Karl's wishes were in serious jeopardy. The Emperor, while prepared to be generous with the British and French, was not going to concede anything to the Italians, who had thus far been unable to take the territories that they desired from him by military action. If they were incapable of winning ground on the Italian Front, he reasoned, why should he simply give them what they desired? Besides, everyone including Karl knew that Rome's territorial demands far exceeded that which Austria had been willing to negotiate over, before the Italians had gone over to the *Entente*. Sixte managed to induce one more dialog with Lloyd George on the 18th, but the Prime Minister was adamant about consulting the Italians if any deal was to be made.

Sixte had good reason to be worried. At the St. Jean de Maurienne Conference which took place on April 19th, Boselli and Sonnino attended for Italy, and were very cool to suggestions that perhaps Austria-Hungary could be induced to sign a separate peace. Sonnino in particular resisted any such opinion, stating flatly that Italy had entered the war to realize certain ambitions which she would not now, after so much bloodshed, be willing to bargain away. He further claimed that a Revolution would sweep away his government if a peace which was not favorable to Italy were negotiated. Following these statements, Lloyd George and Ribot did not press the matter. Sixte was not informed of the outcome of the Conference with regard to peace until it had adjourned, and a few days later the French assured him that his secret had not been betrayed to Sonnino. All hope of success for his mission had by now pretty much evaporated, but the Prince returned to Switzerland to meet Count Erdödy, Karl's emissary, and handed him a letter of explanation for the Emperor. Dutifully, Sixte waited at Neuchátel until Erdödy returned on May 4th, bearing Karl's response, which was conciliatory, but not submissive. Sixte then forwarded the reply to Paris with a trusted companion, while he traveled once more to Vienna for one last personal conversation with his brother-in-law, remaining there for nearly a week while no stone in the talks was left unturned. Finally he returned to Paris via Neuchátel where he and Erdödy made what would be their final exchange of notes. Although the Prince was back in the French capitol by May 16th, he was not granted an audience with Ribot until the 20th and Lloyd George until the 22nd, which is some indication of the low priority which his mission was by then receiving. In the event, neither of the western powers were much impressed with Karl's appeals, and even less with Czernin's rigid diplomacy. They were convinced that Italy and Austria could not come to terms. For two more weeks, Sixte lingered in London, hoping for a breakthrough which never came; at last on June 5th he departed for the front, to rejoin his comrades in the small Belgian Army. On the same day charges that secret diplomacy was being carried out by the government were raised during a debate in the French Chamber. Ribot promptly denied the accusations, but the facts had somehow leaked out.

Sonnino and the Italians were eventually informed of all the shenanigans by their allies at the Paris 'Inter-Allied' Conference held on July 25th, but it is likely that they may have known many of the details at some time well in advance of that event. The whole matter was not finally put to rest, however, until October 12th, when Ribot referred to it during a speech in the Chamber. On that occasion he derisively mocked the Austrian initiative, claiming his nation would never have betrayed Italy. The British Prime Minister in his memoirs repeatedly expresses regret that Karl's peace moves could not have been somehow acted upon.[109] Apparently he forgot that his insistence on involving the Italians was far and away the most important reason that the bid for peace failed. It is difficult to believe that if Austria could somehow have been taken out of the war, that anyone really believed that Italy would be the least bit interested in engaging herself on any of the other war fronts. There can be no question but that to remove Austria was to remove Italy as well; when the *Entente* leaders finally agreed upon this conclusion, Karl was left with nowhere to go, except deeper into the arms of his German allies. From mid 1917 on, Austria-Hungary would either be victorious or be destroyed.

After the fact, of course, Lloyd George or Ribot or anyone else could claim completely scrupulous behavior towards the Italians. If Karl is to be believed, the Italian government did not reciprocate. On or about the 12th of April, an Italian offer of peace with Austria was communicated to *Alliance* ministers in Switzerland. The Emperor later told Prince Sixte that it came directly from King Vittorio Emanuele with the knowledge and approval of Giolitti and Tittoni; he further claimed that the Italians asked only for the Italian-speaking districts of the southern Tyrol and a very small area at the head of the Adriatic, which included the ancient town of Aquileia and a few square kilometers west of the Isonzo. According to Sixte, Karl had put the offer on hold while the exchanges with Paris were being considered. If this is true, one is left to wonder why the King's offer was not negotiated once the Sixte mission had failed. The Prince believed that Karl was unwilling to surrender any ground to people whose armies had been consistently unable to conquer it, but we know for a fact that the Emperor was desperate for peace, and it hardly seems likely that he would have allowed any opportunity to end the fighting on his main front to so easily slip away. What is more likely is that once word of the Sixte mission had leaked out, and Sonnino and some of the other incorrigibles were informed, the Italian King quietly let the matter drop.

What is still unclear to this day, is the question of whether Chief Cadorna was aware of the efforts for peace which so freely floated around the hostile governments in early 1917. If Cadorna knew, it certainly explains the change of heart which seemed to seize him as of late 1916. If he did not, then we are left to conclude that the King's initiative was probably based on the fact that he recognized that his Commander-in-Chief seemed to be losing faith in his own ability, and that of his soldiers, to defeat the enemy decisively and force a victorious conclusion to the war. One thing that is for certain is that many Italian leaders, by early 1917, were beginning to regret that they had not accepted Austrian territorial offers made in the effort to keep Italy neutral in 1915. For Italy as well as for Austria-Hungary, all bridges to the past had been burned by mid-1917. Only two possibilities remained, victory or defeat. For Sonnino and his like, victory meant exoneration and defeat meant ruin. The same could be said of Czernin, and even Karl, in Austria.

Czernin, like his master, was trying to find a way out of the war for Austria-Hungary, a nation beginning by spring 1917 to slip into internal turmoil. On April 12th, he presented a memorandum on the overall national well-being to the Emperor, which was by no means written in optimistic tones. Two days later, hoping to take advantage of the tumult in Russia in the aftermath of the overthrow of the Czarist government, he sent an offer of peace to Petrograd. The lack of any real authority who might have considered the proposal doomed the effort. But forces unleashed by the Revolution soon spread to Austria, and soon the Poles, Czechs, and South Slavs alike were starting to embrace ideas which were not generally what proponents of the Dual Monarchy wanted to hear. A rather sympathetic Karl did nothing to suppress this murmuring treason; to the contrary he allowed minister after minister to fall. Count Tisza, long a symbol of Hungarian interests and Prime Minister of the Magyar half of the Empire, was toppled in late May. As a Monarchist and a Germanophile, his age was passing. Clam-Martinitz, another old-school Czech who refused to be intimidated by the mob, resigned in mid-June.

Ministerial changes could not, of course, much alter the effect of the war on the Austrian economy. During the years of conflict, the Dual Monarchy is said to have mobilized 31.5 percent[110] of its male population, or about 16 percent of its total. With one man in six (including the youthful and the elderly) involved in national service then, the workforce was severely strained. This in turn led to increasing employment of women. It is estimated that about one million females entered the labor force during the war, their numbers rising to roughly half of all industrial workers in Vienna by 1916.[111] Unfortunately, they were paid only half or less than the amount that males earned, and this fact did not tend to decrease the growing labor unrest. And Austria-Hungary could not afford to suffer any disruption in its limited industrial capacity which had been strained since the outbreak of the conflict in 1914. Shortages of all kinds of raw materials had developed and the overtaxed railway network was chronically deficient in engines, rolling stock, and coal. This breakdown of production and transportation affected all commodities, including one of the very most basic— food. We have seen how nutrition had become a problem in the major cities as early as May, 1915; by 1917 it had become a crisis.

Largely self-sufficient in food production prior to 1914, Austria-Hungary slowly slipped into the abyss of hunger that had by 1916 swallowed Russia, Germany, and many of the smaller European nations. Bread rationing was imposed in Austria in April, 1915, and in Hungary in January, 1916. Soon thereafter Austrians were subjected to restrictions on sugar, coffee, milk and meats; Hungary rationed milk in November, 1915. All manner of substitutes were offered, especially horse meat while it was still available. Government efforts to control prices inevitably failed, and a thriving black market sprang up. Friction between the two halves of the Empire increased as time passed and the mostly urban Austrians accused (with some justification) the mostly rural Hungarians of refusing to share their harvests. Strikes and riots became more frequent, culminating in the massive wave of unrest which rocked the cities in January, 1918, following a further reduction in the flour ration. By the final year of the war, Karl's government was experiencing many of the same symptoms which had brought down the Russian Empire a year earlier.

Italy too was feeling the strains of war. At the time of the Kingdom's entry into hostilities, the Salandra government had pushed through a series of edicts comprehensively limiting civil liberties. These tended to be tightened as the war dragged on, despite or perhaps because of, the fact that the average citizen had never been entirely enthusiastic about the fight. Typically, the bureaucracy expanded; in September 1915 the military created a new branch to oversee arms production which was later legitimized when it came under a new Ministry of Arms and Munitions created in June, 1917. Tellingly, a General— Alfredo Dallolio—became the Ministry's first boss.[112] Naturally, once the industrial labor force came under what was effective military control, the workers were forbidden to strike or to bargain collectively.

Like that of its principal enemy, Italian industry suffered from severe shortages of raw materials. The national economy had never been based on manufacturing, but agriculture, however it did have one important advantage over Austria: its allies had access to world markets, and provided enemy submarines could be evaded, merchant ships could be expected to bring in at least some of the necessary material. Food was another matter; the country had imported more than three-quarters of its nutritional needs before 1915. As in the *Alliance* powers, Italy too tried price controls, rationing, and the like, and the result was the same unrest and rioting as occurred elsewhere. Coincidentally with Austria, the longer the war lasted the worse the food problem became. It had reached epic proportions by 1917, when the effectiveness of the submarines was at its peak.

The family-minded Italians bitterly resisted the worldwide trend towards female employment, even when the available supply of males and prisoners-of-war had dried up. Nevertheless, the tight governmental control of everyday life imposed the distasteful measure in mid-1916. Eventually, over 250,000 women would be at work in industry in Italy, a figure representing more than one worker in five of the total. These females, like their counterparts in Austria-Hungary, tended to be more restive laborers than their male contemporaries. Composing only fifteen percent of strikers in 1914, they numbered nearly two-thirds of such demonstrators by 1917.[113] Lower pay for equal work, lack of respect showed them, and exhaustion from long hours both on the job and at the home are generally cited as reasons for the discrepancy in satisfaction with their employment.

For all the belligerents, war weariness had become a definite headache by 1916. The phenomena was nothing new; Europe had been infected by it a century earlier, during the long period of the Napoleonic Wars. Americans had experienced it when the Civil War had dragged on for years, and other nations knew of it as well. Never before, however, had anyone imagined any conflict as widespread and all-encompassing as the Great War was proving to be. In terms of numbers of soldiers and horses involved, huge and powerful navies unleashed, quantities of ammunition manufactured and expended, and financial resources needed to sustain it, this war far eclipsed any other that had ever been waged. For the first time in history, entire populations had been mobilized for a war effort. Entire industrial bases had been transformed into weapons-producing enterprises. Complex machines were being created for use in battle. All national efforts were being channeled for employment against the enemy. And of course, the nation's conscience was clear; the war was a just war, being fought to forestall a wicked enemy whose greed and lust for conquest were without precedent.

Not everyone was buying in to the need for a do-or-die war effort, especially in Italy, where the war had never been popular with large segments of the populace. The nation had been a relative late-comer in the use of conscription to fill the army's ranks and the existing system of 1915 had only been in place for five years. Many industrial workers were exempt, and most Italian industry was located in the north of the country, where the residents were, by and large, better educated than those of the agricultural south. Consequently, many of the army's officer cadre and most of its technical troops were recruited from the north, whereas the rank-and-file infantry tended to hail from the poorer regions south of the capitol and on the islands. This overall situation only compounded the problems of territorial nature which had plagued the country since the days of unification. Not surprisingly many conscripts simply failed to report for duty; over ten percent chose this option in 1914, the last year of peace. During the war, as Cadorna's butcher-bill steadily increased, so too did the numbers of men who refused to be conscripted, and one source lists the extent of the no-shows in 1915 as one man in eight.[114]

The western *Entente* nations always suspected that Italy's heart was not completely in the fight. To a certain extent, that very myth has been perpetrated right down to the present day. These opinions were not arrived at from want of understanding; both the British and French kept a close eye on events unfolding on the Italian Front. Lloyd George, in his memoirs, quoted a portion of a report by the British Ambassador in Rome, Sir Rennell Rodd, which was prepared in November 1916. The document stressed that no such determination as existed in London or Paris to see the fighting through could be noticed in Italy. Britain, Rodd wrote, was considered to be the only country anxious to prolong the war for selfish ends. The endless struggle was causing "certain symptoms of war weariness and discontent"[115] in Italy. Rodd did not elaborate as to how these 'symptoms' were any more serious than those which existed in every country at that time; if he knew something special, the Prime Minister did not record it. Either way, the report was not treated lightly, and it is probably not coincidental that within a month, Cadorna's attitude appears to have changed, and he was soon to issue his appeal for support. Indeed, Lloyd George is perfectly clear that he recognized how slow had been Italian progress in the war and how heavy the losses had been (despite Cadorna's censorship). He sums up the negativity by stating that "Recently there had been a serious setback".[116] He is writing of the November/December 1916 period, but to what 'serious setback' is he referring? Ninth Isonzo had been no more serious a setback than Eighth or Seventh or Fifth, for that matter. Again, we are frustrated to learn the truth. Was he referring to a loss of heart by Cadorna? Could he have known that the King was thinking about a separate peace? Was he afraid that Italy and Austria-Hungary would patch up an agreement and leave Britain and France to face Germany by themselves? It is not the purpose of this narrative to play detective. But the questions do beg for answers. What is for certain is that by the end of spring, 1917, the war had taken on an entirely new meaning for most of the governments involved. We have seen how the efforts for peace came to nothing, due to a definite lack of interest on the part of certain individuals. Other men like Karl would continue to do whatever they could, short of surrender, to put an end to the madness which was clearly sweeping away the world in which they had lived their entire lives, and which was the only world that they could imagine. As is so often the case, however, the relatively few voices of reason were drowned out by the roar of prejudice and hatred. The war would continue.

We left our story of the fighting at the end of January, 1917. Bitter winter weather did not much affect events in the Adriatic and Mediterranean Seas, where *Entente* shipping continued to be sent to the seafloor at an alarming rate. By the beginning of February, 27 German and 15 Austro-Hungarian submarines were stalking these waters,[117] intent on the destruction of enemy vessels. Well over 78,000 tons had gone down in January, and nearly 106,000 tons the following month.[118] During the two day period of the 15th to the 17th, two troop transports were sunk, one Italian and one French, with the loss of nearly 2,000 lives, off Greece's Cape Matapan. No *Alliance* ships were reported lost during the same time period, and the one-sided war on (and under) the waves continued, much to the distress of *Entente* naval leaders.

On February 1st, the weather was clear and calm, if cold, along much of the front. Italians probed Austrian defenses in the Sugana Valley at Mt. Maso and in the Astico and Posina Valleys near the old frontiers. They were greeted with artillery fire and poison gas. Worsening weather put an end to the action for a few days, before the Austrians counterattacked in the Sugana north of the river on the 6th and south of the stream on the 7th. This time it was Italian shellfire that shattered the assaults, even pre-empting one near Mt. Pasubio. In the Carnic Alps, heavy guns tore gaps in the forests on Mt. Freikofel, provoking counter-battery fire. Along the Isonzo, an Austrian ammunition dump was ignited with a terrible explosion during a barrage in the upper valley on the 2nd. There was some fighting near Zagora on the 7th. Then on the 10th, Boroevic's men carried out a fairly heavy surprise attack east of Gorizia, between Mt. St. Katerina and the Wippach River. Combat raged around Sober and east of the Vertoiba for hours before the defenders retired, leaving behind 1,000 casualties including at least 650 prisoners. This defensive success led to an inevitable counter on the 11th; again the Italians prevailed and took 100 Austrian captives. Slightly to the north, an obscure Austrian airman named Franz Gräser was credited with his first victory, in the Tolmein area. Both sides would come to know his name very well. Three days later Raoul Stojsavljevic became an air ace, scoring his fifth 'kill' over the Carso on the 13th.

Italy's aviators were no less active at this time. On the 11th, as enemy airplanes approached Udine, site of Cadorna's headquarters, Francesco Baracca quickly responded to the air-raid sirens, and took off to intercept. A brief aerial combat ensued, in which the ace sent one of the Austrian machines plummeting to its destruction. King Vittorio Emanuele had happened to witness the dogfight, and personally promoted Baracca to Captain and awarded him a third medal. It was the flyer's seventh victory.[119]

February 12th was a day remembered for widespread and energetic artillery activity. Barrages were undertaken at Tonale Pass, on the Zugna *Massif*, in the Lagarina, Travignola, and Cordevole Valleys, in the Valarsa and in the Carnics at the upper But. Near the latter location, the shelling set fire to an Austrian encampment at the foot of Pal Piccolo.[120] The Austrians followed up some of these expenditures with probes near the Tonale and on the upper But on the 17th. On the other hand, the Italians began to concentrate their efforts on railroad stations and junctions. Where the railroad from Udine to Villach crosses the heights between the Tagliamento and Danube watersheds lies the nearby town of Tarvis. Here, the rails branch into a *Y*, with one line leading to Laibach, rendering the place an important location for Austrian lateral communications. A few kilometers to the west the forts around Malborghetto had long been the targets of Italian guns; now the shells rained down on Tarvis itself. From the 13th until at least the 20th, the little town shook and trembled under the persistent explosions, but the railroad was never put out of commission for more than a few hours. Other shells smashed the little station at Santa Lucia, on the Isonzo just below Tolmein, on the 16th. It too was at the juncture of two rail routes. Decent weather from about the 20th to the 24th of the month allowed for numerous minor actions, all along the line from the Carso as far west as the Lake Garda area. Fighting on the high elevations of Mt. Colbricon, the Zugna *Massif*, and Mt. Nero was reported, and other battles in Val Sugana, the upper Ampezzo, and along the Vertoiba were also recorded. Miserable climatic conditions returned again for several days beginning on the 24th, and nothing of much consequence took place until the last day of the month, when a stiff fight developed again east of Gorizia, on the Vertoiba and Frigido streams. During this action, Austrian guns once again shelled the ruined city.

If February was distinguished by a lack of strategic campaigning, men on both sides of the front were still freezing, suffering, and dying. One such example was an Italian sergeant named Benito Mussolini, who was bossing a mortar crew in action during the skirmishing on the Carso. On the 22nd (or 23rd depending on sources) the mortar burst while firing, showering the sergeant and his entire crew with hundreds of razor-sharp fragments of metal. Several men were killed and several others badly injured, including Mussolini, whose body was punctured by dozens of steel bits, a trauma that ended his service and nearly cost him his life. The future *Il Duce* would survive, but never truly recover from the grievous injuries which left him permanently scarred, both emotionally and physically. Thousands of other soldiers endured similar episodes; their lack of notoriety would mean that their ordeals are rarely remembered. Many of the luckier ones were probably killed instantly or sustained only minor wounds, while those less fortunate often died alone, frightened, and in severe pain, among the cruel filth of battle.

March 1917 commenced in much the same manner as February had departed. The imposing Mt. Marmolada in the Dolomites was rocked by Italian artillery fire on the first day of the month; it marked the start of several days of attacks in the district, one of which gained some ground in the upper Pelegrina Valley. Another struck the upper Cordevole near Araba on the 4th, but was repulsed. Battles of a see-saw nature raged from Mt. Costabella to the Cima di Bocche for the next several days as first one side attacked, then the other countered. An Austrian push on Paneveggio was frustrated on the 11th, but the ground lost on the 4th was finally regained on the 17th, following a particularly intense bombardment. As late as the 20th the Italians in the area were still being subjected to heavy shelling, often with gas. An Austrian probe in the Concei Valley on the 11th was turned back, as were similar Italian ventures on the Carso and east of Gorizia on the following day. At the northern edge of the Asiago Plateau, winter-white clad Austrian ski and snowshoe troops probed the defenses on the 15th, then in an impressive tactical exercise on the next day overran several Italian trenches and defensive positions, and scored a minor victory.

Deficiency in heavy artillery had long been one of the chief concerns of the Italian command, a shortcoming which by the spring of 1917 was finally being made good. The relative quiet of the Trentino seemed a good place to test the new weapons in a front-line atmosphere; accordingly several large, new pieces were railed forward up the valley of the Adige, where they were ready for action by mid-March. Roverto had been the enemy railhead on the same river since early in the war, and it had frequently been bombed and shelled from the mountains to the south. Now, the big guns were trained on a station several kilometers to the north, a town called Calliano. The location had been bombed before, but never reached with artillery. All that changed on March 16th, as the heavy shells pounded the train tracks. Pleased with the results, the Italian commanders selected new targets, and soon the town of Arco, north of Lake Garda, was under fire, as was a strongpoint known as Villa Lagarina. On the following day, March 18th, Austrian artillery replied as if in spite, and some of the shells struck a field hospital at Ronchi, affording the enemy a propaganda victory. Several probes and raids were also launched in the Lake Garda region, in a rather primitive effort to locate the big guns. But the Italian command, having satisfied itself of its new tools, withdrew the heavies for transport to the Isonzo, which for Cadorna was still the only sector of much importance.

Chief Cadorna was in fact being slowly prodded into planning a new offensive. As early as the end of January, he had submitted his plans for a new offensive to the French and British Staffs, an attack that was conceived with the expectation of assistance by both troops and guns from the Western Powers. On February 1st, General Nivelle, who was then entrusted with

French strategic planning, had traveled to Italy to meet with Cadorna and remind him of Porro's promise, made at Chantilly, to take the offensive by mid-February, in support of the anticipated attacks on the Western Front that spring. If Nivelle thought he could pressure Cadorna into action for which he had no interest, he was wrong, and went away with only an assurance that Italy would renew the offensive as soon as possible. Such vague statements were as worthless as Cadorna's head-butt strategy. Next it was the turn of Field Marshal Sir William Robertson, the Chief of the Imperial General Staff of the British Empire, to have a go at the stubborn Italian Chief. This latter encounter also took place at Cadorna's headquarters, towards the end of March. Robertson was even less impressed than Nivelle had been, and could scarcely conceal his contempt, after a brief visit to the front, of Italian leadership, methods, and practices. The Englishman, who tended to support the unimaginative Haig, had always opposed plans to reinforce the Italian Front; in March he witnessed nothing which changed his mind, quite to the contrary. The twenty divisions asked for by Cadorna would never be forthcoming. Under extreme pressure from Lloyd George (who after all knew from the Sixte mission that Austria was wavering), Robertson agreed to the transfer of ten batteries of six-inch guns, and their crews, to Italy. In the event, these weapons were in place by the middle of April, well sooner than Cadorna's need dictated. By that time, the French had sent General Foch to have a final crack at Cadorna, and at least a plan to quickly reinforce the Italian Front in case of a major enemy offensive, was worked out.[121] Cadorna was again free to attack whenever he saw fit, as he had always intended he should.

March thus closed with a couple of minor Austrian attacks designed to merely improve local positions. One was delivered north of the Brenta in Val Sugana, against Italian defenses on the Maso River. The second came on the same day, the 27th, but on the Carso, behind a bombardment of some considerable severity. One hill at the latter location was taken. Thereafter the weather warmed noticeably, bringing swollen streams and muddy conditions in the lower-lying areas, which in turn hampered military operations to the extent that nothing of importance was reported from late March throughout April, save a few actions in higher, still frozen, locations.

At the highest levels of Austria's chain of command, an era came to a close in the month of March. Franz Conrad von Hötzendorf had been involved in the military planning of the Empire for a decade, as we have seen. Although he had never quite seen eye-to-eye with Franz Joseph, the old Monarch had maintained faith in his man, correctly recognizing him to be an exceptionally gifted planner and strategist. Karl, on the other hand, considered Hötzendorf to be somewhat of a hothead, and far too hawkish for his own rather pacifistic temperament. There can be little doubt but that Franz Conrad knew from the moment Karl had assumed the throne that his own days at the helm were numbered. The official move came on March 1st. Rather than retire Hötzendorf, the Emperor sent him to command the Army Group in the Tyrol, that area which the ex-Chief had always held so dear to his heart. His replacement as Chief of Staff was General Arthur Arz von Straussenberg, a little-known personality who had been commanding the weak Austrian First Army in Transylvania, when Romania had entered the war. Most senior Austro-Hungarian military men could only shrug their shoulders at the Emperor's selection, but at least Straussenberg was a realist, unlikely to commit gross errors of judgment. Anyway, with the Germans pretty much running every aspect of the war by this time, the new Chief was not going to be allowed much freedom of action.

The sea war continued to go rather well for the *Alliance*. Actual tonnage of enemy shipping sunk was well down in March, when a meager 62,000 or so tons was destroyed. On the 19th, however, the German submarine *U-64* slammed two torpedoes into the French battleship *Danton* off the Italian island of Sardinia.[122] The sinking represented the ninth capital ship of the *Entente* lost in the Mediterranean theatre in the war. The *Alliance* had yet to lose a comparable warship. Worse still, the month of April proved to be one of the most disastrous of all for *Entente* navies, which continued to insist that they held 'command of the sea'. On the 4th, the Italian liner *Ravenna* was sunk off the port of Genoa. In all, an unprecedented 278,000 tons was sent to the bottom of the sea by Austro-German submarines.[123] Naval leaders began to believe that if the unrestricted submarine campaign were not countered somehow soon, some of the more far-flung battlefronts might have to be abandoned, an eventuality that would release Turkish and Bulgarian troops for service elsewhere. Even so, no decisions were taken at the St. Jean de Maurienne Conference, mentioned above, on April 19th. Some new strategies for turning around the war at sea were finally agreed upon at another Conference, held at Corfu, from April 28th to May 1st, but for the time being it was still the U-boats that ruled the waves.

Unfavorable conditions on the ground during much of April did not mean that either army was allowed much rest. The usual artillery duels continued throughout the month. Lake Garda and its surrounds continued to host as a proving-ground for new Italian ordnance. When Austrian intelligence discovered the arrival of some more big guns on about April 10th, counter battery fire was ordered to pound both sides of the lake, and the valleys beyond. This in turn led to Arco and Roverto being shelled; it was not until the 13th that long-range weapons once again targeted the unlucky town of Calliano, where the station, an ammunition dump, and even a train in motion were hit. Casualties were relatively few that day, but when the firing was renewed on the 16th, some assembling troops were caught in the open and killed by the first salvoes. Thereafter, Hötzendorf directed that most such entraining or detraining take place only under the cover of darkness. Both sides took advantage of a few days of fine weather which began on the 20th, for blasting away at each other, firing off older ammunition and generally checking the effectiveness of their weapons and range-finding equipment.

On April 6th yet another mountain peak was blown into fragments, as the Austrians detonated a massive amount of explosives drilled into a spur on the northern fringes of Mt. Colbricon. Apparently both sides had chosen to tunnel on the surrounding heights; six days later the Italians exploded a mine of their own in the same vicinity. The war was literally changing the face of the Dolomite landscape. While such prodigious use of gunpowder derivatives might be good for business in the chemical industries of each nation, it could hardly affect the course of the fighting. In the end the front lines in the Colbricon area shifted a few meters in favor of the Italians. Provided they were willing and able to blow up every mountain in the eastern Alps, one side or the other might sooner or later reach level ground.

Of the three dimensions of the fighting, the air war was probably the most straightforward; here there was no diving beneath the waves or boring into the mountainsides. It was, of course, no less deadly. Following a brief posting in the west, Austrian ace Godwin Brumowski returned to the Italian Front in April, to assume command of *Fliegerkompanie* 41J (J=*Jägerkompanie*=fighter unit), an outfit which one historian considers "arguably the best squadron fielded by the Austro-Hungarians".[124] Certainly, many of its personnel were, or went on to become, aces. One of these, Deputy Officer Julius Arigi, would record five victories in April and May 1917. Flying with a different unit in the air-space over Gorizia, a new pilot, Stefan Fejes, shot down a Nieuport fighter on the 17th, for his first victory.[125] Fejes was probably fortunate to not have encountered Captain Baracca, who was patrolling the same skies at the same time period. Baracca's eighth victim tumbled to the earth near the Isonzo on April 26th; numbers nine and ten followed on May 1st, just east of Gorizia.[126]

With the advent of May, the warming effects of an ever-higher sun removed the last traces of the previous bitter winter. Spring rains nourished the vegetation which in turn greened European landscapes. Flowers began to bloom and birds to sing. Even the mood of General Cadorna, who had entertained such self-doubt throughout the cold weather, improved noticeably. He had long known that he would have to attack again sooner or later, but he had resisted every outside effort to prod him into early action. The French had long since recognized the hollowness of the Chantilly promises and had attacked on their own, into disaster. Nivelle's April offensive would mostly be remembered for the effect it had had on the French army, which was widespread mutiny. A British drive near Arras was hardly less unsuccessful. Russia's new Provisional Government lacked authority, and was pleading for more time to reorganize its forces on the Eastern Front. The war at sea, as we have seen was a disaster. The United States had entered the war, but possessed no army capable of fighting in Europe, and was not expected to do so for a year or so. All eyes turned to Italy, the only theatre where *Entente* fortunes might be redeemed that season. Under increasing pressure, Cadorna was forced to at least pretend that his command represented a strong link in the *Entente* chain, and that he was a team-player ready to coordinate his strategy with that of his allies.

Since Ninth Isonzo, twelve new divisions had been added to the roles of the Italian Army, for a total, by May 1st, of sixty-one, the highest thus far in the war. Equally importantly, the nation's artillery deficiency had more or less been made good, particularly with regards heavy guns, and we have seen how the British had contributed in this manner. Encouraged, the Chief felt he now held a new strategy. The reason for earlier failures, he reasoned, was simple: he had never possessed enough raw force to bludgeon his way past the enemy defenses. Now, after five months of rebuilding and re-munitioning, his forces composed an irresistible force capable of smashing its way to its objectives. All naysayers were silenced; soldiers were severely punished, commanders relieved. A former Corps commander within the Second Army, Luigi Capello, was elevated to Army command. Capello, known to the troops as "The Butcher"[127] because of the reckless manner in which he had previously ordered unit after unit to their deaths, was a man truly cut out of the Cadorna mold, irretractable, aloof, and uninterested in hearing of the woes of subordinates. Capello could be depended upon to achieve his objectives, if it cost him every man in his army. The Duke of Aosta retained leadership at Third Army. He was much more empathetic towards his men than Cadorna or Capello, and had through his horrific experience come to doubt the wisdom of his superior, but a strong sense of duty and a healthy apprehension of a possible backlash from the King kept him from expressing himself too openly.

Throughout late April and early May the Italian buildup commenced. The new artillery was emplaced and sighted, new infantry units were hidden in forests, and thousands of tons of ammunition, rations and supplies of every type were railed to the Isonzo and trucked to the front. Engineers prepared hundreds of miles of new roads to support the effort. An English eyewitness marveled at the skills employed to create some of these roads, which often traversed extremely uneven terrain. He wrote of one which had been specially built for the Tenth Battle, noting that it "came down through carefully selected folds of the mountain side, and through forests that afforded considerable cover from the enemy". Winding its way up the steep slopes east of the Plava bridgehead, the road was dubbed "the thirty-two hairpins".[128]

All such activity did not go unnoticed by the Austrians. Boroevic would not have been surprised had the enemy drive begun anytime after mid-April. He was heavily outnumbered as usual, although chaotic conditions in Russia had allowed for the transfer of some additional units to Italy. Counting the two divisions which would arrive in May, Austria was fielding twenty-nine on the Italian Front, two-thirds of which were under Fifth Army. On the other hand, Austria's erstwhile artillery advantage had pretty much dwindled to nil, and its ammunition reserves were inadequate to sustain an extended battle. Even so, the soldiers of the multi-lingual army were determined to prevent the Italians from advancing into their positions, those trenches, dugouts, and strong points which had been five months in creation. Never before had the enemy been forced to deal with such a strong defense line. On May 1st the Austrian *Landwehr*, which had played such an important role in the war, were officially renamed the *Schützen*, in honor of their remarkable sharpshooting abilities. A day later the Third Infantry Division was renamed the *Edelweiss* Division in another effort to improve morale. The Edelweiss is a flower native to Alpine environment; the unit was being accorded an elite, mountain-worthy status.

Boroevic's men did all they could to discover the enemy plans. Trench raids were conducted for the purpose of taking prisoners for interrogation, and there were numerous instances of Italian troops approaching Austrian lines under cover of darkness or whenever they had a chance to initiate surrender. These were men who preferred captivity to participation in a grueling attack, when death or maiming was likely. Aircraft buzzed the skies, but in general the weather was unfavorable, with low-lying clouds hanging around for many days. A few bombing runs, such as the one on Gorizia on the 5th, could only hope to disrupt enemy assembly behind the front. Finally, the weather cleared and the Austrians could only look on with horror, as they observed the massive forces gathering before them. By then it was too late; the coming of the sunshine meant for that it was time for their adversaries to begin new offensives.

Chapter Eight
No Turning Back

May 10th, 1917 was a beautiful spring day, clear, balmy, and with excellent visibility. It was also unusually quiet at the front, neither side troubling about trench raids or artillery barrages. The skies, too, were nearly free of aircraft, and to the casual observer it would have appeared as though the opposing armies were content to enjoy the long awaited return of lovely weather so typical of springtime south of the Alps. But the impression was deceiving. For the Italians, the hard labor of offensive preparation may have been about complete, however, last-minute briefings, regroupings, and re-munitioning of hundreds of thousands of weapons were the order of the day. For the coming attack, Capello's command was renamed the 'Gorizia Army', and would be first to strike, on a front between Canale on the Isonzo and the north rim of the Carso Plateau. A much-depleted Second Army, still holding the line from Tolmein northward, was not to participate. Aosta's reinforced Third Army still occupied the line from the Carso to the sea; its attack was to be staggered by about a week behind Capello's.

For the Austrians of Boroevic's Fifth Army, the calm of the 10th, which carried over and lasted all day of the 11th as well, was truly the calm before the storm. Desperately, they tried every known method to gain intelligence of the enemy intentions; without any significant movement on the part of the foe, no units could be identified, no prisoners taken for interrogation, no aircraft shot down. About all the defenders could do was try to locate supply dumps and the smoke of field kitchens through their field glasses. They knew something was up, something big, and it was imminent. They would have preferred to know exactly where and when the main thrusts would come, so that they could move all available reserves to locations behind these points before the inevitable barrage rendered all such movements virtually impossible. Many half-suspected that it was already too late. As the sun went down on the evening of the 11th, thousands of men on both sides of the line were enjoying (or suffering) their last hours of life.

Precisely at sunrise on the 12th, all of Cadorna's massed artillery opened fire on every meter of frontline between just south of Tolmein to the shore of the Gulf of Trieste near Duino. It was one of the most intense, and one of the most accurate, of all Italian bombardments of the entire war. Hundreds of thousands of light, medium and heavy shells fell on Austrian forward positions, obliterating trenches, sandbagged machine gun nests, and communication posts. Even deep dugouts, ammunition dumps, and gun-emplacements, where known, were not immune. The terrifying roar deafened Boroevic's troops, some temporarily, some permanently; others were similarly blinded by dust, smoke and debris, still others suffocated from the heat and fumes or from lack of oxygen consumed in raging fires begun amongst all forms of combustible material. The worst part about this hell was that it never seemed to stop. On and on it went, for 54 hours without a pause. The final few hours were the most punishing, as Italian and British gunners, already exhausted, fed their weapons at a frantic pace, to achieve a density of fire designed to shock into impotence anyone who may have somehow survived the first two days of the nightmare. In fact, many thousands of defenders had already been killed in one manner or another, and all semblance of a defense line erased, as though some mighty force of nature had swept through the region. About the only Austro-Hungarian troops to have survived this holocaust were those who had sheltered in one of the many caverns blasted deep into the solid rock of the hills.

Every defender to a man knew that the end of the shelling meant that powerful infantry attacks were soon to follow. Time was very short to file out of the caves, weapons and ammunition in hand, accustom oneself to the daylight, and try to find some rock or tree stump which had not been totally shattered, behind which to take a position and try to identify the oncoming enemy through the still-swirling smoke and unsettled dust. They could forget about being exhausted from lack of sleep, or being hungry, thirsty or in any way uncomfortable; their very lives depended upon their ability to resist the enemy attack. And they would have to resist that attack with seriously depleted numbers and without the benefit of well-prepared positions, the latter having been scattered like dust in the wind.

Two entire Italian Corps surged forward east of Gorizia towards Mts. St. Katerina and San Gabriele into a hilly area north and east of Tivoli. Here, most

Austrian artillery had been spared annihilation during the bombardment, and now it returned a deadly fire upon the attackers, stalling then stopping, the advance. A third Corps, reinforced to near double-strength, assaulted the heights above the Plava bridgehead, scene of so many prior attempts, and so many failures. This time would be different. Despite another heroic defense, which slaughtered Capello's men by the thousands, the weight of numbers, described by one source as fifteen-to-one,[129] finally prevailed, and the tortured mountaintop was secured. Simultaneous flank attacks also succeeded where others in the past had failed, propelled as they were by huge numbers of Italian infantry. A kilometer or two to the south, the village of Zagora was overrun and its defenders wiped out; several kilometers to the north another regiment crossed the Isonzo at Canale and pushed on up the more gentle slopes beyond. Caught off guard here, Boroevic rushed reserves to the vicinity.

Capello's primary objectives were several peaks of the ridge on the east side of the river. The most westerly of these, Mt. Kuk (Cucco), was soon under assault by several converging divisions, as was Mt. Vodice, the next major height to the southeast. Beyond Vodice rose Mt. Santo, then a depression through which ran the road from Salcano into the Val Chiapovano; beyond the road the southerly end of the ridge featured Mts. San Gabriele and San Daniele. This ridge commanded not only the Isonzo valley north of Gorizia, but also miles of rugged, wooded terrain to the east, known as the Ternovanerwald, (Forest of Ternova) a wilderness named for an obscure town to the east of San Daniele. Simply stated, to control the ridge was to control the middle Isonzo region. If Capello could seize it, he could turn the Austrian flanks in both the Baca and Wippach River valleys, and perhaps open the back door to Trieste. Fighting for the peak of Kuk raged all day on the 15th, and in the end the defense prevailed—barely. Undeterred, Capello prepared another attack on the mountain.

Third Army also launched attacks on the 14th, but these were diversionary in nature, as the big push was to be delayed until the Austrians had committed their last reserves into the battles with Gorizia Army. Even so, two Italian divisions struck east between the Wippach and the height known as Fajti Hrib. Boroevic's artillery and machine guns cut down the exposed enemy, ending the attacks in failure. Both sides also threw every airplane they possessed into the battle, hoping to enjoy the tremendous advantages of air superiority. Hundreds of machines made observation and bombing runs, and fought with each other.

Captain Baracca, already the most famous of all Italian aviators, flew dozens of sorties during this time period. He continued to be a successful fighter pilot, and recorded 'kills' on May 13th, May 20th, and June 3rd, all within a few kilometers of the town of Plava. This remarkable string of victories brought his total to thirteen.[130] Other Italian airmen delivered a heavy bombing raid on the enemy airfield at Prosecco on the 12th, and continued to roam the skies over enemy lines throughout the offensive, searching for Austrian artillery and other ground targets. Their opponents were no less active. Hungarian Stefan Fejes outfought a Nieuport over the lower Wippach on the 14th, then bested a SPAD in the same area on the 20th. Fejes was at the time a member of Adolf Heyrowski's unit, which accounted for many enemy planes above those few square kilometers of soil; the leader himself downed one on the 15th and another on June 3rd. Only slightly to the north, Franz Gräser was credited with his second victory over Mt. Sabotino on May 20th.[131] Increasingly, the air war was becoming as deadly as the ground war.

On the afternoon of the 17th Mt. Kuk was finally captured, along with a relative few of its exhausted, emaciated defenders. Capello was pleased, and immediately ordered a fresh attack on Vodice for the next day. The weak bridgehead won at Canale was ordered evacuated in order to reinforce the new drive, which was preceded by another several hours of heavy bombardment. By midmorning, *Alpini* and *Bersaglieri* troops augmented the infantry assaults on both Vodice and Mt. Santo. The barrage had ruined what little remained of the tree cover on the steep slopes, so the Italians charged up relatively barren inclines where they were easy targets for the surviving Slavic and Romanian defenders, who shot them down by the thousands. Nevertheless each succeeding attack wave weakened the defense, however slightly, until munitions and ranks were seriously depleted. Thereafter, the seizure of Capello's objectives became a matter of the degree of his persistence, a matter of his willingness, or lack thereof, to suffer frightful losses in order to prevail. He was not known as 'The Butcher' for nothing, however; the attacks would continue until total exhaustion set it.

Unfortunately for Boroevic, the young Emperor Karl chose this moment in the campaign to appear at Fifth Army Headquarters. This Tenth Battle of the Isonzo was the first one of his reign, and he wanted to experience that which his field commanders were forced to endure whenever the enemy attacked. Boroevic, his hands full trying to dole out his modest reserves to points of the front most likely to be penetrated by the Italians, did not need the distraction. In the event, Karl was gracious and tried not to interfere, and his presence probably tended to steady Boroevic's increasingly shaky nerves. Henceforth, Fifth Army was to be known as the Isonzo Army, decreed the Emperor, in recognition of its having withstood everything that Cadorna had thrown at it for two entire years. Before the monarch had departed, Vodice was announced as lost, and the General dispatched one of his few remaining reserve regiments to the peak to secure its recapture. The attempt failed on the 19th, but so too did renewed Italian efforts to storm Mt. Santo, the logical next prize.

May 20th was a day of battle for the possession of the summit of Mt. Santo. Both sides attacked and counterattacked, shelled and counter-shelled. Several times during the day the ground at the top of the mountain changed hands in the seesaw nature of the fighting, and in the end the shooting died away only because of the total exhaustion of both sides that predictably set in. No one could say for sure who truly held the summit; the place was too thoroughly blasted to shelter many troops, and to occupy the shattered stones and shell craters was useless anyway, since both sides had the peak well-sighted on the range-finders of the big guns. Capello called off further attacks, much to the great relief of Boroevic, who now had no more reserve units to use in counters.

In the Tyrol, von Hötzendorf, who had as early as the 12th been appealed to for diversionary help in the face of the Italian offensive, did what he could to respond. Without reinforcement, his efforts were bound to be rather feeble, but Boroevic was desperate, so a series of minor attacks by local forces was initiated. These began on the 19th, with a barrage, followed by an infantry attack, on the river Maso in Val Sugana, a battle that lasted two days. Other actions took place on the Adamello *Massif*, in the Daone valley, on the upper Posina, and in the Garda-Adige area. The most widely publicized of these spoiling attacks took place on Mt. Pasubio, where a medium-sized Austrian force nearly overran their objective and had to be ejected in close-quarter fighting with bayonets, clubs and grenades. On the 21st another initiative in the Travignolo Valley was beaten off after some hard fighting by the following day[132], a date on which Hötzendorf called off all similar 'diversions'. Not a single Italian soldier had, of course, been 'diverted' from the Isonzo.

A far more important 'diversion' if it indeed could be referred to as such, had taken place in the waters of the Adriatic Sea. We have seen how the considerable numerical superiority in surface ships held by the *Entente* had thus far been unable to neutralize the submarine campaign of the *Alliance* and had been more or less exclusively used to blockade Austria's only seacoast on the Adriatic at the narrow Straits of Otranto, between the 'heel' of Italy and the Albanian mainland coast. The anti-submarine nets employed at the Straits had never been terribly effective. For example, the 65 kilometer (40 mile) wide Straits required approximately 78 vessels to properly cover the gap with nets, each vessel capable of slightly more than eight-tenths of a kilometer coverage. In the spring of 1917, only two-thirds of the necessary boats were employed (50) for the service, and on any given day some of these were likely to be withheld at shore for maintenance and repair. Such was the case in the early morning hours of May 15th, when 47 of the craft were on duty.[133] On several occasions, this line had been raided before but the Austro-Hungarians had always wanted to strike a more powerful blow, and a Hungarian officer had come up with a plan and assembled the means to carry it out. Captain Horthy was a daring and aggressive leader, and a man unwilling to allow the enemy to simply blockade him into port for the duration of the war. Finally given a green light for action, he now steamed towards the Straits with three cruisers and two destroyers, supported by several submarines and torpedo boats. An older battleship and some more warships hugged the Balkan coast, ready to aid the attack force if it should run into unforeseen trouble.

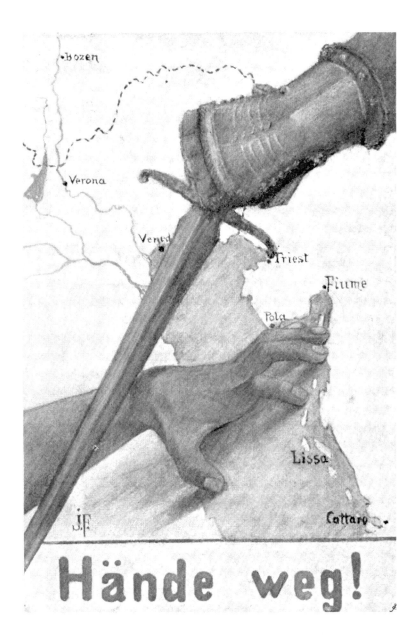

**Hands Off! Is the Response as an Italian Hand
Reaches for Austria's Adriatic Seacoast.**

Horthy's command tore into the line of anti-submarine craft, sinking 14 and crippling three more.[134] Immediately, every British, French, and Italian warship in the area began to close on the Austro-Hungarians, hoping to cut them off from their bases. What followed was the most extensive action of the war in the Adriatic. First shots were exchanged just after daylight; the Austrian destroyers were able to reach the safety of the Albanian coast before they were overwhelmed. Horthy's cruisers, meanwhile, engaged a more powerful fleet of British cruisers in a running battle that lasted two hours. Both groups suffered damage, and Horthy was injured by a hostile shell, and his ship crippled. However, the *Entente* fleet never closed in for the sure kill; bedeviled by mechanical failures and missed signals, it hesitated just long enough for the Austrian reinforcements, led by the old battleship, to discourage any further aggression. Minor, post-climactic maneuvers dominated the remainder of the day. These did not go well for the *Entente*. British light cruiser *Dartmouth* was torpedoed that afternoon by a German submarine, and although it was rescued before it could sink, it had to be towed to port for extensive repairs. Soon thereafter, the French destroyer *Boutefeu* slammed into a mine and was lost.

The Adriatic battle of May 15th is often remembered as 'The Battle of the Otranto Straits', somewhat of a misnomer, but it had begun there and its effects were most noticeable there. For the time being, the *Entente* leaders decided to suspend implementation of the line of nets at nighttime, when the helpless little 'drifters' were most vulnerable. Once again the underdog Austro-Hungarians had won a sea action, a capability for which they had, before the war, never been given much credit. Their fleet, after all, was only the eighth most powerful in the world, and six of the first seven were united in the *Entente*. Strategically, the battle had changed nothing, which was just fine with the leaders of the *Alliance* forces; they still seemed to be winning the sea war with submarines alone. In the month of May, another 181,000 tons of shipping was destroyed in the Mediterranean, and a further 168,500 in June.[135]

If events in the Tyrol or out in the Adriatic made any impression upon Luigi Cadorna, he showed no indication of it during the Tenth Battle. Unperturbed about the fact that Capello's army had been unable to capture all of Mt. Santo or advance due east of Gorizia, he now could think of nothing but the second phase of his one-two punch planned for the Carso Plateau. At dawn on the 23rd of May the Duke of Aosta's Third Army artillery commenced firing for its second major barrage in eleven days. All day the big guns, which included those batteries sent by the British, roared away at the Austrian positions between the Wippach and the sea. Offshore in the Gulf, a number of British light warships joined in, turning all available weapons against the heights above the coast road. Roughly 2,000 weapons of all calibers belched high explosive at any and all suspected enemy strong points, which had already been severely handled by the barrage of the 12th to 14th. According to one source, the rate of fire reached 100,000 shells per hour, which represented "twenty shells for every foot of the front".[136] So lavish was Cadorna's stock of ammunition, that the carnage was ongoing for ten hours, during which hundreds of windowpanes in Trieste were broken by the shaking; the resonating was felt as far distant as Venice. As was always the case as a result of such devastating punishment, all Austrian roads and other means of communication to the rear areas were simply erased by explosions, as were all strong points not actually carved out of solid rock.

In the late afternoon Aosta unleashed his masses of infantry. One target was the town of Kostanjevica at the center of the Carso, where the remnants of the shaken, deafened defenders were able to hold the line. Elsewhere, the Austrians were not as fortunate. As in all previous battles of the Isonzo, the Italian's ability to advance was entirely dependent on whether they possessed sufficient numbers to overrun the enemy line before they were shot down by the limited quantity of projectiles the Austrians were able to fire at them. Two or three-to-one odds had hitherto been insufficient; ten or fifteen-to-one had thus far succeeded. At some level between the two extremes was a break-point, and on the 23rd of May, 1917, it was apparently exceeded. Wave after wave of attackers swept past the indistinguishable old defense line along the coast road and advanced on Mt. Hermada, one of the last few good defensive outcroppings on the short route to Trieste. The ruins of the village of Jamiano were taken, and the assault pressed to gains of nearly two kilometers, a fair amount by Isonzo standards. Overhead, a fleet of 130 airplanes[137] supported the foot soldiers, driving off enemy aircraft and bombing artillery emplacements. Despite a few local repulses, the first day's attack had been a remarkable success.

That night, Boroevic was informed of the withdrawal of his surviving troops to the rear, emergency defense line. Though he had expended virtually all of his reserves in stopping Capello during the prior several days, he demanded a round of counterattacks for the purpose of regaining the lost positions. Despite strong arguments by his staff to the effect that there were in fact very few 'positions' left worth recapturing, 'The Straightrazor' was insistent. Therefore, precious Austrian strength was bled away all day of the 24th in futile counters against overwhelming odds. Some ground was regained, however, especially west of Mt. Hermada, and thousands of dispirited Italian soldiers captured. Aosta hit back on the 25th, his units capturing Flondar and Medeazza, then San Giovanni on the 26th, when they also crossed the Timavo, a small coastal river. Soon, they were countered again and fell back upon the little stream, where the line stabilized once more.

Other battles were raging up on the Plateau. In the center of the front Versic was reached late on the 24th, but Boroevic's counters prevented any further forward movement. A new assault on Kostanjevica dislodged the defenders on the 26th, taking several hundred prisoners and ten artillery pieces, but a desperate counterattack regained the battered town shortly thereafter. By the morning of May 27th, most shooting on the Carso had died away. Once the Austrians had had a chance to reassess what was important to them, they attacked again in a few locations, on the 30th, but these were smaller-scale actions; both armies were too exhausted to do more. Cadorna's net gains for a week of battle stood at two to four kilometers of advance on an eight kilometer front. Once the offensive slowed, Capello was ordered to initiate a further diversion in the hills. Gorizia Army obliged with a fresh effort in the Vodice-Santo area on the night of the 26th/27th; when it failed to gain any ground the attacks were renewed on the afternoon of the latter day.

Italian engineers had once again been working their magic on the newly-won terrain. Within a week of the capture of Mt. Kuk, water supply pipes and *teleferiche* were operable to the summit, and within three weeks a military road had been etched into the mountain, capable of supporting heavy guns, drawn by motor vehicles.[138] *Perforatrici* (power drills) were also hard at work, helping to turn Italy's new conquests into an impregnable defensive position. Well aware that any further counterattacks would have to be delivered before the enemy had time to consolidate his gains, Boroevic, the man who hated to lose a single meter to withdrawal, called an urgent council of war during the lull of the last days of the month, when Cadorna called off his offensive. It met at Laibach, and was attended by Arz von Straussenberg, who promised to appeal to the Germans for more resources for the Italian Front. Meanwhile Boroevic was to make do with what he already possessed, plus the few brigades beginning to trickle in from the Eastern Front.

Collecting every battalion he could somehow scrape up, the Isonzo Army boss prepared a series of short but strong jabs intended to recover lost ground. He rejected the idea of a single, more powerful blow, realizing that the enemy artillery would likely ravage it; instead, small-scale attacks behind concentrated barrages were more likely to succeed, a lesson his opposite number had not learned in two years of carnage. On the 1st of June, Boroevic's artillery began a slow, methodical fire all along the front between Tivoli, due east of Gorizia, and the southern edge of the Carso near Medeazza. It was intended to confuse the enemy, and it did; Cadorna must have wondered just what Boroevic could possibly be up to. Then suddenly the barrage lifted in most areas, and concentrated on only two: San Marco hill just south of Tivoli and the south slope of the Plateau. The San Marco counterattack was delivered on the morning of June 3rd and was successful within a couple of hours; the 700 meter-high hill and 500 prisoners were captured.[139] In the predawn hours of the next day the second assault struck shaken Italian defenders before Flondar and Jamiano. The former was recaptured, an advance of a half-kilometer to a kilometer and a half scored, and 7,000[140] prisoners taken. A third surprise attack by Tyrolese and Hungarian troops parted the enemy lines at Fajti Hrib, took several hundred more captives, and was only beaten back with the aid of heavy artillery and some very hard fighting.

Furious at the loss of ground and the large number of surrenders, Cadorna ordered an immediate backstroke against the counterattacking Austrians. Aosta hurriedly assembled the equivalent of a fresh division and attacked the next morning, before a new barrage could be organized. The attack never had much chance of success; the Italian troops, mostly green and ill-led, were cut down by the hundreds. Other hundreds approached the enemy lines, then dropped their weapons and surrendered. It was an ominous sign of crumbling morale, which even Cadorna could not afford to ignore. To Aosta's great relief, the Chief did not insist on further slaughter following the debacle of June 6th, and both sides had finally had enough of fighting for awhile.

The Tenth Battle was over. It is a matter of opinion as to whether it truly ended on about May 28th, when Cadorna called off his offensive, or on June 6th, when the last of the counters was halted. Either way it had been the costliest of all the ten battles fought to that date. There were hundreds of foreign correspondents in Italy by that stage of the war, and Cadorna was no longer able to easily conceal his true losses, as he had done in the earlier battles. Eventually, an 'official' figure of 159,000 casualties was announced, a total which included 27,000 men taken prisoner. This latter number would never have been admitted had the Austrians not held the proof; they were quick to boast of the number of dispirited enemy soldiers taken. Ten thousand had surrendered during the period of the counterattacks in the first six days of June, alone. Austrian casualties are more difficult to determine, except for the 24,000 or so prisoners seized by the Italians. Most sources list numbers ranging from 65,000 to 90,000. It seems quite likely that the lesser figure is too low, but the actual total of killed and wounded men may never be known. What is certain is that Tenth Isonzo eliminated at least 225,000 and perhaps 250,000 troops from the ranks of the hostile powers.

From a strategic point of view, Cadorna was no nearer either Laibach or Trieste as a result of Tenth Isonzo. What he *was* much nearer to, was the complete breakdown of discipline and morale in his armies. His strategy of attrition was slowly gaining ground, it is true, but at a pace destined to ensure that Italy would run out of soldiers before Austria ran out of ground to lose. At that rate, an advance to Trieste would cost millions of lives, unless, of course, those whose lives were being sacrificed simply refused to go on. On the other hand, Boroevic's strategy of inflexible defense was costing his nation more than it could afford to pay, as well. Stopping the Italians had become a matter of placing a certain number of men, equipped with a certain number of weapons, fed by a certain quantity of munitions, in harm's way. When any of the three elements was depleted to a certain level, it needed to be replaced, or the Italians were sure to break through the defenses. In sum, the war had become a game of mathematics, with morale as the wild card. In fact, Austrian morale was not much higher than was Italy's, by the summer of 1917. It is a matter of historic fact that soldiers are more easily demoralized when forced to constantly fight on the defensive; Isonzo Army had done nothing but defend for two long years, and with no end and no alternative in sight, it too was beginning to grumble. Local counterattacks were no substitute for true offensive action, and the latter was certainly needed if Isonzo Army was to be expected to hold on much longer. Stories of great offensives on the Eastern Front, in Serbia, and in Romania had not failed to reach Austro-Hungarian troops in Italy and these were feeling as though theirs was the only theatre of operations being neglected by the High Command.

Once the Tenth Battle had died out in early June, Chief Cadorna uncharacteristically turned his attention away from the Isonzo and Trieste. As the war dragged on, he came under ever-increasing pressure from the Western Powers to coordinate his actions with those on the Western Front. Italy had always wanted to be considered a principal, not a subsidiary power within the *Entente*. Britain and France, and later the United States, had agreed in principle; Rome was expected to take a leading role in securing the Mediterranean, in contributing to the expeditionary forces based on Salonika in Greece, and generally cooperate in all matters economic and military. All this was well and fine with Cadorna, and we have seen how he had accepted British artillery contingents for the Isonzo and had agreed to accept British and French troops for service on his front should the *Entente* leadership choose to employ them there. Although he was typically unconcerned with others, he certainly knew of the problems which had recently developed in the west, especially the partial breakdown of the French Army. He knew that Russia was in turmoil and not likely to fully recover for the duration of the present war. And he knew that significant American assistance was still a year distant.

Under such circumstances, Cadorna could no longer simply fight his own little war in isolation. He needed to at least appear to be a team player, cooperative when his teammates called. This may well be one reason for the apparent change in his mentality since the winter. The new Cadorna tended to occasionally look over his shoulder, entertained at least some measure of self-doubt, and lived in more of a glass house, aware that others were watching him. We recall that when Hötzendorf had launched his *Südtyroloffensive*, the Chief had quickly created a Fifth Army behind the threatened areas, then stripped it of much of its strength when the enemy offensive had been contained, and demoted it to a 'Command' status, under General Ettore Mambretti. A year later Mambretti's command was once again elevated to the level of Army, only this time, for reasons lost to history, it would be known as Sixth Army. It is quite possible that once Hötzendorf had taken leadership of all Austrian forces in Tyrol, Cadorna suspected a repeat of the earlier enemy move. Hötzendorf would have loved to oblige but he possessed nowhere nearly enough strength. At any rate, the Italian commander decided that once the battle on the Carso was done, he had better appear to be a fully cooperative ally, and initiate an attack somewhere else. Sixth Army was created for this purpose, and in early June Cadorna gave Mambretti the nod. The Tyrol was to be attacked, a move that would preempt anything the enemy was planning there, secure Cadorna's rear once more, and satisfy the *Entente* that Italy was an aggressive partner.

Sixth Army was inserted into the line where Fifth Army had been, the year before, between the First and Fourth Armies, an area in the southern Dolomites drained by the Brenta River. The Brenta Valley cuts a deep trough through the mountains, which on the Austrian side of the frontier was known as Val Sugana. Its upper reaches extend perilously close to Trient, and on the same latitude, the very reason the lovely valley had been the scene of fighting since the war's beginning. On earlier occasions the Italians had simply pushed their way up the valley, and the sub-valleys of the Brenta's tributaries, trying to obtain the height of land from which they could have gazed down upon Trient and the railroad that followed the Etsch. They had never quite reached the extent of the watershed, however, and the Austrian 1916 offensive had subsequently pushed them back onto Italian soil. Fifth Army's counteroffensive had regained much of the lost ground, but it had been unable to retake much of the Val Sugana. Now, in June 1917, Sixth Army was to remedy the situation by finally securing the Brenta Valley and turning the enemy flank from the east, a flank that extended far to south, from Lake Garda across the Etsch to Mt. Pasubio. This time, Cadorna would turn the tables on Hötzendorf.

Mambretti's plan—approved by Cadorna—called not for a direct approach up both sides of the Brenta, but an indirect approach by way of the heights overlooking the south side of the stream, where a lofty ridge dropped sharply down to the water. Control the heights, and you control the valley, with its road and railroad, or so the reasoning went. The ridge was to be captured from the much more gently sloping south side, which was the northern fringe of the Asiago Plateau, scene of so much combat in the previous year. Italian troops already held most of the Plateau, paid for in blood during the 1916 fighting, and the peaks of the ridge were only a few kilometers distant, at least, according to the maps. What Mambretti's maps would have failed to show, even if of the topographic variety, was just how difficult for military movement was the rugged, wooded, boulder-strewn terrain of the northern Plateau. Here was no plateau at all, but a long incline, without roads, into a cul-de-sac surrounded by mountains peaks. Due west lay the 2,047 meter (6,715ft.) Mt. Mandriola, the 2,331 meter (7,648ft.) Mt. Kempel, the 2,110 meter (6,924ft.) Mt. Ortigara, and twins known as Corno di Campo Verdi (2,128m, 6,983ft) and Corno di Campo Bianca (2,105m, 6,908ft) as one's gaze turned counterclockwise. There were other unnamed peaks as well, and several lower mountains helping to block the approaches. For an army to take an objective in this wilderness was a formidable task, even in summertime. The highest elevations were of course devoid of much vegetation, allowing for excellent visibility of oncoming trouble; this was the very reason they were coveted by the Italians.

Following an elementary survey of the ground, it was decided to make the primary offensive effort at Mt. Ortigara, on the most northerly section of ridge. With this summit in hand, all heights to the north shy of the Brenta would be isolated, and a lateral movement westward was a possibility. Apparently Mambretti, like Capello, was Cadorna's type of guy; a less suitable setting for a major attack can scarcely be imagined, for an objective the military value of which was dubious, at best.

On June 9th Sixth Army's artillery opened fire on Ortigara and its southerly approaches, which were little more than goat-trails. The bombardment shattered the bare rock, sending millions of jagged fragments flying in all directions, but especially downhill. Shrubs were uprooted, trees splintered, and their fallen portions hurled violently and repeatedly into the air. Most of the Austrian troops in the area, pressing their relatively new steel helmets to their heads, huddled in ravines or behind rock outcroppings on reverse slopes of the numerous rises, or took cover in the many caves drilled or blasted out of the mountainsides. Once the shelling had stopped, the defenders could hear the din of thousands of enemy voices, as the attackers scrambled up the inclines. Mortar and mountain-gun fire tore into the *grigioverde*, then rifle and machine gun fire. But the Italians were numerous and gained ground; they even threatened to push the defenders from their comfortable positions. Local counterattacks were necessary to restore the situation, and in the end they succeeded.

Undeterred, Mambretti urged his officers to redouble their efforts, and for the next several days wild and confused fighting continued in the smoke and mist, along a front of no more than three kilometers (2 miles). A cut through the main ridge, known as the Agnello Pass[141] was captured, as well as a few of the more southerly heights, but repeated Austrian counters kept the attackers from gaining anything worthwhile. Hötzendorf was soon committing his reserves to the area, and complaining that the enemy had chosen one of the most difficult stretches of frontline to resupply, for his attack. The Italian press had a field day with the Ortigara campaign; soon it had become the second most famous (or infamous) mountain, after San Michele, associated with the war. It need not have bothered. In three weeks of furious fighting, much of which degenerated into savage hand-to-hand combat, Sixth Army failed to accomplish its goals. The summit of Ortigara was in fact captured on the 19th by *Alpini* troops, whose courage and performance is without question, but their foes proved to be equal to the task of defense. On the 25th of the month the mountain top changed hands once again as the Austrians began a series of strong counterattacks designed to regain what little real estate they had lost. These lasted another six days, during which time at least two efforts to recapture Agnello Pass were beaten off with the help of artillery fire. As if to symbolize the expiration of the month, the battle faded away at the end of June. Sixth Army sustained 23,000 casualties in the battles of June; the Austrian units it engaged lost about 9,000 killed and wounded and another 1,000 taken prisoner.[142] One writer on the battle insists that for the Italians, the area of the Ortigara campaign will always be remembered as "la tomba (tomb) degli Alpini or il Calvario (Calvary) degli Alpini".[143]

First Army did what it could to support its neighbor to the east. Diversionary attacks were carried out on June 10th at Tonale Pass, near Chiese in the shadows of Mt. Pasubio, and on the upper Posina near the old frontier. The object, as usual, was to prevent the transfer of enemy reserves to the area of the main attack; the result, as usual, was failure to do so. On the 15th, *Alpini* troops on skis advanced over the snowfields on the Adamello *Massif*, surprised the defenders, capturing some Austria positions, a number of prisoners, and two medium guns. Another action occurred the same day on Mt. Costabella, north of the San Pelegrino Pass. Responding to another Austrian bombardment of Ala on the 27th, First army guns again shelled Calliano on the following day. Artillery fire was in fact the only 'support' Cadorna's two pet armies would contribute to the war in mid to late June, and it was undertaken only occasionally and sporadically, and without much rhyme or reason. The Carso was the recipient of some high explosive, as was the Vodice/Santo area, and on the 28th rail traffic near Santa Lucia was interrupted by damage to the tracks. The only other fighting of any importance along the entire remainder of the front occurred in the Carnic Range, where Italian troops claimed the capture of an obscure crag on remote Piccolo Lagaznoi.[144]

By contrast, the airman of both sides were as busy, or busier, than ever. At this stage of the war, air power had gained the grudging respect of all the High Commands, and air aces were fast becoming the newest heroes-in-arms, as if modern-day versions of medieval knights, whose loyalty, bravery, and gallantry was without question. The summer of 1917 was a great time for many of these men, whose reputations were being enhanced exponentially. Francesco Baracca and his friend and associate Fulco Ruffo continued to claim victims; the latter shot down an Austrian over the Carso on June 7th, the former destroyed his fourteenth enemy airplane near Kostanjevica on July 7th. Kill number fifteen followed on the 31st.[145] Their enemies were no less successful, however. Engaging Italian aircraft involved in support of the Ortigara offensive, Josef Kiss downed one over Asiago on June 10th, then another on the 14th, over nearby Roana. His sixth victory came on July 13th. Stefan Fejes also became an ace that summer. Flying a two-seater over the Wippach Valley, he and his observer accounted for two enemy planes near Sober, but only one could be confirmed, and he was denied ace status for another month, when he scored another victory on July 26th. Airspace over the village of Sober was also the setting for the eleventh and twelfth victims of Adolf Heyrowski on June 26th. And on the Carnic section of the front, Raoul Stojsavljevic was making a reconnaissance run on July 14th, when he was engaged by an Italian fighter. The Austrian won the dogfight, sending the enemy vehicle crashing to the earth between Mts. Crete and Cullar, above the Fella River valley, Nine days later Stojsavljevic was credited with another, his eighth, kill.[146]

Of all 42 months of war on the Italian Front, July 1917 was probably the least active. Both sides were worn down, strategically bankrupt, demoralized and uninterested in fighting, at least for the time being. Artillery actions of course continued, as did the inevitable trench raids, but even these annoyances were reduced in scope. Mostly it was Boroevic who probed, for the purpose of gathering intelligence; a very small-scale attack was delivered on the 9th, against enemy lines west of the Tolmein bridgehead. The biggest Italian initiative was a raid on the 15th on the Carso Plateau, after which a proud announcement of 275 prisoners was made. In general, though, both armies were more than content to rest, regroup, and try to improve their living conditions. Nothing of note occurred out in the Adriatic, either. However, the submarine campaign continued to reap rewards for the *Alliance*. In July another 107,000 tons of *Entente* shipping was sent to the seafloor, and in August the total was over 118,000 tons.[147]

Behind the scenes, the military establishments did continue to evolve however slowly. The Germans had been the first nation to recognize the importance of creating units of specially armed, specially trained assault troops, and on March 2nd, 1915, the first official *Stosstruppen* formations were authorized. The following year Ludendorff himself ordered every German division to raise at least one battalion of these elite soldiers, whose primary task was to lead the way for infantry engaging in offensive operations. This practice soon rubbed off on their allies the Austro-Hungarians, and by early 1917, the latter were training their own *Sturmtruppen* (assault troops). Before long, every division in Karl's army contained hundreds of these fine soldiers, who like their German mentors, were outfitted with equipment deemed most essential when forward movement was desired. In the case of the Austrians, these men carried double food and water rations, a gas mask, a bag each of stick and egg grenades, a dagger and a bayonet, an entrenching tool, wire cutters, and the shorter, carbine version of the infantry rifle with 40 rounds.[148] Had Austria possessed such fine troops at the beginning of her May, 1916 offensive out of the Tyrol, its outcome might have been different.

Only a few *Strumtruppen* had been employed in Italy by summer 1917, but the Italians soon became aware of their presence. Since it was Italy that was the aggressor in this theatre, it was decided at *Commando Supremo* that she, too, needed an equivalent, and the first company began training near Gorizia on June 12th. Within a month, a battalion of *Truppe d'Assalto* was authorized; they were to be ready for Cadorna's next offensive.[149] Soon to be known to their comrades as *Arditi* (intrepid ones), these men were equipped very similarly to their enemy counterparts. They were unique in one regard, however, in that every tenth or so man carried a Villar-Perosa, the world's first mass-produced 'machine pistol', or submachine gun. *Arditi* quickly gained a reputation for being eager to engage in hand-to-hand combat.

Cadorna could hardly expect that innovations such as *Arditi* troops or Italy's growing interest in armored combat vehicles would prove decisive in his quest to attain seemingly unattainable goals. His army was showing signs of the early stages of decay; military desertions, for example had reached the frightening level of 5,000 men a month that summer.[150] Part of the problem was of course his battering-ram strategy and its necessarily lengthy casualty lists. There were other factors at work, though. Principal among these was a growing, worldwide agitation for peace, and despite the fact that pacifism came in many forms and was supported by individuals whose motives were at wide variance, the movement had become a force no longer to be ignored by the middle of 1917. Much talk of peace originated with leaks of information about secret initiatives such as Karl's, and inspired speeches and debates within the political structures of all the leading powers. On June 20th, Baron Sonnino was sufficiently annoyed to deliver a speech in Rome, reiterating the aims for which his country was fighting. Once again he did not reveal the true terms of the Treaty of London. In a prior chapter we saw how he resisted, for months, British and French suggestions for an 'Inter-Allied Conference' in Paris, and it was not until the latter finally was convened on July 25th that his allies could privately inform him, by way of showing him all of the correspondence, of the Sixte affair. When at last he had been fully briefed, the Baron's mood did not improve; he resented the idea of a separate peace because such would have had the effect of cancelling his self-styled crowning achievement, the London Treaty. Sonnino had gone to Paris to talk war, not peace. Thereafter, he suspected (probably correctly) that Giolitti was behind the idea of a separate peace, and he believed that now he would need to struggle with his new rival for the attention of the King.

Unfortunately for Europe, very little of the hot air released in Paris in late July addressed the recent sincere efforts for peace, or the increasing need for it. The Western Front remained unbroken, despite three years of the best intentions of the British and French. Ditto the Italian Front, where eleven major attacks by Italy and one by Austria had failed to make much of an impression. According to the High Commands of both warring groups, the Balkan fronts were useless sideshows (so why did they continue to maintain large numbers of troops there?). The war against Turkey could never achieve anything of importance (again, why bother?). At sea the fortunes of war were too depressing to consider. America could do little for the *Entente*, at least in 1917. And worst of all, the one and only offensive of the Provisional Government on the Eastern Front had ended in disaster, with tens of thousands of Russian soldiers flinging away their weapons and running off to desertion. These were indeed dark days for the *Entente*.

Even before the Conference at Paris convened, Cadorna had renewed his request for ten British or French divisions for his theatre, plus more heavy artillery. This time the message was delivered in such a manner as to imply that the French, who so far had been unresponsive, were perhaps jealous of possible Italian success. The implication was that Paris did not want to see Rome defeat the Austrians before it had defeated the Germans.[151] The Chief knew that the British Prime Minister was at least sympathetic; he had been urging a combined offensive in Italy since the winter. Apparently the barb had some effect on the Paris talks, as the French, without further ado, promised six batteries of big guns for use in Italy. However, the obstinate British Chief of the Imperial General Staff, Sir William Robertson, flatly rejected the idea of sending any troops to support Cadorna. Robertson was a firm supporter of Haig, who always panicked at any ideas which might deprive him of every last soldier he 'needed'. Haig's ideas were reducible to a simple formula, which he recorded in his diary as the only "sound plan to follow. 1. Send to France every possible man. 2. Send to France every possible aeroplane. 3. Send to France every possible gun".[152]

The formula was not unlike that of Cadorna, with regard to his Isonzo front, and it was welcomed by Foch, who had taken over French strategic planning, and was anxious to cure all manifestations of mutiny in the army before France could commit herself to any new adventures. Having felt somewhat stung by their allies, the Italians departed Paris without much satisfaction.

A second Inter-Allied Conference of the summer took place in London on August 7th and 8th. This time Lloyd George had a new ally pressing for an offensive against Austria-Hungary. Baron Sonnino had been maneuvered into a position from which he now had no choice but to advocate a fight to the finish, a victory-or-defeat stance; those of his countrymen who would have preferred a negotiated peace represented the only viable alternative to this point of view, and all other possibilities had been swept away in the rising tide of political polarization. Nevertheless, the idea of a decision in Italy was still considered preposterous by the hard-line Western Fronters, and even Cadorna's representative in London, General Albricci, wanted to stall any multinational enterprises until 1918. Albricci went on to say that Italy would attack again in the near future, using all the artillery lent from the West. Led by Robertson and Haig, an effort to squash any idea of an Italian Front attack for 1917 easily succeeded, and once again the head-butting, battering-ram boys would be allowed to squander British, French, and Italian lives.

Even Austria's overbearing ally Germany was not immune from convulsions for peace that summer. Her military position had never been stronger, and many Germans felt the hour appropriate to bargain from a position of strength. A follow-up to the peace proposal of the past December was desired and enjoyed widespread support. With Russia virtually defeated, German troops everywhere on foreign soil, and the U. S. A. not ready for battle, the time for a now-or-never negotiated peace seemed ripe. Chancellor Bethmann Hollweg was certainly leaning towards talking, but Ludendorff held the real power in the nation, and the Chancellor was replaced by a man more willing to tow the military line. The new man's first speech indicated a guarded readiness to talk peace, but was pounced upon by the *Entente* leaders as proof that Germany's real rulers were not sincere about ending the war. They demanded, as usual, a number of preconditions (German gains to be forfeited) be met before negotiations could commence. When the Germans once again refused to give up anything without receiving something in return, the move fell flat. Thereafter the *Entente* governments refused to parley with their enemies until the latter had changed their government to one suitable in the minds of the former. Historians have ever since glossed over this outrageous stance, generally preferring to parrot the wartime *Entente* leadership by referring to German exertions for peace as 'vague and insincere'. A comparison might reasonably be made to campaigns to negotiate the end of the Vietnam War of the nineteen-seventies, if the Vietnamese government had demanded, as a preliminary to talks, that the American people topple their own administration and replace it with a Communist regime more amenable to enemy sympathies.[153]

Peace never had a chance in the summer of 1917, or at any time thereafter. The war was to be fought to a conclusive military victory, despite the contrary sentiments of millions of people on both sides of the fighting.

Into this atmosphere came, on August 16th, another sincere quest to end the insanity, this time from no less a moral authority than the Vatican. Once again taking the initiative as he had three years earlier, Benedict XVI addressed the belligerent governments, deploring the years of bloodletting and calling for them to consider proposals which could lead to 'a just and lasting peace'. The pontiff suggested mutual disarmament, a restoration of political subdivisions as they had existed before the war, international freedom of the seas, and other conciliatory moves designed to allow all of the powers to stop fighting yet save face. As the Vatican did not enjoy formal relations with three of the major *Entente* nations (France, Italy, and the United States), these had to be handed the proposal through the British offices. The French appeared to yawn, suggesting a collective response by all of the allies. In Italy, Sonnino did not care to reply. What was left of a semblance of authority in Russia considered the Pope's ideas 'pro-German'. In Britain, where any mention of 'freedom of the seas' was bound to provoke suspicion, the attitude was 'thanks, but no thanks'. And President Wilson in the United States, after considerable delay, finally responded in polite and respectful tones; he politely and respectfully wrote the Pope that the German government could not be negotiated with. Benedict had long been accused of favoring the *Alliance* (because of the close ties between the Vatican and the Habsburgs); like all other efforts to reign-in a world gone mad, the papal peace more was denounced as somehow favorable to the Germans when, if anything, it was more favorable to the *Entente*, which stood to regain a lot of lost ground, while the *Alliance* would only Recover the German colonies and a few bits and pieces in Europe, such as those that the Italians had captured. Clearly, the Cadornas and the Sonninos had gotten the upper hand in Italy. The Giolittis had lost. For the Austro-Hungarians, there was no longer any choice. Karl knew he would have to bind his Empire ever tighter to his stronger northern partner. The Habsburg Empire would sink or swim with that of the Hohenzollerns.

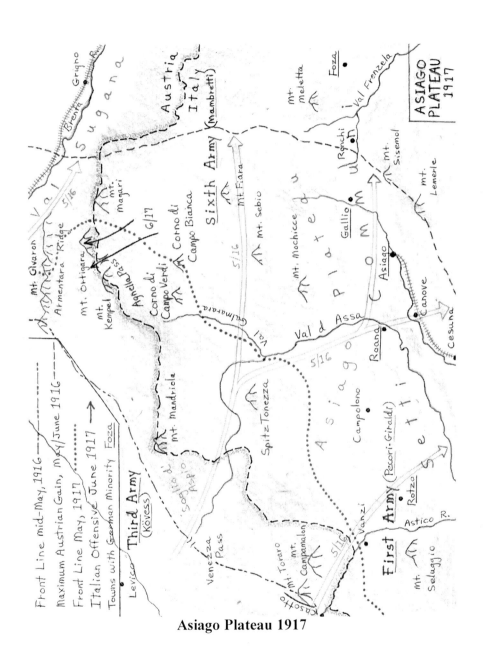

Asiago Plateau 1917

Chapter Nine
The Roles Are Reversed

Now it was August, 1917. On the Italian Front the weather was hot and dry, yet about as comfortable as the soldiers stationed along the lines could expect; at least it was not raining and no one, except a relative few unfortunate enough to be posted on the glacier-clad mountains towards the Swiss border, was freezing. Water levels in the streams were low, allowing for easy fording, and a general lack of surface pools, puddles, and mud translated into fewer insects to battle and smaller numbers of men laid low by disease. Thirst was no particular problem, since the absence of major operations meant adequate opportunity for the engineers to set up water supply systems undisturbed except for the occasional lucky shot from the infrequent, random barrages. More or less left alone to improve upon defensive strong points or living quarters or to conduct the endless routine patrols, the private soldiers on both sides easily settled into roles of passivity and were content to receive new weapons and equipment, and to integrate replacement troops to their units.

Beneath the fairly tranquil surface, the increasing pressure of war-weariness was making itself felt. For the Italians, gung-ho troops like the new *Arditi* were a minority by now; most average infantrymen were having a hard time reconciling themselves to their predicament. Class-consciousness in Italy was nearly as marked as that in Russia, where army morale had all but evaporated. Officers, ever of the wealthier strains of society, were more resented than ever before, and they had never been popular with the mostly agrarian *grigioverde*. Letters and rumors from the home front told of terrible privation due to lack of fuel and a host of foodstuffs. More and more women were entering the workforce, yet still unable, thanks to runaway inflation, to make ends meet. Better educated industrial workers and administrators became popular targets of biting sarcasm. Any males who for whatever reason had not been conscripted to share in the dangers of common soldiers were denounced as criminals who enjoyed the benefits of high wartime wages, safe and secure employment, and a lonely female population anxious for companionship. Tales of strikes and riots in the cities did not impress the troops; they knew a firing squad awaited all who urged indiscipline in the army, while a striker was likely to be forgiven, if not rewarded with higher pay or better working conditions. Consequently, desertion increased sharply that summer. Most deserters simply wanted to go home, instead of facing enemy machine guns in hopeless assaults, and most tried to make their way back using stealth and deception as tools. Others, not wanting to risk detection and execution, gave themselves up to the enemy, a fate they believed equated at least to survival.

Morale was not much better on the Austro-Hungarian side of the front, where men shared many of the same complaints as their enemies, though usually for different reasons. Officers were not generally hated as a group, but the multinational nature of the Habsburg Army ensured that units of men speaking one language often were led by commanders who spoke another, and certain resentments were inevitable. For example, Romanian troops disliked being bossed by Hungarian speakers; Czechs often resisted commands coming in German. Additionally, as more and more of the multi-lingual officers were killed off, many units became unable to understand their leaders. As the war progressed, the various ethnic groups began to think in terms of nationalistic aspirations, and the more extreme advocates of these were less and less troubled at the idea of an Austro-Hungarian defeat. But the biggest problem faced by Karl's legions in Italy was the endless defensive nature of their fight. No sooner had they established themselves in new positions by digging trenches, sighting machine gun nests, establishing communications, and the like, than a fierce enemy artillery barrage was undertaken, and all of their efforts obliterated in a matter of hours. They knew that the barrage would kill a certain number of them, the attacks would kill a certain number of them, and the remainder would be ordered to initiate a dangerous counterattack, or a series of counterattacks, after which most of the original unit would be casualties. Since the enemy would never cease his attacks, and since they themselves were never strong enough to launch a major offensive of their own, the prospects for surviving the war seemed slight. If they did not fight, the hated enemy would win, but if they did fight, they would be killed or crippled and the enemy might win anyway. In addition, they were constantly outnumbered, outgunned, out-supplied. Historians have rarely been kind in evaluating the worth of the Austro-Hungarian armed forces, but with even a most basic examination of the facts, one cannot help wondering how these soldiers were able to maintain their grim determination to resist the enemy. After eleven major attacks in two-and-one-quarter years, ten on the Isonzo alone, Austrian forces on the Italian Front were still holding their own, and then without hope of relief.

At the offices of *Commando Supremo* in Udine, Luigi Cadorna was already planning an eleventh battle on the Isonzo. He was well aware of all the failed peace moves by now, but uninterested; he was also well aware of the serious decline in morale in his armies, and only somewhat more interested. Certain that all the trouble was the work of cowards, traitors, and spies, he felt that what was needed was another attack. This time, of course, things would be different. Tenth Isonzo, the most powerful of all prior offensives, had been almost successful, and ground gained; for a completely successful breakthrough all that was required was more men, more guns, more of everything. This time he would destroy the enemy and advance to Trieste. Accordingly, he gathered the largest attack force yet assembled in his theatre for the war. By this time he disposed of 67 divisions, only one shy of the highest total that Italy would ever achieve in the war (68 for October-November 1917). Of these, 52 would be thrown at the Isonzo,[154] split between Second and Third Armies once again. Capello's 'Gorizia Army', having failed in its debut performance, was disbanded, and 'The Butcher' given control of Second Army, the group that would spearhead the attack. Backing up this three-quarters-of-a-million man force lurked 3,400 field pieces, including the British and French contingents, and 1,700 mortars.[155] This massive grouping was to advance over a broad front, from Tolmein in the north to the sea, a distance of some 56 kilometers (35 miles). An advance up the Idria River Valley with the left wing was vaguely conceived, to be met with the vanguard of the right, coming east through the Ternovanerwald.

Eighty-five kilometers (53 miles) to the southeast of Udine lay the town of Adelsburg, on the railroad between Trieste and Laibach, and slightly closer to the former. This little Slovene locality was the site of the headquarters of Svetozar Boroevic, the man still in command of Isonzo Army and still charged with preventing further enemy inroads to *Küstenland*. Boroevic continued to direct the lion's share of Austrian strength on the front; he could county twenty of the twenty-nine total divisions in Italy, a force that should have fielded 2,000 guns, but all his units were under-strength and the real count probably did not much exceed 1,500. Moreover, these weapons were still under-munitioned, an indication of just how seriously the national economy was being strained; they had, after all, had two months of relative inactivity in which to have been resupplied. But transportation had become a problem. Austria had nowhere near the number of trucks as the Italians possessed, and even horses, now regularly being killed for their meat in the interior of the country, were in short supply. To make matters worse, the enemy bombing campaign against railroads and stations, was beginning to slow train traffic, and manpower and materials for repair-crews was scarce. Frontline soldiers lacked sufficient quantities of everything from water bottles to hand grenades and all other essentials for fighting off a major attack. Boroevic, it may be recalled, had always been loathe to give up ground, and insisted that every meter lost be regained in counterattacks. Now, for the first time, he doubted the wisdom of his own strategy, and was prepared to retreat slightly, if absolutely necessary. First indications of a massive enemy buildup began to reach Adelsberg in July, and by the end of the first week of August, Isonzo Army was bracing for the impact of sudden bombardment.

As both armies awaited the countdown to the offensive, air activity logically increased. On August 2nd, an Austrian reconnaissance plane was shot down by ace Lieutenant Colonel Pier Ruggiero Piccio. The unfortunate Austrian was forced to crash-land, a gamble from which he walked away unhurt. His name was Frank Linke-Crawford and he would not shoot down an airplane of his own for another few weeks, but would eventually rank fourth in total kills, among Habsburg airmen.[156] Piccio would live to rank third for Italy. A day later, on the 3rd, Francesco Baracca and Flavio Baracchini shared a 'kill' near Mt. Nero. For Baracca, it was victim number sixteen.[157] Waves of big Caproni bombers were regularly sent to attack Austrian targets, particularly the railroads, and one of their favorite destinations that summer had become the branch line that ran eastward from the Idria River junction with the Isonzo at Santa Lucia. Benno Fiala was able to shoot down one of these machines on August 10th, as it returned from doing its devilish duty. The following day he destroyed a reconnaissance plane, and on the 19th another Caproni became his sixth victory over the Carso near Fajti Hrib.[158] Even this impressive performance was outdone by Fiala's squadron leader, Godwin Brumowsky, who is believed to have accounted for eighteen Italian aircraft during the month. Several of Brumowski's kills could not be confirmed, however; even so, before August was over he had wrung up a score of twenty confirmed victories.[159] By comparison, Italy's leading ace Francesco Baracca achieved his seventeenth, over the Carso on the 19th.

Another sizeable Caproni raid hit the Idria valley railroad and stations again on the 11th, and this time caused considerable damage. No doubt somewhat frustrated, Boroevic retaliated by sending three dozen Austrian bombers to attack Venice, a deed done on the 14th. The island-city had been bombed many, many times before, and a large percentage of the populace had long since evacuated into the countryside, but this raid of mid-August seemed to annoy the remaining citizenry more so than had previous attacks. They, like the soldiers at the front, were tired of the war, and were not much consoled when the official damage report, issued shortly thereafter, boasted of two of the raiders having been shot down.

Boroevic was somewhat surprised as the fine flying weather of early to mid-August came and went without bringing the expected enemy offensive. Normally possessed of a much calmer demeanor, he now paced about the rooms and grounds of his headquarters, lunging at every intelligence report as it was received and constantly reminding his subordinates to check and double-check with the front commanders to be sure every possible defensive measure had been implemented. It seemed as though the Isonzo Army boss was having as many doubts about his ability to continue to hold ground, as his counterpart Cadorna was having about his own ability to conquer it. The waiting was agonizing for all of the Austrians, but every man from Boroevic on down to the lowliest private knew that the real agony would begin only when the attack was delivered. At the end of the second full week of August, their wait was over.

Two hours past midnight on Saturday the 18th, Cadorna's gunners were given their orders to fire. The night was hot, and before long the artillerymen were soaked in sweat, as they rammed round after round into the gun-breeches, tossing the warm, empty casings to the side, into piles which steadily grew in height and spread out in circumference. So intense was the barrage that individual explosions were not discernable; the terrifying roar was like a hundred simultaneous drum-rolls magnified a hundred times over. As had long been the case during these bombardments, all traces of human interference upon the landscape around the Austrian front lines was soon obliterated, pounded and ground into a fine dust which quickly mixed with the smoke of detonations to form an eerie veil over the countryside. Absence of even a moderate breeze meant that the grey pall hung over the tortured ground, where even dud shells were exploded by the dozens of others falling in the same location. Trapped in their man-made caves, tunnels and mines, the only way the Austrian defenders could survive this choking, scorching inferno was by the use of their gas masks. Even so, hundreds of hapless soldiers either smothered or were burned to death. For tens of kilometers distant, the earth shook from the pummeling, while terrified soldiers and civilians alike waited in silence, hoping, praying that the war would come no nearer.

Eighteen hours after it had so abruptly begun, the shelling stopped, shortly following the sunset. Capello's intention was to send his infantry across the Isonzo under cover of darkness, and for that purpose fourteen bridges[160] were frantically thrown across the relatively low water of late summer, ten of which were designed for infantrymen only. These were usable by first light on the 19th when the true assaults began. This, the only stretch of river still overlooked by Austrian guns (except that north of Mt. Rombon), extended from about two kilometers north of Plava to a couple more north of Tolmein, and it was here that the Italians had correctly assessed the enemy line to be the most vulnerable. Accordingly, Capello sent wave upon wave of infantry, including two *Bersaglieri* brigades opposite and south of the town of Canale up the eastern banks of the stream, against under-strength and underequipped Czech defenders. The Czechs acquitted themselves well, but were quickly overwhelmed. Before the day was done a breakthrough had been achieved. Now nothing could stop Capello's men from swarming all over an area known as the Bainsizza Plateau. An upland between the Isonzo gorge and a cut called the Val Chiapovano, the Bainsizza is not really a plateau at all, rather a hilly, wooded region of few villages and even fewer good roads. Its southern section, around the village of the same name, is really an extension of the Ternovanerwald, but is separated from the main portion of the latter by a vale through which a decent road ran from Salcano, on the Isonzo just north of Gorizia, over the ridge between Mts. Santo and San Gabriele, and into Val Chiapovano, thence around the upland to rejoin the Isonzo at St. Lucia. If the entire Bainsizza 'Plateau' were overrun, the Austrians could logically still fall back to the Val, and dig in on its eastern heights, without losing anything of essence except Mt. Santo, which as we have seen was barely being held anyway.

It was in fact about to be lost. Besides the attacks near Canale, Capello hurled several more divisions into the hills east of Plava, towards the southern half of the Bainsizza. Other units attacked from Vodice, trying to outflank Mt. Santo from the north. Although the defenders somehow managed to contain all these moves on the 19th, they were strained to the limit, and with their communications in shambles, all hope of reinforcement was forlorn. Bitter fighting raged all around the mountain for several more days, during which frequent Italian barrages further weakened the exhausted men doggedly holding the line, but in the end, they too were overrun and outflanked. A few dazed survivors staggered back to Austrian positions farther to the east, on August 24th; the vast majority of Santo's defenders chose to die fighting rather than surrender. Since most of these men were south Slavs, their determination and dedication to their cause provides a shining example of just how false is the often-perpetrated myth that the many Slavic nationalities of Austria-Hungary were less than willing to fight for their country.

Second Army's left hand, or most northerly attacking Corps was given the task of eliminating the enemy bridgehead opposite Tolmein, which if accomplished, would have completely shoved Isonzo Army away from all points on the stream south of the spine of the Julian Alps. Despite an all-day battle on the 19th, it could not advance in the face of accurate and sustained enemy artillery and small-arms fire. The Tolmein bridgehead would remain Austrian, as it had for the previous ten battles, until the end of the war.

Third Army's strike on the 19th was nearly as powerful as that of the Second, carried out as it was by twelve full-strength divisions; its breadth of front was much more restricted, however, and the preparatory barrage was, if anything, even more intense. Austrian defensive positions on the Carso simply ceased to exist, and the assaulting infantry entered a moonscape chillingly similar in appearance to the Western Front. Enough of the German, Hungarian and Polish defenders had survived, however, to make most of the attacks stagger, stumble, and stop. Only in one location—around the ruins of the town of Selo—was much ground gained and even there the advance was limited to a maximum of about a half-kilometer. Nevertheless, Boroevic's southern wing was seriously hampered by the shelling of heavy guns, including the British batteries stationed near Lake Doberdo, and by Italian and British warships in the Gulf, whose weapons blasted the coastal road and railroad, and the southern Carso. Fierce battles in the Jamiano/Flondar area weakened both sides, but Boroevic had few reserves with which to relieve his frontline units. And of the more than 200[161] Italian airplanes committed to the offensive, the majority flew over the easier ground nearest the sea, and made all movement on the Austrian side of the line extremely treacherous. Unwilling to risk the wrath of Cadorna lest he disappoint, Aosta continued his attacks, despite a marked lack of progress.

On August 21st Aosta once again attempted to break through along the coast, and outflank the entire western Carso. Here, Monfalcone was a mere three kilometers (2 miles) distant; the line had hardly moved east at all since the first week of the war. The little Timano River still represented the front line and the once-proud villages of San Giovanni and Medeazza had been reduced to a few broken bricks amidst scraps of charred wood. So-called 'Mt.' Hermada, a 323 meter (1,060 feet) high hill overlooked the coast here and was so thoroughly fortified that it absolutely needed to be taken, before any drive to Trieste could be contemplated. Once Boroevic became convinced that his enemy was serious about securing the hill, he sent an entire division to reinforce the troops whose ranks were being steadily depleted, and the critical hill was held. A counterattack even recaptured some of the approaches to Hermada, including the ghostly remains of what had been the village of Flondar. As if to spite the defensive success of the Austrians, the warships in the Gulf turned their attention to other points along the coast road, including Trieste, which was shelled as well as bombed, repeatedly. Infrastructure in the city was soon destroyed, habitation became increasingly dangerous, and on the 28th, Straussenberg was moved to order the evacuation of the entire civilian population.[162] Sadly, the mostly Italian-speaking citizenry took to flight from their beloved homes, seeking shelter and relief somewhere within the Slavic and German portions of the Austrian half of the Empire.

Meanwhile, on the afternoon of August 24th King Vittorio Emanuele, who had been observing the capture of Mt. Santo through field glasses, was called to the summit to celebrate Italian custody of the 'Holy Mountain'. To the stirring strains of martial music played by a band led by Arturo Toscanini, who had once directed at the Metropolitan Opera House in New York, and cheers of 'Avanti Savoia' shouted from thousands of voices, the King accepted honors from his admirers, while Cadorna's artillery was already pounding the next peak to the southeast, Mt. San Gabriele.

Italian Postcard Proclaims "Long Live Italian Trieste."
Vittorio Emanuele Is Pictured in the Insert Photo.

Ironically, another monarch was also inspecting the fighting, but from the other side of the front. *Kaiser* Karl, who had surprised Boroevic during the Tenth Battle, now made another appearance at Adelsberg during the Eleventh. Boroevic begged Karl to use all of his influence to prevail upon the Germans to allow further reinforcement to be sent to the Isonzo; he also stoically predicted disaster for Isonzo Army if help did not arrive at once. Karl listened patiently, professed his empathy, and promised to intervene. He then traveled to the front, arriving in time to witness the battle for San Gabriele. Profoundly disturbed by the entire experience, the Emperor returned to Laibach shortly thereafter, resolving to help Boroevic in his own way. On August 25th General Waldstatten[163] was ordered to travel to German headquarters on the Western Front and somehow, someway convince Hindenburg and Ludendorff of the necessity of major reinforcement for the Italian Front. Karl also wrote a personal appeal to *Kaiser* Wilhelm, asking his brother-in-arms to apply pressure on his senior commanders, and stressing the urgency of the situation.

While the monarchs celebrated and soul-searched, Italian troops completed the occupation of the Bainsizza upland. Broken, wooded terrain and lack of roads impeded the operation which was not undertaken without considerable fighting. A ridge featuring a central peak known as Jelenik was overcome; another spine overlooking the Val Chiapovano rises to 945 meters (3,100 feet) and was only taken after heavy, close-quarter combat. The advance generally spread from Northwest to Southeast, and in an effort to flank the defenders in the southern portions behind the Kuk/Vodice/Santo ridge, Capello deployed a cavalry unit with orders to ride up the Salcano road through the Ternovanerwald and take the Austrians in rear. The luckless horsemen had not even reached the height of land dividing the Isonzo and Chiapovano valleys when they were stopped by heavy enemy fire and forced to retreat. Even so, Boroevic had no more reserves to spare for a defense of the meaningless Bainsizza upland, and he reluctantly authorized a withdrawal to the ridge on the east side of the Val Chiapovano. The Salcano-St. Lucia road was now pretty much the front line, and Mt. San Gabriele was now exposed from the northwest, east, and south east. Few could doubt what Capello's next move would be.

In fact the battle for Mt. San Gabriele had already begun as early as the 24th, when concentrated artillery fire heralded wave after wave of assaults, which were consistently beaten off. The next day the Italians tried again with the same result. For the 26th, Capello ordered another massive bombardment, followed by yet more infantry charges, all of which were shot up before they could approach the summit. The following morning hosted an even longer barrage, of several hours duration, punctuated by more assaults. All the shelling did of course take a terrible toll of the defenders, but it also had the effect of clearing what had been a semi-wooded mountain into a bare-sided incline on which attackers were easy to identify, once the smoke had cleared. For two more agonizing days this repetitive drama of bombardment and attack was played out on the slopes of San Gabriele, which the abused Italian troops began to refer to as *il monte del morte* (the mountain of death).[164] The exhausted Isonzo Army defenders might well have also considered it their own *Totenberg*; one contemporary source states that 247 Italian airplanes[165] assisted the ground troops in these battles. On the 28th, a forty-plane strong force of Caproni bombers attacked suspected enemy artillery emplacements hidden in a nearby forest.

Throughout the Eleventh Battle, Hötzendorf's group in the Tyrol did little in the way of 'diversionary' attacks so typical of earlier battles. No doubt the veteran recognized the utter worthlessness of such wasteful moves, and what little action as did take place was of the local probing variety. In the Lagarina Valley an enterprise which can only be characterized as a large-scale trench raid occurred on the night of the 19th/20th, and in the Carnic Alps Austrian artillery fired slowly but steadily for several days. On August 28th, *Alpen* troops pushed the Italians out of a few frozen positions near the Stelvio Pass, and the next day a small-scale attack behind artillery fire struck Fourth Army units in the lower Travenanzes Valley. None of these movements attracted more than a glance from the high commands of either side.

For his part, Cadorna was beginning to despair of the whole messy business of war against Austria. His most recent and most powerful offensive of the war had clearly stalled by the end of the month of August. All of the manpower and all of the weaponry that his nation had entrusted to him had failed once again to deliver the expected victory, despite the impressive gains of ground on the Bainsizza, and to a much lesser extent, on the Carso. Typically, his first reaction was for more resources with which to work, and about August 30th, he contacted Foch with a request for more big guns. To his initial surprise, the Frenchman was agreeable, and offered 100 pieces[166], but subsequently stalled, citing the need to consult with the British. Cadorna knew Lloyd George would be agreeable as well; the Prime Minister had long wanted to divert a strong attack force to Italy. Unfortunately the red tape ensured that it would be weeks before the guns arrived, so for the time being, Second and Third Armies would have to make do with what they already possessed.

Even as Cadorna wavered in his resolve, both sides prepared to renew the battle, which had never really waned away, but had degenerated into a slugfest between small groups of men for the ownership of some nameless crag or some surviving stand of trees. Boroevic was gathering every available soldier for a series of counterattacks against awkward positions on the new front line. His air arm continued to serve him well, despite the fact that it was depleted, and by now heavily outnumbered. A new pilot, Eugen Bönsch was credited with his first air victory over Mt. San Gabriele on September 1st. Raoul Stojsavljevic claimed a ninth victim on the 7th.[167]

The first of Boroevic's counters was unleashed on the morning of the 4th, behind a short, but most violent, barrage. Two divisions swept forward from Mt. Hermada and drove in Aosta's right wing, capturing over 6,000 prisoners[168] before midday and eliminating all danger of a breakthrough along the coast. Capello had also chosen the early morning of the 4th to resume his drive on Mt. San Gabriele, and here the Italians were nearly as successful as their enemies were being to the west of Hermada. Spearheaded by the new *Arditi* troops, the attack soon gained the summit, along with 1,500 surrendering Austrian soldiers. Horrified, Boroevic quickly ordered all available artillery brought to bear on the mountain, and counterattacked. Thus began a week-long struggle for the possession of the top of this otherwise unimportant height. The scale of the effort easily dwarfed that in the bids to capture Mt. San Michele, Mt. Ortigara, or Mt. Santo; countless thousands of corpses littered the slopes and summit of that awful location. Probably, success at Mt. San Gabriele had become a matter of pride and principle for both armies, or at least both commanders, and no amount of sacrifice was too great to prevail there. When first one side would seem to gain the advantage at the mountaintop, the other would bombard the place with every means at its disposal. Finally, Capello had had enough of the carnage and ordered all of his artillery to shell the summit into oblivion, and for three days the fury of bombardment literally tore away the mountaintop, sending tons and tons of material rolling or sliding down the sides, not entirely unlike the action of a volcanic eruption. No one on either side of the line who witnessed this unbelievable spectacle expected that any living thing on that mountain could have survived such a cataclysm. They were proven wrong on September 11th, when fresh Italian infantry were directed to occupy the summit and met fierce resistance from Austrian troops who had somehow weathered the storm deep within their caves and tunnels. Three additional days of combat proved indecisive, until strong Austrian counterattacks on the 14th and 15th finally shoved Capello's men down the mountain. The weather then turned warmer, and the stench of decaying flesh overpowered those still alive, and prevented further fighting. Mt. San Gabriele remained Austrian.

Concurrent with Capello's drive of September 4th came waves of Italian aircraft, determined to support the ground forces. One group of bombers attacked Pola, Austria's chief naval base, on the 4th. Warships also shelled the port at the same time, hoping to do some damage amidst the confusion, before the crews of the big battleships anchored there could assume battle stations. Raids like this were at first more aggravating than damaging, but as the war progressed, they became more frequent, and therefore more dangerous. Pola would be bombed at least twice more in September, on the 27th and on the 29th. Trieste was suffering even more raids; these were aimed at the railroad facilities but often struck the city proper. The Austrians tried to retaliate by attacking Venice, a favorite target of theirs because it represented everything Italian, and the city was hit on the 5th, 6th, 7th and 9th of the month. Another raid on the 29th was forced to abort the mission, dropping their cargoes instead on Monfalcone and Aquileia. Italian fighter aircraft also caused a good deal of carnage to ground targets, and they accounted for many enemy aircraft as well. A pilot who had been flying for six years, Giovanni Sabelli, shot down an Austrian over the Ternovanerwald on September 6th, and veteran ace Baracca shared a kill with up-and-coming Lieutenant Luigi Olivari over the Julian Alps on the 16th.[169] Julius Arigi achieved his 13th victory for Austria-Hungary on the 15th, while dogfighting near Gorizia. For the Eleventh Battle of the Isonzo, Chief Cadorna had pretty much kept his silence, preferring to allow Aosta and especially Capello to conduct operations and to make all of the strategic decisions. Perhaps he no longer believed in his own abilities or strategy; perhaps he was willing to allow his army commanders to try to do better without any interference. Whatever the case, he broke his long silence on September 18th, ordering all further offensive activity to be suspended. Without a doubt this command came as a great relief to Aosta, and probably to Capello as well, whose army was utterly exhausted. Cadorna then informed the British and French that Italy would undertake no more strategic attacks for the remainder of the calendar year. It was probably his way of saying that the Western Powers could keep the guns and supplies he had previously requested, and that the Italian Army, like that of the French, was desperately in need of a long resting period during which it could recuperate, rebuild, and recover its waning morale. The statement was not challenged by London or Paris, whose leaders could hardly complain about inactivity on the Italian Front, a theatre they had repeatedly preferred to ignore. The guns that Foch had promised two weeks before were, of course, recalled (they were already in transit) for use in the West. Up until the end of September, 1917, Cadorna had sacked "217 generals, 255 colonels, and 335 battalion commanders"[170] for failure to comply with his whims. Following Eleventh Isonzo, he may have mentally dismissed himself.

In terms of numbers of troops and equipment involved, as well as in casualties, the Eleventh Battle had been the largest yet, larger even than the Tenth, which had easily eclipsed all of the others. In time Italy would officially list her losses as 166,000 men killed, wounded or missing. Of the latter category the Austrians claimed to have captured 9,000. Austro-Hungarian losses are unknown; estimates range from 85,000 to 110,000. Rome insisted that its troops had taken nearly 31,000 prisoners, 150 artillery pieces, 100 mortars and well over 300 machine guns, and there is little reason to doubt this claim. The blow to the Italian armed forces was staggering, but given time, it could be made good. On the other hand, the damage to Boroevic's command—the equivalent of eight or ten entire divisions wiped off the order of battle, nearly three divisions in prisoners alone—was a wound which could only be healed as a result of the greatest care over an extended time-period. Under no circumstances could Isonzo Army take another punch from Cadorna for many months to come, at least for the foreseeable future. Every year so far in the war, Cadorna had attacked well into November, and Boroevic had no information which led him to believe that this year would be any different. During the lull of late September he could only speculate as to the fate of his army. Drawing on his experience he reasoned that he would either be heavily reinforced, or he would be defeated.

Elsewhere about the front in September, fighting was very limited. West of Lake Garda, Austrians probed Italian lines in the Concei Valley on the 7th, without result. Three days later they tried again, behind an artillery preparation and gained a few trenches until counterattacked only hours later.[171] On the 15th, energetic barrages into the upper But and Fella River valleys in Carnia caused the Italian troops nearby to brace for an attack that never came. Extensive tunneling efforts by Fourth Army units on huge Mt. Marmolada culminated in a giant explosion in the wee hours of the 22nd, which tore a huge gouge into the *Massif*, allowing for an improvement in the Italian positions there. Marmolada, like so many other mountains along the front line, had come to resemble an elevated version of some Western Front battlefield, complete with an endless honeycomb of trenches, dugouts (perhaps blast-outs is more accurate) barbed wire and the like, and devoid of vegetation yet littered with all the debris of 20th Century war. Burying bodies on these peaks was practically impossible, so whenever possible corpses were transported down the slopes; when not possible, they were often covered by piles of stones. Two days following the blast in the Dolomites, it was the Austrian's turn to partially destroy a topographic feature when they detonated a mine drilled into Italian-held ground on Mt. Nero in the Julians. Once again, hundreds of tons of shattered rock were lifted from the peak to tumble down the slopes, smashing trees and shrubs and crushing men and machines which happened to be in the way. The Italians were quick to insist that 'no advantage' had been achieved by the enemy for the Nero blast; one might reasonably have asked whether any 'advantage' had been gained by either side thus far in two and one-half years of fighting. By September 27th the worst of the combat on both Mt. Nero and Mt. Marmolada was over. The snow season had begun, and both armies were compelled to restrict all movement.

Improving the front line positions with respect to winter quartering was also the motive for a series of relatively minor Italian attacks east of the Isonzo during the last few days of the month. Once again the Bainsizza upland, Mt. San Gabriele, and the Carso area were scenes of Italian assaults, albeit on a much smaller scale than before. When they, and the inevitable counters were over, Rome announced the capture of another 2,000 enemy troops. Vienna did not comment.

September 23rd was a day of fine flying weather, and both sides were active. Italian airplanes and dirigibles bombed the railroad and stations in the Idria Valley again, as well as enemy troop concentrations in the Chiapovano Valley. To the south, over the Carso, Ernst Strohschneider destroyed two enemy planes, one a reconnaissance machine and one a fighter. Frank Linke-Crawford became an ace that day when he outfought an Italian seaplane over Grado, on the coast. Strohschneider needed three more days to become an ace himself. On September 26th, he dispatched a SPAD for his fifth kill.[172] Other aces were in the making. Eugen Bönsch survived both enemy airplane and ground fire to shoot down an observation balloon in the Plava area on the 28th, then destroyed an Italian fighter in the same area on the very next day. Kurt Gruber scored victory number four behind the enemy lines over Cormons, on the 29th.[173]

The relative calm of late September 1917 along the Italian Front was deceptive. Behind the scenes, the wheels of change were turning, and gaining momentum. Waldstatten's appeals to Ludendorff had not much impressed the German general, who had also become hypnotized by the prospects of success in the West, but to satisfy Straussenberg, a plan to assist Austria in Italy was hastily drawn up and submitted to the Habsburg Chief on the 29th of August.[174] Hindenburg, the figurehead warlord, approved the plan and ordered General Otto von Below, a competent veteran of both Eastern and Western Fronts to be prepared to take command of a new army in Italy if any possibility of success there could be determined. Below in turn sent General Krafft von Dellmensingen, one of Germany's foremost experts in mountain warfare, to the Isonzo area to survey the ground and make a report on the chances of success for offensive action designed to relieve Boroevic. With winter approaching, time was of the essence. Dellmensingen hurried to the front, made his observations, spoke with a few local commanders, then reported. His submission stressed the difficulties of build-up and supply in the rugged terrain, absence of good roads and other communications, and the inability to count on reasonably good weather for a battle of movement so late in the season. "Success", he wrote, "lives only just on the border of possibility".[175] It was hardly a summation likely to instill enthusiasm in the minds of its readers.

Nevertheless, other factors were at work for a German effort in Italy that autumn. *Kaiser* Wilhelm had been very moved by the personal appeal sent him from Karl; first and foremost, Wilhelm was a monarchist through and through, and could always be counted upon to be empathetic to a fellow monarch in need. He pressured Hindenburg, who he liked and respected (and who was also a staunch monarchist) to convince Ludendorff, the real authority in the

High Command (and who he did not care for), to support their Austrian allies at that critical time. Ludendorff grudgingly agreed, and a new Fourteenth Army was created with Below as the commander and Dellmensingen as his Chief of Staff. Preparations for an offensive could now proceed.

Conditions were in fact ripe for an *Alliance* offensive in Italy. It would do wonders for the sagging morale in Austria's armed forces; virtually every man in an Austro-Hungarian uniform considered Italy the main enemy and wanted desperately to see her beaten. An advance onto Italian soil would be a cure-all for the Empire's woes, and was bound to re-energize even the home front, which had lately taken heart from the apparent collapse of Russia. One by one the nation's enemies had been forced to pay for their folly of making war: Serbia and Montenegro in 1915, Romania in 1916, and now in 1917 it appeared as though Russia was beaten. Only Italy remained, and for the first time in the war, Germany was willing to help south of the Alps. Even Boroevic could not suppress a smile when he learned of the enterprise through Straussenberg. His Isonzo Army was to be split into First and Second Isonzo Armies, massively reinforced and become a new Army Group, of which he was to be the boss. 'Army Group Boroevic' was to assume a secondary role in the coming attack by simply supporting Fourteenth Army's left. The weak Tenth Army would cover the right.

Even before any offensive activity had been agreed upon, German divisions had begun arriving in Italy. Before August was out, the Fifth Infantry Division moved in from the Western Front and the 200th Jäger Division from the Eastern Front. In September came the Twelfth Infantry from the West and the so-called Alpine Corps, which in reality was only a division. The Alpine Corps had a unique history. It had been raised in March of 1915 and trained in the Austrian Tyrol until October of that year, at a time when Germany and Italy were not yet at war. No doubt this formation was the cause of the many reports coming out of the mountains that stated categorically that Italian troops had encountered Germans during the course of the fighting in portions of the remote Tyrol, from the Swiss frontier to at least as far east as the western Carnics. Certainly some of the Italian reports may have been inaccurate; Rome's soldiers always carried a certain phobia regarding Germans. On the other hand, in many instances German prisoners were reported as having been taken, and there is no reason to disbelieve such claims. Throughout the years of war, most Italians remained convinced that there were always Germans opposing them somewhere along the line, even when their own superiors emphatically denied such rumors. We do know that the Germans were not above cheating a little bit with regards their former partners in the *Triple Alliance*, even before war between them was official in August of 1916. For example, on July 31ˢᵗ, 1915, the town of Cortina in the Ampezzo Valley, so recently captured by Italian Fourth Army units, was bombed by aircraft based on Toblach, to the north. The pilots flying the bombers were Germans.[176] At any rate, in September 1917, the Alpine Corps had come again to the Italian Front, this time to fight, for sure. It had recently been in action in the Carpathian Mountains of Romania, and was a fine veteran unit. In October, the 26ᵗʰ Division arrived from the Western Front, and the 117ᵗʰ Division was railed in, also from Romania.

To these six German outfits was added five Austrian divisions, all of which were composed of good veteran troops. The First, Third (Edelweiss), 22ⁿᵈ, and 50ᵗʰ Infantry Divisions had all been raised before the war with Italy had begun, and the 55ᵗʰ (formerly the 93ʳᵈ) was formed during the month of its outbreak. Probably five better-quality Austro-Hungarian outfits in late 1917 could not have been found. They would acquit themselves well, and earn the admiration of their German comrades-in-arms. An excellent fighting force had been assembled for von Below by the middle of October.

It is perhaps worthwhile to take a fresh look at the orders of battle for the entire Italian Front for the eve of the *Alliance* offensive, now code-named *Waffentreu* (faithful under arms). Beginning with the Italians, First Army still held the line from the Swiss border to the Val Sugana, although because of the extended length of such a front, two divisions responsible for the stretch from the Stelvio Pass to Lake Garda were considered independent of Pecori-Giraldi. The total of divisions to the Brenta was fourteen. Beyond the Val Sugana Fourth Army under General de Robilant possessed six and one-half divisions and extended to the western Carnics. Then came the two divisions of the Carnic Group, bossed by General Tassoni, who had recently replaced Lequio. Capello's massive Second Army was next, holding the front from Mt. Rombon to just south of Gorizia; it contained twenty-five and one-half divisions. The Duke of Aosta's Third Army held by far the shortest piece of line, from the Wippach to the Gulf, yet it could account for nine divisions. A further eleven divisions were being held by Cadorna in a strategic reserve, and most of these represented units of the defunct Sixth Army. All told then, Italy had placed sixty-eight divisions on the battle line by October. No one could know it yet, but it was a total that would not be surpassed.

Looking at Austro-Hungarian dispositions for the same time period, we find two Army Groups in existence. The westernmost of these was commanded by the ex-Chief of the General Staff, Franz Conrad von Hötzendorf. It disposed of a weak 'Group' under Archduke Peter Ferdinand in the extreme west without any divisional-sized formations, and next came Eleventh Army of General Scheuchenstuel with five-and-one-half divisions in the south Tyrol. A weak 'Command' of four divisions covered the line opposite the enemy Fourth Army. Next to the east lay the under-strength Tenth Army led by General von Krobatin, the in Carnic Alps. Tenth Army would be transferred from Hötzendorf's Army Group to Archduke Eugen's before the month was over. It possessed only one division-sized unit at the time. Eugen was entrusted with Below's Fourteenth and Boroevic's First and Second Isonzo Armies in his Group. Below's eleven divisions were inserted into the line to cover the sector from Mt. Rombon to the southern end of the Tolmein bridgehead. From there, the ten divisions of von Henriquez's Second Isonzo Army stretched to the Wippach valley, and the eleven divisions of First Isonzo Army (von Wurm) faced Aosta's Third. Altogether, forty-two *Alliance* divisions now faced the Italians. For the first time in the war, the Italian numerical superiority had been reduced to less than two-to-one. It may be remembered that Austria had begun the war at a three and one-half to one disadvantage, a handicap that had by October 1917, been cut in half.

Reducing odds does not, of course, equate to overcoming them, and the Austro-Germans were well aware that attacking a numerically and materially superior enemy was not a task to be taken lightly. For one thing, there was simply not enough artillery to lay down a barrage of the magnitude that Cadorna was used to enjoying; consequently a couple of weeks were needed to transport additional weapons and munitions from the now-quiet Eastern Front. As a result, Austria's rail network, always taxed to the limits, was severely strained. More precious days were lost moving the enormous quantities of military equipment from railheads now well behind the lines because of the Italian advances. In the end, though, Fourteenth Army was built into a formidable combat force. By mid-October it could count over 2,000 guns, howitzers and *Minenwerfer*; the lighter weapons were supplied with 1,000 rounds of ammunition, and the super heavies 200 rounds.[177] The medium-weight pieces could expect to fire 500 shots. All this was very frugal by Italian standards, but for the Austrians it was a rare bonanza; they were accustomed to being subjected to enemy barrages which lasted for days, but themselves would not have chosen to do the same, even if they possessed the necessary ammunition. Boroevic's men, for example, had always done well behind short, intense bombardments, when some element of surprise could still be expected. And now, more than ever, they needed to catch the enemy off his guard.

To that end, every effort was made to conceal *Alliance* intentions from Cadorna. Naturally, all preparatory movement was done at night, but this practice was fairly normal, except that this time every man in Fourteenth Army was instilled in the belief of the need for absolute secrecy. Communications methods were severely restricted, and the old-fashioned means of using runners and message pigeons reinstated. Every available airplane was kept in the skies as much as possible, to prevent enemy aviators observing and photographing the buildup, and to prevent them bombing or strafing as well. Flights over Italian airspace were at the same time limited to a degree which was considered normal, to avoid arousing suspicion. Boroevic's airmen joined in the game, and on October 9th the celebrated ace Brumowski enjoyed his 22nd confirmed victory when he sent an observation balloon down in flames.[178]

Italy's aviators continued to indulge in the bombing campaign. Pola was attacked twice in the first two days of the month, and the Austrian naval facilities at Cattaro were the object of raids for the next forty-eight hours or so. Rain and snow on the 5th and 6th grounded most aircraft, and thereafter, the troublesome flights over the Idria Valley were suspended, much to the great relief of Below, whose left wing was trying to assemble in the area, undetected. Then on the 13th, ace Luigi Olivari, with twelve kills to his credit, was killed when his SPAD crashed during take-off. Italy had lost another fine pilot. About one week later, Major Baracca, who had been a friend and associate of Olivari, was determined to avenge his loss. So well protected had the airspace over the Tolmein bridgehead become, however, that he was driven off by five Austrian machines, and retired to the south. Not long thereafter, he attacked two enemy machines cruising near Mt. San Gabriele, and shot both down. Baracca was now four times an ace, with twenty-one air victories.[179]

If Straussenberg was reinforcing the Italian Front with every available man and weapon, it was all being sent to the Isonzo. Nothing could be spared for Hötzendorf's Army Group, but it was directed to carry on 'as usual', and it did so, hoping to convince the enemy that nothing out of the ordinary was up. Probing and trench raiding continued in the Tyrol and in the Carnic range. A minor attack was delivered in the upper Pellegrino Valley on the night of October 11th/12th, and artillery actions were lively most everywhere in mid-month. Even Boroevic's armies participated in this ruse. Only the front of the new Fourteenth Army was quiet. Then on the 14th, successful Italian trench raids captured a group of prisoners near Selo on the Carso, and more ominously, another group just south of Mt. Rombon.

The weather, incompetence on the part of the enemy, praiseworthy efforts by Below's men, good luck—all these combined to assist in making the efforts to conceal *Alliance* intentions for the coming offensive a remarkable success, at least as late as the middle of October. Then the campaign began to unravel. Prisoners taken in chance trench raids were only part of the problem; before any big attack a certain number of men, not wanting to face the upcoming rigors and dangers, always voluntarily surrender to the enemy about to be attacked, often by simply approaching his lines with arms upraised. It had happened with the Italians for every one of their twelve large offensives, it had happened to the Austrians in the Tyrol affair of 1916, and now, inevitably, it happened again. Just how much intelligence could be provided by a few war-weary soldiers is questionable, but at the same time, reports of German troops moving through the Pusterthal were arriving at Udine. On the 19th came still more evidence; German divisions had been observed by spies while passing through Laibach. By the 21st, reports made by Italian airmen were confirmed: units fresh from the Russian Front had been positively identified.

For the most part, all the intelligence received which pointed to an impending enemy offensive was kicked upstairs, and upstairs was not at home. Chief Cadorna had left Udine on October 4th for a two-week leave, a move no doubt inspired by his lack of interest in the defensive nature of the operations which expected to prevail at least until the spring of 1918. No sooner had he returned to headquarters than it was Capello's turn to be absent; Second Army boss was ill and was requested by his physicians to retire to Padua for some rest. In the event, Capello was not gone for long (19th to 22nd), but it was at a critical time, only days before the offensive would begin.

In fairness to Cadorna, it should be remembered that he did issue directives to all of his army commanders, which spelled out in some detail how a strategic defensive posture was to be implemented. As we have seen, he simply dismissed any subordinate who complained or protested his policies. Aosta, for one, knew better than to offend the Chief, and his Third Army was well dug in, according to Cadorna's 'book'. Capello, on the other hand, was a much more offensive-minded, hard driving boss who distinctly disliked the idea of defense, with all of its entrenchment and boring routine. Moreover, he commanded the largest by far of all of Italy's Armies and could not believe that the enemy could possibly scrape together any force capable of challenging his twenty-five and one-half divisions. In fact, the very size of the army made it a most unwieldy force, as large as most Army Groups (and a good deal larger than some), and difficult for a single individual to properly control. To make matters worse, the Second Army was poorly positioned; for the most part the bulk of the troops still lingered in areas of the most recent attacks, without regard for the rest of the front. So while it contained adequate strength for its length of front line—roughly one division per kilometer-and-a-half—its units were not fanned out in such a way as to prevent a breakthrough by the enemy, if he happened to strike at the right location. Unfortunately for Italy, it was a case of whatever could go wrong, did go wrong.

As if lack of resolve at the highest levels of army command was not enough of a handicap for the luckless *grigioverde* holding the line in the dreary autumn weather, a similar crisis within the government was coming to a head. The Boselli administration had never been popular; he was too elderly, unenergetic, and seemed to lack the leadership qualities necessary for wartime. Opponents from all political strains had become increasingly restive and vocal in their displeasure. Socialists, neutralists, and the numerous supporters of Giolitti had not, since the war's beginning, been entirely silenced and with every day since that Italy's war aims had not been achieved, their voices grew louder and bolder in antagonism to the existing policies. On October 16th, the Parliament was reconvened, and soon heated debates were raging within. Many speeches were made, and the one which would best be remembered by a majority of the Deputies was given on the 23rd by *Signor* Orlando, who strongly supported the war, but hotly opposed the dictatorial hold then enjoyed by the military over all national interests. These debates and speeches may well have continued for an extended period, had they not been interrupted, suddenly, by news of the enemy offensive, which unwittingly assisted the wranglers in Rome to again put politics aside, and form a government suitable to provide for the successful defense of the nation.

Austro-German artillery of Fourteenth Army had begun to fire ranging shots as early as the 20th, and was prepared to herald *Waffentreu* for the start date, October 22nd. Miserable weather caused Below to postpone, reluctantly; he was well aware that pleasant days would become ever scarcer as the calendar advanced. Still, Cadorna had always attacked well into November, and time was not so much a concern as was maintaining secrecy of his intentions. Below must have suspected that Italian intelligence had done its job, and that strong reserves were being rushed to the upper Isonzo. He knew he could not afford to wait for long, weather or no weather.

In the event, it was another attack which was featured in the press reports of the 22nd. It was carried out by Austrian troops, though the defending Italians insisted that German units took part, and if this is true, it may well have been a purely symbolic movement, timed as it was to coincide with *Waffentreu*. Early in the war, Austrian Kaiserschützen (Emperor's men-at-arms) troops had captured 2,296 meter (7,532 feet) high Mt. Piano, a peak on the Italian side of the border, overlooking the Misurina Pass, and had held it ever since. Now they attacked here again, driving back the bewildered Fourth Army elements, and precipitating a two-day battle which ended up favoring the attackers. The whole affair was very minor compared to the storm about to break farther east, but memories of Mt. Piano have always been a matter of pride for the Austrians.[180]

On the afternoon of the 23rd, Otto von Below inquired of his staff officers as to weather forecasts for the next twenty-four hours. The replies were not encouraging; more rain and fog expected, snow in the higher elevations. Next the general asked for opinions. Following a brief pause, Dellmensingen urged the attack be ordered for the following day. Security, he reminded Below, would soon be a problem, and the weather would hamper the enemy at least as much as Fourteenth Army. But Below hardly needed any convincing, he nodded, adding "give the order", and the Chief of Staff immediately contacted his Corps commanders. The artillery was to commence fire at 2:00am. Operation *Waffentreu* was underway.

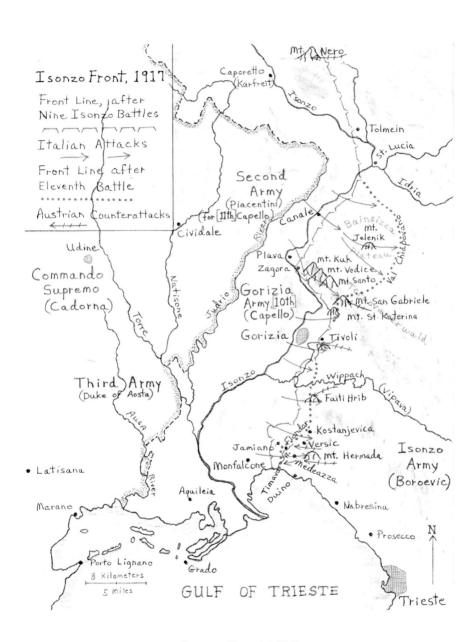

Isonzo Front 1917

Chapter Ten
Beyond All Expectations

At precisely one hundred and twenty minutes past midnight on the morning of October 24, 1917 with Teutonic punctuality, the artillery of the German Fourteenth Army opened fire on Italian positions along the front line between the *Massif* of Kanin/Rombon in the north to the northern edge of the Bainsizza upland to the south. Here, the Isonzo River runs generally northwest to southeast, as did the battle lines. In fact the only stretches of the stream's water still in Austrian hands were found at both extremes of this portion of the valley; above Zaga at the gap in the Julian Alps, the headwaters had never been taken by the Italians, and at the sharp bend just south of Tolmein, a few kilometers from this village to slightly south of St. Lucia, this so-called 'Tolmein bridgehead' had resisted every one of the numerous efforts to conquer it. Below's Army did then have toeholds at each end of its sector which extended all the way into the gorge of the river, and there did exist a few secondary roads over the Julians which lead to the same. Dellmensingen's plan called for advances down the valley from Zaga, up the valley from Tolmein, and into the valley over the mountains. The latter route was of course considered the most difficult and the strongest divisions were allotted for it. If the pincers from the flanks could join with the center somewhere near the village of Karfreit, half of Capello's Second Army could be caught in a vise and destroyed.

At 4:00am the barrage lifted, after two hours of pounding with high explosive. At first the Italians were not too concerned; bombardments of the short-term variety were not unusual anywhere along the front, at any time. But then it began again following a short pause, and the second round consisted of a large percentage of chemical shells, chlorine and phosgene gas. Although a mixture of snow and sleet was falling in the mountains, at lower elevations it was drizzle and mist, with fog in the valley, and the gas mixed into the milky-grey atmosphere perfectly, and was scarcely detectable until the luckless soldiers began to choke and gag. Under such conditions, it was certain that daylight would be delayed somewhat, but by 7:00am visibility was sufficiently good to begin the assault, and the multi-national army began to move towards its objectives.

To the north the attackers broke through the enemy defenses at Zaga, and proceeded downstream, bypassing and ignoring Italian units holding the heights on both their flanks; other contingents behind were to deal with stubborn strong points. In the center, deep snow in the Julians hampered all movement and soon tired the Austrian troops attempting to sweep by the ridge and begin the much less exhausting descent into the gorge, and they gained ground only slowly. It was in the south, at the Tolmein bridgehead that the most remarkable progress was made by the aggressors that day. Here three German and one Austro-Hungarian divisions, shrouded in the fog and mist, scored an immediate breakthrough upon the heights in their path. Ironically, it was here, due west of Tolmein/St. Lucia, that the pre-war Italian frontier was closest to the front line; only one low ridge separated the attackers from the headwaters of the Judrio and enemy soil. The Italian 19th Infantry Division was holding the front in that area; it had spent the entire war as part of either the Second or Third Armies, and its morale had slipped to a low level. By the hundreds, its soldiers simply threw down their weapons and surrendered to the advancing Germans, and within a few hours, the unit had practically ceased to exist. Divisional commander General Villani is said to have shot himself, so complete was the disaster; he no doubt preferred death to dishonor and disgrace at the hands of Capello or Cadorna. A gaping hole was thus torn in the Italian line, and through it poured the crack troops of the *Alpenkorps*. At the end of the first day of fighting, the value of the new *Sturmtruppen* and *Stosstruppen* was evident, as even in the high mountains they had begun to pry open the enemy defenses. Before darkness fell the outskirts of Karfreit had been reached in the center, Rombon had been isolated in the north, and the lower slopes of Mt. Colaurat approached in the south.

The following day, October 25th, was the critical day of the battle. Had Capello positioned his reserves properly, energetic counterattacks might well have retrieved the situation, and stalled Below along the border ridges. But the Second Army boss was absent again, having made a gloomy report to Cadorna at Udine late on the 24th, he cited continuing illness and departed for Turin, leaving his command in the hands of his senior Corps Commander General

Montuori, who could hardly be expected to retrieve stability in the face of chaos. The advance from Zaga had reached Mt. Maggiore before noon, where *Bersaglieri* resisted bravely alone after their compatriots had abandoned them to their fate, which was eventual annihilation. Resistance on the Kanin/ Rombon *Massif* was also difficult and time-consuming to overcome, but was accomplished by Austria's *Edelweiss* veterans. Once Karfreit and its intact stone bridge over the Isonzo had been taken and secured by noon, all remaining Italian forces in the Julians were cut off, and could be starved into submission. Most defenders did not care to wait that long, although isolated groups of *Alpini* often resisted until their ammunition was exhausted. One such body of troops was reported by Italian airmen as still holding out eleven days later.[181] To the south, the 1,243 meter (4,077 feet) Mt. Colaurat was captured without much of a fuss, and all eyes turned to Mt. Matajur, the last peak as yet unconquered, on the ridge above the Isonzo. To take Matajur, the Austro-Germans knew, was to carry the offensive into Italy. To encourage his commanders to take the initiative in securing the early fall of the mountain, Below (a Prussian) offered Prussia's most prestigious military decoration the, *Pour le Mérite,* to the officer whose troops first reached the summit.

In support of Fourteenth Army, the guns of Boroevic's two Isonzo Armies also opened fire on the 25th. Regimental-sized assaults were launched against the Bainsizza upland, in the San Gabriele area, and on the Carso. None gained any ground, but they did provoke considerable artillery counter-fire. Overhead, every available aircraft was sent to assist the ground forces, by both sides. Consequently, dogfights raged everywhere, contributing to the general din and confusion of the battle, and adding to the volume of metal propelled through the air. Benno Fiala achieved his eighth confirmed victory near Mt. San Gabriele on October 25th. Franz Gräser shot down one Italian on the 25th, then another plus an observation balloon on the 26th. Within two days of the start of *Waffentreu,* he had scored three times and had become an ace.[182] Another unknown Austrian aviator bested Giovanni Sabelli on the 25th, when the latter's score stood at five victories. Sabelli was killed, but other Italian pilots would avenge him. Lieutenant Guiliano Parvis enjoyed his first air victory also on the 25th, and on the very next day he and the famous Baracca shared a kill over Italian soil. Not to be outdone, Baracca would also be credited with three enemy aircraft for the two day period of the 25th/26th.[183] As against this, his squadron suffered three losses, Sabelli and two others, one of whom was downed by Godwin Brumowski. Apparently Baracca and Brumowski, the leading aces of their respective nations, had come ever so close to a face-to-face encounter, but aviation history was somehow deprived of such an interesting possibility.

Another Italian airman to survive those fateful days was Bortolo Constantini. Although an experienced flyer, Constantini had never recorded an air victory before the enemy offensive had begun. He, too, was to change his fortunes by achieving kills on both the 25th and 26th. Other Italian aces who added to their totals at that time were Fulco Ruffo, who scored his 14th and 15th on the 25th, and Pier Ruggiero Piccio, who accounted for his 13th on the same day.[184]

Airmen were not the only officers seeking the glories of armed combat. A young German Lieutenant was captivated by the idea of General von Below's offer of the 'Blue Max' for the first commander whose unit ascended Mt. Matajur. His name was Erwin Rommel and his company was among the vanguard of the *Alpenkorps* advancing past Colaurat, and in ideal position to push on to Matajur. At some point late in the day of the 25th, Rommel determined that he should take the mountain; his troops were tiring now, but one more effort might just bring success. Following a brief overnight rest, the lieutenant led his men up Mt. Matajur with first daylight on the 26th, a daring exploit later described by Rommel himself. He claimed that most of the defenders threw away their rifles and approached him, even hoisting him onto their shoulders, screaming 'Evviva Germania' all the while. One officer who refused to join in the treacherous behavior was gunned down by his own soldiers.[185] Before noon on October 26th, the 1,644 meter-high (5,392 feet) Mt. Matajur was in German hands. In 52 hours of full-scale attack, Rommel's men alone had inflicted roughly 10,000 casualties on the Italians, for negligible losses of their own. Both the young lieutenant and his battalion commander were indeed awarded the coveted *Pour le Mérite* for the conquest of the peak. Now the front line was everywhere on or beyond the Italian frontier, all along Fourteenth Army's stretch of front.

At about the same time as the storming of Matajur, Mts. Maggiore, Kuk and Santo were also declared as secure for the *Alliance*. Second Army formations had already begun a hasty evacuation of the Bainsizza upland, covered by several local counterattacks. Boroevic's two Armies were also beginning to stir, their soldiers invigorated by the news of Below's breakthrough. The enemy Second Army was dissolving, and they were anxious to at long last take the war into Italy. Aosta's Third Army did not budge until the morning of Saturday, October 27th when an order for a general retreat finally arrived from Cadorna, who had been slow to grasp the seriousness of the strategic situation. Thereafter a frantic effort was made to save the Army, before Below could abruptly turn to the south and cut off its line of retreat. All the artillery was ordered to fire nonstop until all of the ammunition which could not be evacuated was used up; it was this curtain of fire that kept Boroevic's men at bay, for all day of the 27th, while the men of the Duke's nine divisions scrambled to abandon, as quickly as possible, all of the ground that had been gained in eleven major battles over the past two and one-half years of bloodshed.

Back in Rome, debates in the Chamber of Deputies were still raging when the politicians were informed of the debacle begun at Caporetto (Karfreit). The news was too much; heads had to roll. Sonnino spoke on the 25th, denouncing the increasingly pacifistic mood of the country and lobbying for an increased national war effort, apparently now necessary for victory. The Vatican peace initiative was finally addressed, and denounced as pro-enemy. On the following day the Boselli government could not survive a vote of confidence, and several of the leading figures were forced to resign. Orlando became Premier, but interestingly, Sonnino was retained as Foreign Minister. Italy's answer to defeat would not be submission, rather increased resistance. Britain, France, and the United States were immediately appealed to for economic and military assistance. Even the King, who much preferred to spend time behind the front rather than in his capitol, returned to Rome on the 27th, hoping his presence might steady the nerves of his excitable countrymen.

That same afternoon, Below's advance units began to debouch from the hills down into the Natisone Valley and to the edge of the Venetian Plain. Here lay the town of Cividale, the easternmost rail terminus of the nation. Because of its advanced location on the railroads, Cividale had become the site of enormous warehouses containing supplies of every sort destined for the armies on the Isonzo. Now, on that dreary Saturday afternoon with rain beginning to fall, these were put to the torch, to prevent capture by the Germans. When the latter approached in the last hours before darkness, they found a raging inferno, but were helpless to fight the flames and instead could only watch as millions of man (and woman) hours worth of labor was destroyed in the conflagration. The inferno later spread to the town itself, which was utterly destroyed;

photographs of its ruins cannot have failed to evoke pitiful feelings in all those who viewed them.

On the Carso at the same time were other scenes of devastation. One eyewitness noticed that most of the British big guns were successfully evacuated, even though a shortage of tractors necessitated that each tractor was unhitched several times and driven back for other pieces. He saw fires and heard explosions everywhere as the Italians abandoned equipment and stores, calling his visions an "apocalyptic spectacle".[186] Apparently millions of rounds of ammunition had to be exploded and the detonations shook the earth so mightily that he believed nothing short of a volcanic eruption could have reproduced the effect. All the while Austrian artillery fire rained down upon the scurrying soldiers and claimed many victims. A rearguard force was hastily assembled and installed in the Vallone ravine, to halt the Austrians while the last of the Third Army could escape across the lower Isonzo.

Chief Cadorna may have been slow to grasp the significance of the Austro-German offensive, but once the first enemy aircraft began appearing in numbers over Udine, he quickly gave the order to evacuate his headquarters. The man who had callously sent hundreds of thousands of frightened young Italian soldiers into suicidal charges against enemy machine guns was taking no chances with his own life. *Commando Supremo* would eventually re-establish itself in far-off Padua, well out of danger. Needless to relate, Cadorna did not order himself shot for cowardice, but he did insist that all deserters, agitators, and even stragglers be executed during the retreat. To him, the whole calamity was only a matter of indiscipline. That he himself had been a primary cause for the lapse into such 'indiscipline' was a fact that would never have occurred to him.

October 28th dawned with the Italian Second and Third Armies both in headlong retreat. Austrian troops entered the shattered city of Gorizia (now Görz again), for which so much Latin blood had been spilled. Pushing on, they even reached Cormons that day, then were stopped by rearguards fighting a delaying action on the lower Judrio, the old frontier. Other units reentered Monfalcone, only slightly too late to prevent the evacuation of enemy naval ordnance which had been installed there to threaten the Gulf. It was raining harder now as the Habsburg soldiers stared in amazement at the rusted facilities of the ex-shipyard which the Italians had made no attempt to make use of. On they marched towards the lower Isonzo, needing to cross the river before the driving rain raised it into a torrent. Off to the north German troops were approaching Udine, where like Cividale the Italian Department of Munitions had stocked a large number of warehouses, especially constructed near the railroad. About two kilometers east of the place, the remnants of several Italian brigades made a stand on the Torre River, allowing engineers ample time to fire the fully-stocked warehouses. Throughout the cold rainy night, Below's men could hear the crackle of millions of rounds of small-arms ammunition exploding as it burned, plus a good number of larger explosions of demolition charges. At first daylight on the 29th the rearguards had retreated, and the once-thriving city was entered. Most of the inhabitants had fled with the mini-army of staff officers connected with Cadorna's Headquarters, only they were not whisked away in automobiles, but rather were forced to join the ever-increasing exodus now jamming the roads of eastern Venetia, roads rapidly being churned into deep, sticky mud.

On the same day, units of the Carnic Corps in the upper Tagliamento watershed began to join the retreat. They had a long way to go to reach safety, having gotten such a late start, but in fact, Rohr's Tenth Army was too weak to offer much of a pursuit. Even so they needed to clear the mountains and enter the plain near Gemona, then skirt the northern edge of the lowland if they were to avoid trouble. In the event, the Italian 36th division was fallen upon while trying to cross the Tagliamento on a rather flimsy bridge west of Gemona and all but destroyed. The other division of the Corps, the 26th, would suffer a similar fate at Lorenzago, farther west in the Piave watershed.[187] Both these formations had to be scratched from Cadorna's order of battle, and would not reappear for many months.

Following the German seizure of Udine, which cost them a Corps commander (General Berrer) killed by Italian cavalrymen, and the Austrian crossing of the lower Isonzo, nothing could prevent the capture of all of Friulia. For Below and Boroevic, the next logical target was the line of the river Tagliamento, a stream which did not flow in a single channel, but was spread over a series of small courses choked with gravel and in places forming a swath several kilometers broad, across the coastal plain. It was during the race for this river that the retreat became more of a rout. For many Italians, fed up with the war, overawed with tales of German military superiority, and made miserable by the long marches through the rain and mud, surrender had become an acceptable alternative. Most accounts agree that the flight to the

Tagliamento probably represented the critical moment in the campaign when most Italian soldiers either resolved to do their duty come what may, or decided that one way or another, the war was over for them. Some bodies of troops, even large ones, hurled their rifles into the waterlogged ditches and collectively resolved *"Andiamo a casa"* (We're going home).[188] Thousands deserted in this manner. Other thousands scoured the towns for civilian clothing with which to somehow make their way home. Still others sought shelter within the numerous dwellings which had been abandoned, as the local populace fled behind the army. For many, however, the simplest means to ensure survival was surrender; they were confident that the Austrians would at least feed them and care for their wounds. As the *Alliance* armies advanced, they found the roads lined with these dispirited soldiers standing silently, huddled under the downpour. Sometimes the invaders were greeted with gestures of friendship or cheers of *"Evviva l'Austria"* or *"La Guerra é finita"* (The war is over). Few Austrians showed much sympathy for these wretched ex-soldiers; they had always despised the Italians and here for them was proof positive of their treacherous and fickle nature.

Only three railroad bridges crossed the Tagliamento between the mountains and the sea. These constituted the only structures sure to be strong enough to bear the weight of heavy guns and other military traffic. One was at Pinzano, on Below's extreme right, a second west of Codroipo on the German's direct path, and the third lay at Latisana, in ideal position for Boroevic. For two entire days, the eastern approaches to these spans were like the narrows of a funnel, collecting masses of soldiers and civilians alike, all frantic to cross the river to safety. With far the shorter distance to travel, the Italians were first to reach the stream; they crossed and fanned out on the western banks, expecting to form a new defensive line. They hesitated to destroy the last of the bridges too quickly, knowing that thousands of stragglers and civilians were certain to continue to arrive, seeking salvation. But the enemy was approaching rapidly, and his vanguard first viewed the swollen waters of the river late on October 30th.

On the last day of the month, fighting raged at several key locations along the Tagliamento. German troops, moving quickly, battled their way across the river west of Codroipo and somewhat farther north at Dignano, site of a decent crossing place and a partially destroyed road bridge. These actions stranded a large number of Italian troops, who soon surrendered. For seven days of battle in October, Berlin claimed 180,000 prisoners and 1,500 artillery pieces taken by its forces alone. To the south, Boroevic's Second Isonzo Army assaulted the crossings at Latisana and San Michele, where all the bridges had been blown into the water. In the face of stiff Italian resistance, including a counterattack by armored cars[189], the multi-channeled stream was only partially crossed. Cadorna's battered armies had bought him a few more precious hours, perhaps days, in which to make a command decision. Britain's Chief of the Imperial General Staff Sir William Robertson was hastily dispatched to Italy once the news of the disaster of Caporetto had reached the West. He duly arrived at Treviso on the 31st, met with Cadorna, "observed the condition of the retreating troops",[190] and telegraphed his report to the War Cabinet. Shortly thereafter, both men were informed of an emergency Conference being called for Rapallo, near Genoa, within a few days, and asked to attend. Robertson was more than happy to do so, but Cadorna, with a disaster on his hands was not. The Chief was already nervous about an enemy landing somewhere on the coast to his rear, and concerned that the Tagliamento line would soon be turned from the north.

The Austro-Hungarians already had raised several companies of naval troops (roughly equivalent to U. S. Marines), and on November 1st these took part in an amphibious operation from Trieste against Grado, the island-town lost in the first days of the war. Apparently the populace of Grado was pleased to see the return of Habsburg rule.[191] Flushed with success, the troops were sent against Lignano, a port town near the mouth of the Tagliamento, which they secured on the 3rd. Minor though these operations were, they seemed to confirm Cadorna's worst fears. And when the fighting on the river line began to slowly go unfavorably for the defenders during the first two days of the month, Cadorna lost his nerve. Still, he delayed in issuing any concrete orders.

On the morning of November 3rd, both Below and Boroevic began to break free of the Tagliamento line. The Germans poured over the river at Pinzano, while the Austrians won bridgeheads over the lower stream and began to advance again. They reached the rail town of San Vito the next day, instigating a new battle, while German troops raced down from the north to turn the Italian left. Even Hötzendorf's command was stirring by now, and began a minor, and obviously diversionary, attack west of Lake Garda. The whole idea of another enemy strike from the Tyrol terrified Cadorna; he gave the order to retreat to the Livenza, the next river-line to the west.

The Conference at Rapallo convened on November 5th, during the mass exodus from the Tagliamento to the Livenza. Italian, French, British, and American political and military leaders were gathered to discuss the catastrophe overtaking Italy. British and French troops were already on the way, in accordance with a previous agreement. Cadorna, not surprisingly, did not attend, instead sending General Porro to again represent him. Porro claimed the Germans had committed 35 divisions to their offensive, backed by nearly as many Austrian ones. He demanded at least 15 divisions from the West, if Italy was to survive. Fortunately for the *Entente*, not all its leaders were so easily convinced; most suspected that Cadorna was the real problem with the nation's armed forces. Accordingly, a meeting of the military leaders was called for at Peschiera on the 8th.

While the fate of the Italian front was being decided behind the scenes, hundreds of thousands of people, both military and civilian, were in motion on the Venetian Plain. The weather had finally cleared, bringing new terror to the masses of humanity fleeing along the roads: enemy aircraft. Desperate to prevent what would amount to catastrophic bombing or strafing runs on the overcrowded byways, the Italians sent every aircraft skyward to engage any enemy looking for easy targets. Austria's Frank Linke-Crawford engaged several of these, and shot down two near the coast on November 5th.[192] They became his eighth and ninth kills. The following day brought good fortune to Italy's Francesco Baracca, who accounted for two Austrians. Then on the 7th, he destroyed another enemy airplane, raising his total to twenty-seven.[193]

On November 6th, German troops reached Maniago, at the edge of the mountains and Sacile, on the railroad to Conegliano. The Austrians were fast closing on the lower Livenza, and in one of his last decisions as Chief, Cadorna discarded all hope of standing east of the Piave. All planning thereafter revolved around the Piave as the new, and final, defensive line. For one thing, it was a much larger river than the Livenza, with greater volume than the Isonzo or the Tagliamento; a larger stream short of the Adige could not be found. But to retire to the Adige would have meant abandoning Vicenza, Padua, and above all, Venice—a scenario too bitter to contemplate in the minds of most Italians. Second, the Piave flowed mostly in a single channel, extending with few exceptions, from the mountains to the sea. Another advantage to a Piave line was that it made for a fairly straight and 'clean' course from the south Tyrol to the Adriatic. For once, most everyone agreed with Cadorna; the enemy would have to be stopped on the Piave.

He need not have concerned himself. At Peschiera the King criticized Cadorna publically for the first time, then dismissed him as Chief of *Commando Supremo*. Cadorna was furious and hurt, and said so, but he was not sacked altogether, rather kicked upstairs. One of the decisions reached at Rapello was the creation of a Supreme War Council to coordinate *Entente* military strategy, and the ex-Chief was named as Italy's representative, a fate he no doubt regarded as punishment for failure. Vittorio Emanuele had been considering a replacement for some time and now, on November 8th, he announced his choice: General Armando Diaz. For the first time since the beginning of the war, the Italian Army had a new Chief.

Diaz was, of course, a selection quite acceptable to the Western Powers; the King had made sure of this fact in advance of his announcement. His service record was good though not outstanding. Most recently he had been a Corps commander within Third Army, and had endured the Tenth and Eleventh Isonzo offensives, when his men had gained some ground. Of an entirely different mindset from his predecessor, he was known to be compassionate towards his men and concerned for their lives and comfort. Under no circumstances would he sanction the scope of executions and other punishments that Cadorna was so well known for. In fact he believed that the breakdown in morale in the army had been one result of the plight of the troops at the front, who had only rarely been granted leave or entertainment, but were always subjected to the harshest discipline. Diaz became a sort of Italian Petain, dedicated to the idea that the troops had often been badly misused, and now needed a period of rest and relaxation necessary to allow them to regain their self confidence and recover their faith in their officers. Simultaneously, the army could be rebuilt materially. These, he knew, were long term goals, and he had no intention of resuming offensive operations for many months to come.

First, of course, the enemy had to be stopped on the Piave. Fortunately for Diaz his appointment came just at a time that the enemy offensive was running out of steam. Beset by logistical problems inherent in attempting to supply a rapidly advancing group of armies, the Austro-Germans were also becoming badly in need of rest and refitting. *Waffentreu* had already exceeded all expectations, but it was simply good strategy to try to exploit success to the maximum degree. To this end, Ludendorff had allowed a host of replacement battalions to be sent to Italy in order to form a new unit, which became the

Jäger Division. He also sent the 195th Division from the Western Front, but by the time it arrived the line had stabilized and it was soon returned. Even the relatively short retreat from the Livenza to the Piave was not accomplished without a new disaster. On the same day of his appointment, Diaz learned another 17,000 Italian soldiers had surrendered in the hills.[194]

Then there were two other major headaches to deal with. First, if the Piave was to become the new battle line, all of Fourth Army's front between the Brenta and the Mt. Croce Pass would have to be abandoned and all the efforts of the last two and one-half years in that sector written off. And Fourth Army had not even begun to retreat until the 6th, when Cadorna had finally made up his mind regarding the Piave. That meant it had only one avenue of retreat, down the upper Piave, where theoretically it could be attacked in flank by either Hötzendorf or Below. And the further south it moved, the closer to the oncoming Germans it would become. Speed was now imperative, if it was to escape destruction. Second, Hötzendorf had decided that he should attempt a repeat of the 1916 offensive, and drive across the Asiago Plateau and onto the plain, taking the disorganized Italians in flank. Without reinforcement, Eleventh Army struck on November 8th from the northern reaches of the plateau to the south, and in Val Sugana. That same day, Below's right wing captured Vittorio, a small city at the edge of the uplands only 32 kilometers (20 miles) from Feltre, from which point they could cut the retreat of the Italian Fourth Army.

Hötzendorf's drive caught two commanders off balance. One was his opposite number Pecori-Giraldi of First Army who was horrified to learn of enemy troops swarming all over the Asiago Plateau again. The other was Below, who had expected the Austrian to make an effort to cross the Dolomites and crush De Robilant. Instead, only weak elements of Eleventh Army engaged in a half-hearted pursuit of Fourth Army, from down the upper Piave and the Cordevole, and Below was obliged to send part of his *Alpenkorps* into the hills to attack De Robilant's left. Once again Lieutenant Rommel was in the forefront of the fighting; at the town of Longarone, the relatively small group of South Germans encircled a much larger enemy force, which soon surrendered without much fuss. Only after the Italian commander was confronted did Rommel realize that his men had taken 8,000 enemy troops with 20 artillery pieces prisoner.[195] This occurred on November 10th, the same day Austrian units captured Belluno and that Hötzendorf's soldiers took Asiago again.

Ironically, both Below's and Boroevic's men began arriving on the Piave on November 9th, as if by some prior agreement or planning which was not the case. In fact the Austrians had far less distance to cover; from Monfalcone to San Dona, for example, is about 88 kilometers (55 miles), while Karfreit to Vidor is more like 138 kilometers (86 miles), so the Germans had moved more quickly. Neither group, though both were exhausted, had any intention of stopping on the Piave when they first reached it. As early as the 10th, Austrian troops had crossed the river at Zenson and created a small bridgehead, which was subsequently counterattacked and could not immediately be expanded. For the moment, their advance was stalled while they waited impatiently for additional forces with bridging equipment to arrive. Many kilometers upstream the Germans were experiencing similar difficulties. Also on the 10th, Twelfth Division vanguards surprised a small Italian unit guarding the bridge at Vidor and sprinted across the nine-span stone structure, only to be driven back by machine gun fire. Taking no chances, the defenders blew three of the spans into the river that night, and although the Germans made another serious attempt to cross the river the next day, they were beaten off.[196] The battle of movement had reached its limits.

It is worthwhile to pause here and consider the remarkable success of Operation *Waffentreu*. In over two years of ramming and tearing at the Austro-Hungarian defenses along the Isonzo, Cadorna had achieved gains of two (near Tolmein) to twenty-five (from the Ausa to Hermada) kilometers, and had never scored a breakthrough to his objectives. In eleven major offensives which cost him at least three-quarters of a million casualties, all he had accomplished was the demoralization of his army, and that of the enemy. By contrast, by committing six (later seven) German and five crack Austrian divisions to the Fourteenth Army offensive, the *Alliance* had, in just over two *weeks*, advanced an average of 113 kilometers (70 miles) on a 65 kilometer (40 mile) front. For a loss of about 35,000 soldiers, the Austro-Germans had captured over 300,000 Italians, and killed or wounded another 40,000. Five thousand artillery pieces and mortars had also been taken, and 3,000 machine guns. France's Clemenceau wrote a bitter indictment of Italian incompetence, which he claimed caused the loss of 300,000 tons of wheat "into the hands of the famished enemy".[197] Perhaps most disturbing of all for Rome was the gigantic number of deserters who simply melted away into the countryside; the actual number has always been hotly debated, but estimates run as high as

400,000.[198] What is certain is that Second Army and the Carnic Corps were practically destroyed, and Third and Fourth Armies severely mauled. By December 1st eleven entire divisions had to be stricken from the Italian order of battle, and half of those that remained were seriously under strength. While it may be true that many of the so-called 'deserters' eventually returned, both willingly and forcibly, to service, neither they nor anyone else in Italy would ever forget the agony that was the retreat from Caporetto.

Sometimes referred to as the Twelfth Battle of the Isonzo, history more often remembers the events begun on October 24, 1917 as the Battle of Caporetto, or simply Caporetto. It is a terrible misnomer; very little fighting actually took place at that little village on the Isonzo, the Slovene inhabitants of which at any rate refer to their hometown as Kobarid. Udine or Latisana or San Vito would have been equally appropriate, but Caporetto is the reference that has endured, for nearly a century.

Whatever the battle is called, it was really more of a campaign, and an extremely successful one by the standards of the Great War. It should unquestionably rank as one of the best executed actions of that conflict, on a level with the defense of East Prussia in 1914, the Golice-Tarnow offensive of 1915, or the Romanian campaign of 1916. It remains for posterity as proof of what a relatively small force of well-equipped, well-trained, and determined individuals can accomplish when used properly, and under the right circumstances.

Soon after the fact, Caporetto became a legend, and has remained so, especially for the Italians. It inspired poetry and it inspired art, which often depicted images of the grim, wearisome retreat across the rain-soaked, wind-blown plain. In some strange way it also inspired the spirit of Italy as well. For the first time in the war, the nation had been invaded and Italians were fleeing their homes. Despite the awful defeat, the nation seemed to be shocked from its apathy and lethargy, and a new will to resist the enemy was inspired. There was also a new sense that the nation was not alone against the powerful foe; British and French troops would henceforth fight alongside their Italian allies.

For the *Alliance* Powers what *Waffentreu* had achieved was beyond all expectations. A desperate Austria had finally defeated the hated southern enemy and carried the war onto his soil. *Kaiser* Karl, who had marched with his troops on several occasions, was genuinely relieved by the astounding successes. With Russia now likely to leave the war, it seemed that a new hope of victory was not unreasonable. Italy, the last neighboring enemy of Austria was staggering, and there was every reason to believe she could be knocked out.

The end of the war of movement finally achieved about the 10th of November, did not ensure that the fighting was over, even for a temporary period. Between Vidor on the Piave and Asiago on the *Setti Communi*, a large salient in the line now extended to the north, beyond Fonzaso and Feltre. Hötzendorf did his best to drive in the western edge of the bulge by continuing his attacks on the plateau, but a skillful and intrepid defense of Mt. Longaro by *Alpini* troops foiled the plan. Two days later, however, on the 13th, the defenders were being outflanked on both sides and were forced to retire. On the same day other Austrian infantry advanced down the Brenta and its tributary the Cismone and took Primolano and Fonzaso. The latter location was only a few kilometers west of Feltre on the Piave railroad, which was entered by a mixed Austro-German force almost simultaneously with the fall of Fonzaso. Within a few hours, elements of Austrian Eleventh and German Fourteenth Army were shaking hands near Mt. Tomatico. The trap had snapped shut on any Fourth Army stragglers still remaining in the Dolomites.[199]

On the lower Piave, Boroevic's men continued in their efforts to force a crossing in depth. Besides the bridgehead at Zenson, attempts were made at Folina, Fagare, San Dona and Grisolera using rafts, pontoons, rowboats— anything that would float. A Hungarian regiment was able to force its way past Grisolera and into the marshy delta area of the river, where over the years numerous channels resembling canals had been cut into the silt, sand, and sediment. The effort at San Dona was frustrated, and large numbers of Austrian troops remained in the city, centered on the left bank of the stream. Tales of excesses by the invaders had been circulating amongst the Italians since the great breakthrough, and some were not without foundation. Years later a story from "a small city on the Piave", which was almost certainly San Dona, was confessed by an ex-Austrian soldier. While searching the homes for weapons, he said, his group came into the home of a fortyish woman with three teenage daughters. The man of the house was apparently in military service, and the lustful Austrians assaulted the four helpless females "until far into the night". Later, the horrified women escaped the house only to be detained by other troops who were no less aggressive than the first bunch.

After two days, the four, "scarcely recognizable", were left alone.[200] Just how many times incidents like this one were occurring all across the invaded territory is anyone's guess, but they boded ill for Austria-Hungary if she should lose the war.

Fighting on the lower river raged on for days and even weeks, but with diminishing intensity. Another bridgehead was won at Fagare on the 16th; for a time it seemed that the river-line could not be defended. Then the rains came again, swelling the current and washing away floating bridges, effectively cutting off the units that had crossed from their sources of supply. Italian artillery soon had the range, pounding the panic-stricken soldiers on the right bank, and destroying at will the bridges that remained. Soon the Piave was running red as had the Isonzo before it; when the waters receded, hundreds of Austrian corpses littered the sandbars. Hundreds more, perhaps thousands, must have been swept out to sea.

Diaz's chief concern at this time was for the safety of Venice, now a mere 25 kilometers (15.5 miles) behind the battle line. Its loss would have been a terrible psychological blow for Italy, and it seemed for a time to be likely. The enemy advance had enabled the Austrians to move their most forward naval base to Caorle within easy striking distance from the island-city. Venice had long since been the most frequently bombed locality in Italy, and its architectural landmarks had been shored up, encased really, with millions of sandbags. Now the bulk of the remaining population was evacuated; only essential workers remained. All approaches to the Venetian Gulf were mined, and a special fleet of shallow-draft gunboats was created for the surrounding lagoons and delta marshes. These vessels were camouflaged to appear from the air as tiny islands, but were in effect floating batteries, accompanied by floating munitions dumps, and so forth. Their purpose was to engage any prowling enemy machines with a few shots, then sail away into the inland waterways before they could be located or ranged. As the enemy advanced into the Piave delta area, many of these boats were employed in hit-and-run actions against even ground troops.[201]

While Boroevic's men struggled to break out towards Venice, Below and Hötzendorf were slowly pinching out the salient in the hills. Once Mt. Tomatico had been secured and the town of Cismon on the Brenta taken—both occurrences accomplished on the 15th—an advance down both sides of the river was possible. Even so, the Italians resisted bitterly on the eastern portion of the Asiago Plateau and in the mountains due west of the big bend of the Piave. Josef Kiss served his country well during this fighting, shooting down five Italian airplanes in the four-day period of November 15th to 18th.[202] Twelve aircraft had now been destroyed by the Hungarian ace. Flying within the same *Flik*, Julius Arigi was also credited with two victories in the same time period. For Italy, Silvio Scaroni sent three enemy Albatross airplanes down in flames between November 15th and 19th, the last one near the bridge at Vidor. Major Baracca scored his twenty-eighth kill nearby, also on the 15th. By November 17th the Germans had accumulated sufficient bridging material as to try to cross the Piave again. Two attempts were made after darkness had set in that evening, one at Vidor and one at Fener, some kilometers upstream. Both were caught in the glare of Italian searchlights and flares and were shot up in a hail of machine gun and small arms fire. An eyewitness noticed troops using a new weapon, a "deadly Fiat machine pistol, which fires faster than any known weapon".[203] Frustrated, the Germans could take little satisfaction in the knowledge that a supporting attack from the north, along the far bank of the river, captured Quero the next day, making the Fener effort somewhat unnecessary. On the following night it was achieved without much difficulty. For their part, the Italians fell back upon Mt. Tomba, which became the site of heavy battles for several more days. In the end the peak remained in Italian hands. Mt. Monfenera was also successfully defended, despite three days of Austro-German attacks beginning on the 19th. Clearly, the line had begun to stabilize.

Farther west Hötzendorf was likewise unable to gain much more ground. After two weeks of desperate fighting in the broken country of the *Setti Communi*, his troops were tired and vulnerable to an epidemic, which soon had sidelined 7,000 of them.[204] On November 22nd, they were repulsed at Mt. Meletta, and on the 26th a seesaw battle at Mt. Pertica brought no strategic gain, but did add thousands more to the casualty lists. Thereafter *Kaiser* Karl personally intervened, ordering Hötzendorf to desist; the Emperor was shaken by a wave of strikes and demonstrations that rocked Budapest on the 25th, many angry protestors demanding an end to the war. His order extended to Boroevic as well, and was probably unnecessary, as both Army Group commanders were well aware that the time for strategic gains had passed. As if to punctuate the end of most movement in the Tyrol, heavy snows in the mountains on the 27th effectively ended the campaign.

There were other reasons for the failure of the *Alliance* attacks after the middle of November; considerable reinforcement was on its way for the Italians. Britain sent two Corps from the Western Front under the veteran General Plumer, from the same. Eleventh Corps included the 5th and 48th divisions, while Fourteenth Corps disposed of the 7th, 23rd, and 41st divisions. These troops assembled around Mantua, and when all of their equipment had arrived, were moved into the new front line on the left of Third Army, a location which had become a critical sector owing to the destruction of the Second Army. Their stretch of front covered the Piave from the railroad crossing east of Nervesa to a couple of kilometers sort of Vidor. The repositioning was not undertaken by all of the troops, some of whom were retained behind the front for reserves, but it did take up the latter part of the month, and it was early December before the British were fully ready to engage the enemy. Meanwhile the French had also pulled five divisions from the West in late October, grouped them into a Tenth army under General Duchéne, and railed them to the area between Lake Garda and Verona. The units were the 23rd, 24th, 47th, 64th and 65th Divisions. When no enemy attack down the Adige materialized, they too were moved to a critical sector—perhaps the most critical of all—in the still-unstable front where the line left the Piave near Alano, just south of Quero. An Italian division divided them from the British; they took over the front from Onego to Mt. Grappa.

If the war of movement was over for the ground forces, the same could hardly be said of the air forces. With both sides repositioning, there was plenty of need for increased air activity to locate new enemy railheads, artillery emplacements, airfields and so on. Whenever weather permitted both sides flew innumerable sorties, which in turn led to a lot of aerial combat. Air aces had become heroes by this time in the war, glamorized knights of the skies, despite their notoriously short life expectancy. But the leading aces of both main combatants did not disappoint. Major Baracca claimed his 29th victory on November 23rd, and before the year was out had raised his total to the astounding number of Thirty. Austria's immortal, Captain Brumowski, was credited with two kills also on the 23rd, for a personal total of 25. One of his comrades, Linke-Crawford, also shot down two enemy planes that day, near the mouth of the Piave; he was now twice an ace with eleven Italians to his credit. Flying in the same vicinity, Franz Gräser downed an enemy fighter on the same day, but he would have to wait for another week for his tenth kill, which came on the 29th. One of these Austrians, or perhaps an unknown pilot, shot up the machine Pier Piccio was flying, forcing him to crash-land. Piccio was not seriously injured, and was in the air again by the 30th. Italian aces-to-be Parvis, Costantini, and Novelli also brought down one enemy airplane apiece on that most remarkable November day. Aces or future aces had been credited with nine victories on that Friday, the 23rd! Ferruccio Ranza did not score on the 23rd, but he did shoot down an Austrian near Bassano on the 21st, and another on the 30th, raising his total to ten kills. Costantini victimized his fourth on the last day of the month. Over Feltre, Raoul Stojsavljevic destroyed his tenth enemy aircraft on the 21st. It would be his last victory.[205]

As of December 1st 1917, the *Alliance* could count 37 Austro-Hungarian and 8 German divisions on the Italian Front. To oppose them stood 57 Italian and 10 British and French divisions, although the latter were not yet completely positioned and the former included many under-strength, battered units. Indeed, the disparity of force had been cut to one and one-half to one, the most favorable thus far for the Austrians against their principal enemy. One man, at least, was unwilling to allow the perceived opportunity of the moment to pass unexploited. Franz Conrad von Hötzendorf thought he saw a golden chance to realize his long-desired plan to strike at the enemy rear. Circumstances now seemed even more favorable than in May of 1916 when he launched his *Südtyroloffensive* from the same area for the same purpose. On that occasion, however, his troops had been on Austrian soil, and were obliged to attack over the mountainous border areas, and even so, had reached the very edge of the Asiago Plateau. Only the lack of sufficient means had stopped him then, but now his soldiers stood on a line nearly as advanced as that which they had achieved at the end of the last drive. A mere two ridges, and in some places one ridge, now stood in the path to the lowland, and Hötzendorf was sure the plains could be reached with just one more push before the worst of the winter set in. He had been restless in his headquarters ever since the Emperor's order had put an end to all offensive action, but despite some heavy snows in the higher mountains, the weather had generally held, the roads were passable, and he was desperate to move forward from the Plateau, where there were no decent winter quarters, onto the much milder lowlands, where small cities such as Asolo, Bassano, and Thiene could shelter his army. The problem, of course, was finding others to agree with him; the Emperor, with whom he was in no special favor, was clearly a dead end. Boroevic's command was too far distant to be of much help, save perhaps some diversionary actions. Swallowing his pride, he appealed to Straussenberg, his replacement as Chief of the General Staff, and was surprised to receive a sympathetic response. Straussenberg sanctioned a 'limited' attack, promised to fix it with His Majesty, and would direct Below to assist with his right wing. Astounded but pleased, Hötzendorf hastily prepared a new attack. There was no time to lose.

In fact, Straussenberg was not quite as happily cooperative as his ex-boss may have imagined. He had other reasons for wanting some last-minute action in 1917, not the least of which involved the Germans, who he suspected were preparing to withdraw all of their troops for the Western Front. Now that Russia was no longer a combatant, virtually everyone on the continent fully expected Ludendorff to throw all of Germany's strength against the French and British, before the Americans could arrive in sufficient numbers to tip the scales irretrievably to the *Entente*.

Scheuchenstuel's Eleventh Army began a lengthy bombardment with all available artillery on December 2nd. It concentrated on the eastern half of the Plateau, where it could pave the way for attacks down the Brenta, and better support Below's attacks on its left. Minor supporting assaults began on the 3rd near Asiago, but the main blow was delivered on the 5th, using *Sturmtruppen* and veteran soldiers, who bypassed strongly fortified Mt. Sisemol, isolating its *Alpini* defenders, who only surrendered several days later when all hope of relief had passed. Austrian troops swept into the Val Frenzela, which led to the Brenta at Valstagna, but in several days of bitter fighting were unable to reach the river town. Some accounts of the battle record huge numbers of Austrian airplanes droning overhead, seeking air and ground targets. Apparently Julius Arigi was one of these; he was credited with having destroyed two enemy machines on the 7th. A friend of his and another multiple ace Josef Kiss also upped his total on the 7th, and then again on the 16th.[206]

While the battle in the Brenta Valley was at its height, both Below and Boroevic began supporting attacks. Little was expected or accomplished on the Piave, however, Below's Austro-German divisions striking south between the rivers, caused Diaz some very nervous times. Only one ridge, centering on the Mt. Grappa *Massif*, stood between the aggressors and the plains, and the Italians, now reinforced by the French on their right, were desperate to hold. Hötzendorf, who had personally gone to the front on the 4th, was claiming

15,000 prisoners and 65 guns. A solid defense of the *Massif* was critically needed. Mt. Spinoucia was overrun on December 11th and Col. Caprile, at the north edge of Mt. Asolone, was taken on the 14th. A savage attack on Mt. Monfenera on the 13th was accompanied by a particularly heavy barrage; the German gunners were ordered to fire off all their ammunition in anticipation by their officers of being transferred out of Italy.[207] With French support, the Italians were able to frustrate the assaults. Grappa itself was such a massive protrusion and at 1,775 meters (5,822 feet) high it was deemed too formidable an obstruction to be successfully assaulted directly, so *Alliance* attention was shifted to the westward extension of the *Massif*, a lesser peak called Mt. Asolone, which overlooked the Brenta. Control Asolone, the reasoning went, and the valley could be forced and Grappa outflanked.

To this end one final offensive commenced on December 18th, mostly by Austrian forces, the Germans limiting themselves to some supporting moves to the east, around Mt. Tomba. For five days the attack nibbled away at the mountainous terrain, and Hötzendorf claimed 2,000 prisoners. Only in the Val Frenzela was much ground captured, and here it was limited to a few kilometers. By the 23rd, Col del Rosso had been overrun, and Austrian troops were on the outskirts of Valstagna. Most of Mt. Asolone had also been secured when on the 22nd French and Italian troops counterattacked, driving the Austrians away from the lower slopes of Mt. Grappa and re-conquering most of Mt. Asolone. Heavy snows on the 24th stopped most of the fighting, by which time Austrian reports insisted 9,000 enemy troops including the first Frenchmen had been captured since the 18th. It was small consolation, however, for strategic failure, and Austrian troops would once more be forced to winter in the mountains.

On the 26th, the weather was clear again if cold, and the Austrian command sent a force of 25 aircraft—bombers escorted by fighters—to attack an Italian airfield located at Istrana, west of Treviso. When the alarm sounded, as many aircraft as possible were hurriedly sent aloft, to intercept. One skillful pilot, Silvio Scaroni, was able to shoot down three bombers while his colleagues shot down five other Austrians. Scaroni racked up two more kills on the 28th, and brought his personal total for the month to a remarkable eight.[208] Other Austrian formations raided Padua on the 28th, 29th, 30th and 31st, completely terrorizing the populace. Treviso, Vicenza, Castelfranco and Bassano were also bombed on the 31st. For their part, the Italians concentrated on the enemy bridges over the Piave at the various bridgeheads, pounding them to the point that they needed constant repair. On the 28th the Zenson bridges were utterly destroyed.

Two final attacks, both limited in scope, took place in the last days of December. On the 30th the French, as if to remind the Austrians that they would not be outdone, sent a regimental-sized force down the slopes of Mt. Monfenera, following a five-hour barrage.[209] It was a quick success, pushing the enemy away from the mountain and nearly capturing Alano. Twenty-five hundred Austrians became casualties for one-tenth that number of Frenchmen. Also on the 30th, Third Army elements attacked the Zenson bridgehead, precipitating several days of fighting. Their backs to the now bridgeless river, Boroevic's men fought back as best as they could but were subjected to heavy artillery fire without proper shelter. The carnage was awful and most of the defenders were killed; a few jumped into the icy waters and tried to reach the other bank, but most of these men were overcome by the chill. By early January 1918, the Zenson bridgehead force had been wiped out. It was during these operations on the Piave that ace Fiala achieved his tenth victory, by destroying a Caproni bomber near the river. The 1917 campaign was over, and both sides pretty much suspended further ground activity.

Before the year ended, the war at sea had at long last begun to turn in favor of the far-superior *Entente*. Following the initiation of unrestricted submarine warfare by the Germans the previous winter, the tonnage of shipping lost to subs had increased tremendously at first, then settled into a slow decline as the *Entente* navies developed effective anti-submarine measures. The use of aircraft, the convoy system, an improvement in sound detection equipment, and other practices ensured that fewer ships were being lost at sea. By contrast, the German response was characteristically *Entente* in nature: simply send out more U-boats. In December the first of these had begun to augment the Mediterranean fleet, and a not inconsiderable 148,300 tons was sunk that month. But the writing was on the wall; Austrian vessels sank nothing in December, following meager totals for the two previous months.[210]

It may be recalled that prior to November, Austria-Hungary had not lost a major ship to the war, though the Italians had lost several. When the advance of the army as a result of *Waffentreu* had begun to falter on the Piave in mid-month, the old battleships *Wien* and *Budapest* were ordered to Trieste, thence to the mouth of the Piave where they tried to support the ground forces by eliminating threats from the sea, and shelling enemy positions. However, once at Trieste they were within striking distance of smaller craft based in the Venetian lagoons. After darkness had fallen on December 9th, several torpedo boats made the journey between the ports and attacked the big Austrian warships. A torpedo slammed into *Wien* and the battleship quickly sank. Early, overoptimistic reports that *Budapest* had also been destroyed, or severely damaged, turned out to be false, but after thirty-two months of war, the Italian Navy finally had something to cheer about. On the morning of the 10th, the Austro-Hungarians could only morn the loss of such a huge machine, and most galling of all was the fact that all of the raiders had apparently escaped unhurt. No doubt, many of the Habsburg sailors wondered if the turn of fortune in the naval war was a portent of things to come with the new year. By January 1918, with all hope of a true victory fading rapidly, all attention began to turn to Germany and the anticipated renewal of offensive action in the West. The question on everyone's mind was: Could Ludendorff still deliver victory?

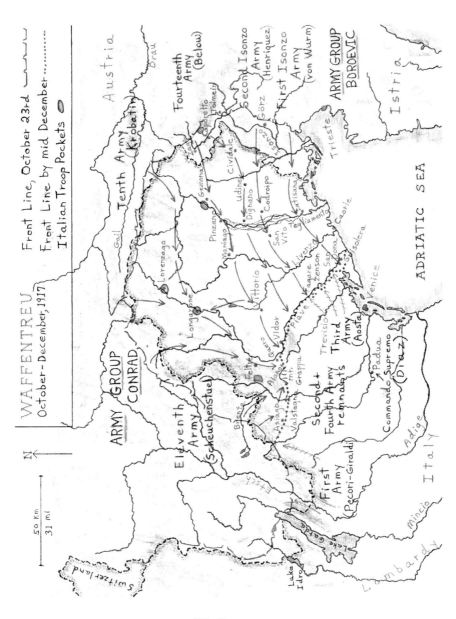

Waffentreu

Chapter Eleven
The Penultimate Round

In the months following the great Italian retreat of the autumn of 1917, the Italian Front became a secondary, almost peripheral theatre of war, at least in the minds of many military leaders of both the *Alliance* and the *Entente*. With the stabilization of the line by the advent of winter it seemed nothing more could be expected there, at least until summer, if ever. Those who understood the temperament of General Diaz realized that no more Cadorna-like offensives could be expected south of the Alps. On the other hand, the front needed to be defended, by both sides. For the British and French, who had weakened their holy Western Front by ten divisions, it was a matter of preventing the defeat of Italy. One by one their other allies had fallen at the hands of the enemy: First Serbia and Montenegro, then Romania and Russia, now if the Italians were to be beaten, only the lines in France would stand between them and an enemy-dominated continent. At all costs, Italy had to be kept in the war.

Had the leaders of the *Alliance* been as determined to smash in the Italian Front as their enemies were to prop it up, they may well had ensured their side could not lose the larger contest. Six German divisions had been sufficient to break Cadorna; what might twenty-six have been capable of? So many divisions were being released from Russia at this time, that finding another two or three dozen for the Alps would have been easy enough. Had these attacked in Italy in the spring instead of in the West, how could the Roman government have survived? Another much less demanding effort could have cleaned up the Balkans, where without German leadership, the Bulgarians were wavering. Had Ludendorff chosen to drive to the Mediterranean that fateful spring instead of into the strongest grouping of *Entente* forces, he could hardly have failed. The Western Front might have been difficult to hold, it is true, but Germany could always withdraw to shorter and shorter lines if need be, without directly endangering herself. And once all forces had been deployed there following the conclusion of the southern campaigns, all the American reinforcement the enemy could muster could never have broken the line in the West. The war may not have been won, but it would not have been lost, either.

Unfortunately for *Kaiser* Karl and his Empire, the German command fell into the same magnetic pull that had attracted the Schlieffens, the Moltkes, the Falkenhayns—not to mention the Haigs, Joffres, Robertsons and so on. The war *had* to be won in the west, an uncompromising, unimaginative, and illogical point of view which cost them all their reputations and would have cost all of their nations a terrible defeat if at least one side had not to win. But Ludendorff was gambling on breaking the line in France before the Americans could intervene in great strength, and once again, as in the Schlieffen timetable, the German war effort would have to race the clock. The 195th Division which had hardly figured in the Italian campaign, was withdrawn to the West in December, as was the 12th Division. In January the 5th Division and the *Alpenkorps* entrained, and in February it was the turn of the 200th Division. That left only the 26th, 117th and *Jäger* Divisions, all of which left Italy by early March. The Austro-Hungarians were thereafter on their own, whereas the Italians still could count on British and French support. The state of affairs gave a major psychological advantage to the armies of Diaz.

Besides feeling somewhat used by their German allies, the Austro-Hungarian people were also feeling increasingly strangled by the effects of the enemy naval blockade. Almost every conceivable product, especially foodstuffs, was in short supply, and prices of everything had inflated to levels unaffordable for all but the wealthiest strata of society. Wintertime was certainly the most trying; lack of fuel and lighting ensured a miserable, cold existence throughout the long, dark months. Anti-war sentiments had always simmered beneath the surface of everyday life, and now they began to boil over as never before. On January 16th, strikes, demonstrations, and even riots in Vienna and Budapest disrupted business-as-usual in the Empire's two largest cities. *Kaiser* Karl was not unsympathetic to the demonstrators, in fact, he generally agreed with them. Although desperate to end the war, Karl knew that either his soldiers must secure victory soon, or his Empire would be torn apart from within, and at the mercy of its enemies. On the first day of February, a serious mutiny rocked the naval base at Cattaro in southern Dalmatia. The sailors demanded immediate peace, better food, and improved service conditions among a long list of grievances, and it took loyal forces three days to suppress the unhappy men, who at bottom were susceptible to agitation due to inactivity brought on by the unwillingness of their superiors to engage a perceived superior enemy fleet which was confining them to port. In short, the long periods of boredom and routine had undermined their morale. Like their German comrades bottled up in North Sea bases for fear of challenging a more powerful foe, the Austro-Hungarian sailors, had they been asked, would probably have preferred to engage the enemy somehow regardless of the risks, rather than sit out the war on idle warships while their nation's future was in peril. Interestingly, three of the leaders of the mutineers escaped retribution by flying a seaplane to Italy.[211]

While the unused navy rusted away, the sea war began to turn against the *Alliance*. In January the U-boats were able to sink 103,000 tons of *Entente* shipping in the Mediterranean, but the totals fell to 84,000 tons in February, a new and ominous trend.[212] Worse still, two submarines, *UB 69* and *UB 66*, were lost in January alone, as many as had been lost in the entire year of 1917. About the only thing the Austro-Germans could cheer about that winter occurred when the raider/cruiser *Wolf* arrived at Pola after a fifteen month cruise of the Atlantic, Pacific, and Indian Oceans, having sunk or badly damaged some thirty *Entente* ships. The *Wolf* was damaged itself when it limped into port, to the cheers of the sailors and marines posted to the harbor. The official German announcement of the vessel's return was issued on February 24th, but the cruiser may have arrived as early as the 17th.

Ground actions at the front over the winter months were few. Artillery fire from the Austrians was reported to be extra heavy on January 5th, and their probes were numerous on the Plateau on the 18th. The Italians attacked at Mt. Asolone on the 14th, prompting two days of fighting, and tried to improve their positions in the Brenta Valley and the Piave delta at the same time. Another battle at Mt. Tomba began on the 23rd and continued sporadically until the end of the month. On the 28th two obscure heights, Mt. di Val Bella and Col del Rosso made the headlines; the Italians claimed some ground gained and 2,500 prisoners during the waning days of January, until heavy snow stopped the nonsense on February 1st. Another action near Asiago was begun on January 29th and lasted in phases until February 11th. No gains of any consequence were achieved by either side, although the Italians claimed another 2,600 prisoners taken on the Plateau.

On January 8th the Italian government announced that Venice was out of danger. Presumably this meant that it was no longer apt to be captured by the Austrians, who had long since been stalled on the Piave and the canals just south of it; no one was so foolish as to believe that it was out of danger from a naval raid, and especially from air raids. To the contrary the advance of the enemy deep into Venetia exposed dozens of population centers to bombing that had hitherto been out of the range of Austrian aircraft. The latter were well aware of their newfound advantages, and soon began to exploit them. Bassano, Treviso, and Mestre were raided on New Year's Day, then Castelfranco and Veneto on the 2nd, Treviso again and Padua on the 3rd, and Mestre, Bassano, and Castelfranco were re-visited on the 4th. Weather grounded the bombers for a time in the middle of the month, then on the 26th they again struck Mestre and Treviso, both on the railroad inland from Venice. Finally, on February 3rd the island-city itself was hit again, along with nearby Padua. Two days later the bombs were falling again; another run of poor weather halted the campaign until the 20th, when it began again and included Padua once more. Mestre, Castelfranco and Venice trembled for the umpteenth time on the 25th. The final raid in February came on the 26th, when witnesses claimed to have counted impact locations of 300 bombs in the old Republic-city, which if true, suggests that this latter raid was indeed a heavy one for the time. Throughout the winter, the Italians for their part did not retaliate much, as they had previously been apt to do; the entire armed forces were concentrating on building up strength. One remarkable exception occurred on February 20th, when long-range Capronis unexpectedly bombed Innsbruck, deep in the Austrian Tyrol.

Neither were the fighter-pilots given any rest that winter. Having risen from obscurity only a few years earlier, they were now considered fixtures by all of the combatant Powers and were very popular with soldiers and civilians alike. January 10th was a notable day for Austria's Linke-Crawford and Gruber, both of whom were credited with two victories near Valstagna. Linke-Crawford's total had now reached fifteen, Gruber's, eight. For Italy, it was Silvio Scaroni who scored on that same day, then again on the 12th near Asiago. Scaroni would destroy two more Austrian airplanes on February 11th, bringing his number of kills to thirteen.[213] Gruber too would go on to outfight two more enemies in February, one on the 1st and one on the 26th over the same stretch of front, between the Plateau and the Piave.[214] Not all pilots, even aces, were so fortunate. Josef Kiss's luck ran out after he had accounted for his 19th enemy machine on January 26th. The following day he was himself shot down, and although he was able to land at his base at Pergine, he was badly wounded and needed many months to recuperate. Raoul Stojsavljevic suffered a similar fate on the 12th, barely managing to survive a crash-landing. He did survive, but for him the war was over; his final tally was ten confirmed victories.[215] And Austria's leading and most famous fighter pilot Godwin Brumowski was shot down twice in a four-day span (February 1st and 4th), the second time again avoiding injury even when the battered machine flipped over, and came to a rest on its top wing. Shaken, Brumowski was advised to refrain from further flights for a while.

Other Austro-Hungarian aces who upped their victory totals for January/ February were Franz Gräser on January 26th and February 24th for fourteen kills, Ernst Strohschneider (14) on January 26th, and Eugen Bönsch (5) on February 21st over the middle Piave.[216]

At the beginning of the month of March, 1918, the Kingdom of Italy fielded 53 divisions along the front with Austria-Hungary, the fewest since January of the previous year. The ten British and French divisions were still present as well. Opposing this force were 41 Austrian and three German divisions; the latter three were soon withdrawn but were replaced by three more Habsburg formations from the East. Virtually everyone on the continent expected a major German offensive on the Western Front at any time. Even the Germans themselves made no particular effort to deny that they intended to attack in the West before American troops could appear on the line in great numbers. The only secret was where and when they would strike. Cringing, the British and French prepared to meet the mighty blow to the best of their ability. Expecting nothing to be brewing in Italy, three French and one British division were recalled from Venetia and hastily railed back to France where every man was sure to be needed. In April, a second British division made the return trip, leaving three, with two French, still in Italy. This arrangement would last until the end of the war. For her part, Italy would manage to maintain 55 divisions again by late June, and this number too would remain constant for the duration. Sixty divisions then was what the Austrian command would have to deal with during most of the 1918 campaigning season.

Straussenberg well knew that he was expected to attack some time in the spring, in support of Ludendorff, in order to ensure that not a single *Entente* soldier more be transferred from the south to the north of the Alps. The question was: when would Ludendorff strike? And what could Austria-Hungary do to help him win? Straussenberg wrestled with the problem, consulted his colleagues, consulted Karl, and all were agreed on one thing. The war had to be ended soon. And the only way to end the war was to force the Italians to negotiate, which in turn meant a successful attack in Italy. Otherwise the nation would be defeated and might break apart—already some enemy leaders were hinting as such. Karl might lose his throne, indeed the throne itself might be swept away forever. Worst of all, the treacherous enemy would win and undoubtedly annex all of the land he wished; land inhabited by Germans, Slovenes, and Croats. By now the Habsburg leaders knew of the Treaty of London (Published by the Bolsheviks in Russia). All were agreed; come what may, the war against Italy had to be won.

To this end, the early months of the year were spent in much the same way the Italians were spending them, building up strength, regrouping, resupplying, and so forth. Neither side was interested in any hard fighting, at least for the time being. Both were determined to be ready, however, when the time should come. Consequently, the early spring months were devoid of any major ground attacks. Patrolling and probing, of course, continued as did artillery exchanges, the latter reported as especially heavy on March 8th in the mountains between the Adige and the Piave. As time passed, more and more encounters between French and British on the one hand, and Austro-Hungarians on the other, took place. The Westerners, however, were soon transferred, part of a major regrouping that Diaz initiated in the spring.

Third Army, still commanded by the Duke of Aosta, and still holding the line of the lower Piave, was least affected by the reshuffling. It held the line from the sea to Papadopoli Island, largest in the river and about midway across the plain. To its left, a new Eighth Army, built around remnants of the destroyed Second, was responsible for the rest of the front on the Piave, to where the line left the river; General Pennella was the boss. From the Piave to the Brenta lay Fourth Army, under De Robilant. Then came a new Sixth Army (Montuori) from the Brenta across the Asiago Plateau, and it was to this formation that the British and French divisions were now attached. To their left the old First Army stretched to Lake Garda. Pecori-Giraldi had remained in command.

From Garda to the Swiss frontier now existed a Seventh Army (Tassoni) as of March. Lastly, a Ninth Army was being created by Diaz to be held behind the front so as to be available in the event of a new emergency. To sum up, six armies now held the front, and these were somewhat smaller than the unwieldy formations sanctioned by Cadorna. They also held (except for Third Army) much shorter sections of front line.

Across no-man's-land, the Austrians were also busy. Boroevic's two Isonzo Armies were once again combined and placed under the leadership of von Wurm. It stood opposite the enemy Third Army. Out of the remains of the German Fourteenth Army was created a new Sixth Army, which faced the Italian Eighth. Archduke Josef was the commander. Then came the two armies of Hötzendorf's group, the Eleventh (Scheuchenstuel), as far as the Astico, and the Tenth (von Krobatin) to the border with Switzerland. There was one inherent disadvantage to this arrangement; no single headquarters commanded the entire theatre, and Straussenberg had other responsibilities besides Italy.

At sea the effectiveness of the U-boats in the Mediterranean continued to decline, due in no small part to the fact that enemy shipping was being much better protected. Nearly 104,000 tons were sunk in March, but less than 76,000 tons in April.[217] Only once did the Austrians attempt to repeat their considerable success against the anti-submarine line of boats at Otranto Straits; five destroyers steamed towards the narrows on the night of April 22nd/23rd. They were challenged by British destroyers off the Albanian coast, and following a brief exchange in which the Austrians gave better than they received, the raiders turned and headed for home. It was a good decision, as the action had caused a small fleet to gather to meet them.[218]

As it had done in the winter, air action dominated the minor actions of the spring. Venice was bombed on March 10th, and on the following day a remarkable raid was carried out on distant Naples. It seemed as though the Italians were not the only ones capable of long-range bombing. March 3rd was a memorable day for an English pilot, who shot down six Austrians before he himself was shot down by ace Benno Fiala. The Englishman, a certain Lieutenant Jerrard, survived and was awarded the Victoria Cross[219]; Fiala went on to claim other victims on the 11th, 13th, and 30th of the month, bringing his total to fourteen victories.[220] Franz Gräser enjoyed a very successful month in March as well. He burst a balloon on the 8th, then destroyed airplanes on the

12th, 16th, and 23rd, all on the lower Piave. Gräser was now able to boast of 18 confirmed victories. Others, like Eugen Bönsch, spent much of the month engaged in attacks on Italian airfields, harbors, and railroad facilities. As March turned into April Bönsch found himself involved in mostly ground-attack missions, not nearly as notorious, and just as dangerous, as combat with other aircraft. He was able, however, to perforate an observation balloon on April 3rd, and down a reconnaissance aircraft on the 17th, for his 7th kill.[221] Upstream on the Piave, Stefan Fejes achieved his 10th and 11th victories on March 22nd and 30th, respectively. Aces-to-be Friedrich Navratil and Franz Rudorfer both scored their first confirmed kills on April 17th, the latter over Mt. Grappa.

If aces were being made, they were also being eliminated. Ernst Strohschneider shot down his fifteenth enemy aircraft on March 16th, but it would be his last. While flying at night in an attack on enemy positions near Zenson, the veteran pilot was killed when he attempted to land. The Austrians also lost the services of Kurt Gruber on April 4th, shot down and killed a short while after he had gained his eleventh victory.[222]

Fortunately for the Austrians, three of Italy's leading aces, Baracca, Ruffo, and Piccio were inactive at this time; they were being presented to grateful crowds in several Italian cities and received wild, enthusiastic acclaim. Other men continued to serve their nation very well in the air. Flavio Baracchini, who had only been flying for one year was quickly running up an amazing total of enemy aircraft. Soon to be shot down and killed himself, Baracchini had destroyed twenty-one Austrian machines at the time of his death. Ferruccio Ranza increased his total by at least two, to thirteen at this time, as well. Silvio Scaroni, scoreless in March, could celebrate his sixteenth victim on April 3rd, when he set an observation balloon on fire.[223]

The aces may have been given much of the publicity, but the outcome of the war was still in the hands of the politicians and the generals. Ludendorff began his long-awaited offensive in the West on March 21st, although it was to be only the first of five such blows, designed to win the war. Hoffmann and many others who were never consulted would have preferred one mighty effort, and if it failed, retreat to a shorter, more defensible line. But Ludendorff was convinced it was a matter of winning now or never, and the Western Front attacks became symbolic of Germany's future: if they succeeded, the war was won; if not it was lost. Caught up in all the frenzy were, of course, the rest of the *Alliance* nations, especially Austria-Hungary, which was expected to support the grand scheme with all of its remaining strength. When Straussenberg, supported by Karl, still had enough self-respect to refuse Austro-Hungarian divisions for the Western Front, the Germans demanded a supporting attack in Italy. Straussenberg was obliged to agree, but in reality attack was the only option for the Italian Front in 1918; the war could not be won with passivity. But both Boroevic and Hötzendorf had been made field-marshals by now; who would lead the attack?

Hötzendorf knew he was no favorite of the Emperor, therefore he bombarded Straussenberg with requests for reinforcement with which to carry out another of his pet offensives from the mountains. Boroevic had no such grandiose ideas; the whole idea of attack did not appeal to him, as he had, it will be remembered, fought off many major offensives undertaken by a far superior enemy. He preferred to make only a moderately strong effort on the Piave, to placate the Germans and pin down the enemy. Logic dictated that one Army Group be strengthened at the expense of the other, as the nation could not provide the necessary resources for two all-out attacks in 1918.

Unfortunately for the Austro-Hungarian cause, it was not logic but *Kaiser* Karl that decided the issue. Calling his Field Marshals to a conference on April 11th,[224] Karl listened one final time to their respective points of view, then announced he had made a decision. All available manpower, munitions, and supplies were to be split between the two Army Groups. In effect, both would be strengthened somewhat, but neither sufficiently so to ensure success. For Boroevic, the new operation would be known as *Albrecht*. Hötzendorf would call his *Radetzky*, after an historic Habsburg soldier/leader who had more than once defeated the Italians. Both blows were to be delivered in the second half of May, if all went well.

At long last the Emperor was burning his bridges. Only a few days after the military conference, Karl confronted Count Czernin, his Foreign Minister, in Vienna. Czernin, who had recently been negotiating the surrender of Romania in Bucharest, had been unable to resist the pressure of the Germans and Hungarians, both of whom favored a harsher peace than he would have imposed. The Minister was aware of the Emperor's displeasure, and learned he was about to be dismissed; it was he who had recently advised Karl to assert his independence of Berlin (and who had worked hard to promote the Emperor's peace initiatives) to which the Monarch allegedly responded "Ich möchte schon, aber wie?" (I would like to, but how?). Now, the Emperor no longer had any use for this man, who had worked so diligently for moderation and peace. Czernin was asked for his resignation, and a heated argument ensued. Apparently the Count was truly hurt by his Monarch; with nothing to gain and everything to lose, he leaked details of the Sixte affair to the bellicose Clemenceau of France,[225] who published the material following initial denials of its authenticity by Karl. The Germans were incredulous, and Karl, without a friend to turn to, was forced to apologize to *Kaiser* Wilhelm and promise to never enter into secret negotiations again. If anyone still doubted that the survival of the Habsburgs depended on victory by the Hohenzollerns, the whole mess put all such misgivings firmly to rest. Czernin's career was of course over; he was replaced by Baron Burian von Rajecz, a Hungarian.

In fact, the foundations upon which the Habsburg Monarchy was built were already being seriously undermined. One case in point involved an Englishman, Wickham Steed, who was foreign editor of the London *Times*. Like many westerners Steed did not at first contemplate the break-up of the Austro-Hungarian Empire, he only participated in what amounted to a propaganda campaign against it. However, as the war progressed and he was made increasingly aware of the goals of various radical groups of the many different nationalities of the Empire, he was increasingly exposed to ideas which, if promoted, would assist the *Entente* cause by weakening one of the principal enemy states. Eventually, Steed was urging the War Cabinet to humor Czech, Polish, Serb and Croat, Slovak and even Romanian separatists of Austro-Hungarian nationality by proclaiming *Entente* support for independence of these peoples from German and Hungarian landlords. One of the biggest problems with this sort of activity had always been the Italian participation on the side of the *Entente*, cemented by the Treaty of London. Italy had been promised extensive areas inhabited by Slovenes and Croats. How then could the South Slavs be courted without offending the Italians? Already, peace with Austria via Karl's feelers had basically been rejected because of the Italian connection. Yet the South Slavs were spoken for by the Serbs, another *Entente* people, and their voices could not be ignored. Matters came to a head in early 1918, and in the middle of March, Steed left London for Rome to attend a Conference called for in an attempt to iron out differences between the Italians and the Austro-Hungarian dissidents, especially the South Slavs. Steed wanted Sonnino to attend this 'Congress of Oppressed Nationalities', but the

Italian Foreign Minister refused, citing his refusal to compromise the London Treaty. Instead Senator Ruffini chaired the meeting and although not all of the various nationalistic aspirations were sanctioned, the separatist movements were pretty much legitimized.[226] By the time the Conference broke up on April 10th, the Empire of Austria-Hungary was doomed, unless it won the war, an outcome that was increasingly unlikely with every passing day.

May 1918 action in the Mediterranean went decidedly against the *Alliance*. On the night of the 4th/5th the Italian Navy transported *Arditi* troops across the Adriatic, where they raided and destroyed several electrical sub-stations on the Dalmatian Coast and Islands. Two nights later a tiny torpedo craft was able to sneak into the harbor at Pola. It was discovered and sunk before it could do any damage, but the portent was ominous. When the Austrians attempted to retaliate with another destroyer raid on the Otranto Straits on the night of the 8th/9th, they were detected well before they approached their destination and had to withdraw quickly to avoid being run down and destroyed by superior forces. At this stage of the war an overwhelming enemy fleet had begun to patrol the Straits, and its vigilance was a strong deterrent to future raids. Worse still, of sixteen submarines on patrol in the Middle Sea and its offshoots that month, five were lost to enemy action.[227] As against this, the *Alliance* could boast of 112,700 tons of enemy shipping sunk, but it was the last calendar month of the war in which over 100,000 tons would go down.[228]

On May 3rd General Foch, by mutual consent of the *Entente* nations, was made Supreme Commander of all *Entente* ground forces. For the first time in the war, the *Alliance* powers faced a unified (in theory at least) enemy coalition, a state of affairs that they themselves had enjoyed for nearly two years. Simultaneously, the Western and Italian Fronts were merged into one so-called 'Entente Battle Line'. Beyond the fortifications *Kaiser* Karl paid another personal visit to some of his front-line troops, in an effort to help build morale for the coming offensives, on the 5th. Suspecting something was in the wind, British troops raided Austrian defenses near Stella, on the Plateau. They were subjected to an artillery barrage as retaliation. A few days later the Austrians counterattacked, but the move was expected, and it accomplished little. When beginning on May 13th Diaz was receiving numerous reports of an impressive enemy buildup, he concluded something resembling a spoiling attack was called for. Seventh Army, as the one least likely to be at risk, was ordered to engage the enemy; an attack in the rugged mountains of the west end of the line began on the 26th. One ridge beyond Tonale Pass was reported as taken, along with 870 prisoners and twelve guns,[229] within 48 hours. In addition, Seventh Army forward units insisted that all signs seemed to indicate that the enemy Tenth Army had been preparing a similar assault at the Pass. In fact, *Radetzky* had been expected to begin on the 28th, but owing to unfavorable weather conditions in the mountains, it had been postponed. The only other moderately heavy fighting in the month took place in the channelized waterways of the lower Piave floodplain where Austrian troops battled for more favorable jump-off points from which to begin *Albrecht*. These actions centered around Capo Sile, a town located at the junction of several canals and a delta arm of the Piave, and occurred toward the end of the month.

Milder, clearer weather typical of the month of May tended to encourage a good deal of aviation. For Benno Fiala the first day of the month brought success as amazing as any experienced by a pilot in the war. In a single sortie, the ace destroyed two enemy airplanes and two observation balloons. Another Austrian of Fiala's unit, Franz Rudorfer, also accounted for one airplane and one balloon on the same day.[230] For Frank Linke-Crawford, May 10th was a day of two victories, his 20th and 21st. Other airmen, however, were not so fortunate. On the 13th, the Italians claimed to have shot eleven Austrian aircraft out of the sky. Franz Gräser's final flight took place on May 17th, as he escorted a reconnaissance plane over Treviso. Both Austrian aircraft were shot down by three enemy fighters. Antonio Chiri, a man who would also become an ace before the war was over, is believed to have caused Gräser's machine to have caught fire. The Austrian's final tally was 18 confirmed kills. Within a week, it was the turn of Josef Kiss, whose 19 victories were fifth best among his countrymen. Kiss was killed by a British fighter, while flying over the lower Val Sugana.[231] Over nearby Mt. Tomba, but a day or two later, Silvio Scaroni dispatched his seventeenth victim. And with Major Baracca again airborne for Italy other enemy machines were bound to fall. Baracca lived up to his reputation that month, by shooting down an enemy on May 3rd, and another on May 22nd. Italy's leading ace was by now a legend, and held 32 victories to his credit.[232] Slowly but surely, the Austro-Hungarians were yielding air superiority to their enemies over the Italian Front.

A fairly heavy air battle was reported over the middle of the northern portion of the Adriatic Sea, west of Pola, on May 18th. Apparently, seaplane groups from each side had blundered into each other, and one plane from each was lost. Two days later other Italian naval aircraft bombed targets at Durazzo and on Lagosta Island. Avoiding the vigorous anti-aircraft fire, the groups returned unmolested.[233]

Ludendorff had begun to unleash the German Army on the Western Front as early as March 21st, when the first of the hammer-blows designed to achieve victory was struck. Impressive gains of ground followed for a week, then a week of slight advances was suffered before the first attack was brought to a halt. Amiens was almost, but not quite, taken, an occurrence that might have led to a German dash to the English Channel. In April, a second thrust drove in the front south of Ypres, but similarly failed to reach the coast. Then on May 27th, a third offensive fell upon the French, driving them back to the Marne River and to a point at which the *Kaiser's* men were closer to Paris than at any time since September of 1914. However, American troops were beginning to arrive at the Front in considerable numbers; there were 18 U.S. divisions in France by June 1st. Ludendorff's staff, at the behest of their chief, began to appeal ever more loudly to Straussenberg to begin his own attacks, anything to divert or distract the *Entente* from the Western Front.

Originally, the Austrian brass had planned to take the offensive on or about the 20th of May; then the 28th had been agreed upon, but as we have seen, it too came and went without action. The new date became June 11th, itself discarded when miserable weather hung over much of the front. Hötzendorf was the only one itching to go; he was certain that his long-range objective— Verona—could be reached easily enough, probably within a few days. This was indeed a very curious belief for him to have entertained; he had already been the architect of two prior attacks from out of the southeastern Tyrol, both of which had failed to reach the plains due to lack of sufficient strength. He must have know that *Radezsky* would be his last chance to fall upon the Italian rear, yet it too had not been heavily reinforced, because of the need to send half of all available resources to Boroevic. No doubt, the Field Marshal's undue optimism was born of the fact that for him, and for the country he had served for so long, the offensive simply *had* to succeed. Failure was not an option.

For his part, Boroevic well knew that his chances of smashing the Piave Front and pushing on to the distant objective of Padua, were slim. Both he and Straussenberg agreed that the attack was necessary, for a number of reasons, the most important of which was the survival of the Empire, but neither man was expecting success of war-winning magnitude. Rather, they hoped for at least a limited advance, from which morale might be improved, or at least maintained, and quantities of enemy supplies captured. Hunger had become a real problem even for the army now, and the soldiers were convinced by a clever propaganda campaign that to advance into Italy meant to advance into a land of plentiful food and drink. When the assaults were again postponed on the 11th, all commanders agreed no further delays could be tolerated, and a final, definitive date was set for the 15th.

The final delay allowed the Italians to score a huge psychological victory in the meantime. Fearing a further deterioration in the morale of the sailors if the Navy continued to remain idle, the aggressive Admiral Horthy, of Otranto Straits fame and now in command of the Austrian fleet, ordered his big ships into action. The idea was to lure enemy small and medium sized warships out to sea with another raid on the Straits by his smaller vessels, then destroy them with his battleships. Accordingly, the capital ships left the relative safety of Pola and steamed out across the Adriatic where they were seen by Captain Rizzo, the man who six months earlier had sunk the *Wien*, in his small torpedo boat. Rizzo, certainly one of the luckiest boat bosses of the war, was able to torpedo another battleship, and escape unharmed. The vessel, one of Austria's largest and most modern warships, named *Szent Istvan*, sank within a few hours, taking 90 men to their deaths. Stunned, Horthy cancelled the entire operation. The date was June 10th, 1918. Rizzo, already a hero in Italy, was now treated more like a saint. If the demise of the *Wien* had signaled a turning-point in the war at sea, the sinking of *Szent Istvan* meant that Austria-Hungary no longer possessed sufficient sea power to challenge the *Entente* even in the Adriatic.

June began with an especially heavy amount of air activity on the part of the Italians and their allies. Spies, deserters, and intelligence reports of all varieties had long since warned of the Austrian intentions, though the latter had done a remarkably good job of concealing their troop movements, concentration areas, and artillery pads. More information was urgently needed, and all available aircraft flew sortie after sortie, bombing roadways and railways and machine gunning all apparently worthwhile targets, and many that were not. Even individual automobiles and supply wagons were attacked. Austrian airmen did their best to defend their ground forces, but they were well outnumbered by now and rarely crossed into enemy airspace. Two fighter pilots shot down two Italian airplanes apiece on June 6th. Benno Fiala raised his total to 21 near the Piave that day, while Franz Rudorfer became an ace even though his second kill of the two could not be confirmed, due to poor visibility.[234] Two days later, it was Silvio Scaroni who scored when he destroyed an Austrian machine defending airspace over Mt. Grappa. On the 9th, Austrian naval aircraft bombed Brindisi harbor as part of the operation aimed at the nearby Straits which had ended in disaster.

Finally the waiting for both sides was over. Tenth Army's sole contributions to the spring offensives were two weak attacks in the mountains on the far west of the front line. The larger of the two struck Monticello Ridge, above the Tonale Pass, on the 13th. The other came south of the Ademello *Massif* in the hills of the western Val Guidicaria. Both were stopped almost immediately; the only ground gained was an obscure height called Col di Rosso near Mt. Albriole. Like so many 'diversionary' attacks undertaken by both sides over the past three years, Tenth Army's efforts were a waste of precious resources that should have gone to the main effort farther east.

Hötzendorf prepared an address to his troops which was distributed to units at the smallest level; every man was to understand the importance of the coming attack. It appealed to their sense of duty and reminded them of the long, proud history of their Empire. Most soldiers needed no prodding, and were as eager as their officers to finish with the *Welsce* once and for all. They did not have long to wait. In the event it was the Italians who struck first on that very day, at fifteen minutes before midnight. Having learned that the Austrian attack would commence on the 15th, the *Entente* troops on the Asiago Plateau began barrages of their own, for the purpose of destroying the enemy assault troops as they assembled. Besides the affair immediately before the new day began, another at 2:45am followed, and this was only fifteen minutes before *Radetzky* was due to begin.

At precisely 3:00am on the 15th, the massed artillery of three Austro-Hungarian Armies opened fire, using all available calibers and types of shells. High explosive, shrapnel, gas and even 305mm armor-piercing[235] were reported as raining down on the front lines between the Astico and the sea. On Eleventh Army's front the cannonade was quite accurate, and in four hours of pounding destroyed enemy trenches, communications and barbed wire. Along the British sector it even exploded an ammunition dump in a thunderous staccato of detonations. The Austrian command had chosen a 30 kilometer (18 mile) stretch of line between Canove and Mt. Grappa for the assault, which began punctually at 7:00am, led by well trained and well equipped *Sturmtruppen* using the infiltration tactics that had worked so well for *Waffentreu*. This time, however, they encountered not demoralized Italians, but British, French and determined Italian troops who knew they must not retreat, lest the enemy reach the plains. Even so, the attackers made two or three kilometers in some sectors and about one kilometer against the British. Despite fierce fighting, often at close quarters with grenades, flame-throwers, and even knives and clubs, the attack stalled. Mt. Lemerle once again, as in 1916, became the high-water mark of Austrian fortunes. The French barely budged at all, and the British counterattacked and regained what little they had lost within 24 hours. Soon, the Italians too had recovered, countered, and repaired the line in their area. It is not unfair to state that before darkness fell on Sunday the 16th, Eleventh Army had lost its chance to break through the enemy front line. *Radetzky* had already failed.

To the east Boroevic's two Armies also attacked on the morning of the 15th, along a 75 kilometer (47 mile) front from the sea to near Vidor on the Piave. Aside from a stretch of land a few kilometers inland from the mouth of the stream which had been captured the previous November, the river in its wide channel was still pretty much the front line. All sorts of bridging equipment had been brought forward in the weeks preceding the offensive, and behind the powerful artillery barrage the engineers worked frantically to span the waters with enough structures to allow for the passage of large numbers of troops. Bridgeheads were seized at Saletto, Fagare, Zenson, and Fossalta and every attempt was made to link these and the established ones opposite San Dora and Grisolera, with lateral movement. Once the right bank of the Piave had been secured, the heavy guns could cross and the advance could proceed across the plain toward Padua, or so went Boroevic's reasoning. Unfortunately for the Austrians, the floating bridges were very vulnerable to Italian artillery fire and airplane attacks, and were damaged or destroyed as fast as the exhausted engineers could repair them. Nevertheless, the river was crossed in force along the front of the Isonzo Army. To its right, Sixth Army crossed in several locations opposite the Montello, and began to storm the heights.

'Il Montello' is an oddity on the Venetian Plain. It is a low height too big to be referred to as a hill immediately south of the river where the stream enters the coastal plain, forcing the waters to flow in a gentle arc around its north edge. Apparently a moraine left in the wake of the last Ice Age, the Montello is not part of the Alpine chain, but rather is detached from the hills to the north and forms a very conspicuous height from the surrounding lowland. Perhaps 12 kilometers (8 mile) long, half as wide, and at its highest point 368 meters (1,200 feet), the mountain was well eroded, therefore fairly smooth-sided and relatively flat-topped. It was heavily wooded[236] and crisscrossed with several secondary roads, and many more wood roads. As a vantage point in the surrounding lowlands, the Montello was well worth possessing and its capture . by the Austrians might just unhinge the whole Piave line.

While desperate fighting raged for the Montello and the river crossings, airmen of both armies tried hard to support their comrades on the ground. Silvio Scaroni dispatched an Austrian on the 15th and Major Baracca shot down two, his 33rd and 34th victories. With these, Italy's ace of aces was finished scoring. Four days later he was dead, the event beginning a long controversy about his demise. No doubt his airplane was shot down, but the fact that his body was found detached from the wreckage and not burned, led some to believe he had in fact shot himself[237]—there was a bullet wound through his forehead—to avoid capture by advancing Austrian troops, at the foot of the Montello. Others claimed he was victimized by a large group of Austrian fighters; whatever the case, another fine pilot was dead. Meanwhile, Austria's leading ace Brumowski achieved his 32nd kill near Spresiano on the 16th, and three days later was able to score twice more. Stefan Fejes shot down a SPAD on the 15th for his fifteenth victory. Eugen Bönsch broke a balloon on the 16th, then destroyed an airplane over the Montello on the 20th, for his tenth confirmed victory.[238]

Beginning on the 17th, the waters of the river rose considerably, as the volume from the recent rains upstream in the watershed reached the plain. Soon a raging torrent, replete with floating logs and all sorts of debris, some of it deliberately pushed into the stream by Italian troops upriver, was slamming into the precarious floating bridges, sweeping many away. A German observer at the Montello sector claimed that "six times are the bridges and footways completed, six times are they destroyed."[239] The main Austrian concern at this time, however, was to push the Italians far enough away from the river as to make the crossings out of the range of the most numerous medium artillery. If this could be accomplished, the crisis of the bridges would be considerably eased. By the 17th at least half, possibly two-thirds of the Montello had been taken. A French observer even wrote that the town of Montebelluna, on a railroad just off the southwest edge of the mountain had been captured by the enemy;[240] he may well have been mistaken. Apparently the place was like a ghost town, completely evacuated and even under hostile shell-fire from some of the few mountain guns the Austrians had been able to manhandle over the Piave, but every other account has the Sixth Army units on the heights stopped before they could desend the southern slopes. The situation had become critical for Diaz however; on the same day Isonzo Army was able to link several of its bridgeheads, and the only area where the front had not been pushed away from the Piave was a short stretch where the two Armies of Boroevic flanked each other. For a few days it seemed as though *Albrecht* might succeed where *Radetzky* had failed. On the morning of the 18th, von Wurm's men were only 18 kilometers (11 miles) from Venice as the crow flies, and Archduke Josef's soldiers were but six or seven from Asolo. At General Headquarters, Straussenberg ordered Hötzendorf to send all available troops to Boroevic, but these would require several days to be moved. In the event it was too little, too late. Italian Ninth Army reserves began to pour into the line, fulfilling the very duties they had been expected to. The Austrians had advanced as far as they would ever be able to.

Diaz's counterattacks first hit the Sixth Army on the Montello and on the River on the 18th; that same day Isonzo Army was attacked at the Salletto and Zenson sectors. And more rain began to fall, slowly swelling the Piave. The situation at the bridges was critical with the shelling, bombing and flooding taking its toll. So many Austro-Hungarians had crossed the river by now that maintenance of the supply-routes was absolutely essential, yet despite all efforts many of the structures could not be safely used. Dozens, perhaps hundreds of the brave engineer troops were killed while trying to support their countrymen, but nature seemed to be on the side of the Italians. The last forward movement of *Albrecht* occurred on the 20th south of Capo Sile, only a few kilometers shy of the north tip of the Venetian Lagoon. Boroevic had now committed the last of his reserves and had not managed a true breakthrough.

June 21st brought a renewal of the Italian counter on the Montello. Heavy fighting, often at close quarters, raged in the woods of the huge hill; without fresh reserves joining them periodically, the Austrians were forced to yield once their ranks were depleted. To the southeast, all of the artillery Diaz could muster was sighted against the wide, deep enemy penetration beyond the Piave, and began to systematically blast away at the Austrian infantry, who of course had not had a chance to dig in or seek shelter on the mostly flat, open plain. With his bridges disappearing one by one, von Wurm appealed to Boroevic for permission to withdraw before it was too late. On the following morning he had his answer: pull back over the river, nothing more was to be gained in *Albrecht*. For the next 36 hours, under constant air and artillery attack, the ravaged units retreated over the Piave, whenever circumstances allowed. In some cases the desperate, harassed men, denied by the enemy or the flooding of a floating bridge, discarded their equipment and jumped into the water, hoping to swim to safety. Many of these soldiers were swept away in the strong current or were machine gunned by roving Italian airplanes. Nevertheless, the majority were able to cross the stream, before an enemy infantry attack on the 23rd closed up to the water-barrier, having pretty much punched at empty space. By the 24th, the only Austrians south of the Piave were holding a line Fosetta Canal—Sile Canal—lower Sile River.

His left flank now exposed, Archduke Josef had no choice but to pull back as well; the Montello was given up on June 24th. Hoping to cause further carnage at the few remaining bridges, the Italians sent all available aircraft to the river, as did the Austrian command, determined to prevent such a calamity. What followed was three or four days of intense bombing and strafing runs, and a good deal of aerial combat. Over Conegliano on the 25th, Silvio Scaroni dispatched two enemy fighters, bringing his victory total to 21. Scaroni had now replaced the deceased Baracca as Italy's highest-scoring ace. On the very same day, Austria's leading fighter pilot was ordered away from the front "on extended leave". Godwin Brumowsky, with 35 confirmed victories would fly no more combat missions, but he did survive the war. His status as the top Habsburg scorer on the Italian Front was soon taken by Benno Fiala, whose squadron engaged an air fleet of 26 hostile airplanes in the notorious 'Air Battle of the Montello'. When the dogfighting was over, five Italians had been shot out of the sky, three of whom were credited to Fiala, who now could claim 24 confirmed victories.[241]

Encouraged by the headlong retreat of the enemy, Diaz authorized local counterattacks all along the line. Little could be expected on the Piave front, but a limited attack at Mt. Grappa on the 26th took a large number of dispirited prisoners, and 2,000 more were reported captured as a result of an assault at Mt. di Val Bella, before the month was out. Even Col di Rosso, in the extreme west, which had been lost earlier in the month, was retaken in a surprise attack on June 30th. But the best news for most Italians in late June was the appearance of another contingent of foreigners allied to their cause. During the height of the Battle of the Piave, General Pershing had ordered, at the request of the Italians, American troops sent to Italy. For reasons still unclear, the 332 Infantry Regiment of the 83rd Division was selected, a meager force to be sure, but the gesture was more symbolic of *Entente* unity than it was designed to reinforce the Italian Front. On June 28th, an advance party of 2,000 mostly medical personnel and staff officers landed at Genoa[242] to considerable local enthusiasm. Soon, these people were involved in setting up facilities in cities behind the front such as Padua and Vicenza. Another month and more would pass before they were joined by the combat troops.

Italy's defensive victory on the Piave and on the Plateau in June of 1918 symbolized a sort of rebirth of national will so very badly injured by Cadorna's inane strategy and by the awful disaster caused by Below's offensive of the preceding October. For the first time in the war, the average Italian soldier genuinely believed he could defeat his Austro-Hungarian opponent. Moreover, he no longer doubted that his side would win, and now sooner rather than later. British and French blood had been shed in his cause, and Americans were on the way. His nation was not fighting alone, was certainly not isolated. The tide had turned at sea, in the air, and on the ground. His countrymen were united as never before, determined to drive out the invaders and conquer *Italia Irredenta*. Domestic factories were producing record numbers of weapons and munitions of all types, and the quality thereof was not inferior to that of the foe. *Entente* nations were supplying that which could not be found or produced at home. True enough, there was still a serious food and fuel shortage, but the situation was not desperate, as it was—if the enemy prisoners were to be believed—in the ranks across no-man's-land. Perhaps most importantly, unrest on the home front was subsiding, as the populace did its best to get in step with the war effort. And Italian troops were confident that their lives would not be wasted in unnecessary, suicidal attacks. Given a short while from which to recover from the June fighting, the army would be ready to once again assume the offensive and avenge the defeat of Caporetto.

Losses for Italy during the June fighting were 85 to 90 thousand men. Three new divisions entered the line that month, raising the front total to 55 once again; for the rest of the war no attempt was made to increase this number, however, existing units would for the most part be kept up to full strength. In addition, two so-called 'Czech' divisions were raised in June out of former Austro-Hungarian prisoners of war who were mostly Slavs desiring to fight for the 'liberation' of their 'subject nations' within the Empire. All told, then, fifty-five Italian, three British, two French and two 'Czech' divisions would constitute the *Entente* order of battle on the Italian Front from June until the end of the war.

Across the front lines, the beaten divisions of *Kaiser* Karl's Army had lost their last chance to win the war, and they knew it. Having begun the war with Italy at a three and one-half to one deficit in terms of numbers, they had slowly closed the gap until May, when their 55 had faced 58 *Entente* divisions, the closest to parity they would ever enjoy. As of July, their 55 had to deal with 62 enemy formations, and the difference remained constant thereafter. Estimates of Habsburg losses for the June offensives range from 118,000[243] to 152,000 men, and these figures represent some of the best soldiers the Dual Monarchy had possessed at that time. Thereafter many if not most units remained under-strength in men and weapons. Ammunition, never a plentiful commodity in Italy, became scarce, as did most supplies and wares. Food was perhaps the biggest problem of all; by the summer of 1918 malnutrition had become a factor even in the army. Industrial output in the nation was down, due to lack of raw materials, fuel, and labor. Transportation, of course, also suffered the privations. In some cases, locomotives were forced to burn wood for fuel, due to a shortage of coal. Stocks of gasoline and kerosene all but dried up. Needless to relate, the populace was restive and ready to strike and even revolt. Most discontents were demanding peace, at any price.

Oddly enough, the Army, though defeated, was still not ready to quit. Despite dogged efforts by propagandists to portray the Austro-Hungarian forces as soldiers of suspect loyalties to the Empire, excepting the Germans and Magyars, such was not the case. All of the various linguistic groups had fought well during *Radetzky* and *Albrecht*, and it was not for a lack of loyalty or determination that these attacks failed. It was more like a lack of good leadership, that problem that had always bedeviled the Italians under Cadorna, that doomed Austria's last offensives. Had either Hötzendorf or Boroevic been heavily reinforced instead of both being lightly reinforced, one or the other may well have broken the front; instead the last reserves of national strength were frittered away piecemeal at a time when success was absolutely critical. After the Battle of the Piave, all the soldiers knew they would never attack again. Defensive warfare, waiting for the enemy to strike, with all its dangers to morale, was now the order of the day. No longer victory, but preventing defeat was the goal.

Among the many Austrian leaders who knew the end could not long be delayed was Franz Conrad von Hötzendorf, the old advocate of preventative war against Italy. Perhaps more than any other figure in the Habsburg Empire the Field Marshal epitomized conflict with the Latins. Three times in the war he had attempted to attack from the South Tyrol and into the enemy rear, and each succeeding effort had been weaker and less effective than the previous one. Three times a very sound strategy had been frustrated for lack of sufficient force, and it is only fitting that after three strikes, Hötzendorf was out. Karl no longer had need of his bellicose ex-Chief of Staff. On July 15th, the Emperor dismissed his warrior and sent him into retirement. No wonder that during that depressing summer derogatory expressions aimed at Karl through his Italian wife could be heard in Vienna and other cities. "Pfui Parma" (Down with Parma, meaning 'the Empress's family Bourbon-Parma) and "Die Welsche hat uns verraten" (The [insulting term for Italian woman] has betrayed us).[244] No doubt the Empress Zita's feelings about the war were mixed, but she certainly did not want to lose her throne. As for Karl, he was at least intelligent enough to realize that the war was lost, and that his actions no longer really mattered.

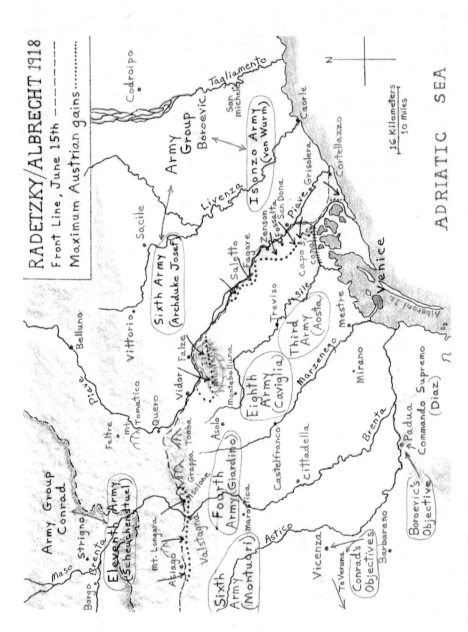

Radetzky/Albrecht 1918

Chapter Twelve
An Empire Disintegrates

That General Armando Diaz would be an entirely different sort of leader from his predecessor was immediately apparent following the defeat of the Austrian June offensives. Cadorna had, after all, launched four major attacks in 1915, five in 1916, and three in 1917 before his enemies had begun the massive stroke which would knock him off the top spot at *Commando Supremo*. Most commanders of the day would almost certainly have followed up the enemy withdrawals of late June with a campaign of strong counterattacks, such as those unleashed by Cadorna on the heels of Hötzendorf's May 1916 drive. But Diaz was of another mindset; genuinely concerned for the lives of his men, conscious of the extraordinary sacrifices necessary to create the military machine he had been entrusted with, and cautious almost to a fault, he was not willing to gamble on enterprises which offered only a marginal chance of success. Content to merely clean up the line in a few areas which made defense awkward for his Armies, he wisely resisted every petition from his own subordinates and his *Entente* allies to go over to the offensive during the primary campaigning season of 1918, the summer months. For well over three months, while gigantic military operations commenced on the Western Front, the Italian Army would engage in an active defense of shelling, bombing, probing, and raiding; it was nevertheless a defense, while the front-line units were rested and brought up to full strength, reserves were created, and weaponry of all sorts was replaced or refurbished and supplied with lavish stocks of ammunition. Defenses were improved to the point where Italy needed not worry about future enemy offensives.

At bottom, Diaz's strategy was an intelligent one, and the right one for the circumstances of the time. He realized that grand offensives were foolish in this, a war when defense prevailed. He knew that big attacks against a still-formidable opponent would only serve to weaken his forces and destroy whatever gains he had made in the improvement of the morale of his troops. And perhaps most importantly, he understood that his enemy was incapable of further offense, and was slowly being weakened by decay on his home front and attrition on other battle fronts. As the submarine threat was gradually overcome, food and raw material shortages in the *Entente* nations improved tolerably, while for the *Alliance*, the enemy blockade had practically strangled the national economies. Clearly, time now favored the *Entente*, and Diaz was not going to sacrifice his men to accomplish a goal that now seemed within reach simply by virtue of patience.

Meanwhile, Ludendorff was still busy expending the last of Germany's strength on futile offensives in the West when for a fraction of the effort advanced there, he could have driven in both the Italian and Salonika Fronts and made his position virtually impregnable. Instead, having learned nothing from the drives of March, April, and May which gained impressively large but militarily useless salients of ground, he insisted on further dissipation of his strength with a fourth attack in June, and a fifth in July. Both of the latter gained very little, but predictably, tended to destroy the morale of his army. Having been promised victory that summer, his soldiers now faced a numerically and materially far stronger opponent, without reserves or new weapons on which to fall back and regroup. Now incapable of any more offensive activity in the West, Germany was forced, like her ally Austria-Hungary, to assume a strictly defensive posture while her home front deteriorated, yet her enemies grew ever stronger. The war was all but over; it had not so much been won by the *Entente* as lost by the *Alliance*.

At sea in the summer of 1918 the effectiveness of the submarine campaign began to evaporate. For the Mediterranean area, 76,600 tons of *Entente* shipping was lost in July, 65,400 tons in August, and 35,900 tons in September. In October 28,000 tons were sunk; in November 10,200.[245] The plummeting totals were not so much due to an absence of means—the Germans still had 28 U-boats in the area as of August—but increasingly effective anti-submarine practices by the *Entente* navies. Even the nets at the Otranto Straits contributed to the victory at sea when on August 1st *UB-53* was caught and damaged, then destroyed by its crew. Three days later, however, the Germans felt some sense of revenge when the French sub *Circe* was torpedoed and sunk by the *U-47*.[246] Even so, by autumn 1918 the war at sea was pretty much over but the shouting.

We left our story of the ground war at the end of June, the Italians having retaken the right bank of the Piave as far south as the Fosetta Canal. Thereafter, Diaz allowed Aosta to continue to attack the still-considerable bridgehead in the canalized delta area of the lower river. For several days, battles involving shallow-draught boats, rafts, and nearly anything that could float were fought on the waterways and in the marshes. Without much incentive to hold on to their hard-won gains south of the main stream, the Austrians generally engaged in a fighting retreat, and sought shelter on the north side of the Piave, where they dug in. Rome claimed nearly 2,000 prisoners on July 2nd, and announced it enjoyed complete control of all the right bank on the 6th. Subsequently the fighting on the lower river was limited to artillery and air actions.

On July 8th, one of the first Americans to bleed on the Italian Front was not a combatant but an ambulance driver named Ernest Hemingway, wounded while visiting Italian soldiers on the west end of the line. A random Austrian mortar round exploded nearby, but Hemingway was shielded from the worst effects of the blast by a less fortunate soldier, who was killed. Even so, the future novelist was peppered with dozens of small shell fragments to his head, legs, and feet. He was immediately hospitalized.

At about the same time, and towards the middle of the Front, Silvio Scaroni and Romolo Ticconi tore into a group of Austrian aircraft and shot it up badly, without injury to themselves. When the day was done Ticconi had destroyed two and Scaroni three, of the enemy planes. Five days later on the 12th, Scaroni was at it again, and two more Austrians became his victims. However, on this occasion, the famous pilot was himself hit by a hostile round and was forced to crash-land. He survived, but the injury was serious enough to sideline him for the rest of the war. His final tally was 26 confirmed victories, second only to Baracca as Italy's best in the war.[247]

July was also the end of the war for another notorious ace, this one Austrian. Frank Linke-Crawford achieved his 27th victory on the 27th, over Valstagna, but two days later he became a victim over the Montello, and was killed. The war had claimed another fine aviator, and they were getting harder and harder to replace. Other men did their best to fill the shoes of their lost comrades. Friedrich Navratil became an ace that month by adding three enemy machines to his credit; two of these were dispatched on the 16th, another on the 23rd, over the south Tyrol.[248]

Italy's King had become quite enamored with aviation in general and fighter-pilots in particular, and once the Americans had become all the rage that summer, he decided that photographs of an Italian Monarch decorating American aviators would make for excellent press. Accordingly, five U.S. pilots who had been serving with the *Entente* air arm in Italy were awarded the Italian War Cross. Vittorio Emanuele did the honors personally, on July 4th, a date all Americans were sure to notice. It would be another three weeks before the 332nd Infantry Regiment reached Italian soil; it finally crossed the frontier via the railroads on the 26th, and was parading in Milan on the 28th. On August 1st, America's mighty contribution to the war on the Italian Front was marched past the King, flanked by Premier Orlando and the U.S. ambassador to Italy, Nelson Page. Later that month the Regiment was attached to the Italian 37th Infantry Division, at that time part of the Ninth Army in reserve. In October, the 37th would be transferred to a new Tenth Army, which also absorbed the British and French divisions. It in turn was placed under the command of British Lord Cavan, and inserted into the line on Aosta's Third Army left, on the Piave. Therefore, the Americans would not see action until the final month of the war.

Inactivity at the front that summer also caused the British, who desired additional troop strength in France, to reduce the three divisions remaining in Italy (7th, 23rd, 48th) by three battalions apiece. They apparently understood that Diaz was not going to initiate any major action there, and believed as did most of the Italians by then, that the enemy was incapable of any big attacks. There were nuisances, to be sure, such as a fairly strong trench raid by the Austrians on July 25th which rather surprised the defenders and captured a few emplacements, with their accoutrements, before the raiders were driven off, but all in all the Front was very quiet.

The probing and raiding was to continue throughout August. At Alano on the 1st, an Italian move scattered some advanced enemy outpost troops. Asiago was rocked by *Entente* artillery a day later, beginning a week of skirmishing on the Plateau. On the night of the 8th British troops probed as far as the outskirts of Asiago, behind a three-hour barrage. The English would return with several hundred prisoners.[249] The following night the French made a similar effort which produced similar results. By the 10th they had reported the capture of Mt. Sisemol and 500 prisoners in two days.[250] Within a few days, attention had shifted to the Tonale Pass area, where fighting had erupted once more, and to a large island in the Piave that the Italians were attempting to capture. An Austrian attack on the lines at Lake Ledro was frustrated by accurate artillery fire on the 19th; a repeat performance on the 28th met much the same fate. On nearby Lake Garda, an Austrian patrol boat was sunk by the fire of big guns, on the 27th.

One of the most remarkable feats of war in August was accomplished not on the ground, but in the skies over the Alps. The Italian poet/adventurer Gabrielle D'Annunzio led a fleet of nine airplanes on a mission to Vienna and back, a total distance of 1,000 kilometers (620 miles) over the most difficult mountains on the Continent, an extraordinary achievement for the year 1918. The mission: drop thousands of propaganda leaflets exhorting the Viennese to throw off the 'Prussian uniform' and topple their 'cruel' government. Just how effective this enterprise could be rated would be difficult to assess; in the event only one plane was lost and D'Annunzio had given his countrymen one more example of dashing behavior they could be proud of.[251]

Over the battle line Friedrich Navratil was perhaps the proudest fighter pilot of those days; his skills earned him five more kills in August, for a total of ten. He too was fast acquiring a reputation, though his country was losing interest. Benno Fiala, Austria-Hungary's third most successful ace, ended his scoring with a victory on August 20th, south of Papadopoli Island in the Piave. Fiala was grounded not long thereafter, until the war ended. His record revealed 28 confirmed victories and five unconfirmed. Ironically, the third of the three top Habsburg aces was also retired from combat at about the same time, he having downed two Italian seaplanes on the 6th and his final, and 32nd, enemy destroyed shortly thereafter. Julius Arigi then joined Fiala and Brumowski as Austria's most successful pilots no longer on combat duty. Perhaps this was done purposely by some high-ranking bureaucrat, military or civilian, who realized what had become of the 4th, 5th, and 6th-ranked aces—Linke-Crawford, Kiss and Gräser—who had been killed. By late summer, the *Entente* ruled the skies just as surely as it ruled the waves.

Following the 'Conference of Oppressed Nationalities of Austria-Hungary' held in Rome in the spring, extremist members of the various ethnic groups residing in the Empire began propaganda campaigns designed to convince rank-and-file members of their linguistic brethren that the Habsburg realm was doomed, and destined to break up. With the defeat of the June offensives, this sort of activity became more prevalent and more pronounced, yet less and less suppressed by the government. For example, a meeting of representatives from the various South Slavic groups in Laibach in early June had been broken up by the local authorities, but when a similar gathering convened in the same city on August 16th, the delegates were left unmolested. Much of the reasoning for the change of heart could be traced to a change of administration; on July 24th the Austrian prime minister Ernst von Seidler who had replaced Clam-Martinitz in June, was himself succeeded by Baron Max von Hussarek, a man quite willing to see the Dual system of the Empire replaced by a triple arrangement in which the South Slavs would comprise the third element. It was an idea which had long since been discussed, and had been favored by the Archduke Franz Ferdinand, before he was assassinated by the very people it was supposed to have satisfied. Hussarek was prepared to allow all sorts of discussion regarding the future of the Monarchy even by those who would otherwise have been considered subversives. Unfortunately this new liberalism came far too late to placate the restive peoples of Austria-Hungary, who at bottom were demanding an end to the war, and with it the privations they were suffering. In fact Hussarek's policies only invigorated the centrifugal forces that were tearing apart the various nationalities which had long been loyal to the Habsburg Empire and had so recently fought and died for it.

When in July Emperor Karl granted a general amnesty to all political prisoners, a new wave of nationalists, especially Czechs, were loosed to begin anew their work of undermining the state. Significant efforts were made to assist in new nation-building by *Entente* agents, diplomats, and spies. The idea, of course, was no less than the destruction of the Empire by its very citizens, an outcome that would surely drag Germany into the abyss as well. The one stumbling block for the *Entente* was the apparently conflicting interests of Italy and the South Slavs, both of whom coveted certain territories which had been promised to Italy by the London Treaty of May, 1915. Having suffered such heavy losses in the war the Italians, led by Sonnino, were nixing all suggestions that they abandon their claims to lands peopled by South Slavs, in the interest of the new campaign to enlist the latter in the anti-Imperial schemes.

The *Entente* need not have worried. Hussarek's new permissiveness, according to one historian, "opened the floodgates of Separatist tendencies."[252] Before long Czechs and Slovaks were openly discussing plans to create a new independent state, and Serbs, Croats, and Slovenes anticipated a union of all South Slavs, including those of Serbian, Montenegrin, or Austro-Hungarian citizenship. The Imperial government, weakened by war and defeat, could do nothing.

Although very determined efforts were made in the summer of 1918 to recruit Austro-Hungarian prisoners of war to the cause of the new national groups coalescing around the ruins of the dying Empire, a comparatively few of these soldiers took the bait, despite offers of decent pay and certainly a better diet than they endured in the overcrowded, disease-ridden prisoner of war camps. We have seen how the Czechs were able to raise two divisions, though these were definitely under-strength by *Entente* standards. But the Czechs were in general better educated and more nationality-conscious than any other Habsburg minority; the South Slavs were unable to persuade but a handful of Croats and Slovenes to take up arms against their land of birth, and the ongoing resentment against the Italians was the chief reason. Nevertheless it is estimated that as many as 400,000 Austro-Hungarian troops deserted their units during that awful summer. Defeatism, disease, and the spread of revolutionary ideas from soldiers who had been infected with such from the Eastern Front were the principal reasons.

With his Empire and his armed forces dissolving around him, *Kaiser* Karl took a grave decision. On September 14th he contacted *Kaiser* Wilhelm, and informed him that his nation needed peace—immediately. It was the last thing that the German Monarch needed to hear at that time; his own armies on the Western Front were reeling from fresh and powerful *Entente* offensives. Karl, however, was adamant. His army was still willing to fight the Italians, he reported, but no one else, and it could not hold out much longer. Peace needed to be negotiated, and as soon as possible. Austria-Hungary was at the end of her strength.

The army was in fact about the only institution of the dying Empire that still continued to function as it had throughout the war. As of the first of September, it was still an unbroken, formidable force, still willing to defend the front against the Italians, who for the time being continued to play a waiting game. September 1st hosted an Austrian probe at Stelvio Pass; it was also the day Stefan Fejes recorded his last official air victory. On the 12th, the ace claimed another Italian opponent destroyed, but this one was unconfirmed. Fejes's final count was 16 confirmed and 4 unconfirmed victories.[253] He would survive the war. Most of the remainder of the month saw only minor actions such as these. The Asiago Plateau was the scene of much patrol and probe activity by both sides. On the 1st, 6th, and 13th the Austrians were the aggressors, and on the night of the 6th/7th it was the French, then the British on the night of the 9th/10th. Also on the 10th, random Italian artillery fire ignited an enemy ammunition dump near Grisolera[254] on the lower Piave. Determined Italian probes on the Grappa front between the Brenta and the Piave over a three-day period (14th-16th) yielded 1,000 Austrian prisoners. Artillery fire of a harassing nature killed a British regimental commander on the 23rd.

One other interesting story came out of late September. Apparently a unit of Czech troops was holding a sector of line just east of Lake Garda, and when the Austrians learned of it, they decided to attack the traitorous soldiers as punishment for their having gone over to the enemy. Following a bombardment employing chemical shells, the assault was made. A bloody, desperate, hand-to-hand struggle was the result, in which neither side took any prisoners. Having satisfied their honor, the attackers eventually broke off the engagement; the Czechs claimed a defensive victory. When thus informed, Premier Orlando sent a congratulatory telegram to the Czechoslovak National Council, a new body the French were proudly hosting in Paris.[255]

Czechs were not the only Austro-Hungarian national group which had decided to boldly sever its ties to the Habsburg Empire. We have seen how Italian intransience had long been the most important stumbling-block to South Slav national desires. As time passed, however, the Italians, under tremendous pressure from the French, British, and Americans to arrive at an accommodation with the Slovenes and Croats, gradually began to yield somewhat. On September 25th a giant leap forward was achieved when the Rome government agreed to recognize the South Slavs as an *Entente* co-belligerent, a status equal to that granted the Czecho-slovaks. Having won the battle for recognition, the South Slavs announced, on October 6th, their intention to develop a national consciousness independent of the Empire. This status did not last long either, given the rapidly-moving events of the autumn, and on October 17th, complete independence of a South Slav state was declared. With this declaration, Austria-Hungary had in essence lost the provinces of Bosnia, Herzegovina, Croatia, Slavonia, Dalmatia, Krain (Carniola), Küstenland, and half of Styria. Even so, the army remained remarkably unaffected, except for an increase in the desertion rate.

Not to be outdone, the Czechs and Slovaks, now pretty generally referred to as the Czechoslovaks, also voiced their own intention to go their separate way regarding the Empire, on the 11th. A provincial government was formed on the 14th, and a Republic was proclaimed on the 17th. Within a couple of days this 'Czechoslovak Republic' had also declared itself totally independent of Austria-Hungary.

Typically, *Kaiser* Karl missed the boat. Still hoping against hope to somehow save his inheritance by placating the various national groups within his crumbling realm, he issued a 'Federal Imperial Manifesto' on October 16th, with the full support of Hussarek and others still grasping at straws. What the Manifesto amounted to was a federalization of Austria into autonomous linguistic components. But because Karl knew his Hungarian subjects would never have agreed to it, he exempted the Hungarian half of the Empire, an act which in itself was guaranteed to render the whole exercise as worthless, since both the Czechoslovaks and the South Slavs resided in both halves of the Dual Monarchy. It is perhaps needless to relate that the Manifesto excited no one and was almost universally ignored. After October 16th, all that remained to Karl was his Army, and few doubted that it too was now existing on borrowed time.

Back at the Italian Front, there were few signs of an impending collapse on the part of the army, despite the nagging drain of desertions, which for October had reached an estimated 70,000 soldiers. Much of the discontentment on the part of these men could probably be traced to the long period of inactivity since June; all armies have always been more susceptible to drooping morale during times of relative quiet, with all of its boring routines. In general, though, the units on the lines were somehow fairly well maintained, in spite of the crippling shortages of everything from rations to radios to razors.

The Navy was another matter. Karl's Manifesto had a definite detrimental effect on the morale of the sailors, and they began to exhibit signs of indiscipline. On October 17th, Austrian submarine crews refused to venture farther than the limits of the Adriatic; other personnel longed to be sent home, and others expressed a loyalty to one or another of the new states now growing out of the ruins of the Empire. Clearly, the fleet was no longer capable of any sort of offensive action. Not that it mattered much anymore; the *Alliance* had been all but neutralized in the war on the Mediterranean. On the 6th, a German submarine, the *UB 68*, had attacked a convoy off Malta and been sunk when the convoy escorts opened fire and damaged it beyond repair. The sub's commander, Karl Dönitz, scuttled his vessel and surrendered.[256] Dönitz would one day succeed a man named Hitler as leader of Germany.

Austria's faltering air arm lost the services of yet another ace on October 21st, when Friedrich Navratil was severely injured in a test flight, of all things. This accident meant the end of the war for Navratil, whose total stood at ten victories. At the time of his enforced retirement only one Austrian pilot still active could claim of a higher score. But by October of 1918 most pilots cared less about their scores than they did about their survival. As in the case of all wars, no one wanted to be the last to be killed.

As late as early October, General Diaz continued to be uninterested in going over to the offensive. He was soon to change his mind, however, overtaken as it was by the implications of the consequences of unfolding events. In late September, Bulgaria, threatened by an *Entente* offensive on the Salonika Front, sued for peace and was granted an armistice. Ottoman Turkey, thus geographically cut off from its allies by Bulgaria's defection, was already wavering from the steady advance of British forces in Mesopotamia and Syria, and it too would obviously need to quit the war. With her southern partners dropping out of the struggle, Austria-Hungary was exposed to invasion from the Balkans, and lacked the necessary strength to build another new front there. Suddenly, it appeared that the Habsburg Empire would be the third of the dominoes to fall, and with the Poles, Czechoslovaks, Romanians, and South Slavs already demanding large pieces of its corpse, Italy would have to act fast if she was to participate in the dissection. Orlando, Sonnino, and even the King joined the Western Powers in urging Diaz to act swiftly if the nation was to have a strong voice at the peace table. Against his own wishes and instincts, the General agreed to abandon the defensive posture he had become comfortable with and go over to the attack, as soon as possible.

Of course, contingency plans for just such an emergency had already been worked out by Diaz's staff, led by Pietro Badoglio. A major regrouping was initiated, and had been completed by the third week of October. First, Third, Seventh and Ninth Armies, the latter still in reserve, were more or less left alone, but into the middle of the line was inserted two new Armies. Sixth Army of General Montuori and Fourth Army now under General Giardino were squeezed slightly to their left and a Twelfth Army (Graziani) was inserted between the Piave and Mt. Grappa. To its right stood Eighth Army (Caviglia), then another new force, the Tenth Army (Lord Cavan) held the middle Piave. The British Corps and the American Regiment were transferred to Cavan; the French divisions went to Graziani. The Czechs were assigned to the reserve Ninth Army.

Italian intelligence was fairly well informed as to the dispositions of the enemy. Straussenberg had recently regrouped as well. Von Krobatin now controlled the western group of two Armies, consisting of the six divisions of his own Tenth Army and the eleven divisions of Scheuchenstuel's Eleventh Army. Two other divisions were held in reserve. Boroevic still commanded the eastern group, including von Wurm's fourteen-division-strong Isonzo Army, the Sixth Army now under Schönberg-Hartenstein with seven divisions, and a new force known as the 'Belluno Group' with thirteen divisions, under General Ferdinand Goglia. Two more divisions were held as army group reserves. As Badoglio surveyed the situation, he could easily rule out offensive action in the difficult, mountainous west, where lateral communications were poor; he also disliked the idea of attacking Isonzo Army on the lower Piave, where the stream was wide and deep and flowed in a single channel.

The center of the Front looked much more promising, where five Armies—the Sixth, Fourth, Twelfth, Eighth and Tenth—faced the Asiago Plateau, the Mt. Grappa area where the Italians held good positions, and the middle Piave, a broad but shallow trench overlooked by Eighth Army defenses on the Montello. Soon, a battle plan had been worked out and approved by Diaz. It called for Sixth Army to advance on the Plateau, Fourth Army to push up the Val Sugana, Twelfth to attack up the gorge of the Piave into the Dolomites, Eighth to cross the river opposite the Montello and make for the Vittorio area, and Tenth to seize the large Papadopoli Island in the stream and secure a general crossing. The Italians were quite certain that the enemy did not possess sufficient reserves with which to counter all of these assaults. Somewhere, a breakthrough was bound to occur, and Ninth Army could be fed into it, if necessary. With the front thus broken, Straussenberg would have little choice but to withdraw deep into the mountains, that is, out of Italy altogether. By October 18th all was ready, but then it began to rain, and the river began to rise. Diaz ordered a postponement.

While the rains stalled a new round of violence at the front, the internal condition of the Empire went from bad to worse; it had in fact ceased to exist as a political entity. His Imperial Manifesto having been thoroughly trashed, Karl could only shake his head as one by one his lands slipped away from legal Habsburg possession. On October 21st deputies from the German-speaking areas of the ex-Empire formed a 'Provisional National Assembly' and proclaimed the birth of an independent German-Austrian state.[257] With this action, only Hungary had not severed all ties to the dynasty. Two days later former Imperial Croat troops occupied Fiume, a city of mixed Italian and Croatian population, and Hungary's only seaport.

Finally anxious to get going, Diaz ordered Sixth and Fourth Armies to attack when the rains had stopped. The others would have to wait until the waters of the Piave receded somewhat; two additional days was deemed sufficient. The first action of the campaign kicked off on the night of the 23rd/24th, when Cavan's men assaulted the gravel-covered, brush strewn island of Papadopoli, that five kilometer long by one and a half kilometer wide piece of real estate that had been the site of so much fighting in June, when the Austrians had crossed the Piave there and were subsequently thrown back by the Italian counterattacks. Since then it had been a sort of no-man's-land, occasionally patrolled by both sides but belonging to neither, though the Austrian presence was the heavier of the two. On the morning of October 24th, the island was firmly in the hands of the British, they having taken many prisoners and caused the remaining Austrians to retreat to the left bank of the river. Bridging operations from the right bank to the island were begun immediately.

At 5:00am on the morning of Thursday the 24th, more than 1,700 guns, Sixth and Fourth Armies' share of the 7,700 now in the hands of Diaz, opened fire on the line between Asiago and Mt. Grappa. The barrage was a comparatively short two hours long, but what it lacked in longevity it made up for in intensity. Coming as it did at the juncture of Krobatin's and Boroevic's sections of responsibility, it caused some consternation within the Austrian command, but there was no time to switch reserves; the infantry attacks commenced at 7:15am. Immediately, savage fighting raged all along the tortured front, often at close-quarters. Mt. Asolone was stormed by *Arditi* troops and won, but was lost again the same day to strong Austrian counterattacks. North of Grappa the army without a country acquitted itself so well that, according to a British observer, "Some of the heights were captured and recaptured alternately eight times."[258] The battle soon began to resemble one of Cadorna's Isonzo offensives, as attack after attack by the brave Italian infantry was shot up by the Austrian defenders, for very little gain. Chilly air and darkness stopped the fight temporarily, but it was renewed on the 25th. Again Schwarzlose machine guns and artillery and mortar fire took a terrible toll on the attackers, who slowly crawled forward, trading thousands of lives for a few meters of advance. Much the same story was told of the 26th, although the crawls were accelerated slightly as attrition took its toll on the defense.

On the third day of the battle in the hills, Diaz received reports that the Piave had somewhat subsided in volume and could be bridged. It was still raining on the plain, but lightly, and both Cavan and Graziani were eager to attack and Caviglia was not opposed. Diaz gave the nod to allow the second phase to begin. Accordingly Tenth Army troops packed Papadopoli under cover of darkness, and were waved off one-half hour before midnight. Eighth Army, meanwhile, began to lay seven bridges over the river, covered by a pounding artillery bombardment. High water, floating debris, and Austrian counter-fire hampered the effort, however, and only two had been completed by morning. Cavan was more successful; two separate overnight efforts behind powerful barrages were followed by a third at 6:45am on the 27th. Heavy fighting commenced; despite skillful resistance, both the Italian Eleventh Corps and the British Fourteenth Corps were able to advance several kilometers, until stopped by counterattacks at Roncadelle and San Palo. Tenth Army reported 9,000 prisoners and fifty guns taken for the day. By contrast, Fourth Army was able to capture only 150 of the enemy.[259]

Austria's outnumbered and beleaguered airmen did their best to assist the ground forces, but they were being overwhelmed. Eugen Bönsch destroyed two Italian airplanes on the 27th, then one each on the two succeeding days, after which he was shot down into the thick of the fighting. Bönsch would survive, but he was done flying and finished with 16 confirmed (and one unconfirmed) victories, seventh best among Austro-Hungarian pilots. Another of the dwindling number of Austrian aces still flying at this time was Franz Rudorfer who also downed two enemy aircraft on the 27th, over Papadopoli Island. Rudorfer had burned a balloon on the 24th over the river and these were his last kills as well, eleven confirmed and two unconfirmed victories was his final total.[260]

Kaiser Karl, horrified by the awful fighting resulting from the massive Italian offensive and unwilling to allow his loyal army to be pounded to pieces, ordered his diplomats to arrange an armistice on whatever terms as could be forwarded from the Italians. Any outcome, even surrender, was now acceptable, he explained. For some reason lost to history, he waited until the next day, the 28th, to inform his one remaining ally, *Kaiser* Wilhelm. The last German Emperor's response, if indeed he offered one, cannot have been of surprise. At any rate he never replied. He, too, knew that the war was long since lost.

On the night of October 27th/28th both Twelfth and Eighth Armies broke free of their bridgeheads over the river Piave and began a general advance; the former would capture Valdobbiadene that day, the latter, Susegana. At Pola, the remaining German naval personnel began an evacuation, scuttling five U-boats in the process. Another was self-destroyed at Trieste. In the distant Austrian province of Galicia, authorities announced their intention to allow their homeland to be attached to a new Polish state. At Austrian General Headquarters, orders were issued to the various units at the front to initiate contact with the enemy for the purpose of obtaining a truce or cease-fire in all localities. And on the crumbling Piave front, American troops were finally committed to battle.

October 29th was the decisive day of the battle. Italian Sixth and Fourth armies were still being held in the hills, despite the fact that Scheuchenstuel had committed his last reserves. On Eighth and Twelfth Army's front, however, Belluno Group was beginning to waver. Graziani's troops took Alano and pushed on to the outskirts of Quero. Caviglia, who had had a very difficult time in bridging the river, and had even diverted some of his divisions to the south in order that they might cross two of the nearest Tenth Army structures, was at last able to begin to press on towards Vittorio. Cavan's Tenth Army reached the Monticano River on a front of several kilometers, threatening Fontanelle on the far bank. Desperate Austrian counterattacks still prevented a true breakthrough, but it was clear to all that Piave line would not be restored. That evening the Hungarian leadership sent a message to all Hungarian soldiers in Italy: Disengage and begin to fall back. It did not want any more of its troops killed or captured; they were needed on the home front to suppress the rising tide of revolution. And at Austria's naval bases twelve U-boats would depart over the next 36 hours, to avoid a takeover by the South Slavs. Five more would be scuttled by their crews at Pola, and one each at Trieste and Fiume. Three more submarines escaped from Cattaro, so a total of fifteen attempted to return to Germany via the long, dangerous sea route. Two minelayers were also sunk at Pola. Amazingly, only two of the fifteen escapees were intercepted by *Entente* action; the others eventually returned to German ports.[261]

As Eighth Army troops poured over the Piave at Falze, north of the Montello, they came upon a badly wounded enemy officer who had fought hard against the *Arditi* leading the assault. They tried to help, and even carried the officer to a field hospital, where nevertheless *she* died. Austrian prisoners were filed by the body in the hope she could be identified, to no avail. The dead female was buried in the cemetery at Falze di Piave, her grave marked by a stone which read: "An Unknown Woman who cannot be better identified than with the words, Clothed as an Austrian Officer."[262] We do not know if the anonymous woman was a wife, a mother, or a sister, but we do know she was a daughter, and that she felt strongly enough about her cause to fight and die for it, as did millions of other Austro-Hungarian citizens. It is perhaps altogether fitting that her death came roughly concurrent with that of the country she loved, well after most of the rest of the world had decided that it must take place.

October 30th was the final day of battle for the old Austro-Hungarian Army. Unable to contain the breach over the Piave, Boroevic ordered the river line abandoned. Straussenberg was prepared to do one better; his Hungarian troops already falling back, he ordered his Austrian soldiers to evacuate Italy. The order stunned commanders at the front and threatened to turn a somewhat orderly retreat into a rout. Only with the greatest difficulty were many officers able to maintain some semblance of control over their men. Eleventh Army and Belluno Group, which had been very effective in holding the Italian Sixth, Fourth, and Twelfth Armies, began to give ground. Eighth Army, having taken Conigliano, pushed all the way to Vittorio before nightfall. Tenth Army, advancing at a frenetic pace, reached the upper Livenza River at Francenigo and the rail town of Oderzo, while cavalry on its left glimpsed the town of Sacile before darkness fell. The lengthy and costly battle for the north slope of the Grappa *Massif* finally came to an end as the Austrians retired and Fourth Army elements recovered Mt. Prassolan, while Twelfth Army units drove on past Quero. On the Asiago Plateau units of the British 45th Division—which had been left behind while most of their countrymen were transferred to Tenth Army—assisted in the recapture of Asiago. Other Sixth Army elements carried Mts. Asolone and Spinocia.

Straussenberg, meanwhile, was trying desperately to contact the man entrusted with the task of entering the enemy lines with a truce delegation, as ordered by the Emperor on the 27th, but this General Weber had had a difficult time in making contact with an enemy who was not terribly interested in talking peace until their offensive had run its course. Everyone on the Italian side now was talking about avenging Caporetto, and few wanted to see the advance reigned in before all Italian soil had been cleared. Finally, Weber was allowed to cross the lines at an inactive part of the front in the Adige Valley. He was then shuttled, via automobile towards Diaz's headquarters in Padua. While Weber bounced over the Venetian countryside, Karl decided to put an end to the threats of violence at the dying Empire's naval bases. That evening, he declared that the Danube Flotilla was now granted to Hungary. The main ocean-going fleet in the Adriatic ports was given to the South Slavs.

Karl's gesture was less motivated by a desire to be generous to the South Slavs, than by the desire to prevent the Italians from seizing the fleet. All of the Empire's main ports—Pola, Fiume and Cattaro—except Trieste were peopled mainly by Serbs and Croats, and the move seemed logical enough; two days earlier these cities had been declared by the new South Slav National Council to be a part of its lands. All the more shocking, then, was a declaration by the authorities in Fiume to be an independent city-state, with intentions of seeking incorporation into Italy. This bombshell hit all interested parties even before Karl's 'gift' could be accepted, and immediately Italian government involvement was suspected.

Most Austro-Hungarians had a good deal more to worry about than the fate of the Imperial fleet. The enemy, having broken the front, was now pursuing the retreating army. Italian cavalry and armored cars overtook many an infantry unit, forcing thousands of men to surrender. Overhead, *Entente* aircraft prowled the skies, shooting down many of the remaining Austrian airplanes, which by now were short of fuel and often piloted by inexperienced aviators. Roads crowded with Austro-Hungarian army units were pitilessly bombed and machine-gunned, destroying thousands of vehicles of every sort, from supply wagons to artillery carriages. Dead horses and men soon littered these arteries, making passage along them extremely slow and arduous. To make matters worse, the air attacks wrecked every bridge, both road and railroad, that the fleeing troops needed to make good their withdrawal across Venetia and Friulia. Many an Italian ace was made during the ghastly campaign of the last days of the war.

While the armies in Venetia faced disintegration, the Weber delegation was delivered to an estate known as Villa Guisti, not far from Diaz's headquarters at Padua. The Austrian General knew that every moment lost meant further destruction of the hapless elements of the army, who were becoming increasingly incapable of defending themselves. To his horror, Weber realized early on that his erstwhile enemies were in no hurry to call off their offensive and thus save lives; they had political reasons for wanting the war to last a little longer. For one thing, Italy had not yet properly avenged its defeat and rout of the previous year; for another, it would be impolitic to end the fighting before certain objectives were in Italian hands. Another entire day would pass before his opposite numbers would even present their terms.

At the front most movement on the final day of the month took place on the plain, where Boroevic had managed to retire behind the Livenza and destroy the last of the bridges over that stream behind him. His divisions were still more or less intact, and offered strong rearguard actions which held the line of the lower river for the time being, while the main body of troops set out for the Tagliamento. Upstream, however, Sacile had been lost in the morning, and an enemy drive on Pordenone begun. All the other Italian armies advanced only slightly. The retirement had still not degenerated into a rout, despite another command from Budapest that day, ordering all Hungarian soldiers to immediately return to their homeland. Some measure of the state of affairs in the Hungarian Capitol at that time might might be taken by the cold-blooded murder of Count Tisza, once the most powerful man in Hungary, by disgruntled soldiers at this time. Apparently, some men forced their way into his home, and upon finding him standing speechless, simply gunned him down. Ironically, Tisza was one of the few men in power in August of 1914 who had opposed the decision to go to war. Having been unable to prevent it, however, he had been enthusiastically cheered by crowds who were unaware of his stance, and who clambered for hostilities to begin. On that occasion, he had remarked to an aide, "If only they knew how little I deserve their cheers".[263] Now, four years and a lost war later, he was killed by revolutionaries who believed he was responsible for the war. Another staunch Habsburg supporter had been removed from the new political climate.

Also on the 31st came the formal end of the Imperial Navy. At Pola, fleet commander Nicholas Horthy, as per his orders from the Emperor, handed over control of his ships to representatives of the new South Slav government. He waited for the old Imperial flag to be lowered, then folded it and carried it away with him as he left for Hungary.[264] Most of his ex-sailors had already departed for home or parts unknown; a few even attempted to reach Germany, from which they hoped to carry on the war. At about the same time, Austria's last remaining seaport—Trieste—was taken over by its Italian and Slovene residents, who ran off any remaining German or Hungarian administrators. Both Austria and Hungary were now land-locked countries.

The South Slavs did not have long to enjoy their new-found sea power. That night, Italian frogmen slipped into the harbor and attached mine-like devices to two battleships, the older *Wien* and the larger and more modern *Viribus Unitis*. Both devices were detonated, and both ships were sunk. *Viribus Unitis*, flagship of the Imperial navy, capsized and took many men down with her. By dawn both vessels rested on the bottom of the harbor. The South Slavs were incredulous, and needless to relate, the incident did nothing to improve the thorny relations between them and the Italians, who they always suspected of duplicity in the matter. The latter protested that the war was still on, and that their men had been unaware of the proceedings at Pola of the prior evening.

At the same time that battleships at Pola were filling with seawater, Italian airships bombed railroad stations in Val Sugana. Fourth Army artillery soon joined the action, and a drive up the Brenta and its tributary the Cismone was begun. The old frontier was passed that evening. To the west, Sixth Army renewed its offensive toward the western Plateau and First Army, hitherto inactive, joined in the drive, and a pitched battle for Mt. Cimone soon developed. Twelfth Army captured Feltre, joining hands with Fourth east of Fonzaso. Graziani could now either push up the Piave towards Belluno, or move due north against the Cauviol-Cardinal-Rolle Pass ridge. Eighth Army was already headed for the former, via the Vittorio-San Croce defile. Tenth Army took Pordenone and raced to the Meduna, crossing it without bridges. Third Army was crossing the lower Livenza. All along the line the Austrians were attempting desperately to disengage.

General Weber, on the other hand, was just as desperately trying to engage the Italian delegates in peace talks. On the evening of the 1st of November, he was finally presented with Rome's demands: total Austrian demobilization, immediate withdrawal from all territory Italy desired to annex, and *Entente* occupation of any Austrian lands it deemed necessary, with the right to move freely through Austrian-controlled ground. In return, the *Entente* offered an immediate cease-fire and end to the war. What the terms amounted to, of course, was unconditional surrender; even Karl, who had for so long sought peace, balked at this idea, as he felt the conditions were dishonorable. Another day was wasted while the Austrians twisted and squirmed, trying to contemplate a more acceptable exit from hostilities.

Another factor regarding Italian rigidity was fast manifesting itself in the minds of many of the Latins, both military and civilian. As the Army recaptured large swaths of territory, the population of the occupied areas anxiously told tales of the brutality of the enemy. Everything Austro-Hungarian, Habsburg or Imperial was vilified; no tale of woe too extraordinary as to be unbelievable. No doubt, much of what the inhabitants spoke was true, or at least based on truth, especially when they charged theft of food, destruction of crops, and the like. The occupation had come at a time when the enemy troops were practically starving. One eyewitness claimed that "Everything movable of any value had been packed up and sent off to Austria-Hungary." He did add, however, that "there had not been a systematized destruction of what could not be taken",[265] and observed that most of the enemy troops had "behaved tolerably". That there had been excesses can be taken as for sure; that the Imperial soldiers' stay in Venetia had been any less tolerable than, say, the Russians in Galicia, is doubtful. At any rate, once atrocity stories began to circulate around northern Italy, the chances that the Italians would be willing to go easy on their collapsing enemies began to be reduced.

November 2nd was the day on which the battle broke up into what amounted to a headlong retreat followed by a determined pursuit. Seventh Army, the last of the Italian Armies to move, added its weight to the offensive by striking in four places, at Stelvio Pass, Tonale Pass, in Val Guidicaria, and immediately west of Lake Garda. Its neighbor First Army surged ahead to Roverto in the Etsch Valley and crossed the old border in the Astico Valley, as well as advancing on a broad front in the mountains between the two. Sixth Army captured Mts. Majo and Cimone and all but the most northerly reaches of the Plateau. Fourth Army pushed past Grigno and on to the outskirts of Strigno. The Twelfth Italian Army advanced to Belluno by midday and was well up the Agordo Valley by nightfall. Eighth Army armored cars and infantry in trucks raced past Belluno to the east and were able to reach Longarone. And Tenth Army closed up to the line of the Tagliamento, between Spilimbergo and San

Vito. Aosta's Third Army made Portogruaro, and a little beyond.

Everywhere on the plain the scenes were described in much the same manner. The skies full of Italian and *Entente* aircraft, constantly bombing and strafing the enemy columns as they tried to flee, yet scarcely an Austrian airplane to be seen. Smashed and wrecked wagons, carts and automobiles everywhere amidst the dead horses and men, whose corpses were so numerous that they needed to be cleared before the lanes were passable. Huge heaps of ammunition and stores abandoned in the ditches or dumped into streams to help effect a crossing; war material and equipment of every sort strewn across the countryside. Bridges and culverts had all been blown to oblivion, by one side or the other. Then there were the bits and pieces of uniforms, especially helmets, which had deliberately been tossed aside to lighten the burden of the soldiers who were obliged to escape on foot. Whenever they had had time, or perhaps the means, roadside trees had been felled across the ways, in an effort to slow the pace of the pursuit. The sights were simply horrible and the smell was unbearable.

Having waited a day for a response from the Austrian command which had not come, the Italians added one more stipulation for Weber to deal with. Accept the armistice terms within another 24 hours, they informed him, or they would advance on to Vienna, if necessary. Only half-surprised, Weber informed Straussenberg, who was still waiting for Karl to render a decision. The Emperor had meanwhile come to terms with his own new impotence, and renounced his position as Commander-in-Chief of the Army, leaving his Chief of Staff to deal with the mess. Straussenberg stalled and soul-searched for hours, but despite his extreme reluctance to do so, in the end he knew that he must give the order to capitulate. There was really nothing much else he could have done; at the front, men were still fighting and dying for no worthwhile purpose.

Taking full advantage of the opportunity for further advance, all the Italian Armies drove deep into former enemy ground on November 3rd. Beyond Tonale Pass, Seventh Army reached Ossana on the upper Noce and Tione, well into the Val Guidicaria. First Army armored cars led the way into Trient and arrived only a short while before the left wing vanguard of Sixth Army also entered the city from the east. The right hook of Sixth Army was in Borgo before sundown, a maneuver that nearly surrounded a large portion of the mountainous border area to the south. Fourth, Twelfth and Eighth Armies continued their drives up the Piave watershed, while Tenth and Third spread across the eastern plain. The river Tagliamento was crossed on a broad front; American troops fought their only major action in Italy when they were temporarily halted on the middle course of the stream by an effective rearguard action. By far the most remarkable gains of the day were achieved by Italian cavalry on the upper Tagliamento, when they galloped past Pinzano, bypassed Gemona, and reached Venzone, well into the mountains on the railroad leading to the Pontebba Pass. Farther south Udine, the principal city of Friulia, and site of Cadorna's headquarters for two and one-half years, was entered just as darkness began to fall.

Eager to occupy Trieste, that fateful city which had been the main unresolved issue between the two nations when they had parleyed before the war, Diaz authorized a naval expedition to sail from Venice and seize the coveted city. A destroyer carrying a company of *Bersaglieri* was duly dispatched, and arrived at Trieste that afternoon, to the ecstatic cheers of much of the port's remaining population, which had long been a majority of Latin-speakers. The Italian nation had paid a terrible price to do so, but it had finally won its prize, and the Italian flag flew over the onetime main rival of Venice.

Back at Villa Guisti, General Weber at long last received the message from General Headquarters that he had been waiting for. Italy's armistice terms were to be accepted. Then, having worked out the details of the surrender, the Austrians signed the documents. The war was to officially end on the afternoon of the following day, the 4th. It was 6:30pm at the time, and that left twenty or so hours of continuing hostilities. Both sides planned to use this time to their advantage; Weber hoped many Austrian units could withdraw to points beyond the enemy's reach, while Diaz's staff wanted to capture as many enemy soldiers, and as much equipment, as possible. In the event, the one additional day of war favored the Italians.

Badoglio, Diaz's Chief of Staff, urged his armies to energetically advance as far as they could on the 4th. The defeat of the previous year was to be avenged to the fullest, even surpassed, but of course in reverse. Many Austrian units, informed of the armistice, assumed the fighting was over and laid down their arms. Some of these continued to retreat as quickly as possible, others did not. Either way few expected to be overrun and taken as prisoners of war in those final hours, yet that is exactly what happened to many, if not most, units of two entire Army Groups on that particular Monday. Hundreds of thousands of soldiers, expecting to be sent home, were systematically rounded up and sent to prisoner of war camps, from which they would be used as laborers for the purpose of clearing the debris of war.

Italian Seventh Army achieved some of the most spectacular advances on the 4th. The force from Stelvio Pass drove down a tributary of the Etsch and reached the extreme upper valley of that stream, while the units beyond the Tonale conquered the entire Noce watershed. A third column coming out of Val Guidicaria reached the Etsch far to the north of Trient, joining up with First Army troops along the river. Sixth Army conquered all of the Val Sugana, including the lakes in the Pergine/Levico area; British troops of the 48th Division could look from the heights into the Fersina Valley. The Fourth Army got as far as Primiero on the Cismone; Twelfth Army boasted the capture of Cencenighe, in sight of Mt. Marmolada. A few kilometers north of Pieve di Cadore was the limit of Eighth Army's push. To the northeast, cavalry were able to ride as far as Pontebba on the old frontier. Third Army, with a much shorter distance to travel, was able to cross the pre-war border and take Monfalcone once more. The most incredible gains of the day, however, were made on the front of Tenth Army, which somehow was able to close up to the Isonzo on a broad front. Just as the 3:00pm armistice time approached, the vanguard was within reach of some objectives for which many Italian soldiers had died. Not surprisingly, the clock was ignored, and the advance ended where the nation would have demanded it end. Flitsch, Karfreit, Tolmein and Görz were entered before darkness stopped the forward movements, and from that moment on would be called Plezzo, Caporetto, Tolmino, and Gorizia, respectively. The Italian Army had had its revenge.

For the one Regiment of Americans on the entire Italian Front, the last day of the war was relatively uneventful. Having been stopped on the Tagliamento the day before, the Regiment received orders to cross the stream at 3:15am on the 4th. Apparently the operation took several hours to accomplish, but was completed by 9:00am.[266] It then marched off to the east and took custody of a good deal of abandoned war material, but did not overtake the enemy.

In fact the Isonzo area was the conduit for the retreating troops of von Wurm's Isonzo Army, the only one of the Austrian formations in Italy that more or less escaped capture, intact. Tenth and Eleventh Armies and the Belluno Group had pretty much been taken prisoner, hampered as they were by mountainous terrain with few roads and fewer escape-routes. Sixth Army's positioning was awkward for a speedy withdrawal, and it too, had been largely destroyed, but much of Isonzo Army crossed the stream for which it was named and fell back into Carniola, from which it could disperse and try to make its way home in small groups. Of course 'home' was now in one of six different independent states now holding territories of the defunct Austro-Hungarian Empire, and many a soldier truly did not know exactly where he wanted to go. But at least he retained somewhat of a choice, whereas hundreds of thousands of his erstwhile comrades, now in Italian captivity, did not, at least until their 'hosts' decided they no longer wanted to feed them.

With the South Slav movement gaining strength and international recognition, the Italians deemed it wise to also capture much of the territory along the Adriatic coast that had been promised to them by the Treaty of London. To this end several expeditions similar to the Trieste affair of a day earlier were undertaken on the 4th, before the armistice took effect. The ports of Fiume, Zara, and Rovigno were thus occupied, as were the islands of Lagosta, Curzola, and Meleda, none of which were peopled by a Latin-speaking majority as Trieste was. Nevertheless all these locations had once belonged to the Venetian Republic, and still contained small numbers of people of Italian speech. By the end of the day, Italy had taken possession of most of the ground that was of her main concern.

The fighting from October 24th, when Diaz launched his offensive, until the armistice is remembered in most histories as the 'Battle of Vittorio Veneto', an odd title for a campaign that began between Asiago and Mt. Grappa, and ended with advances all along the Italian Front. Perhaps the name is no less accurate that is 'Caporetto' for Operation *Waffentreu* and its aftermath, but it is certainly more misleading since no great amount of fighting occurred at the city of Vittorio. Moreover the city itself does not need to be qualified as resting in the province of Veneto any more than say New York needs to be referred to as New York, New York (State). Even the most detailed maps of Italy do not indicate another Vittorio in some other province (i.e. Vittorio-Calabria); even if some villages do exist around the country, it would be for them to qualify their location, not the larger settlement. The point is that if at some time in the far future archaeologists were to search for evidence of the Battle of Vittorio-Veneto, they would have a hard time finding it. The same could of course be said of Caporetto, and it is curious, to say the least, to see how certain name-tags are attached to important historical events.

At any rate the final campaign of the war, which might more logically be referred to as the Diaz Offensive had cost both sides dearly. Italy suffered at least 60,000 casualties in the early battles in the mountains alone, a third of these dead. The second phase of the offensive was less deadly; perhaps 30,000 dead and wounded were lost in the Venetian campaign. Overall then, 90 to 100,000 casualties for the *Entente*. As usual, the defending Austrians incurred far fewer men lost in the fighting, however, they lost many thousands of prisoners even before the mass surrenders of the 4th, which far exceeded in number those taken as a result of combat. Actual totals have always been a matter of dispute, but at least 400,000 and possibly a half million men did not leave Italy that November. Of these, only 30 to 40,000 were killed or wounded and the remainder became guests of Rome. Later, the Austrians would claim about 360,000 men had gone into captivity; Italian sources insist on a figure nearer 430,000. All of the linguistic groups of the ex-Empire were represented in this mass of humanity, including Italians from areas coveted by Rome, who apparently were less enthusiastic about becoming citizens of the Kingdom of Italy than the government in Rome would have cared to admit. Incredibly, as many as 7,000 Italian-speakers may have been amongst the captives, and their captors subsequently considered them as "allies of the Entente".[267] In addition to enemy soldiers, the Italians also seized between 5,500 and 6,800 artillery pieces (depending on what was considered artillery), about a quarter-million horses, and 12,000 motor vehicles. 'Caporetto' had indeed been avenged.

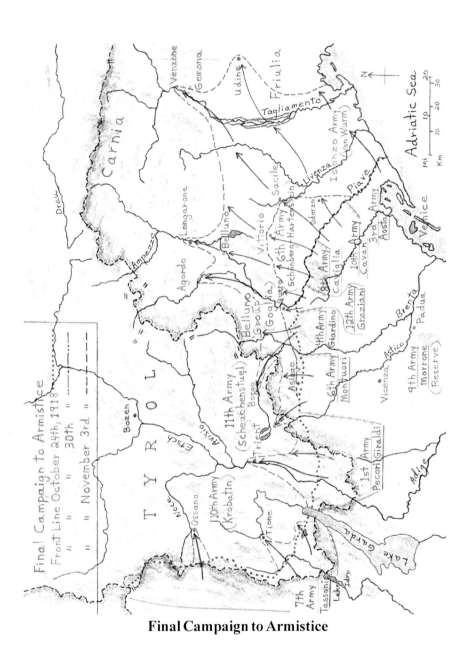

Final Campaign to Armistice

Chapter Thirteen
Making Peace…Sort Of

With the signing of the armistice on November 3rd, 1918 and its implementation a day later, the war on the Italian Front had come to an end. Already, the Empire of Austria-Hungary had ceased to be, broken as it was into several nationalistic components at the behest of the *Entente* powers, yet its formal removal from the war represented the third of the four *Alliance* nations to fall into defeat. Thereafter, only Germany remained, and there was no longer the slightest doubt in the minds of anyone interested in the outcome of the conflict that she too, would soon give way to the inevitable. One additional week of slaughter on the Western Front would be necessary before all involved parties agreed that the Great War should come to pass. While politicians wrangled, soldiers bled and died.

Having destroyed the Austro-Hungarian armies in Italy, and having taken prisoner perhaps forty percent of the entire enemy order of battle there, the Italians were fairly well disposed to allow the remainder of the ex-enemy force to make its way home without further molestation. A few units were able to retire over the Brenner Pass or trek eastward out of the Pusterthal and thus escape the South Tyrol. The bulk of the surviving forces, however, principally of the Isonzo Army, were obliged to outrun their pursers on the Venetian Plain and retreat over the river for which Boroevic's main force had been named. Even then, most knew they were not safe, and the exodus continued nonstop to Laibach, provincial capitol of Carniola, from which the railroads ran east or northeast, towards Budapest and Vienna. But the entire province was now claimed by, and in the hands of, the South Slavs, and most officers were not comfortable until they had taken their men into land populated with German or Hungarian speakers. Boroevic himself, a Croat by birth, traveled to Villach, then to Klagenfurt, from where he tried to extricate the bulk of his command from those areas in which he knew the troops would not be welcome.

To the lasting credit of the Slovenes, who populated Carniola and a good deal of Styria as well, there were few incidents involving hostility towards the ex-Imperial soldiers, for it was a month or so before all of Isonzo Army's troops could be evacuated, given their large numbers and the limited capacity of the railroads. Of course, not all the men wanted to 'escape' from the clutches of the Slavs; many thousands of Slovenes, Serbs, Croats and even some Italians made their home in these areas, and given their recent camaraderie with the other nationals of the old Empire, there was little desire among them to confront the Czechs, Poles, Slovaks, Ukrainians, or even the Germans, trying to make their way home. It was not until the Serbs who hailed from the old Kingdom of Serbia, who were quickly taking control of all South Slav interests, began to assert themselves that trouble with the Germans, Hungarians and Italians began, and by that time most if not all of these men had long departed the Laibach area. At first, Boroevic's intention was to regroup his Army and advance on Vienna in an effort to save the Empire or at least the Dynasty. When such dreams proved to be illusory, the loyal Field Marshal disbanded his own headquarters and began contemplating his own future.

In distant Vienna, the local authorities had lost control of an angry public reeling from hunger, deprivation and defeat. Only with the greatest difficulty was Straussenberg able to collect an odd assortment of officers, officer candidates and loyal police with which to protect the Emperor and his family. But Karl was well aware of his new irrelevance and harbored no desire to attempt to retrieve his authority by force; once it had become clear to him that bloodshed would surely accompany any effort on his part to retain his throne, he needed no persuasion to abandon all of his privileges. On November 11th, the last Habsburg Emperor issued a statement from his family palace at Schönbrunn, just south of the capitol. In it, Karl claimed "unalterable love for my peoples", acknowledged that the German-speaking areas of Austria were about to become an independent state, and declared his wish to "relinquish every participation in the administration of the State". He subsequently left the palace for Eckartsau, a hunting lodge northeast of Vienna, on the advice of his friends, who were afraid that it had become too dangerous for him and his family to remain at the palace. Although he did sign some paperwork at the behest of his ministers, he would always insist that he had never formally abdicated. At the same time, Italian troops closed up to the Brenner Pass in Tyrol, deep inside German-speaking territory. Here they stopped their advance, as at all locations on the spine of the watershed between the Adriatic Sea and the Danube River.

Curiously, it was not until the 13th that the Hungarians were able to obtain an armistice, similar to the one signed between the Austrians and Italians ten days earlier. It did not amount to much, since as we have seen, Budapest had ordered its troops to walk away from the war a few days before its end, and most of these men had had a good head start on their erstwhile comrades for the long journey home. Karl's 'abdication' was announced at the same time, as a sort of *fait accompli* for him; one that apparently was effective when three days later the ex-Monarch sent notice that he had indeed quit as Emperor. No one much noticed, as the chaos in Budapest at the time was even worse than that in Vienna, before a liberal government under Mihály Károly was able to emerge briefly. The next day, the 14th, a 'Republic of Austria' was proclaimed in the old Habsburg capitol. The so-called Austrian National Assembly unanimously approved a resolution calling for union with Germany.

It would take only a little longer for the South Slavs to begin to implement their plans for a new, independent state. Flanked by formerly hostile powers in Bulgaria, Hungary and Austria, and an obviously expansive Italy, representatives of the various ethnic and religious groups from all of the lands generally referred to as having a South Slavic population met at the capitol of the ex-Imperial province of Croatia, until recently a part of Hungary. The city, Agram, was renamed Zagreb, and on the 23rd it was announced that the old Kingdoms of Serbia and Montenegro were to be united with the provinces of Bosnia, Herzegovina, Croatia, Slavonia, Carniola, and portions of Styria, Carinthia, and Dalmatia. It was assumed, though not desired, that the Italians would annex Küstenland and much of Dalmatia, but the latter, in particular, was to be contested. Serbia's Karageorgevich dynasty was to inherit all of the lands; thus from its inception, the South Slavic state took on a distinctly Serbian character. On December 1st the new nation was proclaimed as the Kingdom of the Serbs, Croats, and Slovenes. Its capitol, of course, was that of Serbia, Belgrade. To many people, the new nation represented a simple enlargement of old Serbia, a view most Italians had come to espouse. Before the end of the year, a new map of Europe had largely been drawn. All that remained for the victors was to tidy up a few details, or so it seemed.

The war on the Italian Front was over. It had lasted from May 23rd, 1915 to November 4th, 1918, a total of 42 months or 1,261 days. Its effects were felt for decades afterward, and have not entirely been removed even to this day. Foremost among losses suffered on this major warfront were the human beings, each one of whom represented a unique personality forever removed from whatever rendezvous with destiny he was to have experienced had the war not broken out. Even many of the moderately wounded and a large percentage of the prisoners of war were so traumatized by their misfortunes that they would be very slow to re-assimilate with with the general population once they had returned home. The dead and in many cases the severely wounded were of course removed from the status of productive citizenry, but for the thousands of unemployed who battled deprivation and depression in the feeble post-war economy, a 'normal' life was scarcely conceivable. For untold thousands of young men, be they Austrian, Hungarian, Slav or Italian, the experience of the Great War was so shocking, so unbelievably brutal, no easy or straightforward return to civilian life was possible. For untold thousands more, it was not even desirable. Many would eventually succumb, following lengthy periods of depression or illness or both, to dementia and suicide.

Battle casualties of the war have always been and will always be unknown. This account has offered figures for the sixteen major campaigns alone, which no doubt involved at least ninety percent and probably more, of the total losses, but on each and every day of the conflict, men suffered and died. Nevertheless by using both minimum and maximum numbers for these struggles, we can arrive at a reasonably good estimate of the human cost of the Italian Front. Cadorna's eleven offensives on the Isonzo, his Plateau attack of June, 1917, and Diaz's final offensive, along with Austria's *Südtyroloffensive, Waffentreu* and *Radetsky/Albrecht* comprise the sixteen. Minimum Italian losses in killed, wounded, and captured reach 1,303,500; the maximum is 1,468,000 or so. For Austria-Hungary, the respective numbers are 970,500 and 1,160,000. All told, we have at least 2,274,000 and perhaps 2,628,000 casualties in just the main battles. To this, at least five percent can be added for those soldiers lost to ordinary attrition as it affected both armies during the 1,261 days of conflict. Even then, we still need to consider losses incurred by the Germans, estimated at 10 to 15,000 during October/November 1917, the French (approximately 1,000 killed, 2,500 wounded, 100 captured) and the British, who are believed to have sustained 2,100 killed, 4,700 wounded, and 200 captured.

Czech and American units also took some casualties though their number was comparatively small.

In addition to the army losses, naval and air personnel were injured in fairly large numbers. One source offers 3,169 Italian naval killed and 5,252 wounded,[268] but does not mention those of Austria-Hungary, which, presumably were somewhat lower. For the first time in history, airmen had played a considerable role in battle, and they had suffered proportionately, for their efforts. Italy had produced 43 air aces, who collectively accounted for 398 air victories.[269] It should be remembered that not every pilot shot down was killed, but usually his valuable machine was wrecked, and in many cases aircraft shot down took two or more men with them. Austria-Hungary hosted 49 aces with 477 confirmed and 40 unconfirmed kills,[270] but some of these victories occurred over the Eastern and Balkan Fronts. Still, the majority were achieved in Italy.

As for the prisoners of war, the terms of the armistice required that all Italians in Austro-Hungarian captivity be released immediately, a stipulation that was doubtless a blessing in disguise for the captors, who simply lacked the necessary supplies with which to maintain them. It also undoubtedly saved many of their lives; the global 'Spanish Flu' pandemic was at its height just then and the prisoner camps were notorious targets for its wrath. By contrast, Austro-Hungarian internees in Italy were hard hit by the germs. Of the prisoners taken in the final campaign alone, 30,000 would never leave detainment,[271] and for the war as a whole, probably 50,000 men perished while captives of the Italians. It is not known just how many Latins died while enduring Habsburg hospitality in camps such as Mauthausen, somewhat east of Linz, but the total certainly reached five figures, and possibly well into five. Rome continued to work its captives in clearing the debris of war and repairing the extensive damage to the infrastructure of the invaded lands for months after the cessation of hostilities. Once the final peace treaties had been signed they were gradually sent home, preceded only by those who had been too badly injured or were too sick to work. Eventually most men returned to their homes, only to find the local economy in shambles and very little in the way of employment opportunities, and another group of individuals was added to the ranks of the post-war discontented.

We have seen how the problems between the Italians and the South Slavs were rather pronounced long before the war had come to an end. Both groups wanted Trieste and Istria as well as Dalmatia and the islands in the Adriatic; both also had designs on Albania and in other areas of the Balkans, and these issues did not disappear with the end of the fighting. To the contrary, the new rivalry was about to manifest itself with renewed passion. For one thing, Rome bitterly resented the Austrians' handing over of their ex-battle fleet to the South Slavs, for another, the Treaty of London had awarded much territory to Italy in which the inhabitants were Slovenes, Croats, or Serbs, the three groups now apparently uniting into a single state. Rome refused to recognize the new nation. The Slavs responded by allowing the Kingdom of Serbia—a country with which Italy had been an ally in the war—to absorb all lands peopled by Croats and Slovenes. This infuriated the Italians, who well remembered how bitterly Slovene and Croat soldiers had fought them on the Isonzo front. They considered these people to be ex-enemies who should be treated as defeated nationalities, like the Austrians and Hungarians; certainly, they believed, the Slavs should hardly now be rewarded.

This territorial dispute along the Adriatic littoral was one of the most serious of all those in the wake of the Great War. The Germans at least realized that they were going to lose a good deal of territory, at least Alsace-Lorraine if not more, to France and their Polish-speaking districts to the new Polish State. Even so, they were granted several plebiscites in disputed areas (though none in the West), and the country was left more or less intact. In the case of Austria-Hungary, the Empire was entirely removed and replaced by a hodge-podge of newly independent states and much-enlarged neighbors, all hungry for as much land as possible. Romania, for example, more than doubled in size, mostly at the expense of Hungary. The new nations of Poland and Czechoslovakia were taking vast swaths of the old Empire. And if the South Slavs had their way, old Serbia would nearly triple in size. Under the circumstances, the Italians felt that they were being quite reasonable, asking only for that which had been promised to them by the London Treaty, though they assumed early on that they would also be granted the port city of Fiume. But the South Slavs countered that at the time of the signing of the Treaty of London in April, 1915, no one expected that the Habsburg Empire would disappear as a result of the war. Circumstances had changed, they argued, and invoked one of the most popular phrases of the day: self-determination. If the principle of self-determination were to be applied to the disputed areas, these Slavic-speaking lands would never agree to incorporation into Italy, given that they now had a South Slavic state to associate with.

All Europe and in fact all the world was wild with the idea of 'self-determination' during those waning days of 1918. Now that the *Alliance* powers had been defeated, or so went the reasoning, the principle could be applied to all peoples who were governed without their consent. In fact, no one really knew what self-determination meant. It had never been defined. The term had been coined by American President Woodrow Wilson, and was used in his famous Fourteen Points, on the basis of which both the Germans and Austro-Hungarians had lain down their arms. But beyond the obvious connotations, nobody could define it or indicate how it would affect the peacemaking process. Wilson himself had made many statements since leading his nation into war in April of 1917, on the "rights and liberties" of small nations. He talked of "autonomous development" for all peoples, the rights of the governed to "have a voice in their own governments" or to "determine their own institutions". And of course his repeated use of the slogan about making the world "safe for democracy" resonated around the developed world. For all that, however, Wilson never intended his principles to be universally applied. These were political expressions designed to rally his skeptical nation to the fight. If they could also be used to undermine the will of his nation's enemies, so much the better.

Wilson has always been a controversial historical figure, as most successful politicians are, yet no one doubts that at bottom, he was an idealist who tried to make his world a better place in which to live. His was an uphill battle against corruption, self-interest, and greed, yet he himself was by no means free of faults. For one thing, he utterly refused to believe, once he had made a decision on an issue, that he could be wrong. Although he professed an undying love of American democracy, when the time came to select five plenipotentiaries for the Peace Conference, he chose only those who agreed with him politically, thus angering his powerful opposition, the Republican Party. He claimed to abhor war and in fact had been re-elected in 1916 to a second term of office under slogans such as the rhetorical question "Who keeps us out of War?", but he never hesitated in sending military forces into Mexico when he felt American interests there were being threatened. At one point, Wilson let a remark slip about teaching the Latin Americans "to elect good men". This is a strange utterance from someone committed to self-determination.

Once the United States was involved in the World War, Wilson felt almost as a crusader, fighting ignorance, greed and injustice, so that fair play, civilization, and peace might prevail. Almost immediately, his nations' enemies became wicked, like pawns of evil. The United States, he insisted, sought no new territory, reparations, or revenge, it only wished to extend its image to the world of the oppressed, so that the latter might be inspired to emulate America. It might justly be said that Wilson was beginning a long tradition of American attitude in which Americans like to believe that their values were universal values, that their government and society should stand out as a model for all others. The Fourteen Points certainly were received as Wilson had intended them to be, and practically overnight, he had upstaged all other politicians the world over. By the time of the end of the war, the American President was being looked to as the one leader in the world most capable of bringing about a just and honest peace.

There can be no question but that the *Alliance* countries had agreed to armistices based on the Fourteen Points because they genuinely believed that Wilson would give them a fair deal at the peace table. In fact, Wilson was not terribly concerned about the ex-enemy peoples, or others, for that matter. When a group of Irish nationalists approached him for support in their endeavors for independence from Britain, Wilson showed no sympathy or patience for them. He was not about to offend the British for the sake of a comparatively few Irishmen. Lloyd George, who was easily just as shrewd a politician as Wilson, soon had the measure of his American colleague. Thereafter, the two got along fairly well though they never completely trusted one another. Clemenceau and the French were somewhat slower to adapt to Wilson's condescending style, but thankfully no serious rift ever developed between them. Unfortunately for the Italians, Wilson's relations with their leaders would not be so cordial.

Italy's ambassador to Washington at the time was Baron Macchi di Cellere, a man who one notable historian describes as possessing "an extraordinary capacity to ignore facts".[272] The Baron had repeatedly assured his government that all was very well with Italian-American relations; Wilson had been shown a copy of the Treaty of London and had raised no objections to it. All this was true enough, but the President subsequently convinced himself that he knew nothing of the secret Treaty and was therefore not bound to respect it. Moreover, Wilson took a position identical to that of the South Slavs, insisting that the unplanned but subsequent break-up of the Austro-Hungarian Empire rendered the London Treaty obsolete, and therefore void. The people in Rome did not, of course, agree.

Wilson's worldwide popularity in late 1918 was a major factor influencing his decision to break with tradition and travel to Europe for the Peace Conference. He was the first American President to travel abroad while in office. Landing at Brest, France on December 13th, he was received with much pomp and ceremony by the French, who had every reason to court his good graces. Following ten days of conferences, speeches, and handshaking, he then traveled to Great Britain for several more days of much the same. Italy was third on the President's itinerary; on January 2nd, his train reached the Alpine frontier. Huge and wildly enthusiastic crowds assembled along Italy's roadways and filled her city squares, with untold thousands of citizens attempting to obtain a glimpse of the man who would deliver the world from evil. By the 4th Wilson was in Rome, where he called for ten thousand tons of food for delivery to the starving peoples of Central Europe. Next day he visited Milan. An estimated one million people turned out in Turin, and another huge crowd waited in Genoa. By all accounts, never in living memory had any politician, much less a foreign public figure, been held in such high esteem by the Italian nation.

Besides his enormous popularity, Woodrow Wilson could confront his European colleagues from a position of great material strength. Although the United States had been a latecomer to the war, the nation had been profiting from it since its beginning in 1914, and by the time of Wilson's European sojourn the continent owed the United States Government and private banking concerns some 10.5 billion dollars, an unheard-of sum in those days. In addition, American military strength had grown exponentially during the year and a half of hostilities and had not peaked before the Armistice. United States naval power now rivaled that even of Britain, long since the world's strongest sea-power. American resources seemed 'inexhaustible'; by contrast Europe had been bankrupted, decimated, and devastated. Even without his newfound popularity, the President's will was bound to have a profound influence upon the peacemaking.

Once all the delegates had assembled in Paris and the business of making peace could commence, American-Italian relations soon were strained. Initially, the French had assumed that all business would be conducted in their language alone, but since the British Commonwealth nations and the United States all insisted that English be adopted as a second 'official' tongue, Clemenceau, who spoke English well, and his delegation soon gave way. This act prompted Orlando and the Italians to push for their own language to be a third vernacular in use, but the move garnered no support and was quickly ignored. From that moment Orlando, who did not speak English well and did not easily understand it unless it was spoken slowly, felt himself at a disadvantage *vis a vis* Wilson, Lloyd George, and Clemenceau. Sonnino, who was a delegate for Italy, was fluent in both English and French, but the necessity of his constantly relaying information to Orlando was an obvious detriment in Paris. Then, as early as February, the United States recognized the new South Slavic State, an action that considerably angered the Italians.

On the 1st of December 1918, Prince Alexander of Serbia declared the existence of the Kingdom of the Serbs, Croats and Slovenes. It was no accident that the Serbs were named first; the new state was basically an enlargement of old Serbia, which was also allowed to swallow up Montenegro (though not without bitter opposition). The Serbian government became the South Slav government, the Serbian army became the South Slav army, and so forth. The Croats and Slovenes would have preferred a federated state of roughly equal subdivisions or provinces, but Serbian prestige was too great. It had been the first nation to have war declared against it in 1914, and it had subsequently been overrun, but managed to preserve a small army with which to oppose the *Alliance* throughout the war. The Croats and Slovenes had of course been a part of Austria-Hungary and had generally fought on the Italian Front, though the Habsburg authorities were careful not to pit them against the Serbs, and only reluctantly against the Russians. Britain and France did not immediately follow the American example by recognizing the South Slav Kingdom; they had, after all, made generous promises to Italy in the Treaty of London. Consequently, the Croats and Slovenes looked to Wilson to argue their case against the Italians. 'Self-determination' was the phrase they most often preferred to quote when discussing the future.

Besides being terrified of the Italians and resentful of the Austrians and Hungarians, the Croats and Slovenes were suspicious of the Serbs, who immediately disbanded all Croatian and Slovene units of the ex-Imperial army. To make matters worse, the two peoples lived in areas that had never been well-defined historically. Croatia had been a province of Hungary, but large numbers of Croats also lived in Austrian Dalmatia and Küstenland. As for the Slovenes, the province of Carniola was overwhelmingly Slovene, but many others dwelled in Küstenland, Styria and Carinthia, and they butted against Italians in the Isonzo area. The southwest tip of Hungary also was Slovene in speech. In early 1919 these people wondered who would support them in their efforts to obtain a national identity. On February 18th, the Italians notified the peacemakers in Paris of their refusal to accept arbitration over South Slav claims against lands that had been promised them by the London Treaty.

Before long the Slovenes countered by insisting that the old Italian-Austrian frontier should remain the border between Italy and themselves. They and the Croats would share the Küstenland, and they wanted the Slovene-speaking areas of Styria, Carinthia and Hungary, plus a little more, such as the distinctly Austrian city of Klagenfurt. Rome could not have cared less about Styria, Carinthia or Hungary, but it was determined to get Dalmatia and Küstenland, which included the Isonzo valley plus Trieste and the Istrian peninsula with the naval base at Pola. Soon a new slogan was heard all over Italy: "The Treaty of London plus Fiume", a sure indication of what Italians expected as their fair share of the spoils of war. About the same time, the ever-restless D'Annunzio began to fill the newspapers with articles defending Italy's right to conquest, and calling for ever more extensive annexations. Anything short of complete Italian satisfaction, D'Annunzio wrote, would constitute a "mutilated victory". The words were quoted and re-quoted, and another catch-phrase had been forever coined.

Behind the scenes more ominous events were taking place. As early as December, General Badoglio, who had been Diaz's second in command, had drawn up plans for military action against the South Slavs. Having protested loudly against the South Slav occupation of Pola and their possession of the ex-Imperial fleet, the port and the ships had been turned over to the Italians, who subsequently controlled the necessary means and bases from which to launch a strike against Croatia/Dalmatia had they so chosen. Fortunately, cooler heads prevailed, at least for the moment. On February 23rd, however, a new party was formed in Italy among individuals who were not likely to be considered cool-headed. Within a month, the party was under the control of an ex-sergeant who had been been badly wounded in the fighting on the Carso Plateau. His name was Benito Mussolini and his party were known as the Fascisto (Fascists). They were militant nationalists, bent on achieving glory for Italy at any price.

Extremely upset about the hardening national attitude in Italy, President Wilson became determined to support the South Slavs against the claims of Rome. Citing self-determination as a reason, he steadfastly refused to allow Dalmatia or Fiume to go to Italy. The British and French did their best to convince the Italian delegates to give up their claims based on the Treaty of London. Surely, they argued, Italy could see that circumstances had changed; the existence of Austria-Hungary, on which the treaty was based, was no longer a reality. Depriving a neighboring powerful Empire of its ports and naval bases made good military sense, but to strip an ex-ally and a friendly power of the same would only gain a new enemy for Italy. The arguments were valid but failed to move Orlando and especially Sonnino, who could always reply that his nation had gone to war for certain, specific ends, had suffered terrible losses for three and one-half years, and was now entitled to demand that the provisions of the Treaty be respected. Never mind trying to change the rules after the game had been played. Italy had done her part, and now expected to receive her reward. The nation would tolerate nothing less; to deprive Italy of her promised lands would probably cause such internal disturbances as would bring down the government. Before long, the French and British realized that Sonnino was not to be budged. Thereafter the Americans took up the task of debating the poker-faced Italian Foreign Minister. They quickly began to understand what the Austro-Germans must have gone through while trying to keep Italy neutral during the winter of 1914-1915. In the end, Colonel House, Wilson's closest associate in Paris, declared negotiating with Sonnino as "hopeless".

There were, of course, other problems to deal with as well. On February 16th the infant Republic of Austria held elections the results of which clearly showed that the vast majority of its German-speaking population desired a union with Germany. Of the fifteen provinces of Imperial Austria, the Republic had a firm grip on only four—upper and lower Austria proper, Salzburg and Voralberg. Three others were partially under its control, Styria and Carinthia were disputed with the South Slavs and Tyrol disputed with the Italians. All the others had been irretrievably lost and were already being administered by foreign governments. Under the circumstances the Austrians, without much arable land and now a landlocked nation, were anxious to join their ethnic brethren in Germany. The *Entente* nations, not wanting to see the Germany they were busy weakening be strengthened in any way, forbade the union.

Wilson, conveniently forgetting his principle of self-determination when it suited him to do so, supported his erstwhile allies, and the Austrians had no choice but to try to survive as an independent state. Soon, the Vienna government demanded that ex-Emperor Karl renounce forever his rights to the throne and leave Austrian soil. This Karl dutifully accomplished, and on March 23rd departed his homeland for an estate in Switzerland owned by his Empress's family. Four days later the new state abolished forever all rights and privileges of the Houses of Habsburg and Bourbon-Parma, to which Zita belonged, and confiscated all family property accumulated over the long centuries of Habsburg rule, excepting Karl's personal fortune. Habsburg family members who wished to remain in the Austrian Republic were required to take an oath of allegiance to it. At the stroke of a pen, a ruling House stretching back to the Medieval period had been dispossessed.

If hunger, unemployment, and inflation stalked Austria, the situation was even worse in Hungary, which was even more isolated from the comparative order in the West. Invaded and intimidated by Romanians, Slovaks and Serbs, the fledgling Hungarian state soon collapsed and was replaced by a Communist dictatorship similar in nature to Soviet Russia. Its leader, Bela Kun, had in fact been captured by the Russians during the war and been subjected to Bolshevik propaganda while a prisoner. On March 22nd Kun's revolutionary regime nationalized all big business and industry and appealed to the Soviet Union for support. By April 2nd Kun had notified Paris that he would honor the armistice with the *Entente* that Hungary had signed on November 13th. The Western Powers responded by looking the other way while Romanians, Czechoslovaks, and Serbs renewed military operations, intending to occupy all of Hungary and perhaps divide its remains among themselves. The Italians, of course, welcomed the Serbian distraction in Hungary.

The one area in which Sonnino was able to score a fairly easy success was in the Tyrol. It may be recalled that before the war, Austria had been willing to surrender the southern third or so of the province, where Italian speech prevailed, in order to purchase Italy's neutrality. The *Entente* had outbid her, however, offering the entire Adriatic watershed, or roughly two-thirds of the province, for Italian participation. It was easy to give away that which belonged to someone else, and the provision had been written into the Treaty of London. Wilson, once again ignoring the principle of self-determination when it would have favored German-speakers, was willing to accommodate Sonnino in this area, and the Italian Foreign Secretary drew up the new boundary line, which was approved without much fuss, except for a few murmurs from Lloyd George. Apparently no one bothered to study the new line; if they had they would have noticed that Sonnino had outwitted the others. Although the Italians had always insisted that they needed a watershed border for security reasons, and because they enjoyed a watershed frontier with France, the new line in the Tyrol did not in fact completely adhere to the stream divide. From the Swiss border to the Pusterthal all lands drained by the streams running into the Adriatic became Italian property, and those where waters ran into the Danube remained Austrian. But farther east, where the western end of the Carnic Alps is broken by valleys leading into the Pusterthal, the headwaters of the Drau (Drava) River were also to become Italian. The upper valley around Sexten had been the scene of much activity during the war, and had it remained Austrian it would have created a small bulge in the frontier which jutted into Italian territory. It was also the site of a portion of the railroad connecting the Drau and Adige systems; therefore Sonnino simply drew a cleaner line through it, and no one noticed. It is interesting to note that he did not round off a similar salient which jutted into Austrian ground by leaving it for Vienna, and therefore what remained of Tyrol was cut into two pieces, separated by a portion of Salzburg province. Although the Austrians later protested vigorously at this amputation of so much German-speaking ground, they were quietly ignored, and about a quarter-million Germans passed into Italian citizenship. The revelation caused such intense disappointment in Austria, that the head of the American mission in Vienna was obliged to solicit both Paris and Washington to define just what 'self-determination' meant, as applied to the Austrians. Despite repeated requests, no response was ever granted.[273]

With the Tyrol problem having been rather easily solved, the peacemakers could turn their attention to the far more difficult matter brewing between Rome and the South Slavs. Although most of Küstenland was inhabited by Slavs, the Italians not only wanted it in its entirety, they wanted to push its eastern edges well into Carniola. In addition they demanded Fiume, a part of ex-Hungarian Croatia, and much of Dalmatia. The idea was to reclaim these former Venetian lands and limit the new (and potentially rival) South Slav state to a short seacoast without a major port. Only then could Italy be assured of Adriatic supremacy.

In Paris the Italian delegation pleaded their case on grounds of strategic needs and historical precedents. Rome, then later Venice had once owned these areas. They reminded the Conference that Italy had brought civilization to these 'barbaric' areas and pointed to the prevalence of Latin influence up and down the coastline, and produced maps showing a dozen coastal towns and cities as having significant Italian-speaking minorities. They also argued that Serbia had already been granted Bosnia, Herzegovina, Hungarian Croatia/ Slavonia, and would probably soon be given much of southern Hungary and pieces of Austria. Italy, then, as the larger, stronger power the war effort of which had undoubtedly hastened the defeat of the *Alliance,* should be equally rewarded.

Neither the Americans nor the British and French were much impressed by the Italian demands. Already irritated by reports that Italian military units were preventing the transportation of food sent to Adriatic ports to the Slavic hinterland, they refused to rubber-stamp Rome's desires. Wilson in particular dug in his heels and determined not to allow Italy to annex much Slavic soil. Thus began a protracted battle of wills.

By the advent of March, 1919, the Council of Ten at the Paris Peace Conference had begun to lose control of the powers with which it had been invested, namely the remapping of Europe. Finding the larger council unwieldy and somewhat impotent, Wilson, Lloyd George, Clemenceau and Orlando began to meet as a group by themselves. Lacking these heads of state the Council of Ten lost much prestige and was soon eclipsed by these so-called 'Big Four' who went on to hold 145 private sessions, twice the number held by the Council of Ten. Before long, all the world looked to the 'Big Four' to iron out a just and lasting peace. Once again, because of the language barrier, and because he represented the weakest of the four (Italy owed the *Entente* approximately 3.4 billion dollars in 1919). Orlando was a sort of odd man out. He would indeed be out, literally, by an act of his own making, once the discussions about Italian expansion heated up. On March 21st, the entire Italian delegation gave notice that unless its nation's demands were met, they would leave the Conference. The ultimatum did not enhance Italy's standing at the Conference, quite to the contrary. When the Italian demands came up for discussion in April, the nation was more isolated diplomatically than ever. And Orlando stood alone amongst the 'Big Four'.

The brutal truth was that the Italian military was already occupying a good deal of ground inhabited by Slavs, and nothing short of war was going to eject its troops. When Wilson and the others were forced to recognize this fact, they gave way on the areas under Rome's control and instead became determined to prevent any more Slavic territory from a similar fate. Since Fiume and Dalmatia remained relatively free from occupation, it was these regions that Wilson decided to defend for the Slavs, come what may from Italy.

It should also be remembered that not all Italians favored aggressive expansionism. Many politicians were far more moderate, and a handful even tried to convince their countrymen to accept annexation of only those areas where a clear Italian-speaking majority was evident. These men wanted to preserve Italy's close alliance with the Western Powers, and warned against future problems with the Germans and Slavs if these groups were not treated with understanding and respect. Unfortunately, when such moderates tried to speak publically, they were shouted down by militants, nationalists, and particularly Fascists. Democracy in Italy had been badly weakened by the war, with its resulting privations, hysteria, and rigid regimentation. It is altogether possible that the Western leaders realized the nature of the new Italy, and therefore did their best to contain it. At any rate, by April 1919, the Italians had managed to alienate Wilson and Clemenceau, and were fast losing the sympathies of Lloyd George.

The rift opened wide in mid-April. No one wanted to deny Rome the Latin-speaking areas of Küstenland, the triangle from Aquileia to Gorizia to Trieste. But Italy demanded not only all of the province, but a substantial piece of neighboring Carniola—almost entirely Slovene in speech and sentiment—as well, which included Boroevic's old headquarters—town of Adelsberg and an important piece of the railroad running from the Slovene capitol of Ljubljana (formerly Laibach) to Trieste and Fiume. Nor was this all. Such a line if drawn would still have missed the inclusion of Fiume, which was not in either Küstenland or Carniola, but at the western tip of Croatia. As mentioned above, Wilson, aware that the Italians were in possession of all this ground save Fiume, did not bother to contest most of it, but he drew the line at Fiume, and made up his mind that he was not going to allow Italy to have it. There the matter deadlocked; neither party would be moved.

With his nation firmly behind him, and indeed as he received almost daily communications from Rome exhorting him to stand fast on Fiume and

Dalmatia, Orlando confronted Wilson on April 14th. The meeting was not cordial, and solved nothing. Lloyd George and Clemenceau tried to affect a compromise by suggesting that Italy receive the Adriatic islands but not the Dalmatian coast and that perhaps all the Dalmatian ports be made free cities. Meanwhile, the South Slavs began to drop hints that they were prepared to fight the Italians if the latter were awarded any more territory of Slavic speech.

For several days, Orlando and Sonnino fenced with Wilson. This struggle of wills began to strain Orlando's nerves, with Sonnino becoming increasingly irritated; he would accept nothing less than his precious Treaty of London had allowed, plus Fiume. Wilson appeared to age rapidly, looking haggard and tired. Even Lloyd George began to lose patience and Clemenceau was positively disgusted, especially with the Italian intransience. With no agreement apparently on the horizon, the Italians had finally had enough and walked out of the Peace Conference on the 24th. They returned to Rome to cheering crowds and a most supportive press, which caricaturized and denounced Wilson. It is perhaps needless to relate that in the semi-hysterical political climate in Italy of those days, extremists like the Fascists and dramatists like D'Annunzio gained greatly in popularity.

Besides weakening Italy's already shaky democracy, the impasse at Paris did not create a positive situation for the Italian government. The British and French could point to the walk-out as a good reason, finally, for them to not honor the terms of the Treaty of London. The Americans held it up as proof of Italian unreasonableness and discontinued the flow of credit to Rome. Soon aware that their tactics had failed, Orlando and Sonnino returned to Paris on May 6th, only to find that the 'Big Three' were capable of functioning without them. For his part, Wilson was reluctant to enter into any further negotiations with the Italian leaders, and took his case directly to the Italian people in a series of press releases. This tactic also proved unsuccessful; the people were both furious with Wilson and unhappy with their own leaders for failing to secure what were seen as the nation's just rewards. Wilson, who was growing weaker physically, washed his hands of Italian sessions and left the whole messy business to Colonel House, while he himself concentrated on the Treaty with Germany. Of course House, who enjoyed far less prestige than his boss, could hardly be expected to accomplish much.

On June 2nd, 1919, a preliminary Treaty of Peace was handed to the Austrian delegation at Paris. It was published a day later. The new Austrian Republic was to recognize the independence of Czechoslovakia, Hungary, The Kingdom of the Serbs, Croats, and Slovenes, and Poland, as well as the enlargement of Romania and Italy, at the expense of the defunct Empire. Bohemia, Moravia and Silesia were to go to Czechoslovakia, Galicia to Poland, and Bukovina to Romania. Tyrol had already been broken up as we have seen, and Styria was divided along a line roughly Ebiswald-Spielfeld-Radkersberg-St. Anna, points south going to the Slavs. Carniola, except for the piece already in Italian hands, also went to the Slavs, thus isolating an 'island' of German speech, similar to that around Asiago, of several towns and villages centered around Gottschee in the southern part of the province. That left only Carinthia to be dealt with; it contained large numbers of Slovenes within its southeastern frontier, but the Italians were also interested in the area where the three language groups converged. Ultimately they were awarded a triangular shaped piece of real estate containing Slovenes and Germans, but few Latins. It not coincidentally straddled the railroad that negotiated the Pontebba Pass and the Karawanken Mountains and led into the Gail River valley. About half of this area was drained by a tributary of the Tagliamento, and therefore a portion of the Adriatic watershed, but the other half was sloped to the Gail, in the Danube system. Once again, the Italians had managed to surpass their ambitions for a watershed boundary. The Slovenes, on the other hand, were not granted outright Klagenfurt and the frontier area of mixed German-Slovene speech; the final border was to be decided by plebiscite.

In addition to the land grabs, Austria was to forfeit all of her salt-water fleet (long since confiscated) and up to twenty percent of her Danube flotilla. Six thousand milk-cows were also to be surrendered, 4,000 to Italy and 1,000 each to Romania and the South Slavs. Two thousand of other bovines were to go to Italy, 1,025 to Romania, and 825 to the Slavs. The Italians were also to receive 2,000 pigs and the Romanians and Slavs 1,000 horses and 1,000 sheep apiece from the diminutive new Republic. Other reparations included 'property of predominant historic interest' which the Habsburg government had, over the centuries, transferred from its possessions to Vienna. For example, the Crown Jewels and some Medici heirlooms were to be returned to Tuscany, artwork and manuscripts to Modena, Norman artifacts to Palermo, 'ninety-eight' manuscripts to Naples, just to mention that which would be surrendered to Italy. The Poles, Czechoslovaks and Belgians also had their hands out.[274] The entire list of the terms of the Treaty are numerous and perhaps irrelevant here; suffice to say that it completely disarmed and impoverished Austria, a now-landlocked country of few natural resources and only seven million people, a third of whom resided in greater Vienna.

Totally stunned by the terms of the Treaty they were expected to sign, the Austrians protested vigorously and to no avail. Particularly galling to them was the loss of the over three million German-speakers who lived in Bohemia and Moravia, in areas mostly contiguous to either Germany or Austria, and therefore in areas which could have been awarded to either. The Czechs, of course, cited economics, tradition, and anything else they could think of to be granted the disputed territory just as they did regarding the million or so Hungarians they were planning to absorb. Their arguments were convincing to an audience that was being told what it wanted to hear, and were strengthened by the fact that Czechoslovak troops had served the *Entente* on the Eastern, Western, and Italian Fronts. In only one instance were the Austrians allowed a concession, and then only because it came at the expense of the Hungarians. Applying for ownership of a narrow strip of land of German speech just over the Hungarian border known as the Burgenland, they were more than half surprised when it was assigned to them, minus the city of Odenburg. It was the only instance when any of the defeated nations were able to gain territory it had not owned before the war (Although if one considers Austria-Hungary as a whole, the point is moot), and was probably only done to somewhat offset the shock of the loss of the Bohemian, Moravian, and Tyrolese Germans. The Hungarians, naturally, were not amused.

Most South Slavs were displeased with the idea of a plebiscite in Carinthia, but knew they needed to proceed with moderation, particularly once their state had been formally recognized by the French and British, an act which also occurred in June. Thereafter, the dispute with Italy took center stage, and the Austrian question weakened in importance in the minds of most interested observers. In the meantime, the Belgrade government decided it could solve the Carinthian territorial dispute with force. Quietly, it assembled a force of fourteen Serbian and four Slovenian battalions, complete with cavalry and artillery, and advanced into the province beginning on May 28th. Despite skillful resistance by a much smaller Austrian force, it advanced to the Drau on a front from Arnoldstein to Lavamünd. By June 6th Serb troops were in Klagenfurt, the only sizeable population center in the disputed area. According to those who lived through the Slav occupation, it was marked by a reign of terror in which slogans like 'Death to the friends of the Germans' (Tod den Nemcuri) were heard constantly. The brutal occupation probably did the South Slav cause more harm than good in the long run, however, and led to the formation of resistance groups like the Carinthian Homeland Service (K.H.D.) who countered with expressions of their own. "Carinthia for the Carinthians" and "Carinthia remains undivided" was soon being heard behind the backs of the nervous occupation forces. When at last the plebiscite was held on October 10th, 1920, just shy of sixty percent of the voters chose to remain Austrian, in spite of an intimidating presence of South Slav troops watching the polls.[275] Only two small areas of southeastern Carinthia went to the Slav Kingdom. These included the towns of Drauburg (Dravograd), Gutenstein (Ravne), Miesdorf (Mezica), Schwarzenbach (Crna), and Oberseeberg and Unterseeberg (Zgornje Jezersko/Spodnje Jezersko). Frontiers for the new Austria had finally been defined. Slovenia was also awarded a small area of western Hungary, northeast of the Mura River containing about a dozen towns; it was due south of Austria's new Burgenland. Subsequently, only the South Slav border with Italy still needed to be settled.

It would prove to be the most difficult issue arising from the war on the Italian Front. On June 19th, Orlando's leadership could not survive a vote of confidence in Rome; Francesco Nitti replaced him, although somehow Sonnino retained his post. Domestic problems dominated Italian politics that summer, and by August, Tittoni was prepared to allow Fiume to become a free city and forgo all claims to Dalmatia. No doubt the French, British and Americans would have been very happy to settle the matter at that, but before any such agreement was signed, the restless and flamboyant D'Annunzio propelled Fiume back into the headlines.

A number of extremist groups, the fascists among them, had been considering a forcible takeover of Fiume throughout the summer, while Italian public opinion clambered for its annexation in defiance of the Western Powers. Of all Italians most likely to take such action, D'Annunzio, with his undying flair for the dramatic, stood out. As of late summer he had collected an odd force of perhaps two hundred adventurers, all anxious to seize the last outpost of *Italia Irredenta* (Reports as to which ethnic group was more numerous in

Fiume often differed considerably, but it is safe to consider that Italian-speakers and Croat-speakers both claimed a majority in the city. The surrounding countryside was almost entirely Slavic in speech and sentiment). When the signing of the peace treaty with Austria was announced as having been performed at St. Germain en Laye on September 10th, they decided to strike before a similar accommodation with the South Slavs could be undertaken. The next day the unlikely army made its move, and other Italian troops sent to arrest it joined D'Annunzio instead, on the 12th, and the soldier-poet occupied all of the main buildings of Fiume's infrastructure. Subsequent threats from Rome failed to impress the rebel 'army'; deadline after deadline came and went without effect and the city quickly lapsed into a state which can only be described as an ongoing drunken orgy. All the while militarists, criminals, and misfits of every description continued to swell the ranks of the 'crusaders' while the Italian public cheered and delighted in the news.

The crisis threatened to bring down the Italian government, which was obliged to condemn D'Annunzio and impose a blockade of the port city. Even the King got involved, calling for a general election later, and an immediate vote of confidence in the government, an appeal that was entertained, on September 27th. Premier Nitti survived, as did Tittoni as Foreign Minister, but once again D'Annunzio upstaged everyone by declaring war on the South Slavic State on the 30th. The Serb leaders needed little provocation to send a military force to Fiume, and by his impetuous act, D'Annunzio had in fact crossed the line of tolerance. Warned on no uncertain terms to back off, the Italian hero began to moderate his statements. On October 3rd the 'National Council' of Fiume requested the blockade of foodstuffs be lifted, as the city faced starvation. Two days later another address assured the Slavs of free access to the sea through the port, and complained of foreign intervention in the solving of the Adriatic question. As late as September 29th, the Chamber of Deputies in Rome had demanded that Fiume be annexed by Italy, but suddenly on October 10th with war against the Slavs and without Western support a real possibility, it agreed to the solution of making the city a free port on the border of both Italy and the South Slavic State, belonging to neither. Even the rebel leader, his support within Fiume beginning to wane, agreed to this solution on the 16th.

He did not, however, leave the city, and within a few days seems to have recovered his nerve. On October 27th, he announced that the citizens of Fiume, in a 'practically unanimous' vote, had decided for annexation to Italy. A week or so later he was boasting of 50,000 followers and a proposal to conquer all of Dalmatia. In reality, his only Dalmatian adventure turned out to be a dramatic landing at Zara on November 15th, a location he must have known had been assigned to Italy (the one and only Dalmatian town that had) in the latest deal being cut between Rome and Belgrade. Although D'Annunzio boasted of grandiose plans to invade other Slavic lands, including Montenegro,[276] a remark that prompted the Serbs to send an entire division to Spalato on the 22nd, he in the event soon returned to Fiume, where he continued to live a life akin to that of a Prince of the City.

Tittoni forwarded a fresh proposal to the West to solve the crisis, in mid-December, but it was rejected by President Wilson. As a result, the Italian Foreign Minister resigned his office. On the 24th a fresh—and internationally supervised—vote on the future status of Fiume by its citizens was held, and the results showed that seventy-five percent of the people favored a Free-City arrangement for the municipality for the time being.

New talks in Paris on the Adriatic area commenced on January 11th, 1920. The Italians, weary of the controversy, declared that they would withdraw all claims to Dalmatia except for Zara, the only town there with an undeniable Italian-speaking majority. Furthermore, they agreed to Free City status for Fiume. All the Adriatic islands would go to the Slavs, except Lagosta in the south and Cherso, Lussin and a few tiny specks immediately east of Istria. Satisfied, the French and British sent the proposal to Belgrade where it was partially, but not completely accepted. Wilson, long since back in North America, warned that any settlement reached without United States concurrence might cause the nation to reject the other recent treaties. Then on February 29th, the Italians and South Slavs were brought together in London for direct bargaining. Following two months of accusations, threats, pleading, bickering, and even begging, the two sides came to agreement on April 24th. The final decision regarding the 'Adriatic Question' was at long last published on May 12th. It was not until November 12th, however, that an actual document, the Treaty of Rapallo, was signed between the Kingdom of Italy and the Kingdom of the Serbs, Croats, and Slovenes. Two weeks later the Italian Chamber of Deputies ratified the agreement; all that remained to be done was to oust D'Annunzio and his 6,000 associates from Fiume, after which the place could become a true 'Free City'. No one expected it would be easy. A 20,000 man force under General Caviglia surrounded the port from the land side on

December 1st, while a naval force closed in from the Gulf. Caviglia sent D'Annunzio an ultimatum; the latter responded by declaring war on Italy. Three more weeks of wrangling and negotiating achieved nothing, except to reveal that none of the Italian troops and sailors wanted to fight the rebels, and a fair number actually deserted to them. But on the 21st D'Annunzio informed Caviglia of his 'unalterable' decision to not recognize the Rapallo Treaty. After two days grace, army units and warships opened fire instigating several days of half-hearted fighting. On December 29th the insurgent leader surrendered. Only on January 14th, 1921 was the city declared as free of its erstwhile guests. D'Annunzio himself departed for France on the 18th. Peace had finally come to the shores of the Adriatic.

Eastern Boundary of Italy as agreed by the Treaty of London, 1915 – – – – –
Actual Boundary by 1924 (where different) – – – – –
Post 1954 Border · · · · · · · · ·

Italian Cities Bombed or shelled from the Sea, 1915-1918 · Ancona

Boundary Changes

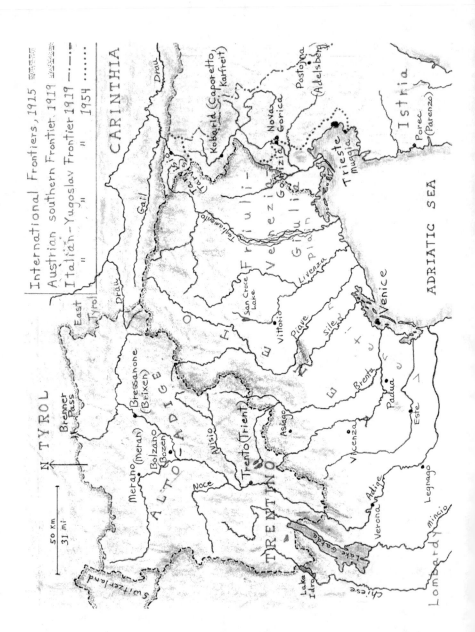

Boundary Changes

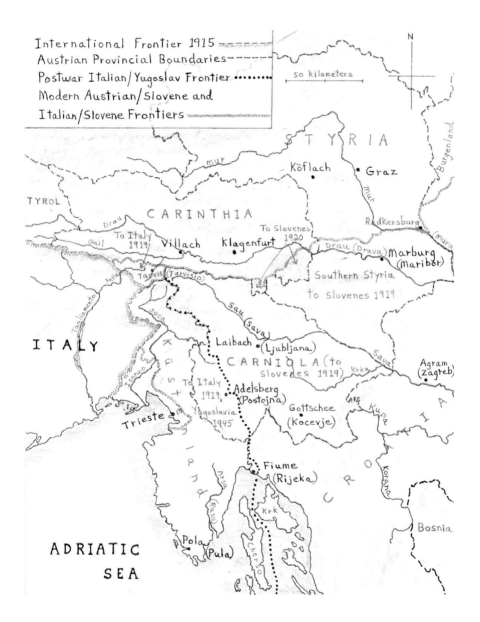

International Frontier 1915
Austrian Provincial Boundaries
Postwar Italian/Yugoslav Frontier
Modern Austrian/Slovene and
Italian/Slovene Frontiers

50 kilometers

N

STYRIA

Köflach · Graz

TYROL

CARINTHIA

Burgenland

To Italy 1919

Villach   Klagenfurt   To Slovenes 1920

Radkersburg

Drau (Drava)   Marburg (Maribor)

Southern Styria to Slovenes 1919

Tarvis (Tarvisio)

ITALY

Laibach (Ljubljana)

CARNIOLA (to Slovenes 1919)

Agram (Zagreb)

To Italy 1919   Adelsberg (Postojna)   Gottschee (Kocevje)

Yugoslavia 1945

Trieste

Fiume (Rijeka)

CROATIA

Bosnia

ADRIATIC SEA

Pola (Pula)

Boundary Changes

Chapter Fourteen
Legacy

It is often charged that the settlement of Versailles, which ended the state of war with Germany in 1919, satisfied no one. The statement is not quite true, but had it been redirected at the peace-making process resulting from war on the Italian Front, it would have been much closer to hitting the mark. *Almost* no one in Rome, Vienna, or Belgrade, or in the remainder of those respective countries for that matter, felt that the Treaties of St. Germain and Rapallo represented the final word for the Alpine or Adriatic frontiers. The Viennese easily had the most to complain about; once the capitol of Europe's second largest nation, an Empire of more than fifty million subjects, their city now appeared on maps as the eye of a tadpole-shaped country of less than seven million with only one eighth as much land. And the ground that was left was mostly Alpine terrain, high mountain peaks separated by the innumerable gorges cut by icy, fast-flowing streams. Only the Danube plain and the newly-acquired Burgenland offered much possibility for agriculture. Right from the start, the country was unable to feed itself, as the victorious powers must have known it would be, yet they continually denied its wishes to join with Germany, because had the two united, the territorial and population losses so recently imposed on Germany would have been made good, and they wanted to see her weakened, not remain equally strong, self-determination be damned. And the addition of the German-speaking Austrians to the larger group might actually have been more desirable for Berlin than retaining the largely foreign-speaking elements that it had lost. At the end of the first year of peace, Vienna was on the verge of starvation; the bread ration had been reduced to four ounces per person per week.[277] The economy, not surprisingly, had been reduced to chaos. Left without much arable land, Austria had also been left without the types of natural resources necessary to sustain a modern economy, much of which, with accompanying industry, had gone to Czechoslovakia. At the tip of the tadpole tail, the small province of Voralberg, the most distant of all from Vienna, expressed its desire to join the neighboring Swiss Confederation.

Particularly disturbing to the Austrians was the loss of the Tyrol, perhaps fifty percent of the area of the entire province, which as we have seen, split the remainder into two sections, and the loss of the German-speaking areas of Bohemia and Moravia, which contained many critical pieces of the old Austrian economy. These latter areas became known as the Sudetenland and they would soon become a major issue between the Czechs and Germans.

In Belgrade, the Serb leaders had every reason to be pleased with the outcome of the war. Serbia had gone from a primitive Balkan nation to a sizeable European state with a long Adriatic coastline and frontiers on the West. Bosnia-Herzegovina, Croatia-Slavonia and Montenegro had all been annexed, as well as portions of western Bulgaria, southern and western Hungary, most of Dalmatia and Carniola, a slice of Styria, and a small piece of Carinthia from Austria. Only the Slavic-speaking areas of western Carniola and the old Küstenland had been denied, by the Italians, to the new and enlarged Kingdom of the Serbs, Croats, and Slovenes. The new state was, however, a strange mixture of ethnic and religious groups who may all have spoken a similar language, but whose customs and traditions were as diverse as was the history of the ground it now straddled. As far back as Roman days the Empire had been split between East and West within the territory of the new Kingdom, and in two thousand years of development since, the old gap had never again been bridged. The Belgrade government certainly faced challenges in administering such a diverse realm, and the fact that several of its neighbors—Hungary, Bulgaria, Albania and Italy—were resentful of it was not going to help. It was not long before several of the various groups within the Kingdom were wondering if they would not have been better off to have resisted the advances of the Serbs and to have remained apart. Many of the Slovenes, for example, felt in some ways closer culturally and economically to Austria, than to Serbia.

Of the three countries, Italy was easily the most populous, the most developed economically, and the strongest militarily. Its powerful army and navy had helped win the war for the *Entente*. It had gained all of the land so long craved as *Italia Irredenta*, indeed had gotten all it wanted except Dalmatia. But legends, once perpetrated, are hard to dispel. Germany had its 'stab in the back' excuse to explain its defeat, and Italy could not forget

D'Annunzio's lamenting of a 'mutilated victory'. For many Italians, their nation had somehow been cheated at the peace table, had somehow been denied the glory that was due it, and Italian politics, never a model of orderliness, became chaotic and hysterical. We have seen how Italy's feeble democracy had been weakened by Cadorna's virtual military dictatorship, without so much as a protest from the King; after the war some sections of the country became almost ungovernable as gangs and mobs of extremists of every persuasion stalked the countryside, terrorizing the inhabitants. Into this vacuum of violence and uncertainty stepped the Fascists with their militant nationalistic messages of might making right. Once again the King was not disposed to oppose the strongmen, and Italian democracy was easily crushed without hardly a protest. Benito Mussolini, the onetime sergeant on the Isonzo, installed himself as dictator of a willing Italian nation.

Once he had consolidated his power, one of Mussolini's first acts of aggression was the annexation of Fiume, in January of 1924. The move displeased the South Slavs, but they never seriously contemplated any counteraction, and the showdown between the two old antagonists was delayed until Italy had a new and powerful ally.

Before the rise of Hitler, Mussolini was certainly no friend to the Germans, though he had learned the language and did admire Teutonic inventiveness and efficiency. Once in power, he turned on Italy's new German minority in the 'Alto-Adige' as the German-speaking area in Italy's half of the Tyrol was now called. Place names were Latinized; the three main towns of Bozen, Brixen and Meran became Bolzano, Bressanone, and Merano respectively. Schools and government offices suddenly had to use Italian to function and even newborns were not to be given names that 'offended Italian sentiment'.[278] Italy retained the area even at the height of Hitler's power as the perceived price of Mussolini's friendship. In 1938 Hitler's Germany annexed Austria and the Sudetenland, but it was not until after Italy's military collapse in the middle of the Second World War that a disgusted *Führer* reattached the Alto-Adige to Tyrol, an arrangement that like all of Hitler's territorial acquisitions, did not survive the war. All throughout the remaining Twentieth Century, the world was reminded of Sonnino's triumph in the Tyrol, at least every four years during the winter Olympic Games, when so many 'Italian' athletes of the snowy sports were announced with unmistakably German names.

Austrian-Italian relations have been relatively good ever since, though a certain sensitivity from the days of the Great War still remains, if well beneath the quiet surface. The famous discovery of the ancient body of a man high in the Ötztal Alps in the early 1990's represents the latest border incident between the old enemies; the 'Iceman' was found by Austrian nationals hiking the watershed frontier area and he was subsequently sent to Vienna for study. The government in Rome protested vigorously and claimed the corpse had lain on its side of the line, and this dispute was only resolved when a surveying team of neutral interest was sent to the area. It concluded that the discovery site was indeed a few dozen meters inside the Italian portion of the watershed, and the 'Iceman' had to be surrendered at Vienna and sent to Rome. A few years later the Austrian government formally requested the Italians to return what is believed to be the last surviving example of an Austro-Hungarian pontoon, the type used in the bridging of the Piave during the final Austrian offensives of June 1918. This relic had been on open-air display near Nervesa, a town on the river and in the shadow of the Montello. Vienna's request was in the words of one writer, "politely declined".[279] Old antagonisms apparently die hard.

Even today the old pre-First World War boundary between Italy and Austria survives as the border of the Italian province of Trentino-Alto Adige. Only its northeastern line has been altered by the incorporation of all of the Piave watershed into the province of Veneto, a not too significant change, but one which transferred the extreme upper Cordevole Valley, north of Mt. Marmolada, and the Ampezzo River watershed, including the scenic region around Cortina, to Veneto.

The long-standing friction between Italy and the South Slavs affected more significant changes. After the war, the Kingdom of the Serbs, Croats, and Slovenes entered into a defensive alliance with Romania and Czechoslovakia, designed to hold down the Hungarians. In 1929, it was officially renamed Yugoslavia, at the insistence of the non-Serb ethnic groups. Following Hitler's destruction of Czechoslovakia, and Romania's adherence to the *Axis*, Yugoslavia found itself isolated and nearly surrounded by hostile states; only Greece was friendly. Hitler himself had no great interest in what he regarded as an Italian sphere of influence, but once Mussolini had taken his nation into the war on Germany's side, the Yugoslavs were given a choice: join the *Axis* or become an enemy. In 1941 the Germans struck, and the uneasy Kingdom was quickly overrun. Montenegro and Croatia, the latter enlarged by the

319

addition of Bosnia-Herzegovina, were to become semi-independent states under Italian protection. Hungary took back what it had lost in 1919. Italy finally annexed much of Dalmatia and southern Carniola, including the German-speaking 'island' around Gottschee. Hitler took northern Carniola and the portions of Styria and Carinthia that had been lost at the end of the First World War. For awhile, it seemed as though the settlement of the Great War had been completely reversed.

However, the Yugoslav problem never went away for the *Axis*. Almost immediately, several Yugoslav resistance groups flourished; eventually Tito's became the strongest and was supported by both the Western Powers and the Soviet Russians. Yugoslavia's resistance was treated as an Allied Power, at war with the *Axis*. This gave the country considerable leverage at the close of the war, and Tito, while ousting the Monarchy, was able to everywhere restore Yugoslavia's frontiers to those of 1919. Zara, Istria and the Adriatic islands were also given to (or rather taken by) Tito's government, and only the line with Italy was left to be determined. This time the Yugoslavs were claiming Trieste, the city for which Italy had gone to war in 1915, and the all-too familiar label of Free City was being applied to it. Trieste thus became the Fiume of the second war and a resolution to the problem was no less difficult. Italy pushed hard to keep at least western Istria and Trieste; the Yugoslavs wanted a pre-1915 frontier.

The dispute dragged on until 1954. Italy kept the Tarvisio triangle of land east of Pontebba that it had taken in 1919; south of it the 1915 line applied as far as the middle Judrio from which it turned east to include Cormons for Italy; then it crossed the Isonzo just north of Gorizia, virtually split the 'City of Violets', then ran due south through the Vallone nearly to the coast road. A very narrow strip of coast was allotted to Italy to allow Trieste to be geographically connected to Monfalcone. The southern suburb of Muggia marked the end of Italian territory. All else went to Yugoslavia. Roughly 300,000 ethnic Italians fled the Dalmatian and Istrian coastal towns to join their fellow Latin-speakers to the west. In the new Yugoslavia, Slovenia and Croatia divided the old Austrian Küstenland; Croatia took the peninsula including Pola (now Pula), while Slovenia took the borderlands with Italy. For the Latins, their net gain since 1915 along the Isonzo after 1954 was: Aquiliea, Cormons, Gradisca, Monfalcone, Sagrado, half of Gorizia and the Trieste/Muggia coast strip. Taken with Tarvisio and the Tyrol, the gains represent, more or less, the minimum demands the nation had sought in 1915. Excepting the raw deal forced upon the Germans, the post-1954 borders probably come as close to being fair and equitable to all as could ever be expected. The once disputed lands now constitute a part of the Italian province of Friuli-Venezia-Giulia. All that remains of the 1915 frontier now is a 75 kilometer (45 mile) stretch along the Carnic Alps at the northern tip of this province and that of Veneto, and from the middle Judrio to the Tarvisio triangle. Across the border lie eastern Tyrol and western Carinthia where, as in the rest of Austria, very little talk of a new union with Germany has been heard.

After the collapse of Communism in the late 20th Century, two of the most unlikely states to have emerged from the ruins of the Austro-Hungarian Empire also disintegrated, they having been artificially propped up throughout the uneasy period of the Cold War. The divorce of the Czechs and Slovaks was not particularly messy, but a diminutive Slovakia still is home to large numbers of Hungarians that Budapest would like to accommodate. For the Czechs, minorities are no longer a problem, inasmuch as about 3.5 million German-speakers were forcibly expelled from the Sudetenland in the aftermath of World War II, but unlike those areas of expulsion in Poland and Russia, the Germans have never foresworn their claims to lands in Bohemia and Moravia, and a small but vocal minority still occasionally agitate for their return. In the case of Yugoslavia, the break-up involved more than just two parties and was a good deal more dramatic. War, punctuated by genocide, again ravaged the land. Slovenia, as the farthest province removed from Serbia became independent with very little bloodshed. The case of Croatia was more difficult, that of Bosnia-Herzegovina more difficult still. In the end, both broke free of Belgrade, as did Macedonia, and most recently, Montenegro. Today's Serbia can point only to Vojvodina, an area taken from Hungary in 1919 and which still supports a large Hungarian-speaking population, for evidence of its gains from the Great War, but it barely makes up for the loss of Macedonia. Most recently, the turbulent province of Kosovo has also declared its independence from Serbia and if this act is in fact accomplished, the new Serbia will be even smaller than was the Serbia of 1914. Yugoslavia then, has become six or seven independent states, and Serbia is landlocked once again.

The last Habsburg Emperor Karl, unwanted in Austria and almost everywhere else in his former lands, began to focus on Hungary, the last remnant of his inheritance which had yet to embrace a stable government. After the overthrow of Bela Kun and his Communist dictatorship, ex-Imperial Admiral Nicolas Horthy was able to gain control of the nation and reinstitute a nominal Kingdom. Horthy, an admiral in a state without a seacoast, was not supportive of Archduke Joseph von Habsburg's serious efforts to restore his family to the throne, though Karl always pointed out that he had never abdicated as King of Hungary. Somewhat misreading the political climate in 1921 Budapest, and influenced by the urgings of a badly-advised small group of loyal followers, Karl tried twice to reclaim the throne. Although support for him was widespread among the upper class, Horthy enjoyed the sympathies of the majority of Hungarians, and was able, by threatening to use force, to prevent a Habsburg restitution. Karl, ever peaceable, refused to allow his followers to engage the government troops and soon left Hungary for good. His spirit all but broken, Karl became sickly and his constitution weakened rapidly. Within a year, he was dead on the island of Madeira, his choice for a residence in permanent exile. He was only thirty-four years of age. Always a pathetic figure who was in no way responsible for the war (or the peace), Karl certainly deserved a better fate. Many decades later, the Vatican announced that he was to be awarded the distinction of 'Venerable'; and a few years beyond, in 2003, he was proclaimed to be 'Blessed', the Church having decided to beatify the last Habsburg Emperor.

Karl's widow, the ex-Empress Zita, long outlived her husband. Returning to Switzerland, she petitioned several times over the years to be allowed to return to Vienna, if only for short visits. Not until she had reached the age of ninety, however, did the Austrian Republic deign to grant her requests, and three separate passages to the capitol were arranged in 1982.[280] The old Monarch was by all accounts quite a hit with the Viennese, appearing at localities she had not seen in sixty-three years. Remarkably, Zita lived on until 1989, expiring only a few months before the collapse of Communism throughout much of her old Empire. Her family was permitted to bury her with the other historic figures of the Habsburg dynasty in the Austrian capitol.

King Vittorio Emanuele had acquiesced in Italy's adherence to the *Triple Alliance* yet made no significant protest when his ministers decided, in 1915, to switch allegiances and join the *Entente*. Similarly, he decided not to oppose Mussolini in 1922 when the Fascists could easily have been crushed by the Army, and thus allowed the nation's curious and feeble democracy to be replaced by an authoritarian government. For once in his life taking a decisive stance, the King in July 1943 informed the Italian dictator that as the Fascist cause no longer represented the will of the Italian people, he would have to step down. The interview was not cordial, and Mussolini took the hint. Vittorio Emanuele lived to see democracy reinstated in his Kingdom, however, the Italian people decided in 1946 to replace the Monarchy with a Republic. The King lost his throne as a result of a plebiscite held in that year. On May 9th, he abdicated, following a reign of 46 years. He died in exile in Egypt during the following year.

Field Marshal Baron von Franz Graf Conrad von Hötzendorf, the military chief who had argued hard for preventative wars against Serbia and Italy long before 1914, was dismissed and retired by Karl after the failure of Operation *Radetzky*, ending 47 years of his service to the Empire. He spent most of the rest of his life in Vienna reminiscing with old friends and arguing for Austria's union with Germany. He also found the time to prepare a lengthy series of volumes of memoirs, which were published a few years prior to his death. On August 25, 1925, in Bad Mergentheim, Germany, he passed into history.

Wartime boss of Italy's *Commando Supremo* General Count Luigi Cadorna had been somewhat disgraced by the 'Disaster of Caporetto', but after the war his reputation was redeemed; the Fascists were friendly and Mussolini elevated both Cadorna and his successor Armando Diaz simultaneously, to the rank of Marshal of Italy, the loftiest military position of the nation. Cadorna busied himself in writing very self-serving memoirs of the war; Diaz was appointed Minister of War. Obviously, Mussolini was courting favor with the two former heads of the Army, as he realized that the military was the one institution capable of challenging his Fascist movement and its chokehold on the country. Diaz needed no cheerleaders; his reputation was somewhat akin to that of a savior of Italy after Caporetto, and he had always been held in high esteem by his soldiers. He lived beyond the glory days of 1918 by nearly a decade, finally expiring in early 1928. Cadorna, ever unrepentant for his horrible mishandling of the army on the Isonzo, also died in 1928, at age 68 two years older than Diaz.

Field Marshal Svetozar Boroevic Edler von Bojna, whose skillful defensive leadership had helped defeat eleven enemy offensives along the Isonzo, found himself a man without a country after the war. As a Croat by birth he had no difficulty in favoring the South Slav cause in opposing Italian expansionism in the Adriatic area. Offering his services to the Belgrade government, he was disappointed when it not only declined to employ him but soon declared that he would not be allowed to resume residence in Croatia; it even confiscated his property there, an act which completely impoverished him. The South Slav authorities, dominated by Serbian influence, tended to consider all former Austro-Hungarian officers and officials as ex-enemies not to be entertained by the new regime. Boroevic had little choice but to settle in Austria, where he was sustained by other ex-Imperial officers and friends. He chose the area earmarked for the plebiscite, where many citizens easily switched from the German to the Slavic language. At any rate he did not long survive the war, and suddenly died while enjoying some recreation at the Wörthersee, the largest lake in the region. The 'Straightrazor' was in his 64th year.

Gabriele D'Annunzio, the 'hero' of Fiume, who had fought on the Italian Front when he felt like doing so, continued to live a flamboyant and outrageous lifestyle after the war. Mussolini tolerated him because of his popularity, but privately complained about his extravagance, comparing him to a diseased tooth which either had to be pulled or filled with gold, the gold being a state expenditure. By 1938 the gold had apparently run out; the onetime poet and playwright was found dead in his home. Murder was suspected, but never proven.

Lieutenant Erwin Rommel, who had won Germany's 'Blue Max' in the early days of Operation *Waffentreu*, decided to remain in the Army after the war. For years he commanded a company of soldiers quartered at Stuttgart, capitol of his native Württemberg. By 1932 he had achieved the rank of Major, and in 1939, that of General. The outbreak of World War II saw him as Commandant of Hitler's Headquarters, and the two men would form a close, if not cordial, relationship. Following the attempt on Hitler's life in July of 1944, Rommel was implicated, however, and chose to commit suicide in order to protect his family from Nazi retribution. At 52 years old he was one of Germany's youngest Field Marshals and a national hero who was given a State Funeral.

Vittorio Orlando, Italian Prime Minister and Italy's contribution to the 'Big Four' at Paris, outlived nearly all of his contemporaries. Never approving of the Fascist regime, he wisely kept a low profile until its overthrow in 1943. He went on to become a well-respected senator for the nation's post-war democracy, and was held as a sort of elder statesman. His death came in 1952.

Baron Sidney Sonnino fell from power and grace shortly after Orlando did, in 1919. He was resoundingly criticized for failing to demand a share of the German colonies, Fiume, and a host of other things, but if nothing else, he was consistent, ever demanding that the provisions of the Treaty of London be respected to the letter. When such did not occur, Sonnino, honest to a fault, did not choose to demand compensation elsewhere, believing such behavior to be shiftless and undignified. Instead, he retired into an icy silence which was never broken by a single word to his detractors until the day of his death in late 1922. Perhaps more than any other individual, the Baron personifies Italy's war effort from 1915 to 1918. Stubbornly honest, dogged and determined, yet never compromising, self-critical, or glory-seeking; all admirable traits to be sure, but unlikely to attract attention or win friends.

Woodrow Wilson, United States President, and author of the famous Fourteen Points on the basis of which the Germans and Austro-Hungarians had asked for armistices, had become probably the most popular man in the world by the end of 1918. While in Europe, his health declined rapidly once he ran into serious opposition from some of his *Entente* allies, particularly the Italians. Subsequently more interested in establishing a League of Nations than applying his oft-stated principle of self-determination to the drawing of the new map of Europe, he was devastated when he was forced to recognize that his own nation was not firmly behind him. In a physically weakened condition, he embarked upon a rail trip around the United States to try to sell acceptance of the peace treaties to the American people. His train had just reached Colorado in September 1919 when poor health obliged him to return to Washington. Within days he had suffered a massive stroke from which he never completely recovered. Soon, his party was out of power and his efforts to rally his nation had failed. Thin, pale, and weak, the President became but a shadow of his former self, but he clung to life until 1924.

Benito Mussolini, the one-time corporal in Cadorna's army, embarked on a foreign policy of unabashed aggression, once he had cemented his power as Italian dictator. His regime did, however, manage to finally reconcile the long-standing dispute between the nation and the Roman Catholic Church. In 1929 Pope Pius XI authorized the signing of an accord which basically acknowledged the *fait accompli* with which the Vatican had been served in 1870. Vatican City became, for all intents and purposes, an independent sovereign entity, with the Bishop of Rome as head of state. Mussolini would declare war on the British and French in June, 1940, and at last the Westerners were made to feel how the Austro-Germans had felt about Italy in 1915. Following the overthrow of Fascism in 1943, he was arrested and imprisoned, but was temporarily rescued by his German allies and reinstalled as *Duce* of occupied Italy. In April 1945, while attempting to slip over the border into Switzerland, he was apprehended and murdered by anti-Fascist Italian irregulars.

Austria-Hungary's most prolific scoring air ace, Godwin Brumowsky, was badly shaken by the defeat and dismemberment of the nation he had fought for. Retiring for a time to a family estate in the province of Transylvania, recently annexed by Romania, he gradually became bored with a rural life and returned to Vienna in 1930 to found a flying school. Six years later he died in a plane crash. He had not been piloting the aircraft in which he was killed.

Julius Arigi, runner-up to Brumowsky, returned to the city of his birth after the war. By then it had become a part of the new state of Czechoslovakia and Arigi helped the fledgling nation establish an air service and an aviation company. He eventually relocated to Austria and was pleased when the small Republic was absorbed by Germany in 1938. Thereafter he became a flight instructor for the German Air Force, a position he retained throughout the Second World War. Continuing to fly until the 1960's, he lived on into old age and passed away in 1981 in Attersee, Austria.

As the highest scoring Italian ace that survived the war, Silvio Scaroni was held in high esteem in military circles throughout the world once the conflict was over. His career was perhaps the most remarkable of any former fighter pilot. He would travel the world over as an aviation expert, spending a good deal of time in many North and South American, European, and Asian countries. In the late 1920's he was commanding a fighter group in the Italian Air Force; a decade later he was Chief Aviation Advisor for Chaing Kai-shek. By the time of the Second World War, he had risen to the rank of General. Scaroni survived until 1977.

The long and brutal war on the Italian Front had cost the nations of Europe, by the figures suggested above, a minimum of 2.4 million casualties, and perhaps as many as 2.8 million. Using a median number, then, we have 2.6 million (mostly) men killed, seriously wounded, missing or captured by the enemy. We have seen how capture often equated to death, disease, or otherwise ill-health, the effects of which were often permanent. Of the missing, the majority were undoubtedly killed and never discovered because their bodies were either blown to pieces by artillery fire, buried by the same, or simply allowed to decay in remote locations where wildlife soon had scattered even their bones. At any rate we have two and one-half million people whose lives were either abruptly ended in violence or terribly disrupted by the same, usually forever. Just how many men suffered ever after from trauma or feelings of terror, guilt or rage can never be known, but such a list would certainly include large numbers of those who survived the fighting without becoming official casualties.

Besides the horrific human cost of the war, the financial reckoning was absolutely staggering, and for the first time in history, monetary figures in the billions were being routinely spoken of. Never mind that millions of human beings had been financially ruined by the war, even their governments were hamstrung by astronomical expenditures. As of the early 21st Century, few nations of the world have ever paid off the debts assumed during the Great War. Even the United States, which is generally assumed to be one of the few nations to have profited from the war, was never paid but a fraction of the value of the gigantic amounts of credit it forwarded its *Entente* allies. Most countries, such as Austria, which was expected to assume a disproportionate share of the debt of the old Habsburg Empire, were unable to pay anything against the huge reparation bills they were presented with. Italy, never a model of financial stability, was left so impoverished by the war that for years thereafter many of its citizens could see no evidence of a working government in their districts at all, and this is a major factor for the relatively easy success of the Fascists during the destabilized conditions of the early 1920's. Moreover, fighting had largely devastated large areas of northern Italy where forests had been cut, towns bombed and shelled, and bridges and other vulnerable parts of roads and railroads destroyed. All of Friuli-Venezia-Giulia had been a war zone, as well as half of Veneto and portions of the newly annexed Tyrol and Küstenland. The debris of war was strewn everywhere, and hundreds of thousands of hastily-buried bodies needed to be collected into military cemeteries and given a properly identified final resting place, if possible. The task was a daunting one, but the Italians did the best they could, especially with regards to their own soldiers. Dozens of new cemeteries were dedicated, and unidentifiable, skeletal remains were gathered into huge ossuaries, especially along the

Isonzo. Millions of unexploded bombs, shells, and grenades also needed to be dealt with, an ongoing process that continues, with constant new discoveries, to this day. As in France, large sections of the old battlefields were cordoned off, and declared too dangerous for visitation. These, too, still exist a century later.

With the passage of time, many of the war's scars on the landscape have healed, though there are still locations at which portions of trenches, concrete emplacements, and of course dugouts blasted into solid rock can be seen. In recent years, coincidental with the rise of popularity of walking tours of the old Western Front, more and more visitors are frequenting the less inaccessible battle sites, but the ruggedness of the terrain along most of the old front line precludes its hosting all but the most determined guests.

If the Italians have made every effort to honor their dead of 1915-1918, the other side has never been given much opportunity to do so. The Austro-Hungarian Empire was a multi-ethnic state, and after the war ended in defeat and dissolution, it became fashionable for its successor-states to distance themselves from the Habsburg era. Slovenes, for example, as a part of Serb-dominated Yugoslavia, had no incentive to remind those in Belgrade that they had once fought hard for the defeated Empire to keep the Italians out of their lands. The same could be said of the Croats. Poles, Ukrainians, Czechs, Slovaks and Romanians had no particular interest in admitting that they too had once fought against Italians, shoulder to shoulder with Germans and Hungarians. The latter two nationalities, anxious to be accepted as new, independent, friendly nations, and not to be considered as heirs to a Habsburg past, were not likely to risk hostility by insisting that their war dead be honored. Consequently there are nowhere near the number of monuments to Austro-Hungarian soldiers along the old front line as there are to Italians, and those that do exist were often neglected over the decades and fell into disrepair. The fact that both the Germans and Hungarians were on the losing side of the Second World War certainly did not help. Even so, the memory of the men who fought on both sides should never be allowed to lapse. They fought for a cause that they believed in or were loyal to, and most willingly gave their lives for it. Their efforts and their sacrifices must never be forgotten.

It has often been said or written that when Franz Joseph died, no one wept, and when Austria-Hungary disintegrated, no one cared. This type of arrogance is not history, it is nonsense. If the old Emperor was not the object of excessive public emotion at his death, it might be remembered that the event occurred at the beginning of a bitterly cold winter while the nation had already been at war for over two years, and when food and fuel were in short supply. Hundreds of thousands of Austro-Hungarians had lost sons, brothers, husbands and fathers in the war and the nation was long since traumatized by the scope of the conflict. People could hardly be expected to burst into hysteria at the death of an 86 year old man. As for the Habsburg Empire, it had experienced some very good, peaceful, prosperous years during the long reign of the old man, and in the years following the Great War, a good deal of nostalgia for Imperial days was felt in most quarters of the old Empire. East Central Europe has certainly not known such stability ever since; if the Empire was an imperfect state it can be considered no different than any state yet created by humans, and it was no doubt far superior in providing for a quality of life than many of its successor-states have been. It did at least endure for many centuries, which says something for its worthiness, as opposed to states like Czechoslovakia and Yugoslavia, which would not have survived the Second World War—that is, a quarter century—had it not been for the rise of Communism. The old Empire, like the family that legally owned and governed it, certainly had its shortcomings, but the fact remains that millions of people were willing to fight for it, as late as the second decade of the Twentieth Century. Even historians have dubbed the Empire as 'ramshackle'; it was in fact anything but.

Of 79 Infantry Divisions raised by Austria-Hungary, 64 saw at least some service on the Italian Front. For Cavalry Divisions the numbers are 8 of 12. Overall, then, 72 of 91 combat Divisions, or 79 percent of the total were committed south of the Alps. Eleven divisions spent their entire life or the tenure of May, 1915 to November, 1918 in the theatre. As we have seen, the Germans contributed eight more, between September 1917 and March of 1918. For the Empire, this was most definitely no 'sideshow', but the main front of the war.

Similarly, Italy's war effort has too often been belittled. For years, in general histories of the conflict, one could read statements like 'Italy was never a vigorous ally' or 'Italy began the war only when the others were exhausted', and the like. Such assertions can only be born of ignorance. Rome was able to raise 78 Combat Divisions for the war—74 Infantry, 4 Cavalry—and all but two were at some time deployed against the Austrians. Only the 38th Division, which was raised in March, 1916 and served until the end of the war in Albania (also opposing Austrians), and the 79th Division, which was raised in October 1916 and disbanded two months later, were not active in northern Italy. While it is true that the British and French each sent five divisions to Italy in the wake of *Waffentreu* (Caporetto), it is much less often noted that the Italians also sent help to the Western Front during the crisis of spring, 1918, in the form of the 3rd and 8th Infantry Divisions, which then served there until the autumn. It should also be noted that although Cadorna always considered the Isonzo sector to be his main front, 51 Italian Infantry and two of its four Cavalry Divisions also spent at least some time in the Tyrol. Only five spent their entire tenure there, however. Another six served on the line in the Carnic Alps. This level of war effort is by no means to be despised, and coupled with the enormous number of casualties sustained there, it is easy to see that the Italian Front represented the third most important theatre of war during 1915 to 1918.

There can be no doubt whatsoever that the outcome of the Great War was decided, indirectly, by the existence of the Italian Front. Had Italy remained loyal to the *Triple Alliance* in 1914, and sent its legions against France, as Cadorna and the King expected she would, the resulting German/Italian invasion could hardly have failed. As events would show, even without Rome's support, Moltke's blow very nearly succeeded, and this with French knowledge that their Alpine border was secure, hence all of the nation's weight could be used in the north to stop the German invasion. Now let us consider that the initial invasion failed, even with Italian support. In such a case, France has to fight a two-front war, and on her Alpine Front she has to commit roughly the same force the Austrians later needed to deploy to halt the Italians. Subtract these French divisions from the Western Front, and what is the outcome there? And, of course, without an Italian Front of its own to defend, Austria-Hungary is able to increase her commitment in Russia and the Balkans. In light of what in fact did happen later on, it seems safe to say that Russia would have been knocked out of the war sooner than she was, probably Serbia as well. With the combined Austrian and Italian Navies giving the French and British very real headaches in the Mediterranean, would the *Entente* have been able to carry out the Dardanelles operation? Would it have been able to establish the front north of Salonika? It seems unlikely. Certainly Romania would not have entered the war against the *Alliance*, indeed she may have joined it. Imagine the situation of spring 1918, in which all of the forces then holding the Italian Front are turned against the *Entente* on the Western Front and in the Alps! Can anyone seriously believe that the *Entente* could have survived such a devastating blow? And would the United States ever have been able to join the 'Allies' in 1917? A large domestic minority of Americans sympathetic to the *Alliance* nearly blocked the country's entrance into the war as it was. Add the already considerable Italian minority to their ranks and American participation seems doubtful; at any rate it would have come too late.

If there seems to be no question, then, that with a loyal Italy the *Alliance* wins the war, what about a scenario with a neutral Italy? Baron Sonnino once (publicly) said that he wished his country had never joined the *Entente*; the statement was made in frustration over the difficulties of the peacemaking process, it is true, but the Baron, perhaps the personality closest to that of Bismarck's by 1919, well knew that Italy would have gained far more in victory as part of a triumphant *Alliance* than he was capable of wresting from his *Entente* partners. A neutral Italy would of course have gained nothing but the ongoing contempt of its former partners. But it would not have lost anything either, and like the United States, may have greatly benefitted in an economic sense. Without a southern front to fight on, Austria-Hungary would almost certainly have concentrated on the Balkans, where her pre-war main interests always lay. Again, with Italy neutral, Romania probably does not enter the war; Austria probably pushes on to Salonika, a long standing ambition thus fulfilled. No *Entente* presence in Greece is ever established, and Bulgaria is not the first domino to fall in September of 1918. Russia collapses, at least as soon as, if not sooner than, she in fact did. In the spring of 1918, Ludendorff's massive strike force is augmented by dozens of Austro-Hungarian divisions which burst through the quiet sector in Lorraine and turn the French right. At best, the *Alliance* wins the war; at worst it battles the *Entente* to a protracted stalemate, and a negotiated peace is worked out.

Admittedly, all this is pure speculation, but nevertheless a very real possibility, if Italy had not signed the Treaty of London in April of 1915. That she did do so ensured an *Entente* victory. Had she not, the *Alliance* would probably have won, or the war may possibly have ended in a stalemate. For those who believed (or may still believe) that the *Entente* victory made the world any safer for democracy, or that it was the first step toward ending all wars, the Italian action is logical, and satisfying. For those who continue to question how by fragmenting the world into an endless number of independent states it can be made any safer or more democratic, or for that matter if being democratic is in fact what it desires, Italy's flip-flop in 1914-1915 will always be one of the great 'what if's' of history. We have seen how the process developed and when the decisions were made. What we may never know is exactly who it was in the Italian government whose weight of opinion was sufficient to bring about the change of direction.

It is often said that every group has a leader, whether he or she be sanctioned and installed or merely consciously or even unconsciously recognized. Generally the magnetism of one's personality, the force of one's will, or the skill in using one's voice and vocabulary as a means of communication, not to mention poise, self-confidence and a whole host of other factors, determine who will emerge as a leader of a particular group. Some persons do, others do not, care to take the initiative. Certainly King Vittorio Emanuele, never a forceful Monarch, was not responsible for Italy's wrangling of the period. Neither was Luigi Cadorna, who as we have seen was prepared to cooperate with the Germans against France. Giolitti fought the change of policy tooth and nail. Salandra was Prime Minister at the time and threatened to resign if Giolitti blocked the government's moves, but this does not indicate that he was, at bottom, behind the new strategy. Though a good politician, Salandra does not seem to have enjoyed the widespread confidence of his peers that would have been necessary to lead the charge for a tilt toward the *Entente*.

In the end, the search will inevitably lead to a man who was widely respected in Italy; he had twice enjoyed tenures of ninety days as head of the government, and had held various ministerial posts. A liberal by nature, he was a tireless scholar, yet he was aristocratic in outlook, despised crowds and tended to disregard public opinion. Son of a Jewish father and an English mother, he was by religion a Protestant in a soundly Catholic nation. When Salandra turned to him in October 1914 upon the death of Foreign Minister Giuliano, the two were able to make an agreement that Italy must associate herself with one or the other of the warring coalitions. First they would try to induce Austria to purchase Italian neutrality, and if the effort failed, they would simply do whatever was in the nation's best interests. And once he had set out upon a course, our man never wavered.

Was Baron Sidney Sonnino the man most responsible for bringing about war on the Italian Front? It seems likely. Was he then, indirectly the man most responsible for the *Entente* victory? Once again the answer must probably be given in the affirmative. Sonnino himself would never have taken credit (or blame) for it publicly; he never aspired to popularity, nor did he particularly relish power and authority. He was in fact not a politician and was certainly no real diplomat, preferring to say little while others did most of the talking. It was his misfortune, in 1919, to have to deal with a man like Woodrow Wilson, one of the few persons he ever encountered who was as intellectual, and as stubborn as he himself was. Bargaining from a stronger position, Wilson was able to frustrate the Baron; hence Sonnino's remark that he wished he had never brought Italy into the war on the side of the *Entente*. This was not sarcasm, but a statement of fact for which the normally silent 'Taciturn' never forgave himself. But was his stony silence of his last years the product of a momentary loss of self-control in Paris, or was Sonnino truly sorry he had not argued for Italy to stay true to the German *Alliance*? The answer went with him to the grave.

Endnotes

Chapter One

[1] The vote in Rome itself was 134,000 in favor of joining Italy, 1,500 against.
[2] Irredentists were those nationalists who constantly espoused the acquisition of *Italia Irredenta*, the 'unredeemed' portions of Austria inhabited by people of Italian speech, who were supposedly chafing for the opportunity to be detached from Austria and annexed by Italy.
[3] Martin, Page 127
[4] Gilbert The *First World War* Page 151
[5] Halpern, Page 143
[6] Horne Vol III, Page 216

Chapter Two

[7] The Germans refer to the river as the Etsch, the Italians call it the Adige.
[8] Sette Communi has been variously translated as Seven Communes or Seven Municipalities, but Seven Communities is, I believe, most fitting.
[9] Mainardi, Page 13
[10] Gray, Page 97
[11] Nicolle, Page 14
[12] In most armies the ranking of units from smallest to largest was: squad, section, platoon, company, battalion, regiment, brigade, division, Corps, Field Army, and Army Group.
[13] Nicolle, Page 22
[14] Powell, Page 78
[15] Mirouze, Page 44
[16] Ellis and Cox, Page 235
[17] Nicolle, Page 36
[18] White, Page 186
[19] Chant, Page 42

[20] Jung, Vol I, Page 21
[21] Ibid, Page 45
[22] Ellis and Cox, Page 227
[23] Manchester, Page 253
[24] Chant, Page 11

Chapter Three
[25] Northcliffe Page 218
[26] *Deutsche Soldatenjahrbuch* 1970 Page 263, Article by Franz Wick
[27] Gilbert *The First World War* Page 166
[28] Jung Vol I, Page 38
[29] Halpern Page 145
[30] The town of Karfreit is located close enough to the junction of lands of the three languages that it is also known as Kobarid to the Slovenes and Caporetto to the Italians.
[31] Reynolds, Vol III, Page 342
[32] Schindler Page 49
[33] Reynolds Vol III, Page 363
[34] Chant Page 85
[35] Schindler Page 59
[36] Halpern Page 149
[37] Reynolds/Churchill Vol II, Page 56 Lewis R. Freeman
[38] Schindler Page 67
[39] Gleichen Page 130
[40] Halpern Page 150
[41] Palmer & Wallis Pages 158-162
[42] Halpern Page 383
[43] Schindler Page 101

Chapter Four
[44] Reynolds/Churchill Vol III, Page 59
[45] Ibid Page 61
[46] Robertson Page 121
[47] Gray Page 104
[48] Halpern Page 383
[49] Reynolds/Churchill Vol I, Page 317

[50] Halsey Page 48
[51] Schindler Page 117
[52] Ibid Page 140
[53] Gilbert *The First World War* Page 235
[54] Robertson Page 121
[55] Chant Page 59
[56] Reynolds/Churchill Vol II, Page 65
[57] King, J.C. from the Diary of Gino Speranza Page 124
[58] Ibid Page 129
[59] Halpern Page 160
[60] Chant Pages 59, 75

Chapter Five
[61] Ellis/Cox Pages 127-129
[62] Reynolds Vol V, Page 204
[63] Dominian Page 69
[64] Halpern Page 161
[65] Westwell Page 100
[66] Gilbert Page 256, Wilmot Page 232
[67] *Deutsche Soldatenjahrbuch 1973* Das Kaiserschützenmuseum im Schloss Ambras bei Innsbruck Page 253
[68] Halpern Page 387
[69] Chant Page 85
[70] Schindler Page 152
[71] The Italian speaking portion of south Tyrol. *Welsch* meant undesirable foreign; for Austrians it usually meant Italians, while for Germans, Frenchmen were often the targets.
[72] Halsey Vol IX, Page 63
[73] Reynolds Vol V, Page 235
[74] Halsey Page 71
[75] Allen Vol V, Page 252
[76] Halpern Page 161, Gleichen Page 49 (1916)
[77] Halpern Page 388
[78] Ellis/Cox Orders of Battle Page 204
[79] Horne Vol IV, Walter Oertel Page 298
[80] Northcliffe Pages 195-196

81 Horne Vol IV, Page 299
82 Chant Page 75
83 Schindler Page 166
84 Northcliffe Page 194
85 Schindler Page 171
86 Northcliffe Page 213
87 Chant Page 65
88 Robertson Pages 125, 131

Chapter Six
89 Chant Page 82
90 Ibid Pages 85-86
91 Reynolds Vol VI, Pages 169-170
92 Schindler Page 177
93 Reynolds Vol VI, Page 157
94 Schindler Page 186
95 Chant Page 73
96 Schindler Page 190
97 Robertson Page 122
98 Reynolds Vol VI, Page 175
99 Halpern Pages 162-163
100 Gray Page 175
101 Halpern Page 388
102 Lloyd George Vol II, Page 949
103 Ibid Page 939
104 Allen Vol IV, Page 211
105 Robertson Pages 122, 126
106 Chant Page 51
107 Reynolds Vol VI, Page 175

Chapter Seven
108 Lloyd George Vol IV, Page 1987
109 Ibid See Volume Four of his memoirs. An entire chapter is devoted to 'The Austrian Peace Move'.
110 Beckett Page 207
111 Ibid Page 330

[112] Ibid Page 249
[113] Ibid Page 333
[114] Ibid Page 208
[115] Lloyd George Vol II, Page 846
[116] Ibid Page 845
[117] Gray Page 176
[118] Halpern Page 390
[119] Robertson Page 122
[120] Reynolds Vol VI, Page 454
[121] Bonham-Carter Pages 231-232
[122] Gray Page 177
[123] Halpern Page 391
[124] Chant Page 52
[125] Ibid Page 71
[126] Robertson Page 122
[127] Schindler Page 201
[128] Horne Vol V, Page 303, Buchan Vol III, Page 530

Chapter Eight
[129] Schindler Page 205
[130] Robertson Page 122
[131] Chant Pages 68, 71, 75
[132] Gleichen Page 210
[133] Halpern Page 163
[134] Ibid See pages 162-166 for a more detailed account
[135] Ibid Page 396
[136] Schindler Page 212
[137] Buchan Vol III, Page 533
[138] Horne Vol V, Page 305
[139] Schindler Page 216
[140] Ibid
[141] Reynolds Vol VI, Page 472
[142] Gilbert Page 339, Schindler Pages 220-221
[143] Richard Galli, *'The Battle of Ortigara, June 1917'* for The Great War Society
[144] Gleichen Page 218

[145] Robertson Pages 122-123, 126
[146] Chant Pages 66, 71, 75, 82
[147] Halpern Page 396
[148] Jung Vol II, Page 20
[149] Nicolle Page 23
[150] Gilbert Page 357
[151] See Lloyd George Vol IV, Chapter LXI
[152] Bonham-Carter Page 257
[153] It might also be recalled that even after its unconditional surrender at the end of the Second World War, the Japanese people were allowed, when they insisted, to keep their Emperor. Americans in 1945 certainly had more justification in demanding a basic change in the structure of authority in Japan, than they did in calling in 1917, for the replacement of the Imperial German government.

Chapter Nine
[154] Schindler Page 223
[155] Ibid
[156] Chant Page 63
[157] Robertson Page 124
[158] Chant Page 60
[159] Ibid Pages 52-53
[160] Buchan Vol III, Page 540; Reynolds Vol VII, Page 197; Halsey Vol Nine, Page 88
[161] Reynolds Vol VII, Page 198
[162] Halsey Vol Ten, Page 448
[163] Taylor Page 216
[164] Schindler Page 240, Jung Vol 2, Page 6
[165] Reynolds Vol VII, Page 199
[166] Bonham-Carter Page 268
[167] Chant Pages 69, 82
[168] Schindler Page 240; Gleichen Page 242
[169] Robertson Pages 127-128
[170] Buchan Vol III, Page 544; Taylor Page 215
[171] Reynolds Vol VII, Pages 204-205
[172] Chant Pages 63, 73

[173] Ibid Pages 69-70, 77
[174] Mc Entee Page 429
[175] Taylor Page 217
[176] Treadwell/Wood Pages 106, 107
[177] Schindler Page 248
[178] Chant Page 53
[179] Robertson Page 123
[180] A three-dimensional model of Mt. Piano was created after the war and installed in the Kaiserschützenmuseum outside of Innsbruck. It was one of two peaks thus immortalized, the other being Mt Marmolada. See *Deutsches Soldatenjahrbuch 1973* Pages 247 to 255

Chapter Ten
[181] Allen Vol Five, Page 55
[182] Chant Pages 60, 68
[183] Robertson Pages 123, 129
[184] Ibid Page 126
[185] Sibley/Fry Page 30
[186] Reynolds/Churchill Vol III, Page 84
[187] Ibid Pages 96-97
[188] Horne Vol V, Page 314
[189] Schindler Page 259
[190] Bonham-Carter Page 298
[191] Jung Vol 2, Pages 6-7
[192] Chant Page 63
[193] Robertson Page 123
[194] Gleichen Page 260
[195] Gilbert Page 376
[196] Mackay Page 39
[197] Horne Vol V, Page 320
[198] Schindler Page 264
[199] Whispers of surviving Italian troops deep in the mountains were commonplace for about a year, until the end of the war. One group of 1,400 men under a certain Captain Arduino is reported to have survived somehow, undetected or ignored, until friendly forces returned to the area in November of 1918. See Allen Vol five Pages 58-59

[200] Hirschfeld Page 310
[201] Horne Vol V, Pages 378-379
[202] Chant Page 66
[203] Horne Vol V,Page 374
[204] Gilbert Page 383
[205] Information for this paragraph is credited to Chant, pages 53 to 82 and Robertson pages 123 to 129
[206] Chant Pages 57, 66
[207] MacKay Page 31
[208] Robertson Page 130
[209] Mackay Page 32
[210] Halpern Pages 396-397

Chapter Eleven
[211] Halpern Page 171
[212] Ibid Page 400
[213] Robertson Page 130
[214] Chant Page 78
[215] Ibid Pages 66, 83
[216] Ibid Pages 69-70, 73
[217] Halpern Page 400
[218] Ibid Page 173
[219] Robertson Page 205
[220] Chant Pages 60-61
[221] Ibid Pages 69, 70
[222] Ibid Pages 74, 78
[223] Robertson Page 130
[224] Mackay *Asiago* Page 43
[225] Martin Page 263
[226] For more on the efforts to bring down the Habsburg Monarchy, the reader may wish to consult Z.A.B. Zeman *The Break-Up of the Habsburg Empire 1914-1918*
[227] Gray Page 181
[228] Halpern Page 400
[229] Halsey Vol Ten, Page 456
[230] Chant Pages 61, 79

[231] Ibid Pages 67, 69
[232] Robertson Pages 123-124, 130
[233] Gleichen Page 54; Reynolds Vol VII, Page 602
[234] Chant Page 79
[235] Mackay, *Asiago* Page 61
[236] Supposedly, trees from the Montello provided the source of lumber with which to build Medieval Venice, and it has been a good source of timber ever since. Mackay Page 44
[237] Halsey Vol Nine, Page 139
[238] Chant Pages 70, 72
[239] Horne Vol VI, Page 222
[240] Ibid Vol VI, Page 217
[241] Chant Pages 54, 61
[242] Mackay Page 164
[243] Schindler Page 286
[244] Martin Page 255

Chapter Twelve
[245] Halpern Page 400
[246] Gray Pages 182-183
[247] Robertson Page 130
[248] Chant Pages 64, 80
[249] Reynolds Vol VIII, Page 105
[250] Ibid
[251] March Pages 589-590
[252] Zeman Page 222
[253] Chant Page 72
[254] Reynolds Vol VIII, Page 110
[255] Ibid Page 111
[256] Gray Page 183
[257] Beckett Page 393
[258] Horne Vol VI, Page 362
[259] Reynolds Vol VIII, Page 182
[260] Chant Pages 71, 79
[261] Gray Pages 183-185
[262] Hirschfeld Pages 122-123

263 Martin Page 75
264 Schindler Page 304
265 Horne Vol VI, Pages 366-367
266 Howland Page 321
267 Schindler Page 307

Chapter Thirteen
268 Gleichen Part III Page 196
269 Robertson Page 131
270 Chant Page 90
271 Schindler Page 307
272 MacMillan Page 287
273 Ibid Page 11
274 Reynolds/Churchill Vol III, Page 374
275 *Deutsches Soldatenjahrbuch 1970* 'Kärntens Freiheitskampf' Pages 266-271
276 King Page 615

Chapter Fourteen
277 Gleichen Part III Page 238
278 MacMillan Page 291
279 MacKay Pages 70-71
280 Palmer Page 348

A Note on Sources

For those interested in further reading or research on the war on the Italian Front, certainly no shortage of available material will await them. Though large numbers of English-speakers did eventually participate in the campaign, they did of course comprise a relatively small percentage of the human beings involved there, and logically, their accounts represent only a fraction of the literature ever produced by those in a position to leave first-hand accounts. Far and away the largest group linguistically were Italian speakers, and given the similarity of Italian to Spanish, this fact is beneficial to Westerners, especially Americans, who with each succeeding generation are becoming increasingly aware of the necessity of abandoning a traditional preference to remain monolingual and often tend to familiarize themselves with the Latin tongues. German, on the other hand, has never been considered a major obstacle for the English-speaker to overcome, and a large percentage of the Austro-Hungarian Army personnel were persons who where either fluent in, or at least familiar with, the original vernacular of the Habsburgs. Hence, some knowledge of these two languages in particular is helpful, almost critical really, if one is to take full advantage of the available information.

On the other hand, a good deal of material has been surfacing from east-central Europe especially since the fall of Communism in the early '90's. Today, many accounts in Hungarian and the many Slavic languages heard in the old Austro-Hungarian Empire are available, but due to the general lack of familiarity with these mediums for the average person in the West, I have refrained from listing any of these in the space below; besides, they are dealt with in other works, and appropriately credited.

The following list of titles represents those which have to a greater or lesser degree influenced the preparation of this history. One point that needs to be made here regards my personal skepticism for for all things official, and both the Austrian and Italian official histories are no exception. Like many

Americans weary of official finds—such as those of the Warren Commission or of Project Blue Book just to name a couple—the very word 'official' has come to take on an entirely new meaning. For us, the definition of 'official' is: Sanctioned Nonsense, and we rarely trust a word of it. Similarly, I believe that the 'official' histories of the war must never be taken too seriously, written as they were by persons whose outlooks were hardly objective of the struggle. Nevertheless, the official histories are listed below, for those who enjoy a good work of fiction based on actual historic events. I would add that the Cadorna memoirs are even worse than the official histories for a shameful distortion of the truth, and I must confess that, having been moved to a state of disgust and perhaps more than just a bit of frustration, I never could bring myself to complete the study of them. Admittedly, Conrad's own works are not a lot better, but they at least leave the mark of a man of reason and *some* humility. At any rate I continue to prefer to conduct research in my own unorthodox manner, piecing together a story from what many consider as unlikely sources.

One such source has now all but disappeared. As a youth maturing in the two decades immediately following the Second World War, I was exposed to countless stories from men who had participated in the latter; they were, after all, the fathers of those in my age group. Almost ignored at the time were the veterans of the First World War, men recognized on Memorial Day or Veteran's Day to be sure but who had fought in a war that was completely overshadowed, at that time, by the later conflict. I was one of the few of my generation who preferred to listen to the older men, and if memory serves properly, I must have spoken to hundreds of these ex-soldiers, many of whom had been conscripted by the English, French, German, Italian, Austro-Hungarian and Russian nations and later emigrated to the United States where they seemed quite willing to tell their stories. Whoever coined the expression that 'youth is wasted on the young' certainly had it right in my case; it would never have occurred to me in those days to make some attempt to record any of these remarkable tales for posterity. For such efforts, there was always going to be time in the future. But today, those veterans are all gone, most long since gone, whereas in 1960 there were probably more World War One participants alive than there are Korean War veterans today. No doubt, over the years I have forgotten many, if not most, of the important details of these stories, but I will never forget the presence of one common denominator in all the tales, one which was readily apparent to even an eager, if attentive youngster.

The Americans, long since disillusioned by the non-fulfillment of the hopes inspired by the 'war to end wars' rhetoric, as well as those who fought on the side of the nations that lost the war, wanted more than anything to believe that their efforts had mattered, for *something*. Even the others were noticeably anxious that the world should somehow remember their sacrifices and those of their comrades who did not survive the contest. As I see it now, it is the duty of those of us who chronicle the Great War to see to it that those long ago hopes and desires continue to be disseminated.

Fortunately, today the world at large possesses a much more realistic appreciation of the relation of the two World Wars to the overall evolution of human civilization, and the First World War has rightly begun to take center stage as the defining moment in all modern history, replete with lessons that no responsible person of our times can afford to ignore.

Bibliography

Abbott, Willis J. *Pictorial History of the World War* Leslie-Judge Co. New York 1919

Allen, George H. (Ed.) *The Great War* (5 volumes) George Barrie's Sons Philadelphia 1915-1921

Andriessen, J.H.J. *World War I in Photographs* Grange Books U.K. 2002

Banks, Arthur *A Military Atlas of the First World War* Leo Cooper London 1989

Beckett, Ian *The Great War* Pierson Education LTD Harlow 2001

Bismarck, Otto von *Reflections & Reminiscences (*2 volumes) Smith Elder & Co London 1898

Bonadeo, Alfredo *D'Annunzio and the Great War* Fairleigh Dickinson U.P. London 1995

Bonham-Carter, Victor *The Strategy of Victory 1914-1918* Holt Reinhart & Winston New York, Chicago, San Francisco 1964

Buchan, John *A History of the Great War* (4 volumes) Houghton-Mifflin Boston & New York 1922

Bundesministerium Für Landesverteidigung Militärwissenschaftlichen Mitterlangen *Österreich-Ungarns Letzter Krieg (*7 volumes each with supplement volume) Vienna 1930-1938

Burgwyn, H. James *The Legend of the Mutilated Victory: Italy, The Great War and the Paris Peace Conference* Greenwood Press Westport CT. 1989

Cadorna, Conte Luigi *Mémoires* Fratelli Trevés Milano 1921

Cavalry School Fort Riley, Kansas *Cavalry Combat* Telegraph Press Harrisburg, PA. 1937

Chant, Christopher *Austro-Hungarian Aces of World War One* Osprey 2002

Conrad von Hötzendorf, Franz *Aus Meiner Dienstzeit 1906-1918* (5 volumes) Rikola Vienna 1921-1923

Czernin, Count Ottocar von *In the World War* Harper & Brothers New York 1920

Dallas, Gregor *1918: War and Peace* Overlook Press New York 2001

Dalton, Hugh *With British Guns in Italy* Kessinger London 1919

Deutsches Soldatenjahrbuch (various authors) Volumes 1970, 1972, 1973 Schild Verlag München

Dominian, Leon *Frontiers of Language and Nationality in Europe* Henry Holt & Co New York 1917

Edmonds, James and H. R. Davies *Military Operations, Italy 1915-1919* Imperial Defense Committee Official History of the Great War London 1949

Ellis, John and Michael Cox *The World War One Databook* Aurum Press London 1993

Esposito, General Vincent J. *The West Point Atlas of American Wars* Praeger New York, Washington and London 1978

Europe at War (various authors) Doubleday, Page & Co 1914

Falkenhayn, Erich von *The German General Staff and Its Decisions 1914-1916* Dodd, Mead & Co New York 1920

Falls, Cyril *The Battle of Caporetto* J. B. Lippincott Philadelphia 1966

Fitzsimmons, Bernard (Ed.) *Tanks and Weapons of World War One* BPC Publishing Beekman House New York 1973

Forty, Simon *Historical Maps of World War I* PRC Publishing London 2002

Gilbert, Martin *The First World War* Henry Holt & Co New York 1994

Gilbert, Martin *Atlas of the First World War* Dorset Press London 1970

Gleichen, Lord Edward (Ed.) *Chronology of the Great War 1914-1918* Greenhill Books London 2000

Gooch, John *Army, State and Society in Italy 1870-1915* Palgrave MacMillan New York 1989

Gray, Edwyn A. *The Killing Time* Charles Scribner's Sons New York 1972

Guernsey, Erwin Scofield *A Reference History of the War* Dodd Mead & Co New York 1920

Halpern, Paul G. *A Naval History of World War I* The Naval Institute

Press Annapolis 1995

Halsey, Frances W. (Ed.) *Literary Digest History of the World War* (10 volumes) Funk & Wagnalls New York & London 1919

Hart, B.H. Liddell *A History of the World War 1914-1918* Faber & Faber London 1924

Hart. B.H. Liddell *The Real War in 1914-1918* Little Brown & Co Boston 1930

Hemingway, Ernest *A Farewell to Arms* Scribners New York and London 1929

Hirschfeld, Dr. Magnus *The Sexual History of the World War* Panurge Press New York 1934

Hook, Alex *World War I Day by Day* Grange Books U.K. 2004

Horne, Charles F. (Ed.) *Great Events of the Great War* (7 volumes) The National Alumni 1920

Howland, C.R. *Military History of the World War* The General Service Schools Press Leavenworth Kansas 1923

Johnson, Douglas Wilson *Topography and Strategy in the War* Henry Holt & Co New York 1917

Johnson, Douglas Wilson *Battlefields of the World War* Oxford U.P. 1921

Jung, Peter *The Austro-Hungarian Forces in World War I* (2 volumes) Osprey 2003

Keegan, John *An Illustrated History of the First World War* Alfred A. Knopf New York 2001

King, Jere Clemens *The First World War* Walker & Co New York 1972

King, W.C. (Ed.) *King's Complete History of the World War* The History Associates Springfield MA 1922

L'escercito italiano nella grande guerra 1915-1918 Italian Official History Rome 1927

Livesey, Anthony *The Historical Atlas of World War I* Henry Holt & Co New York 1994

Lloyd George, David *War Memoirs* (6 volumes) Ivor Nicholson & Watson London 1934-1937

Low, Sidney James *Italy and the War* Longmans Green & Co New York 1916

Ludendorff, Erich von *Ludendorff's Own Story* (2 volumes) Harper & Brothers New York & London 1919

MacKay, Frances *Asiago* Battleground Europe Series Leo Cooper Yorkshire 2001

MacKay, Frances *Touring the Italian Front 1917-1919* Battleground Europe Series Leo Cooper Yorkshire 2002

Mainardi, Roberto and others *Friuli Venezia Giulia* (English edition) Banca Nazionale Del Lavoro Italy 1978

March, Frances A. *History of the World War* United Publishers Philadelphia, Chicago, Toronto 1919

Martin, William *Statesmen of the War* Milton Balch & Co New York 1928

McEntee, Gerard L. *Italy's Part in Winning the War* Princeton U.P. 1934

McEntee, Gerard L. *Military History of the World War* Charles Scribner's Sons 1937

McMillan, Margaret *Paris 1919* Random House New York 2001

Mirouze, Laurent *World War I Infantry in Color Photographs* Windrow & Greene London 1995

Mollo, Pierre and Andrew Turner *Army Uniforms of World War I* Arco Publishing New York 1977

Nicolle, David *The Italian Army of World War I* Osprey 2003

Northcliffe, Lord *At the War* Hodder & Stoughton London, Toronto, New York 1916

Page, Thomas N. *Italy and the World War* Kessinger Publishing London 1921

Palmer, Alan *Twilight of the Habsburgs Emperor Frances Joseph* Atlantic Monthly Press New York 1994

Palmer, Svetlana and Sarah Wallis *Intimate Voices from the First World War* Harper Collins New York 2003

Powell, E. Alexander *Italy at War* Charles Scribner's Sons New York 1919

Raab, David *Battle of the Piave Death of the Austro-Hungarian Army 1918* Dorrance Publishing Pittsburgh 2003

Reynolds, Frances J. and Allen L. Churchill (Eds.) *The Story of the Great War* (8 volumes) P. F. Collier & Son New York 1916-1920

Reynolds, Frances J. and Allen L. Churchill (Eds.) *World's War Events* (3 volumes) P. F. Collier & Son New York 1919

✻Reynolds, Michael S. *Hemingway's First War: The Making of a Farewell to Arms* Princeton U.P. 1976

Robertson, Bruce (Ed.) *Air Aces of the 1914-1918 War* Aero Publishers Fallbrook California 1964

Rolt-Wheeler, Frances *The World War for Liberty* National Publishing Washington, D.C. 1919

Schindler, John R. *Isonzo: The Forgotten Sacrifice of the Great War* Praeger Westport CT 2001

Shermer, David *World War I* Octopus Books London 1973

Sibley, Roger and Michael Fry *Rommel* Ballantine Books New York 1974

Simonds, Frank H. *History of the World War* (5 volumes) Doubleday Page & Co New York 1917-1920

Strachan, Hew *The First World War* Viking Press Penguin 2004

Taylor, A.J.P. (Ed.) *History of World War I* Octopus Books London 1974

Thayer, John *Italy and the Great War: Politics and Culture 1870-1915* University of Wisconsin Press Madison 1964

Treadwell, Terry C. and Alan C. Wood *German Knights of the Air 1914-1918* Barnes & Noble 1998

Villari, Luigi *The War on the Italian Front* Cobden-Sanderson London 1932

Visintin, Prof. Luigi *Atlante Storico Evo Moderno* Instituto Geografico De Agostini Novara undated

Wells, Herbert George *Italy, France and Britain at War* MacMillan New York 1917

Westwell, Ian *World War I Day by Day* MBI Publishing WI 2000

Wilmott, H.P. *World War I* Dorling Kindersley Publishing New York 2003

White, B.T. *Tanks and Other Armored Fighting Vehicles 1900-1918* MacMillan New York 1970

Zeman, Z.A.B. *The Break-Up of the Habsburg Empire 1914-1918* Oxford U.P. London & New York 1961

Zingales, Francesco *La conquista di Gorizia* (Official Italian) Rome 1925

Printed in the United States
134517LV00004B/41/P